Contours of the Theatrical Avant-Garde

THEATER: Theory/Text/Performance

Enoch Brater, Series Editor

Recent Titles:

Trevor Griffiths: Politics, Drama, History by Stanton B. Garner Jr.

Memory-Theater and Postmodern Drama by Jeanette R. Malkin

Performing America: Cultural Nationalism in American Theater edited by Jeffrey D. Mason and J. Ellen Gainor

Space in Performance: Making Meaning in the Theatre by Gay McAuley

Mirrors of Our Playing: Paradigms and Presences in Modern Drama by Thomas R. Whitaker

Brian Friel in Conversation edited by Paul Delaney

Sails of the Herring Fleet: Essays on Beckett by Herbert Blau

On Drama: Boundaries of Genre, Borders of Self by Michael Goldman

Contours of the Theatrical Avant-Garde: Performance and Textuality edited by James M. Harding

The Painted Word: Samuel Beckett's Dialogue with Art by Lois Oppenheim

Contours of the Theatrical Avant-Garde

Performance and Textuality

Edited by James M. Harding

Ann Arbor

THE UNIVERSITY OF MICHIGAN PRESS

Published in the United States of America by
The University of Michigan Press
Manufactured in the United States of America
⊗ Printed on acid-free paper

2003 2002 2001 2000 4 3 2 1

A CIP catalog record for this book is available from the British Library.

Library of Congress Cataloging-in-Publication Data

Contours of the theatrical avant-garde : performance and textuality /
[edited by] James M. Harding.
p. cm. — (Theater—theory/text/performance)
Includes bibliographical references and index.
ISBN 0-472-09727-X (cloth : alk. paper)
ISBN 0-472-06727-3 (pbk. : alk. paper)
1. Experimental theater. I. Harding, James Martin, 1958– . II. Series.
PN2193.E86 .C66 2000
792'.022—dc21 00-008540

To Joe,
an anarchist
who encouraged me

Acknowledgments

I want to take this opportunity to thank the individual contributors to this volume, not only for the marvelous essays that they produced but also for their patience as I pieced the book together. It has been an engaging pleasure both to work with them and to learn from them. I also want to thank LeAnn Fields at the University of Michigan Press for her belief in this project from our very first discussion about it. Her support has been indispensable in making the volume a reality. Above all, and as always, I am deeply grateful to Friederike Eigler for her interest in my work, for her conversations about it, and for her challenging insights. She has sacrificed time that might have been used for her own scholarly work so that I could finish this project.

Of all the essays in this volume only two have appeared previously, one of them in partial form. Patrice Pavis's essay appears here for the first time in English translation. It is taken from the final chapter of *L'Analyse des spectacle* (Paris: Nathan, 1996). A portion of Kristine Stiles's essay appeared in *Siski* 12, no. 1 (1997). The controversy surrounding that portion's initial publication is addressed in the full essay included in this volume.

Contents

PART III. Textual Spaces, Theatrical Spaces, and Avant-Garde Performance

PART IV. Reflections on the Institutions of the Avant-Garde

James M. Harding

Introduction

On Departmental Rivalries, Textual Metaphors, and Avant-Garde Performance

The appearance of this book at the beginning of the twenty-first century is especially appropriate given that the initial idea for it grew out of a response to Bonnie Marranca's "Theatre at the University at the End of the Twentieth Century," published in *Performing Arts Journal* in 1995. Marranca's assessment of the state of academic theater studies in the late nineties is wide ranging in its admonishments and suggestions, but of particular interest to me as a professor of literature specializing in modern and contemporary drama is her harsh disavowal of a curriculum driven by "the traditional interrelationship of Theatre and English departments" and focused on "the best-known canonical plays around the turn-of-the-century, and the early decades, with Williams, Miller, Beckett, perhaps Genet, and Pinter at mid-century, and the trendy American and British plays of recent years."[1] While the text-centered curriculum she criticizes works in literature departments—since courses in modern dramatic literature need literary texts—the history of modern and contemporary drama has been profoundly influenced by various strands of the avant-garde that are "subjects regularly *not* taught" in courses on modern or contemporary drama and theater.[2] Indeed, it would be difficult to imagine the very dramatic canon Marranca criticizes, especially the more contemporary dramas, without the legacy of the avant-garde movements that are typically overlooked. This historical avant-garde is the primary focus of this volume.

Marranca's critique is arguably a product of those avant-garde strands and has much in common with the antitextual sentiments of the avant-garde and with the avant-garde's redefinition of the mise-en-scène and of performance as artistic forms in their own right. In the opening essay of this volume, Laurence Senelick documents much of that redefinition, especially as it evolved in a combative relation to the institutions of culture in general and to literature in particular—but so too does David Graver's essay on Artaud and on the authorities of "the text." At one level, in fact, it is easy, from Senelick's and Graver's discussions, to recognize the legacy of the avant-garde's antitextualism in Marranca's critique of academic theater. This, in part, accounts for her criticism of the interrelationship of theater and English departments and for her criticism of the preeminent position that texts and textual metaphors have enjoyed in theater studies at the expense of other traditions that have impacted theater practice in the twentieth century. Not surprisingly, the examples from those other traditions cited by Marranca have a long affiliation with the avant-garde. She refers to the rich sources that the "visual arts," "dance history," and "the new physics and sciences" have been in the evolution of twentieth-century experimental theater, and the impact of these very traditions on our understanding of the avant-garde are explored here by Mike Sell, Kristine Stiles, Sally Banes, and Michael Vanden Heuvel.[3] Philip Auslander's essay on Fluxus presents, in fact, a convincing case for extending Marranca's list even further so that it includes experimental music as an influential source for avant-garde performance as well.

My comments are not intended to suggest that Marranca's critique is merely a subtle reassertion of the legacy of the avant-garde. On the contrary, her critique attests to the timeliness of the renewed interest in avant-garde performance that this volume exemplifies. It appears at a time when textuality, at the very least as a critical metaphor, has become perhaps the most pervasive of analytical paradigms, and while Marranca's criticism of an "overemphasis on drama and indifference to staging practices," that is, a privileging of (dramatic) text over performance, may generally refer to the dominance that the study of literature has exercised over the study of theater, her assessment has very specific implications for the study of the avant-garde.[4] It suggests that relying on textual metaphors to analyze performative practices may very well skew, if not compromise, analysis. Where Marranca argues by implication, Richard Schechner is more direct. In the interview in this volume, he simply states that the study of literature and the study of performance are entirely different disciplines. They are governed by their own unique requirements. So too is the avant-garde, and for the study of it some resistance to the pervasiveness of textual metaphors would seem to be crucial. If such metaphors blur the distinctions between text and performance, they may not only cultivate an indifference to the performative dimensions or staging practices of avant-garde theater; they may very well elide a crucial dynamic of the historical avant-garde. They may compromise an assessment of the (admittedly problematic) opposition that the avant-garde constructed between text and performance.

This volume is thus based upon the assumption that it is worth considering whether textual metaphors are precalibrated to oversight and thus blind to the very legacies that Marranca admonishes us to teach. One example of such precalibrations and of the extent to which textual metaphors tend to eclipse the tension between text and performance that is so central to the historical avant-garde is Clifford Geertz's seminal essay from the early 1980s, "Blurred Genres: The Refiguration of Social Thought." Geertz speaks of a destabilizing "recourse to the humanities for explanatory analogies in the social sciences."[5] As ominous as this destablization may at first sound, Geertz's assessment is generally positive, and, though careful to demand intellectual rigor, he finds especially encouraging sociological analyses that employ a "text" or "drama" analogy. As helpful as such analogies may be to the social sciences, they lack, in Geertz's discussion, the distinctiveness that characterizes them in the work of theater scholars like those who have contributed to this volume. Though scholars may disagree on the degree to which one can ultimately maintain a distinction between text and performance in the avant-garde, the shift from a "text analogy" to a "drama analogy" cannot come as easily as it does in Geertz's discussion. For, in one respect, the rise of avant-garde performance is premised upon the demise of a text-centered approach to theater. Two immediate examples of this argument occur in this volume, the first of which responds almost directly to Marranca's lament that theater scholarship has been characterized by an "over-emphasis on drama and indifference to staging practices."[6] Christopher Innes's "Text/Pre-Text/Pretext: The Language of the Avant-Garde" maps the gradual separation of text from performance in the history of the avant-garde and explores how this separation was facilitated by innovative experimental workshops. In some respects, Erika Fischer-Lichte's "The Avant-Garde and the Semiotics of the Antitextual Gesture" picks up where Innes leaves off. Her essay culminates in a discussion of how avant-garde experimental performance led to the formation of a new genre of literary text, namely, the director's manual, which is the product of, but distinct from, performance itself.

Though removed from the actual problematic relation of text to avant-garde performance, Geertz's cautious embrace of text and drama analogies has a fundamental relevance to the assessment of that relation. Rather than taking interest in the extent to which the analogies he cites are in conflict with one another, Geertz is—and understandably so—primarily interested in the effect that text and drama analogies have on the quality of analysis produced in the social sciences. His concerns with the potentially delimiting effect of text and drama analogies recently appropriated by the social sciences thus find an interesting echo in Marranca's concerns with the delimiting effect of blurring the hard-fought distinctions between text and performance that have profoundly affected the course of twentieth-century theater. These distinctions, though hard to maintain as clear binary oppositions, are grounded in an historical antagonism between text and performance that has been one of the avant-garde's greatest sources of vitality. Yet the implications of this antagonism, in the final analysis, are not limited to dramatic texts or literature. They extend to institutional texts as well. The antagonism between text and performance in the history of the avant-garde carries an implicit challenge to the institutional practices of theater scholarship itself—especially as these practices relate to those who would assess the history, success, and impact of the theatrical avant-garde. At one level, these practices have already been challenged by critics like Alan Woods, who has suggested that the scholarly interest in the avant-garde is indicative of a "literary bias" that privileges avant-garde performance over popular theater, since "much popular theatre lacks [the] literary value (or even merit)" that scholars have identified in avant-garde expressions.[7] Though the historical avant-garde's interest in cabaret and variety theater tends to undercut the opposition that Woods draws between the avant-garde and popular theatrical forms, his criticism of the bias in theater scholarship is not without precedent. With regard to scholarly discourse and textual practices, one cannot help but ask whether scholars of the avant-garde too easily brush aside provocations like Marinetti's expressed desire "to free this land from its smelly gangrene of professors" and to "destroy the museums, libraries, [and] academies of every kind."[8] At one level, the context of such comments—one that incidentally includes Marinetti's own interest in variety theater—indicts the very institutional framework within which Marranca and other theater scholars work. As is well known, Marinetti's comments are by no means isolated. Historically the theatrical avant-garde has consistently defined itself vis-à-vis a negation not only of text and mimesis but also of author-ship and author-ity and of the academic institutions to whom Marranca addresses her comments. Even Daryl Chin, the associate editor of *Performing Arts Journal,* has argued that the avant-garde "is founded on the oppositional, the adversarial, the antagonistic" and that its "institutionalization," which is tantamount to its demise, "began with the dependence on education."[9] With respect to the avant-garde, the crucial problematic thus faced by scholars even today grows out of their own institutional discursive practices as critics and theorists and out of the relationship that these practices have to the analysis of radical, experimental performance communities that, while not anti-intellectual, have frequently defined themselves in a hostile relationship to academic institutions and their scholarly method. In its simplest terms, the looming question for scholars of the avant-garde becomes how to avoid metaphorically and/or literally reinscribing avant-garde performance into its textual and institutional antinomies.

While much of the work included in this volume suggests that the antinomies between the academy and the avant-garde have never been all that clearly defined—and here I am thinking specifically of Sally Banes's marvelously informative history of university patronage of the avant-garde—the two have had an uneasy working relationship at best. The point here is not to downplay those tensions but rather to acknowledge them and to recognize that, however problematic our institutional accountings of the avant-garde may be, the antitradition of avant-garde theater, in its varied forms of resistance to institutionalization, can still offer us important insights into the industries of literature, theater, scholarship, and culture.

This volume is intended to provide the context for a consideration of these insights and to precipitate an enduring constructive exchange, already begun in the volume itself, between critical theorists, theater historians, scholars of dramatic literature, and members of the performance community. Addressing scholars in both theater and literature departments, it will be especially appealing to those who seek to introduce students to the radical provocations underlying the avant-garde tradition, and to those whose own work focuses on the often strained relations between the arts and the university or, more generally, between the arts and their institutional cultural contexts. Given the nature of the book's topic, it demands that a multiplicity of voices be heard, contrasted, and left unreconciled. Rather than developing a single thesis or seeking closure, the volume thus intends to provide a topology of the contentious negotiations between the contexts of avant-garde performance and the texts to which these contexts give rise.

On the Definition of the Avant-Gardes, or the Definitions of the Avant-Garde

Crucial to this topology is some sense of the range of definitions that are assumed in the different essays included in this volume. It may come as no surprise that my initial answer to the question, "What is the avant-garde?" is not altogether consistent with the answers that emerge from the essays themselves. That is perhaps as it should be. Definitions of the avant-garde are legion. They are tendentious, combative, and contested, and they are elusive, which ironically may be the one thing that all definitions of the avant-garde share. Elusiveness has been a trait associated with the avant-garde since Ortega y Gasset, in his seminal study *The Dehumanization of Art* (1925), argued that avant-garde manifestations split the public not into groups defined by those who like a work and those who do not but rather into groups defined by "those who understand it and those who do not."[10] Any work positioned rhetorically to challenge the comprehension of those who would dismiss its significance lends itself to provocation, controversy, and debate. Such has been the repeated position of the avant-garde and of those who would don its mantle. While unresolved debates over the mantle of the avant-garde may very well be confusing to those who desire precise definition, such debates do have one positive side: they signal an enduring resilience that the avant-garde has sustained in part by fluidity in definition and a willingness to "continually attack itself in order to survive and prosper."[11] In fact, many would maintain that "to be in the avant-garde is to be in a perpetual state of rebellion."[12] Much of this rebellion has developed in opposition to definitions imposed upon the avant-garde, and while this clearly has been a crucial source of renewal, it is important to keep in mind that not only the definition of the avant-garde has evolved in the last century but so too, for better or worse, has its sense of rebellion, and it is this evolving sense that for many, including myself, either distinguishes the historical from the present avant-garde or, in more extreme terms, distinguishes the authentic avant-garde from the experimental theater that passes as avant-garde today.

Regardless of whether one defines the avant-garde solely as an ephemeral movement inseparably intertwined with a modernist past, or whether one recognizes in the radical aesthetic movements from the early part of the century the emergence of what Michael Vanden Heuvel has called an "avant-garde urge" that has continued to thrive in contemporary theater, our understanding of that urge—like Benjamin's theory of allegory, which played a crucial role in his study of German Baroque tragedy—is largely contingent upon a sense of the dynamics that characterized the historical avant-garde.[13] As Peter Bürger notes about the theory of allegory articulated in *The Origin of German Tragic Drama:* "it was Benjamin's experience in dealing with work of the avant-garde that made possible both the development of the category and its application to the literature of the Baroque, and not the other way around."[14] Though Bürger uses these comments to justify his appropriation of Benjamin's theory of Baroque allegory for a discussion of the avant-garde and montage, they also provide a measure with which to assess the objectives and focus of this book. Concentrating primarily upon radical, experimental theater from the turn of the century up to about 1970, this volume pivots on an inversion of Bürger's strategy for dealing with Benjamin. Rather than using the avant-garde to account for a theory of drama from a previous period (like the Baroque), this book intends to explore the dynamics of the historical avant-garde so as to lay the foundation for a consideration of the origins or originality, the debts or departures, and the blunted or cutting edges of contemporary, experimental performance.

But even this agenda is not without its problems—affirming once again Paul Mann's assertion that "the discourse of the avant-garde," characterized as it is by dialectical and polarizing effects, is such that "one cannot hope to rise" above it.[15] These problems are not the result of essays included in this volume (like those by Kristine Stiles, Sally Banes, Patrice Pavis, and Michael Vanden Heuvel) that assume either explicitly or implicitly that there is a contemporary avant-garde. A discussion of the "historical avant-garde" that spans the first seventy years of the twentieth century is for many an unacceptable extension of the term *historical avant-garde,* if not of *avant-garde* itself. Such, for example, were the views expressed by Erika Fischer-Lichte when I first approached her about a contribution to this volume. On this point, Fischer-Lichte's views are in marked contrast to Richard Schechner's characterization of the "historical avant-garde" as encompassing "a period of innovation extending roughly from the end of the nineteenth century to the mid-1970s (at most)."[16] Fischer-Lichte's views have much merit in distinguishing between the politically and aesthetically radical experiments in European theater between the wars and the theater that reconstituted itself after the rise of fascism drove radical theater from the European continent. Though I personally do not subscribe entirely to this view, it does raise some important questions about the highly charged value of the term *avant-garde* as an epithet and titular commodity.

The most fundamental of these questions has to do with what one gains and loses by the continued use of the term *avant-garde,* or conversely with what one gains and loses by discontinuing use of the term. Seeking answers to these questions, it seems to me, is far more important and constructive than attempting to find a solid definition of the term. Clearly, the stakes in the answers to this question remain high, and though one would be hard pressed to effectively counter the implicit assertion in Schechner's rhetorical question "What in today's performance world can be said to be new?" his well-known claims that the term *avant-garde* "no longer serves a useful purpose" and that for contemporary theater the term "really doesn't mean anything today" are belied by the contested, controversial currency the term continues to enjoy.[17] In fact, for those who advocate the continued use of the term, the gains, rhetorically at least, have more to do with constructing a critical opposition to the cultural mainstream than with the production of the uniquely new: hence Richard Kostelanetz's association of the avant-garde with "establishing discernible distance between itself and the mass of current practices,"[18] and Hal Foster's argument that with the absorption of the historical avant-garde into the mainstream of bourgeois society—what for Bürger was the failure of the historical avant-garde—"the institution of art is [now] grasped as such not with the historical avant-garde but with the neo-avant-garde."[19]

Whether indicative of a path that is entirely new or one that is built upon a provocative recombination of techniques once thought to be exhausted, characterizing contemporary aesthetic expressions as avant-garde or neo-avant-garde necessitates a fundamental revision of the concept itself. Indeed, many critics, like David Graver, have forwarded arguments that seriously question whether, after the institutionalization of the historical avant-garde, contemporary experimental theater can legitimately claim to position itself in critical relation to our cultural institutions: "Once the radical, iconoclastic innovations of dada and surrealism are accepted as legitimate forms of artistic expression, no innovation can place an artistic movement beyond the pale of legitimate aesthetic practice and, hence, give it the distinctive otherness enjoyed by previous incarnations of the avant-garde concept."[20] If Graver is correct in his assessment and "distinctive otherness" is now precluded as a possibility for aesthetic expression, the presumption that the neo-avant-garde can grasp the "institution of art" cannot, as Hal Foster maintains, be taken for granted. This is not to say that the neo-avant-garde is a failure but rather to say that it resembles the historical avant-garde only in name. The term itself has undergone a kind of recycling and has been put to different use.

One of the primary differences has to do with politics. Lost in the contemporary concept of the avant-garde is the historical avant-garde's embrace, however problematic, of revolutionary politics—an embrace that Renato Poggioli and Christopher Innes have traced back to the Paris Commune and revolutionary anarchist thinkers like Bakunin, the legacy of which I explore in the essay that I have contributed to this volume. On the one hand, Foster is fully cognizant of this embrace and recognizes that historically the avant-garde has been crucial to the "coarticulation of artistic and political forms."[21] Yet in his critique of Peter Bürger's argument that "the aim of the avant-garde . . . [was] to destroy the institution of autonomous art in order to reconnect art and life," Foster simply overlooks the extent to which in pursuit of this aim the historical avant-garde defined "life" along revolutionary political (either Marxist or anarchistic) lines.[22] After maintaining that a central characteristic of the "neo-avant-garde . . . is to *critique* the old charlantanry of the bohemian artist as well as the new institutionality of the avant-garde, Foster argues that Bürger "fails to recognize the ambitious art of his time" and as a result "can only see the neo-avant-garde in toto as futile and degenerate in romantic relation to the historical avant-garde." This blindness, Foster maintains, is especially ironic. Despite a "grounding in Benjamin," Foster notes, Bürger thus "affirms the very values of authenticity, originality, and singularity that Benjamin held in suspicion."[23] At the very least, the irony here is doubled, for Benjamin's expressed suspicion of authenticity, originality, and singularity—which finds its clearest articulation in "The Work of Art in the Age of Mechanical Reproduction"—is but a preface to an assertion that with the loss of these values art is now prepared to assume a meaningful role in politics, which, for Benjamin, clearly meant revolutionary politics.

Whatever its ambitiousness, the neo-avant-garde that Foster discusses in *Return of the Real* is far from revolutionary, and though one can cite numerous examples from the historical avant-garde that fall short of genuinely revolutionary aspirations, the association of the historical avant-garde's radical artistic expressions with radical politics is important at the very least because it establishes a parallel between the avant-garde's relation to the institution of art and revolutionary activism's relation to the structures of bourgeois society, a parallel that is only implicit in Peter Bürger's arguments. The latter revolutionary activity is not a criticism from within but an attack from outside and is intended not to reform and correct a system that it maintains; rather it intends to topple the existing system. Similarly, Bürger has characterized the relation of the avant-garde to the institution of art as fundamentally distinct from a "system-immanent criticism," that is, a criticism that "functions within a social institution."[24] The historical avant-garde took on the institution of bourgeois art as a whole, exposing its "productive and distributive apparatus and also . . . the ideas about art that prevail[ed] at . . . [the] time and that determine[d] the reception of works."[25]

Good examples of this process were the experimental theatrical workshops of figures like Grotowski and Brook discussed by Christopher Innes in this volume, especially since these workshops underscored the production rather than the finished product or finished work of art. But the point is that once this "self-criticism of art" is absorbed by the institution of art, then the status of movements like the neo-avant-garde acquire the rather dubious hue of "system-immanent criticism." This is by no means to suggest that we today lack a profoundly engaging experimental, political theater, but rather to suggest that to call that theater avant-garde or even neo-avant-garde may not only fail to enhance our understanding of the significance of that theater, but it may also distort our understanding of the historical avant-garde.

Perhaps somewhere in the Althusserian realms of uneven historical developments there are surviving or newly emerging contexts where radical art and revolutionary politics can yet converge into a vital contemporary avant-garde or where avant-garde performances can escape the institutional affirmations of a "system-immanent criticism." Perhaps those same uneven developments demand a multiplicity of definitions, even of the historical avant-garde. I have tried in this volume to accommodate such discrepancies while still maintaining some historical bearing. In proceeding thus, I obviously betray an ironic trust in the lessons of history—ironic because much of the theatrical avant-garde's historical oppositions to bourgeois society and its institutions have pivoted on the ephemeral, elusive nature of performance. It has thus consciously circumvented the mechanisms of historical record, that is, the stuff on which lessons of history traditionally rely. Nonetheless, important registers of the historical avant-garde have endured and have shaped the course of this book.

Among those registers the most paradigmatic has been the avant-garde's positioning of itself in opposition to the mainstays of bourgeois theater, which, as is well known, was a text-based theater. As the object against which the avant-garde was able to define itself, that text-based theater served not only as a foil for the avant-garde's antitextualism but more generally for its opposition to the institutions of bourgeois culture. Certainly, the antitextualism of the avant-garde was a manifestation of that opposition and not merely because it coincided with a rejection of bourgeois theater. That text-based theater was indicative of a bourgeois obsession with the printed word (an obsession that even T. S. Eliot found disturbing), and the antitextualism of the avant-garde needs to be understood, at one level, as a crucial example of the avant-garde's fierce opposition to the underpinnings of bourgeois society and its institutions.

On the Book's Structure

The attempt to provide a wide accounting of that antitextualism and its implications is central to the first section of this collection of essays. The essays included in this section of the book are united by their considerations of the various ways in which the avant-garde resisted institutionalization by defining itself as a negation of literature, text, author-ship, author-ity, and the theater associated with these concepts.

While the theater is greatly indebted to the avant-garde for demonstrating that performance and mise-en-scène are more than mere representation of a text, the essays in the second section of the book explore the extent to which "text" is more than that which the avant-garde negates in its reconceptualization of performance. These essays examine how the avant-garde has not only ironically tended to produce texts even as it attempts to establish a theater liberated from texts. They also consider the extent to which textuality itself is an inescapable dimension of performance.

The essays in the third section of the book examine the question of textuality by shifting the focus of discussion to the avant-garde's defiance of the traditional spatial and textual limitations of conventional drama, that is, to the avant-garde's radical redefinition of theatrical space. The essays in this section, which situate the avant-garde in its various relations to the institutions of bourgeois theater and culture, serve as a crucial primer for the book's final section.

The fourth and final section of the book considers avant-garde performance in its long problematic relation with the academy. The essays not only document how closely tied to the academy the avant-garde has historically been, but they also document how that tie has been and continues to be marred by an overt hostility.

NOTES

1. Bonnie Marranca, "Theatre at the University at the End of the Twentieth Century," *Performing Arts Journal* 50–51 (1995): 56.

2. Ibid.

3. Ibid., 56, 57.

4. Ibid., 56.

5. Clifford Geertz, "Blurred Genres: Refiguration in Social Thought," *American Scholar* 49 (1980): 168.

6. Marranca, "Theatre at the University," 56.

7. Alan Woods, "Emphasizing the Avant-Garde," in *Interpreting the Theatrical Past,* ed. Thomas Postlewait and Bruce A. McConachie (Iowa City: University of Iowa Press, 1989), 168.

8. F. T. Marinetti, "The Founding and Manifesto of Futurism," in *The Twentieth-Century Performance Reader,* ed. Michael Huxley and Noel Witts (New York: Routledge, 1996), 251.

9. Daryl Chin, "The Avant-Garde Industry," *Performing Arts Journal* 9 (1985): 65.

10. Ortega y Gasset, *The Dehumanization of Art,* trans. Helene Weyl (Princeton: Princeton University Press, 1948), 6.

11. Paul Mann, *The Theory-Death of the Avant-Garde* (Bloomington: Indiana University Press, 1991), 11.

12. Marc Aronson, *Art Attack: A Short Cultural History of the Avant-Garde* (New York: Clarion, 1998), 11.

13. Michael Vanden Heuvel, *Performing Drama/Dramatizing Performance* (Ann Arbor: University of Michigan Press, 1993), 25.

14. Peter Bürger, *Theory of the Avant-Garde,* trans. Michael Shaw (Minneapolis: University of Minnesota Press, 1984), 68.

15. Mann, *Theory-Death,* 19.

16. Richard Schechner, *The Future of Ritual: Writings on Culture and Performance* (New York: Routledge, 1993), 18.

17. Ibid.

18. Richard Kostelanetz, *Dictionary of the Avant-Gardes* (New York: A Capella, 1994), xiii.

19. Hal Foster, *Return of the Real: The Avant-Garde at the End of the Century* (Cambridge: MIT Press, 1996), 20.

20. David Graver, *The Aesthetics of Disturbance* (Ann Arbor: University of Michigan Press, 1994), 11.

21. Foster, *Return of the Real,* 5.

22. Ibid., 15.

23. Ibid., 11, 12.

24. Bürger, *Theory of Avant-Garde,* 21.

25. Ibid., 22.

I. Text and Antitext in the Historical Avant-Garde

Laurence Senelick

Text and Violence: Performance Practices of the Modernist Avant-Garde

> *Ciamar a thu, how are you, and hoozit gaun pal,*
> welcome to thi Cabaret Guillaume McGonagall.
> We got: Dadaists, badass gits, shits wi RADA voices.
> Futurists wi sutured wrists and bygets o James Joyce's—
> *Bienvenue, wha the fuck you are, let's drink the nicht away,*
> *come oan yir own, or oan thi phone, or to thi* Cabaret.
>
> W. N. Herbert[1]

> When traditional artistic forms reach a dead end, the products of popular culture are admitted into the drawing-room, raised to the rank of authentic literary art, to wit, canonized.
>
> Viktor Shklovsky[2]

In the Beginning Was the Word

At one point in his precocious autobiography, in which he narcissistically relates all manner of offensive behavior, Salvador Dalí regrets one outrageous stunt he failed to pull off. He had long hoped to arrange things so that one morning the populace of Paris would awake to discover a gigantic loaf of a bread, a *baguette* of Gargantuan length, extending to the Bois de Boulogne. The inexplicable nature of this apparition would, he was sure, *épater les bourgeois* once and for all.[3]

This unrealized *blague* bears many of the earmarks of modern avant-garde performance: mystification, disproportion, and enormity, an everyday object imbued with Freudian symbolism and made a source of wonder and stupefaction. In one respect, however, it is uncharacteristic both of artistic provocation and, in particular, of Dalí, since it is meant to be anonymous. The perpetrator must remain unknown if the victims are to be flabbergasted to the proper degree. This runs counter to the tradition (if such a word can be used of the first avant-garde) of exhibitionism, which places the creator center stage as the "onlie begettor" of his outrages. It was precisely such showing-off that raised the hackles of George Orwell. Granting Dalí's talent, he objected to him as "an exhibitionist and a careerist," and raised the question why should the art world so willingly indulge and nourish these aberrations.[4] Aberrant acts committed privately fell within the mandate of the psychiatrist; aberrant acts committed publicly and greeted with respectful attention required the attention of the sociologist.

Making the public pay attention has, from the outset, been an intrinsic need of the avant-garde, and this has usually been taken to mean a frontal attack. However, as early as 1864, Baudelaire scorned the military metaphorism explicit in the term; to his ears it implied a conformism and discipline inimical to artistic individuality. Michael Kirby has pointed out the term's "directionality," which suggests "a rear guard or at least the main body of troops following behind."[5] In military thinking, however, a vanguard also implies reconnaissance patrols, insidiously infiltrating the populace. The spies Joshua sent into Canaan are early instances of this kind of subversion. The avant-garde does not necessarily rush to engage the enemy, but often underhandedly undermines its foes. A Salon des Refusés can make its mark only if people attend it, but best of all, if the artists mingle with the crowd to savor its reactions. While direct confrontation triggers violent effects, the artist stealthily withdraws from the fray to observe and gauge the nature of these effects. Art as a disruptive "fifth column" may be a more appropriate figure of speech.

Traditionally, an author could gauge the impact of his work only at a remove, by means of press notices, sales figures, fan mail. The avant-garde, however, required the immediacy of performance to test the efficacy of its provocation. Too often, historians have overstated the literary origins of the modernist avant-garde. Even in the case of dada, the most self-consciously iconoclastic of the early movements, Hans Richter insists, "the Cabaret Voltaire was first of all a literary phenomenon." This emphasis is reiterated by Willi Verkauf, who points out that, although dada is valued as a major movement in modern art, the painting and design it engendered were essentially illustrative, and, like its masks and manifestations, ancillary to literature. "The motive power came from literature, from the cerebration of non-painters and, wherever fine art made its contributions, from artists, who knew how to express themselves no less by the written word than by the brush or the engraver's needle."[6]

Without discounting the literary origins and motives of its progenitors, one should point out that from its inception the modernist avant-garde was as performative as it was literary, perhaps more so. The earliest seeds of the modernist avant-garde are, indeed, to be found among literary gatherings of the 1870s, but what constituted "literature" or "literariness" was already under attack: preexisting standards of prosody, subject matter, treatment, and, particularly, decorum were discarded in favor of strong feeling and a more direct relationship to life. How this was presented, the poet's performance, one might say, was what mattered; as Verlaine remarked, slightingly, "Et tout le reste est littérature."[7] The dialectic between artistic intention and public response required a more blatant mediation by performance than had earlier movements. In the taverns and nightclubs that cradled these newborn talents literature was conveyed via performance, or else, in the process, its formal qualities were made to play second fiddle to its efficacy as a vehicle for performance. In the cabaret, as Klaus Budzinski reminds us, "the literary element must lie rather in the author's ability to inspire, that is, to present the interpreter with a subject for performance worked out just broadly enough to open the door for his interpretive imagination."[8] When the avant-garde found its first home in the *cabaret artistique,* the written word had to take its place among skits, songs, recitations, projections, puppet plays, and dance; when it was not performed by its author, the word was reliant for its transmission on expert reciters and *diseuses.* The Italian futurist repudiation of everything academic or conventional made a point in a 1915 manifesto of shouting at the top of its print-font, "EVERYTHING OF ANY VALUE IS THEATRICAL."[9]

The Writer as Performer

Those casual meetings of poets in Parisian cafés in the early 1870s, the Vilains Bonshommes and the Zutistes, disseminated a new version of the bohemian as *poète damné,* the artist self-dramatized as outcast and alcoholic and epitomized by Verlaine.[10] By the next decade the original image of the bohemian as insouciant hedonist had been effaced by that of a more radical rebel who rejected the allure of filthy lucre, cultural uniformity, and the well-being promised by the "leveling of pleasures," refusing any compromise with the mindless herd. This anticonformism, commonly evinced by an avoidance of regular employment, was emblazoned as resistance and challenge to the bourgeoisie. Despite attempts to identify it with the anarchist movement, most bohemian opposition to the bourgeois establishment was more temperamental than political, and as readily linked to such various manifestations of new aesthetic tendencies as dandyism, decadence, and symbolism. Or, less programmatically, to humor (a word, *l'humour,* and a concept borrowed by the French from the English), fantasy, and *fumisme.*[11]

French-English dictionaries translate *fumisterie* as an "imposition" or a "joke," but it is a joke that must be delivered deadpan to have its full effect. To exalt this into a system, *fumisme,* is to organize a skeptical and essentially pessimistic philosophy into a series of elaborate hoaxes. It was the bohemian weapon par excellence for deflating pomposity and exposing hypocrisy. Bohemians playing practical jokes on the bourgeoisie was a favorite topos of fiction: Eugène Sue's immensely popular serial novel *Les Mystères de Paris* (1842–43) and its stage adaptations were punctuated by the gross pranks perpetrated by the artist Cabriole on the witless concierge Pipelet. *Fumisme,* however, was a subtler form of aggression, a charge laid so deep that the victim was often unaware that he had been undermined until it was too late. The composer Georges Fragerolle explained that *fumisme*

> is to wit what operetta is to opéra-bouffe, caricature to cartoon, prunes to castor oil. To be considered a wit, it is sometimes enough to be an ass in a lion's skin; to be a good *fumiste,* it is often required to be a lion in an ass's skin. In the former case, the effect is direct, in the latter it is once, twice, often ten times reflected.[12]

Fumisme was made the defining element in a literary gathering by Émile Goudeau when he transformed the loosely knit poets' clubs into a "grander scale of group entertainment, collaboration and self-promotion,"[13] known as the Hydropathes. Paradoxically, the Hydropathes were not full-time rebels or social pariahs: most were professionals or students of impeccably middle-class background who dabbled in poetry. After paying a visit in the early weeks of the organization's existence, Francisque Sarcey, doyen of French theater critics, gave it his blessing, calling it, "très intelligent tout ensemble et très sympathique." He found nothing dangerous about it, but regarded the atmosphere of mutual criticism more wholesome than in "those little so-called poetic chapels, in which each one plays God in turn."[14] The irony is that Sarcey, the type of all that was most conventional and philistine in French taste, would become a major butt of the Hydropathes, who vied in making up stories that put him into embarrassing situations or issuing outrageous statements in his name.

Sarcey also noted that celebrated actors were attending meetings of the Hydropathes: it was this theatrical admixture that catalyzes the conversion of the literary into the performative. The Hydropathes had from the start organized their meeting place and their program along the lines of the *café chantant* and the variety stage: instead of a group of poets sitting around a restaurant table in an intimate discourse, there was a podium, a master of ceremonies, and, eventually, an invited audience that did not participate. This last factor is crucial. So long as all those in attendance take part, such a gathering may be considered *en famille;* but once a distinction is made between those who recite and those who merely listen, a public performance has taken shape. The result was more convivial than the earlier poets' gatherings, but also more literary than the ordinary variety show.

The performance format also dictated the style of the writing. As Daniel Grojnowski points out in the best account of the Hydropathes in English, texts designed to be performed aloud on a stage strive for immediate effect. The need for bravura pieces that would startle by their virtuosity, paradoxicality, or surprise led the group to work out genuine "routines." Individuals developed stage personae and a set of idiosyncratic inflections to characterize their speech. The spirit of *fumisme* called for a spoken word that revelled in puns, *recherché* rhymes, a mockery conveyed by tone of voice. Grojnowski calls this, somewhat tautologically, the "rhetoric of orality."[15]

The most striking innovation was in the writer subsuming the performer and addressing the audience *in propria persona*. Precursors can be found in the platform performances of Dickens, Thackeray, Mark Twain, and other authors who, with varying degrees of histrionic proficiency, interpreted their own writing in public. In those cases, however, they were reading published works that were familiar to the listeners. The audience attended to hear an authoritative rendition of words and ideas already known to them; the fusion of the author's personality with the prose lent the latter greater validity, as if the voice of the Lord itself were to utter the Sunday service. For the public, the text was authenticated by the physical presence of its creator. Obviously, the impression was strongest when the author proved to be, like Dickens, a talented actor; but, for the most part, the residual effect was reassuring.

The avant-garde writer as performer had a different aim, not to reassure but to defy and undermine the public's assumptions. Rarely were the pieces published, and then usually in small-circulation magazines and limited runs of private presses. The audience had to deal with the bonding of writer and text as it was presented to them for the first time (even though writer-performers might be expected to have "party pieces," which they would reel off on request). It also had to revise its relationship to the author as he challenged its preconceptions on the spot.

The conversion from a group of writers reading their latest productions to one another into a troupe of performers reciting to an invited public was swift. At first, guests might be asked to offer their own contribution, but the dividing line between performer and spectator was quickly drawn, and once the spectator was charged an admission fee, the transition from club to cabaret was complete. However, the commercial factor made it imperative that the audience be "entertained," not simply with refreshments. Therefore an element of spectacle entered the picture. Le Chat Noir not only provided a picturesque ambience of Gothic armor and Valois antiques redolent of Dumas *père,* it became famous for its shadow-theater performances. The illuminated screen against which the shadow puppets played required the hall to be darkened, so that the narrator read the text in a penumbra that obscured his face. Since the narrator was usually the author of the play, this lent his disembodied voice special authority.

The author-performer's voice as the primary indicator of the meaning of the action refers us to the modernist debate about actors versus puppets. At a time when the legitimate theater was dominated by stars and personalities, the avant-garde theater rejected the actor's primacy, and replaced it with the writer's. "Actors spoil plays for me. . . . Their personalities efface the work they represent," declared Anatole France in a statement Paul Margueritte used to preface a brochure meant to win the Parisian public over to puppet plays.[16] A cast of puppets subjugated to the author's will was the logical devolution of the Wagnerian idea that everything in the theater must serve the vision of a single genius. As the Russian symbolist poet Fedor Sologub wrote, in a world in which all humanity is prey to Fate, there is nothing humiliating for an actor in becoming a puppet. Sologub prescribed a theater in which the author sat beside the platform reading his text, stage directions and all, while the actors mimed to his words.[17] The shadow play and the puppet show were perfect realizations of this theater, and the concurrent innovation of monodrama,[18] a play in which the audience was to observe the action and form its opinions by "co-experiencing" the reactions of only one character, shared the same goals.

Very often in early cabaret such a mise-en-scène was evoked to challenge the dominance of naturalism and illusionistic staging. In a parody of Hauptmann performed at the Elf Scharfrichter cabaret in Munich, a narrator speaks a single sentence that runs on for several pages, while the characters enact a series of horrific events that befall them in accordance with the running narrative. In Christian Morgenstern's duologue *Egon und Emilie,* the actor breaks the frame and refuses to carry on in the traditional way to the traditional end.[19] The conventional relationships between author and actor, between author and audience, between author and character, between actor and character all undergo questioning and are rarely allowed to stand.

A similar conflation of author and protagonist is conspicuous in Alfred Jarry's *Ubu Roi* (1896), invariably cited as the first "avant-garde" play. Although at the premiere the role of Ubu was taken by a distinguished actor, Firmin Gémier, Jarry had conceived of his characters as the personnel of a puppet show, and the play itself had evolved from toy theater performances Jarry had mounted when a schoolboy. His essay "De l'inutilité du théâtre au théâtre," published in the *Mercure de France* in September 1896 in advance of the production of *Ubu,* denigrated the virtuosity of actors and called for depersonalizing masks.[20] As Rilke once noted of Maeterlinck, Jarry is best performed by amateurs; his characters resist complicated psychologies or technical expertise. When a great actor such as Georges Wilson or a great comic such as Max Wall portrays Père Ubu, focus shifts from the author's ingenuity to the prowess of the performer.

The play's violence by its very cartoon nature needs the dehumanization of a Punch-and-Judy show to work properly. In this respect, *Ubu Roi* has much in common with the slapstick knockabout of silent movie comedy: the muteness of the actors, the conversion of color into black-and-white, and the oversized image on the screen helped provide a *Verfremdungseffekt* conducive to laughter unhindered by thought of consequences. In their own unaffected way, Mack Sennett and the great Hollywood comics who followed him were unwitting avant-gardistes, as the surrealists were quick to note.

In Jarry's case, however, the role of puppet master extruded into the role of puppet. Over time donning the mask of Père Ubu became habitual, and he could not remove it; he turned into the outrageous caricature plastered with white cosmetics memorialized in chapter 8 of Gide's *Les Faux-monnayeurs* (1925).[21] In this guise he could offend with impunity: assuming Ubu's identity was a means of removing himself from human consequences, a real-life equivalent to the harmless knockabout of the puppet-show and the pantomime comedy.

Another model for the author-performer was the *diseur* of the popular variety stage. Recitation had long been a lucrative form of parlor entertainment for legitimate actors who could amuse a social gathering while dressed in evening clothes; the foremost French dramatists composed monologues with particular artistes in mind. Coquelin *cadet,* the monologue's foremost exponent, modestly called himself merely the genre's "midwife." He identified its "mother" to be Charles Cros, a leading light of the Hydropathes, whose monologues "L'Obsession," "Le Bilboquet," and "Le Hareng saur" are pioneering examples of black humor.[22] The popularity of the *diseur* and *diseuse* on the variety stage suggested a new intimacy, no longer reliant on music, between performer and a more sophisticated spectator. The ability to put across a song through expression, timing, innuendo, and the knowing use of gesticulation had always had more to do with music-hall success than had musicianship. Whatever the locale, the most popular music-hall stars—Marie Lloyd and Dan Leno in London, Mayol and Jeanne Bloch in Paris, Otto Reutter and Claire Waldoff in Berlin—had no voices to speak of, but communicated in an eloquent *Sprechstimme.*[23]

Yvette Guilbert, who did have a musical background but "only the ghost of a voice" according to the composer Gounod, was careful to be billed as a *diseuse,* and the piano behind her texts is a modest *obbligato.* Without "a trace of the rowdy restlessness and forced 'go'" of the music-hall singer, she "makes all her effects in the simplest way and with perfect judgment," Bernard Shaw recorded.[24] The songs that brought her fame, her *chansons grivoises* and *chansons rosses,* narratives and character monologues, were delivered "between clenched teeth." In "Quand on vous aime comme ça," Guilbert sings as a battered woman of the proletariat, who revels in the blows and bruises her boyfriend hands out as love tokens; the delivery is punctuated with ouches and groans, imitations of a swollen lip or a broken jaw. It is *nat-*

uraliste to the max, without abandoning the lighthearted melodic line of the music or ingenious rhymes of the poem. In "Les Vieux Messieurs," Maurice Donnay's hymn to dirty old men, Guilbert catalogs the various species of superannuated lecher lovingly, caressingly, and only at the last does she begin to voice her indignation in the refrain, "Les vieux coch"—but stops and returns to the cooing, "Les vieux messieurs, les vieux messieurs." The subtlety of the performance makes acceptable the inadmissibility of her subject matter. Her masterpiece, "Les Vierges," was carried past the censors by her calm air, slow diction, and coldness; not singing but coughing over the forbidden words, making them considerably smuttier in the process.[25]

Although Guilbert never sang in *cabarets artistiques*—her usual venues were variety theaters and nightclubs— most of the poets associated with the Hydropathes and the Chat Noir wrote for her, and her example was widely imitated. Her mordant style of delivery was frequently commented on as a novelty in an age of golden voices declaiming a *ronron tragique.* As it happened, Coquelin *cadet* recited Cros's pieces in a similar deadpan style, also associated with Jarry (Gide remembered "no inflection or nuance and equal stress on every syllable, even the silent ones"),[26] Lugné-Poe and Firmin Gémier, the trio responsible for the incarnation of Ubu. In line with its preference for puppets over actors, Jarry's "De l'inutilité du théâtre" prescribed a special voice, not unlike the high-pitched drone of the puppet Guignol, and suggested that "the delivery throughout the play be monotone." In a letter to Lugné-Poe on the eve of production, Jarry reiterated the need for a special voice for the lead character.[27]

Among the Hydropathes, Maurice Mac-Nab, said to have no voice for public speaking, became famous for his unsmiling rendition of his poem "Les Foetus," reciting woodenly "as if he were intoning a page from the Office of the Dead."[28] The point was that it was impossible, in this unnudging performance, to determine whether to laugh or feel sad at each stanza. Both there and at the Chat Noir, Alphonse Allais maintained a mien of great dignity that reminded Maurice Donnay of a blond Viking and Jane Avril of an English first mate. With a melancholy smile on his lips, he could fill line after line with a monotonous *grisaille* before detonating a particularly percussive gag.[29]

In Germany, a similar novelty in recitation was associated with Frank Wedekind, who presented his macabre ballads to his own guitar accompaniment; the musical side is remarkably anodyne, as the sheet music reveals. The power must have resided entirely in Wedekind's mordant, impassive delivery, using a voice Brecht described as "brittle, slightly monotonous and quite untrained."[30] It may have had its origins in the style of the *Bänkelsinger,* the street singer who intoned his gruesome, rhymed accounts of dreadful doings *(Moritäten)* while flipping over lurid pictures of the deeds. This almost mechanical narrative of the ghastly was given sepulchral resonance by the female star of the Elf Scharfrichter, Marya Delvard. The frequently reproduced posters of Delvard depict her with a skull-like visage, her mouth drawn down into a reverse rictus, her expression stonily grim, a perfect incarnation of the French term *pince sans rire.*

The performer's poker face and inexpressive elocution proclaimed a new relationship between performer and audience: the former was no longer attempting to ingratiate himself and make things easy by interpretive inflections and gesticulation; the latter was put on its mettle to figure out what attitude to take to the performance. For the first time in the Western theater, irony becomes a major component of the performer's art, rather than the dramatist's.

The Audience as Performer

In his memoirs, the German poet Erich Mühsam provides a vivid description of Wedekind's lesser-known brother Donald performing a variation on this style:

> Donald Wedekind interpreted his brother's songs, masterfully accompanying himself on the mandolin, with the sonorous and insinuating voice of a baritone, and at the same time in a Swiss accent which gave him a harsh expression, almost without modulation. Women were absolutely fascinated by his diction. . . . While he sang, he took a malicious pleasure in making each of his female listeners blush one after the other. He would stare fixedly at a girl, lean towards her over his instrument and hypnotically emphasize the raciest passages in the song's lyrics. The poor victims writhed politely beneath his piercing gaze and finally turned crimson. And when he estimated he had gone far enough, he turned to another with the same surefire effect.[31]

This style of close-range aggression could work only in the presence of a silently receptive audience. When avant-garde performance began to feature "bruitism" and clamorous demonstrations, a more stentorian tone was required. One chronicle of the Café Voltaire notes that on April 9, 1919, the audience howled down Tristan Tzara, who was trying to read a dada proclamation, "la voix en lambeaux" [his voice in tatters].[32] Just such an antiphony of agents provocateurs on stage and an indignantly rebarbative reaction from the house was, for the next wave of the avant-garde, a consummation devoutly to be wished.

To achieve this, the gemütlich and welcoming ambience of the artistic cabaret had to be dispelled. When Max Halbe organized the Intimes Theater in Munich in 1895, he prescribed keeping the masses and their money at arm's length; "let the circle be open only to art and friends of art . . . a specialists' stage by and for artists, a stage free from all nonartistic considerations, an intimate theater, where experts and connoisseurs can be alone among themselves."[33] Halbe's elitism was retrograde; for the writer-performer, insulting the audience was a potent means of testing his effectiveness.

To create a body of taste and opinion conducive to his work, the avant-garde artist had to make himself conspicuously unacceptable and create a state of misunderstanding or virtual warfare between himself and the public. "Provocation is a way of putting reality on its feet," Bertolt Brecht explained.[34] Unlike the actor or the manager inadvertently offending the audience by improper behavior or commercial maladress, the deliberate attempt of artists to affront public taste or morals was a relatively recent phenomenon. Owing to entrenched censorship throughout Europe and to the self-protective nature of theater managements, the stage, as was its mandate, tended to endorse community values and reinforce the audience in its prejudices. In the French theater, long dominated by the *claque* system, a form of spontaneous audience participation had managed to emerge; by the time of the battle of *Hernani* (1830), spectators came expecting to take sides in a war of convictions. The tumults that greeted the premieres of *La Dame aux camél-lias,* adaptations of Zola and the Goncourts, *Tannhäuser* at the Paris Opéra, Hauptmann's *Vor Sonnenaufgang* in Berlin, Chekhov's *Seagull* in St. Petersburg are stops along the road to *Ubu.*

These recurrent eruptions of outrage should not, however, be taken as registering a refinement in public taste; rather, they are outlets for audience activism. Such participation helped restore to the audience its function as an integral factor in the performance. As the audience was made more passive by the prevalence of subdued lighting in the auditorium, by its division from the stage by the orchestra pit and proscenium, and by a general melioration of manners (except in the galleries), its only opportunity to recover its earlier active role was in shows of displeasure against distasteful truths or stylistic innovation. It was a way of impeding the post-Wagnerian trend that turned the audience into a cowed congregation, isolated in the dark, made to concentrate on a framed simulacrum of reality. However, unlike reformers such as the Russian symbolists, who sought to revive the theater by creating a quasi-religious communion between stage and house, the dadaists and futurists preferred to arouse the latent hostility between the artist and the spectator. The cool disdain conveyed by the deadpan style coexisted with more raucous lendings from the amusements of the people.

A constant refrain in avant-garde manifestos lauds the variety stage and circus. These offered powerful and attractive antitheses to conventional theater: nervous sensation rather than reflection, kaleidoscopic variety rather than narrative, outlandish attractions, often vulgar and aggressive, as a polemic to a dominant culture of introspection. The call to replace established theater with an all-inclusive species of performance, capable of embracing marionettes, showbooths, and the grotesque, varies from Jarry's prescriptions in "De l'inutilité du théâtre" and Otto Julius Bierbaum's call for a Dionysian theater in his novel *Stilpe* (1897) to Meyerhold's and Eisenstein's anti-illusionistic fracturing of dramatic structure into "A Montage of Attractions." Predictably, similar pronouncements are broadcast by the dadaists: "The image and artistic ideal as variety program—: that is our kind of 'Candide' against the times."[35]

These encyclicals commonly repudiate the hegemonic text, reinstate the virtuosic player of the prenaturalistic stage, call for unusual performance spaces, and acclaim rhythm as a key device. All means of modern technology and techniques of traditional performance are enlisted in the attack on literary theater. Principles of montage, simultaneity, and speed demand structural elements suitable to a new sensibility. These ideas were so prevalent that, by the 1920s, even Walter Benjamin can be found praising a performance of *Hamlet* as "a revue of passions," and extolling "The virtuosity of the player versus the theater engineers! That will be the Wembley of theatrical art."[36]

Popular entertainment fostered a more symbiotic relationship between the performer and the crowd as well. A prime reason Marinetti hailed the music hall was that it "is the only kind of theater where the public does not remain static and stupidly passive, but participates noisily in the action, singing, beating time with the orchestra, giving force to the actor's words by unexpected tags and queer improvised dialogue." However, in contrast to the commercial variety theater, in which the customers' prejudices and comforts were catered to, the avant-garde theater was to engage them through what amounts to practical applications of *fumisme:*

> To smear gum on a stall so that its occupant may be stuck to his seat and excite general hilarity. Naturally the evening coats or dresses would be paid for by the management. To sell the same place to ten different persons; obstructions, discussions and quarrels will necessarily follow. To offer free seats to ladies and gentlemen who are notoriously cracked, irritable, or eccentric—calculated to provoke immense rows by bizarre or objectionable behavior.[37]

In popular entertainment, the risk is all on the performer's side, and the illusion or actual presence of danger adds piquancy to the spectator's pleasure. In avant-garde performance the danger is transferred to the audience, which finds itself in an anomalous situation, incapable of taking anything for granted, and often under attack.

Disconcerting the spectator was not meant exclusively as an incitement to hostility. The ostensible motive behind the provocation was analeptic or therapeutic. One of the first commentators on dada called it "a stratagem by the artist to impart to the citizen something of the inner unrest that prevents the artist himself from being lulled to sleep by custom and routine."[38] The external stimuli were restoratives for the worthy burgher's lack of inner urgency and vitality, meant to startle him into a new life.

"Give a dog a bad name and hang him," the saying goes. A preliminary step in estranging the audience was to christen it with a term of opprobrium. Preexisting stigmata were plentiful, starting with Matthew Arnold's "Philistines," drawn from the German university slang *Philister* for townies; in *Culture and Anarchy* (1869) Arnold contrasted their "Hebraic" moral earnestness with the "Hellenistic" free play of intelligence. Whether these smug worshippers of the second-rate were called "Children of Darkness," after Carlyle, or, less melodramatically, *épiciers,* to point up their connection to trade, they were the necessary collocutors in the artistic dialogue, the dull whetstone against which the bohemians' wit could be sharpened. In the French theater, they had been incarnated in Henry Monnier's Monsieur Prud'homme, until the avant-gardists turned the bald, bespectacled critic Sarcey into a fictional character to their advantage and his discomfiture. At the Stray Dog in St. Petersburg, the standard term of abuse, "pharmacists" *(farmatsevtsy),* labeled literary dilettantes and mediocrities; but despite the cry of its cofounder N. Sapunov, "Don't let in pharmacists," they tended to make up the bulk of the cabaret's frequenters.[39]

This was an imponderable problem in casting the spectator as stooge. With the establishment of independent theaters at the fin de siècle, audiences arrived expecting provocation and might take offense only when the fare was blander than it expected. To provide stronger meat for jaded appetites, the *tranches de vie* of the Théâtre Libre coarsened into the bloody gobbets of the Grand Guignol. Tourists to Montmartre enjoyed the frisson of attending the Cabaret du Néant, where they were served by undertakers and dined off coffins. At Aristide Bruant's Le Mirliton, they reveled in being called swine to their faces by mine host who specialized in custom-made insults. The aggression of the early *cabaret artistique* was somewhat muted by being licensed. When the minister of public education asked the prefecture of police in 1897 why cabarets were not subject to preliminary censorship like theaters and music halls, he was told that the personnel of the Chat Noir and Le Mirliton were "composed of poets and song-writers whose works had artistic value and who do not seek the vogue enjoyed by smutty productions." Unlike the variety stage, which catered to a lower class of clientele and lured schoolboys, cabarets were deemed not obscene, and the prefecture turned a blind eye toward those situated in artists' quarters such as Montmartre.[40]

The bourgeoisie's ability to absorb shocks and keep apace with its provocateurs has been deplored by Artaud and Genet. To pierce this resiliency and overcome the artist's marginal status, frontal attacks required a higher decibel level and an escalation of the mode of attack. Inexplicable dumb shows and noise, the long-standing means of splitting the ears of the groundlings, were abetted by scatology. The audience was assailed both by the dadaists' bruitistic concerts and the futurists' ensembles of bizarre instruments and by the verbal evocation, if not the sight and smell, of the cloaca. With Ubu's *Merdre!* as rallying cry and his toilet brush as a standard, the avant-garde spewed forth all the words that from childhood had been forbidden public utterance. Apollinaire's manifesto-synthesis *L'Antitradition futuriste* (1913) set "Mer . . . de . . ." to music and wished it on a long list of bêtes noires ranging from critics, Shakespeare, and Siamese twins to "dilettantismes merdoyants" [boring-as-shit amateurishness].[41]

The very first dada soiree at the Café Voltaire on July 14, 1914 had waged these tactics with some success.:

> Before a compact crowd, Tzara demonstrates, we want we want we want to piss in many different colors, Huelsenbeck demonstrates, Ball demonstrates, Arp Erklärung, Janco meine Bilder, Heusser einige Kompositionen dogs bark and the dissection of Panama on the piano on the piano and embarcardero—Poem shouted—*shouts* in the audience, fights, first row approves, second row declares itself incompetent the rest shout, who is stronger they bring on the bass *drum,* Huelsenbeck against 200, Ho osenlatz [*sic,* i.e., Trouser fly] accentuated by the very base drum and bells on the left foot—protests shouts breaking windows suicide demolition fighting police interruption.[42]

In the long run, however, pandemonium has diminishing returns. When Tzara arrived in Paris in 1920, the editors of *Littérature* decided to stage a public demonstration every week, and the first such manifestation in March was a huge success. *Le Figaro* called it "a beautiful hullaballoo," and pointed out that neither *Ubu* nor Marinetti's satiric tragedy *Le roi Bombance* (1905) had ever unleashed such bedlam or been so blackguarded; the public booed and whistled at the "Dadas who welcomed the insults with beaming faces. . . . The Dadas exasperated the spectators and I think that's really all they wanted."[43] A certain weary standardization began rapidly to set in to both the incitements and the reactions. André Breton recalled that the "methods of bewilderment" and agitation developed in Zurich were practiced in Paris without much originality.

> Every time a Dada demonstration was planned—naturally by Tzara who never tired of it—Picabia would gather us in his drawing-room and call upon us, each in turn, to come up with *ideas* for this demonstration. Ultimately, the harvest was not very abundant. The main course would inevitably be made up of the first, or the second, . . . or the *n*th Adventure of M. Antipyrine by Tristan Tzara performed by his friends invariably shoved into cardboard tophats (as a last resort, this was his favorite "idea," Zurich must have been agog at it).[44]

A decrement in excrement was also evident. There is a certain Falstaffian cynicism as well as Rabelaisian ribaldry in Francis Picabia's declaration, "Honor can be bought and sold like your ass. Your ass, your ass represents life the way French fries do, and you serious lot smell worse than cowshit."[45] However, when Wieland Herzfelde publishes a poem called "The Dada-lyripipidon," each line playing on "Pipi,"[46] and Raoul Hausmann dubs Walter Mehring the "Pipi-dada," the source of inspiration is not the water closet but the nursery. Gradually, the audience steels itself to mere simulation and even looks forward to the game, forcing the performer to greater extremes. Even in our own jaded age, pursuit of the "stool for scandal" has led Karen Finley to pour Hershey's syrup down her front to simulate the liquid feces she invokes; but even she is eclipsed by the fecal explosions of Leigh Bowery, who inundated the first rows at his shows with the effects of an enema often mixed with blood capsules.

There is also the unlooked-for result that the audience will outdo the performer in aggression. The press of the early modernist period testifies amply to the active and contentious comportment of spectators in reply to the provocations directed at them from the stage. The beleaguered spectators fought back, showering the futurists with a wide assortment of vegetables and manhandling the performers.[47] Huelsenbeck claimed that he and plants in the audience exchanged blank gunfire at his dada lectures; but unrehearsed mayhem was more common. At the Stray Dog in 1917 St. Petersburg, an anti-tsarist allusion in a recitation by Nikolai Evreinov provoked a volley of gunshots from a sullen tsarist ensign at a ringside table.[48] That same year Jacques Vaché, one of Jarry's fondest admirers (Jarry had been notorious for random fusillades at home and in cafés), came to the opening night of Apollinaire's *Les Mamelles de Tirésias* brandishing a revolver and threatening to fire into the audience.[49] The gunshot that had so often marked the climax of nineteenth-century drama crossed the footlights to become part of an exchange between the public and the spectacle.

The violence of individual spectators grew more predictable but also more dangerous when organized, as in the attacks of the *camelots du roi* and other reactionary groups against Buñuel and Dalí's surrealist film *L'Age d'Or* at the Cinéma 28 in Paris in 1930. By throwing stink bombs at the screen and breaking up the place, they offered physical chaos as an antidote to what they regarded as artistic and moral chaos. The recourse of the *camelots du roi* to brute force is, perhaps, the natural sequence of events. After all, Huelsenbeck had declared that "Dada is the chaos out of which a thousand orders arise, which Dada will swallow up back to Chaos."[50] Willed self-annihilation is built into the avant-garde program, and in the process the individual human being is first reduced to sheer body and then becomes sacrificed to the machine.

The Thing as Performer

The avant-garde was not, in fact, in the forefront when it came to apotheosizing popular entertainment. The naturalists' obsession with corporeality necessarily imputed a fascination to acrobats and gymnasts, the body brought to perfection. For the avant-garde, however, attention to such marginalized performers was part of the urge to embrace all human activity in a global vision. When Jarry began writing a regular column for *La Revue Blanche* in 1902, he announced that he would be concerned with

> *spectacles plastiques.* . . . Perfection of muscles, nerves, training, skill, craft, technique: . . . bare-knuckle fights, horse races, velodromes, skating, car-driving, women's fashions, an operation performed by a great surgeon . . . a tavern, a dance-hall. . . , a drunkard expert in tipples, an explorer who has eaten human flesh. . . , the offspring of a tabby-cat and a squirrel. . . , a sailboat veering to the leeward . . . a squabble among topers . . . the Pope's funeral.[51]

His rationale was that "All these gestures and in fact all gestures are to a degree aesthetically equal"; and in keeping with this idea, his first two contributions covered Barnum's circus and the contortionist Juno Salmo. The body in motion was also emblazoned in Marinetti's proposal to carry to the fullest extreme the physicality and sensationalism of the sawdust ring: "FUTURISM WANTS TO TURN VARIETY INTO A THEATRE OF AMAZEMENT, RECORD-SETTING AND BODY-MADNESS (*physico-follia*)."[52]

One of the more intriguing passages in Marinetti's praise of the variety theater singles out a particular type of physical comedy associated with Americans. His ambition is

> To encourage in every way the genius of the American Eccentric, all his mechanical grotesque effects, his coarse imagination, his immense brutality, his surprise waistcoat and his baggy trousers, deep as a ship's hold, from which will be brought out, with a thousand other cargoes, the great Futurist hilarity which shall rejuvenate the face of the earth.[53]

There was a long tradition of English and American clowns dominating the European circus ring—Sir Edwards, Tom Belling, Footit (and it might be recalled that Footit was another example of impassive foolery); the very word *clown* entered most European languages at this time.[54] But the references to brutality and mechanicality may refer, more specifically, to the ineffaceable but often overlooked influence of the Hanlon-Lees.

An English-born acrobatic troupe that played the Americas in the 1860s, the Hanlon-Lees next performed pantomime scenarios in Russia, Germany, and France. Their scenarios were macabre, ultraviolent revocations of the laws of nature, exhibitions of spring-heeled agility and ingenious "tricks of construction," wringing startled laughter out of reversible decapitations, ceiling walking, shipwrecks, human beings slammed through pianos or their fellow man with speed and dexterity. The Hanlon-Lees became the darlings of the Parisian intelligentsia and in no small degree inspired such naturalist explorations of the circus as Edmond de Goncourt's *Les Frères Zemganno* (1879). Goncourt noted their "glaçante bouffonnerie" [chilling hijinks] and was not alone in finding "something mortuarily funambulatory, a macabre facsimile of the jollity of agile undertakers" in their performances.[55] The rejection of rational explanations and decorous convention had the appeal of down-market anti-Cartesianism that will recur in the cinéastes' praise of Jerry Lewis.

The Hanlon-Lees' combination of unsmiling sadism and slapstick was regarded as peculiarly "Anglo-Saxon."[56] Alphonse Allais invented a Yankee persona, Captain Cap, to purvey his shaggy-dog stories in a disquietingly impassive manner. Goncourt described Paul Margueritte's pantomime *Pierrot assassin de sa femme* as a "pierrotade macabre à la façon d'un clownerie anglais," and Margueritte himself dedicated his *Pierrot Mormon* to the Hanlon-Lees. The latter contains such moments as this:

> Major Bagstock prepares himself a toddy of neat whisky into which, along with some addled eggs, he crushes a pimento the size of a cucumber. He drinks it hot, without batting an eyelash. All of a sudden a tiny blue flame appears like a drop on the end of his nose and a practical-minded Yankee dashes up to light his cigar at it. One masterful uppercut followed by a well-aimed kick sends him catapulting into the india-rubber hunchback, knocking over Madame Lou, who, as she flounders,

> reveals the color of her garters. The rubber-ball-man bounces off the ceiling, flattens a gentleman like a pancake, and floats through the balcony window in a fireworks display of broken glass.[57]

The "American" flavor is to be tasted in the farrago of up-to-date fads (a cocktail, India rubber, boxing) with magical and multifunctional transformations (a nose used as a cigar lighter) and extreme mayhem entailing no serious physical consequences; this last, along with the pyrotechnics of broken glass, persist in current Hollywood action films.

Another manifestation of this vogue is Frank Wedekind's *Bethel,* a burlesque pantomime "in Anglo-American taste" about a racehorse and a beauty with a birthmark; it employs eccentric comedy, acrobats and equestrians, cowboys and Indians, chorus girls and Salvation Army lasses, along with wild beasts played by actors. Worse off than Madame Lou, a matron loses her petticoats; the Sioux blow their noses on a white flag of surrender; and everything ends in a Lewis-Carrolline trial and an Offenbachian cancan. This mythic America would also be drawn on by Jean Cocteau in his ballet *Le Boeuf sur le toit* (1920), set in an American bar, its characters cast from circus clowns; by Brecht for his early plays, and by Voskovec and Werich for their Prague satirical revues. In Wedekind's scenario, however, as with the Hanlon-Lees (and later, Chaplin), objects are made to serve alien functions: a thermometer scans the horizon, gun barrels and a stethoscope staunch a monstrous thirst, an umbrella stands in for a revolver.[58] The sudden metamorphoses, the contortions of the human form, the sexual innuendo, the floating and falling fit most neatly into the surrealist dreamscape.

In these American-inspired farces, the human body loses its mortal fragility and takes on the properties of a soulless thing. Like the comic character in Bergson's theory of laughter, it comes to resemble a machine, efficiently but mindlessly repeating its behavior. One of the textbook clichés about modernism is that, in an age of unprecedented scientific discovery and speed of transport and communication, the artist began to worship progress and the Machine at the expense of traditional "humanistic" values. This is in some degree true after 1910, when the Italian futurists denigrated the art of the past in favor of the machine form. Marinetti's statement that a racing car was more beautiful than the *Victory of Samothrace* was expanded by Apollinaire in *L'Antitradition futuriste,* which advocated "machinism," wherein "every form of expression should contribute a dynamic element of its own to a dynamic civilization."[59] A photograph reproduced in most books on dada shows George Grosz and John Heartfield at the Berlin Dada Exhibit in June 1920 holding up a sign that reads, "Art is dead. Long live the new art of the machine of Tatlin."[60]

The earnestness of these statements is suspect, given the pervasive undercurrent of *fumisme.* The plaint "Les choses sont contre nous" could also be heard nearly as often. Rather than supplanting the human with the machine, the avant-garde seemed to be trying to equate machines to human beings, to bring them both to a point where the machine's vitality could be exploited outside the humanist traditions of subjectivity and emotionalism. Although the new might be embraced in order to subvert the old, the inanimate object in itself was not to be trusted, and was as apt for mockery and alienation as the human body.

The avant-garde apotheosis of the machine was undercut by the persistent concept of the enmity of inanimate objects toward their human masters. This notion had been treated comically in America as early as 1864 in Katherine Walker's *Atlantic Monthly* article "The Total Depravity of Inanimate Things," and gained currency in Europe from Friedrich Theodor Vischer's novel *Auch Einer* (1878), which speaks of "die Tücke des Objekts." The notion seems to be a sublimation of a Luddite unease with a burgeoning material world. In the wake of the Industrial Revolution, rooms become filled with mass-produced furniture, decorations, bric-a-brac. Streets teem with vehicles, public monuments, *ammeublement de la rue* such as Morris columns, kiosks, and *vespasiennes.* The human image is captured by the mechanical method of photography, and the voice by phonography. Social intercourse is mediated by objects from telephones to canned food to condoms. A feeling of alienation from the overpoweringly material sets in. Speaking of the younger generation of the Russian intelligentsia in the second decade of the century, Viktor Shklovsky said, "Things died, we lost a sense of the world, we were like a violinist who had lost the touch for bow and strings."[61] So, while some avant-garde artists were extolling the sleekness and dynamism of the modern machine, others were either deploring the dehumanization attendant on industrialism or equating humans and machines as alike in their vacuousness and futility.

The modernist avant-garde handled this proliferation of things and their inimical relationship to humanity in two distinct ways. In the pictorial and graphic arts, the artist channeled and manipulated the object to create an entity, such as a fur-lined teacup or a urinal labeled "fountain," that thwarted expectations of functionality or aesthetics. The surrealists' violent yoking of disparate objects is a similar technique. In their collages and constructions, Raoul Hausmann, Hannah Höch, and Max Ernst exploited the fetishism of catalog advertisements, using the images of the commercial media to subvert both business and art. Francis Picabia's object portraits made a joke out of "the forced incongruity between the inert objects drawn in [a] generic manner and the titles conferring individual personality, emotion, or sexuality" on them.[62] The machine or object becomes anthropomorphized, but any heroic pretensions are dissolved by an ironic and debunking wit.

In the performing arts, a more common or literal practice was to show the performer at loggerheads with the physical object. The stage property, which in French has the telling name *accéssoire,* stops being an accessory to or extension of the actor and becomes a hindrance and a foe. This was a regular comic device of the great Munich clown Karl Valentin: whether playing in an orchestra, running a photographic studio, speaking over the radio, changing a spotlight, or simply reading a love letter, he found himself engaged in a mortal tussle with every prop he came in contact with. "Objects are perfidious," he wrote:

> The trouble is, they have to be confronted before they can be used, because once aroused from their state of torpor objects take a perfidious revenge. And this creates laughter, because laughing is the only way to react to the fear created by things that come to life in an unpredictable way in the hands of man.[63]

The Panoptikum that Valentin founded featured such improbable exhibits as a nose-picking machine and the apple Eve had offered Adam with a bite taken out of it, poker-faced satires of the scientific pretensions of the natural history museum and the cabinet of curiosities. However, in his sketches, which unravel into a tangle of complications, malice operates on every level: objects, language, and human behavior all display a callous recalcitrance and casual rudeness. Consequently, they all have to be wrestled to the ground and trampled on. Valentin confutes Bergson's premise that human beings become funnier the closer they resemble machines; in his microcosm, things come to seem like refractory individuals.

Valentin's is a theater of estrangement, a void in which persons and objects are alike reduced to signs. For all the surrealism of his visions, however, Valentin remained a popular entertainer, and, although a comic genius, cannot be enrolled among the programmatic avant-garde, because his artful nonsense made no pretence of intellectual defiance or solemn provocation and aggression. Dada and futurism sought freedom in the constant practice of negation, a liberation from any laws, morality, or gravity whatsoever. Valentin, on the other hand, achieved his reductio ad absurdum by functioning within the bounds of convention.

The avant-garde equivalence of human performer and machine is more clearly put in Walter Mehring's *Race between Sewing Machine and Typewriter,* performed by him and George Grosz at a happening of the Berlin Dada Club in December 1918.

> *At the sewing-machine:* BÖFF, *world champion at plugging genital and educational gaps.*

At the typewriter: WALT MERIN, *featherweight.*
BÖFF. "Whirr, whirr—bassalur" (H. C. Andersen)!
WALT. Tocktocktock! Ding! Ping, ping!
BÖFF solo on the ocarina. Tülitetüt! Lüttitü! O, sole mio! Old man river; Mississippi—
WALT. . . . et Rataplan, rataplan!
BÖFF. Willy, willy—Wow, wow!
WALT aside. —by Wolfgang Goethe!
BÖFF and *WALT in unison.* Eiapopeia! Tandaradi! Hip, hip Dada . . . Dada-capo![64]

Here, the human actors speak for and manipulate the machines, but have not yet been merged with them.

The intrusion of the thing itself as a rival or counterpart to the flesh-and-blood performer seems to have begun earlier with Marinetti's "drama of objects," *Il Teatrino dall' amore* (The Toy Theater of Love, 1915). Marinetti explained that the most important characters "are the little wooden theatre (whose marionettes perform in the dark without the presence of a puppeteer), the Buffet, the Sideboard [that] present in a non-human way the temperature, their dilations, the weight that they support, the vibrations of the walls" by their dialogue of creaks and cracks whenever the human *dramatis personae* are offstage. If the object is the leading character in *Il Teatrino,* it gains celebrity status in the futurist "surprise" sketch *Music for Dressing By,* in which an upright piano wearing ballet slippers is groomed by a set of servants.[65]

Avant-garde playwriting subsequently provides us with a showroom of inanimate objects that obliterate their human performer, from the Kiosk in Apollinaire's *Les Mamelles de Tirésias* (1917) to the Curtains in Picasso's *Le Désir attrappé par la queue* (1941), and including the Toothbrush, Cigar, and sugared Pernod in René Daumal's *En gggarrde!* (1924). To perform such objects is equivalent to being imprisoned in Picasso's cubist costumes for *Parade* (1917): the performer's personality is totally effaced, and recourse is had to the uninflected tones of the cabaret *diseur.* When he concocteaued the "characters" of two talking phonographs in *Les Mariés de la Tour Eiffel* (1921), Cocteau did not even allow them the ragtime garrulity of Victor Columbia Edison, the animated gramophone in L. Frank Baum's *The Patchwork Girl of Oz* (1916). His praise for Pierre Bertin and Marcel Herrand, the actors who created the roles, singles out their self-effacement: "Diction black as ink, as big and sharp as the capital letters on a billboard. Here, oh surprise, the actors seek to serve the text rather than serving themselves from it."[66] The actor is no longer even a puppet, but a disembodied voice devoid of distinguishing features.

When the avant-garde artist working in cabaret imagined a world controlled by machines, he painted it in murky tones. The totally mechanized futures envisaged in 1923 and 1924 by Mehring in his revue song "The Machines" and by the Polish poet Bruno Jasieński in his surrealistic novel *The Legs of Isolde Morgan* are bleakly dystopian. But the following year Laszlo Moholy-Nagy's essay "Theater, Zirkus, Varieté" formulated a hopeful fusion of the circus model with the machinal. In it he calls for a theater of pure affect and the ruthless ousting of whatever "literature," "ideas," and "potential truth" persist on the expressionist, futurist, and dadaist stages. The subconscious and dreams of fantasy and reality, hitherto central to the intimate art theater, are rejected. Moholy-Nagy is willing to accept the "human eccentricity" and "mechanics of the body" drawn from circus acts and athletic exhibitions: these are "essentially founded on the surprise or stupor of the spectator confronting the potential of his own organism, revealed by someone else." Unfortunately, this produces "a subjective effect" with mingled elements of sensibility and literature; for popular entertainments are too superficial to eliminate subjectivity entirely. Hence the need for a "uniquely mechanical" eccentricity, a minutely controlled synthesis of contrasting dynamic phenomena, which is capable of excluding the human being from the stage entirely, although it may choose to use him as an adjunct. To this end, talent, craft, or even stage presence were nugatory: Oskar Schlemmer predicted that anyone picked from the audience and transported to the stage would be transformed by its magical nimbus.[67]

As Schlemmer and others experimented with these ideas at the Bauhaus, the leaching of individuality from human beings and their reduction to robotic status was achieved by carapace-like costumes; the "functional elements" of mortals were aligned with puppets, mannequins, and automata. When Hugo Ball had appeared at the Café Voltaire encased in his famous wizard's costume of cardboard, he had experienced a panic—a mixture of claustrophobia, agoraphobia, and helplessness—that propelled him to bizarre but appropriate behavior. The Bauhaus's metallic masks and padded sculptural suits of papier-mâché served a different purpose: they were meant to transform dancers and actors into architecture in motion. The human body in space mutated into geometric shapes or mechanical motions. Schlemmer's *Triadic Ballet* (1922) initiated a type of performance that became increasingly abstract and elementary. By the time Wassily Kandinsky created a "stage synthesis" to illustrate Mussorgsky's *Pictures at an Exhibition* (Dessau, 1928), the whole stage had become occupied exclusively by "objective forms" (with the exception of two "pictures" that employ a couple of dancers in a schematic and almost static manner).[68] The *Gesamtbühnenaktion* (total stage action) called for by Moholy-Nagy marks a return to the Wagnerian *Gesamtkunstwerk,* with the performer's individuality and virtuosity entirely subjugated (or in this case excluded) by the single vision of the deviser, Kandinsky's "spectator-interpreter-creator."

What Then?

With characteristic self-assurance, Richard Huelsenbeck predicted that despite the ephemerality of dada, its laughter would have a future. But there is no trace of *fumisme* or comic virtuosity in the peremptory pronunciamentos of Moholy-Nagy. The metamorphosis of the literary gathering into an industrial showroom was complete.[69] The shunting aside of the author as *auteur* and the relegation of the audience to a passive receptor of stage "magic" is in keeping with the predominating role of the mass media; as live performance itself became obsolete, almost by definition aimed at a mandarin audience, the avant-garde was in danger of seeming retrograde or at least *vieux jeu* in its recycling of stock ploys.

If one reads through C. Carr's collection of reviews of so-called alternative or avant-garde performance for the *Village Voice* over the past decade, the sense of déjà vu is overwhelming. Although putting in play the latest technologies and revelling in a sexual blatancy untapped by their precursors, these artists essentially recapitulate the innovations of the past, usually without the theoretical underpinnings. Coupling exhaustion with excess (which, at the previous fin de siècle, Arthur Symons saw as a sign of decadence), they perform in a social vacuum in which anything goes. Having to cover an evening of "neoism," Carr all but throws in the critical towel.

> Any definition of neoism simultaneously reveals and conceals, because that is the goal—to get where "all mechanisms of logic are broken, control is impossible, the great confusion rules." Neoism dates from the late seventies—an ism that swallowed every modernist ism, then puked out the pieces. Jarry's pataphysics [*sic*], Marinetti's manifestoes [*sic*], Duchamp's readymades, Klein's leap, Warhol's fifteen minutes, Beuys's alchemy, Maciunas's games—they're all floating in the neo soup now. Neoism is the last little gurgle of what we once called avant-garde. Or maybe it's nothing.[70]

What blunts the cutting edge of the current innovators is the absence of a universal ambition in their works. For all their nihilism, the pioneers of the modernist avant-garde made megalomaniacal claims for their insurrections: Fragerolle proclaimed, "'Fumisme' *was* nothing, it *is* everything"; Rudolphe Salis planted his banner with the strange device "What is Montmartre?—Nothing! What should it be? All"; and Otto Julius Bierbaum forecast that the

Nietzschean Superman would be born not in a manger, but in a *manège*. Richard Huelsenbeck rejoiced that dadanarchy "has turned world history into parody and God into Jack Pudding."[71] Jarry, typically the most categorical, announced, "La 'pataphysique, c'est la science," laying claim to all knowledge for his dominion. Perhaps cowed by the extremes to which slogans of "All or Nothing" brought us in the cataclysmic twentieth century, contemporary avant-gardists are comparatively modest in their pretensions and refrain from such absolutism, except as self-parody.

For the artist's presence on stage as performer to have prestige, his person, rather than his art, has to be at stake, to some degree. Wedekind was imprisoned for lèse-majesté for a poem about the kaiser; and the kaiser's eventual successor, Adolf Hitler, proscribed modernism as *Entartete Kunst* or *Kulturbolschewismus*. Cabaret artists and avant-gardists found themselves muzzled, exiled, imprisoned, or murdered. Marinetti penned paeans to Mussolini; and Mayakovsky, who had welcomed the Bolsheviks by calling for the liquidation of all past art, grew so disillusioned with the Stalinist confiscation of the revolution that he liquidated himself. In contrast, the refusal of funding or of gallery space to current avant-gardists is child's play; it highlights their marginality to the life of their society. Iconoclasm ends up as image making, and instead of a direct relationship between the artist-performer and the public, the media, as their name makes explicit, intermediate.

NOTES

1. W. N. Herbert, *Cabaret McGonagall* (Newcastle upon Tyne: Bloodaxe, 1996), 1.

2. Quoted in Victor Erlich, *Russian Formalism: History—Doctrine* (The Hague: Mouton, 1965), 76.

3. Salvador Dalí, *The Secret Life of Salvador Dalí,* trans. Haakon Chevalier (New York: Dial Press, 1942), 128.

4. George Orwell, "Benefit of Clergy: Some Notes on Salvador Dalí," in *Dickens, Dalí, and Others: Studies in Popular Culture* (New York: Reynal and Hitchcock, 1946), 177.

5. Charles Baudelaire, *Mon coeur mis à nu* (1864), in *Oeuvres complètes,* ed. Cl. Pichois (Paris: Editions de la Pléïade, 1961), 1218–19; Michael Kirby, *The Art of Time* (New York: E. P. Dutton, 1969), 18–19.

6. Hans Richter, "How Did Dada Begin?" in *Dada: Art and Anti-Art,* trans. D. Britt (London: Thames and Hudson, 1965), 18; Willi Verkauf, *Dada: Monograph of a Movement* (London: Academy Editions, 1975), 12.

7. Paul Verlaine, *L'Art poétique* (1874), in *Oeuvres complètes,* ed. Charles Morice (Paris: Albert Messein, 1925), 1:296.

8. Klaus Budzinski, ed., *So weit die scharfe Zunge reicht,* in *Die Anthologie des deutschsprachigen Cabarets* (Munich: Scherz Verlag, 1964), 9–10. Unless otherwise noted, translations are my own.

9. Filippo Marinetti, Emilio Settimelli, and Bruno Corra, "The Futurist Synthetic Theater" (1915), trans. R. W. Flint, in *Futurist Performance,* ed. Michael Kirby (New York: E. P. Dutton, 1971), 196–202. For originals of futurist documents, see *Il Teatro futurista a sorpresa: Documenti* (Florence: Salimbani, 1979).

10. Mary Shaw, "All or Nothing? The Literature of Montmartre," in *The Spirit of Montmartre: Cabarets, Humor, and the Avant-Garde, 1875–1905,* ed. Phillip Dennis Cate and Mary Shaw (New Brunswick, N.J.: Rutgers University Press, 1996), 125.

11. Paul Valéry: "The word *humour* is untranslatable. If it weren't, the French wouldn't use it" (*Aventure,* November 1921, quoted in André Breton, *Anthologie de l'humour noir* [Paris: Jean-Jacques Pauvert, 1966], 14). Also see Lionel Richard, *Cabaret, cabarets: Origines et décadence* (Paris: Plon, 1991), 61.

12. "Le Fumisme," *L'Hydropathe,* May 12, 1880.

13. Phillip Cate, "The Spirit of Montmartre," in Cate and Shaw, *The Spirit of Montmartre,* 20.

14. Francisque Sarcey, *Le XIXe Siècle,* December 1878, quoted in Raymond de Casteras, *Avant le Chat-noir: Les Hydropathes 1878–1880* (Paris: Albert Messein, 1945), 55–56.

15. Daniel Grojnowski, "Hydropathes and Company," in Cate and Shaw, *The Spirit of Montmartre,* 106. He points out that this tradition is perpetuated in Céline and Queneau; it is no coincidence that the latter's *Exercices de style* has been successfully dramatized and staged.

16. Paul Margueritte, *Le Petit Théâtre (théâtre de marionettes)* (Paris: Librairie illustrée, 1888), 7–8. Margueritte concludes that the actor's name and familiar face impose an obsession that makes illusion all but impossible.

17. F. Sologub, "The Theatre of a Single Will" (1908), in *Russian Dramatic Theory from Pushkin to the Symbolists,* ed. and trans. Laurence Senelick (Austin: University of Texas Press, 1981), 132–48.

18. For monodrama, see L. I. Tikhvinskaya, *Kabare i teatry miniatyur v Rossii 1908–1917* (Moscow: Kul'tura, 1995), 268–84; and Laurence Senelick, "Boris Geyer and Cabaretic Playwriting," in *Russian Theatre in the Age of Modernism,* ed. Robert Russell (London: Macmillan, 1990), 36–63.

19. Hans von Gumppenberg, *Der Nachbar: Monodrama in einem Satz* (1901), in *Das Kabarett der frühen Jahre,* ed. Volker Kühn (Berlin: Quadriga Verlag/J. Severin, 1984), 98–100; Christian Morgenstern, *Egon und Emilie* (ca. 1901), in *Gesammelte Werke in einem Band,* ed. Margareta Morgenstern (Munich: R. Piper, 1965), 335–36. Translations can be found in Laurence Senelick, ed. and trans., *Cabaret Performance,* vol. 1: *Europe, 1890–1920* (New York: Performing Arts Journal Press, 1989), 110–16, 72–73.

20. In Jarry, *Oeuvres complètes* (Monte Carlo: Editions du livre, n.d.), 4:161–67.

21. Gide's description of Jarry as "a plaster-faced Kobold, got up like a circus clown and acting a fantastic, strenuously contrived role which showed no human characteristic" appeared in "Le groupement littéraire qu'abritait le *Mercure de France,*" *Mercure de France,* December 1946. The pertinent passage is translated in full in Roger Shattuck, *The Banquet Years: The Arts in France, 1885–1918* (Garden City, N.Y.: Anchor, 1961), 211.

22. Coquelin Cadet, *Le Monologue moderne* (Paris: Ollendorf, 1881), 11. Edward Gorey is among the modern admirers of Cros, having issued his own illustrated translation of "Le Hareng saur" (and Allais's "Story for Sara").

23. It should be pointed out that the terms *Sprechstimme,* which Arnold Schoen-

berg described as the voice rising and falling relative to indicated intervals, and *Sprechgesang,* a vocalization halfway between song and speech that Alban Berg employed in *Wozzeck* (1925), are first associated with expressionist acting and twelve-tone music.

24. G. B. Shaw, "Yvette Guilbert," *World,* May 16, 1894, reprinted in *Shaw on Music,* ed. Eric Bentley (Garden City, N.Y.: Doubleday, Anchor, 1955), 242–43.

25. Guilbert's performance can be heard on Yvette Guilbert, *Le Fiacre* (Pearl/Flapper PAST CD 9773, 1991). The lyrics are to be found in her book *Autres temps, autres chants* (Paris: Robert Laffont, 1946). For her comments on "Les Vierges," see Yvette Guilbert, *La Chanson de ma vie* (Paris: Grasset, 1927), 89–91.

26. "A nutcracker, could it speak, would act no differently." Gide, "Le Groupement littéraire."

27. Jarry, *Oeuvres complètes,* 7:269–76.

28. Clovis Hugues, preface to Horace Valbel, *Les Chansonniers et les cabarets artistiques* (Paris: E. Dentu, n.d.), xi–xii.

29. Casteras, *Avant le Chat-noir,* 166; Anatole Jakovsky, *Alphonse Allais "le tueur à gags"* (Paris: Les Quatre Jeudis, 1955), 57, 68, 70, 72, 75. One observer pointed out that the chansonniers at the Chat Noir performed with their hands in their pockets with an insouciant air, like amateur actors trying to give an impression of naturalism. Ch. Baret, *Propos d'un homme qui a bien tourné* (Paris: Gerin, 1909), 22.

30. *Augsburger Neueste Nachrichten,* March 12, 1918, quoted in *Brecht on Theatre,* ed. and trans. John Willett (New York: Hill and Wang, 1964), 3. Brecht was a great admirer of Wedekind's technique; although from all accounts Brecht's public performances were less than polished, the very amateurishness may have lent a special quality of anguished intensity to his epigonism. Wedekind's performances in his own plays were noted for their casualness, his hand in his pockets and his words slurred, working against the intensity of the text. Thomas Mann was so struck by this contrast that he devoted an essay to it, and the theater scholar Kurt Pinthus claimed that Brecht's ideas of *Verfremdung* in acting derived from it. See Tilly Wedekind, *Lulu die Rolle meines Lebens* (Munich: Scherz, 1969), 225.

31. Erich Mühsam, *Namen und Menschen: Unpolitische Erinnerungen* (Leipzig: Volk und Bühn Verlag, 1931).

32. Richard Huelsenbeck, ed., *Dada Almanach* (Berlin: Erich Weiss Verlag, 1920), 26.

33. Max Halbe, "Intimes Theater," *Pan* 1 (1895): 107, quoted in Peter Jelavich, *Munich and Theatrical Modernism: Politics, Playwriting, and Performance, 1890–1917* (Cambridge: Harvard University Press, 1985), 152.

34. Brecht, "Notes to the Opera *Aufstieg und Fall der Stadt Mahagonny*" (1930), in *Brecht on Theatre,* 34.

35. Hugo Ball, *Die Flucht aus der Zeit* (Leipzig: Duncker und Humblot, 1927), 94–95. For relevant documents, see Claudine Amiard-Chevrel, ed., *Du cirque au théâtre* (Lausanne: L'Age d'homme, 1983); and Manfred Brauneck, ed., *Theater im 20.Jahrhundert: Programmschriften, Stilperioden, Reformmodelle* (Reinbek bei Hamburg: Rowohlt, 1986).

36. Walter Benjamin/Bernhard Reich, "Revue oder Theater" (1925), *Der Querschnitt* 5 (1925), II, 1039–43. "I must state quite without prejudice that the variety of these entrances, in which each player makes his effect in isolation, this seamless rolling on of new scenes in which something else is always featured, has pleasantly diverted me."

37. Filippo Tomasso Marinetti, "The Meaning of the Music Hall," *London Daily Mail,* November 21, 1913, a somewhat abridged version of "Il Teatro di varietà," *Lacerba,* October 1, 1913.

38. Udo Rukser, quoted in Huelsenbeck, *Dada Almanach,* 41. Greil Marcus contrasts this statement with one from Elvis Costello, insisting that the artist's vocation is to be an irritant. Greil Marcus, *Lipstick Traces: A Secret History of the Twentieth Century* (Cambridge: Harvard University Press, 1989), 127.

39. Viktor Shklovsky, *Voskreshenie slova* (St. Petersburg, 1914), 12. In the Anglophone world, the passive or resistant audience was dichotomized by gender: spectators who wanted mindless entertainment enlivened by sexual display were called by the trade papers the tired businessman or the bald heads in the first rows; the prudish or narrow-minded, resistant to experimentation, were feminized as Mrs. Grundy, the *New Yorker*'s old lady from Dubuque, Terence Rattigan's Aunt Edna.

40. Report of March 11, 1897, quoted in Elisabeth Pillet, *"Ta gueul', Moignieau! . . . T'es pas un chanteaux officiel" ou la réception critique de l'oeuvre de Gaston Couté* (Paris: Paris-III, 1990), 443–44.

41. The manifesto is reproduced in Claude Schumacher, *Alfred Jarry and Guillaume Apollinaire* (London: Macmillan, 1984), 164–65. In a letter to André Billy, Apollinaire explained that he was shitting not on the great literary figures of the past but on the misappropriation of their names.

42. Huelsenbeck, *Dada Almanach,* 13. In French in the original; the German words mean "Enlightenment," "My pictures," "One's own compositions."

43. Quoted in Richard, *Cabaret, cabarets,* 325–26.

44. André Breton, *Entretiens* (Paris: Gallimard, 1969), 58–59. This passage suggests that Breton was actually unaware of what the Zurich performances had been like.

45. "L'honneur s'achète et se vend comme le cul. Le cul, le cul représente la vie comme les pommes frites, et vous tous qui êtes sérieux, vous sentirez plus mauvais que la merde de vache." Francis Picabia, "Manifeste cannibale Dada," *DADAphone* 7 (Paris, March 1920).

46. Wieland Herzfelde, "Das Dadalyripipidon," *Schall und Rauch,* May 1920, 1 mm [*sic*].

47. Contemporary reportage of futurist performances has been compiled in Giovanni Antonucci, *Cronache del teatro futurista* (Rome: Abete, 1975). One might compare the Living Theatre's chanted plaint, "We aren't allowed to take off our clothes," regularly confuted by spectators' stripping themselves naked.

48. V. Pjast, *Vstrechi* (Moscow, 1929), 288.

49. André Breton, "La Confession dédaigneuse," *Les Pas perdus* (Paris: Nouvelle revue française, 1924).

50. "Eine Erklärung des Club Dada," in Huelsenbeck, *Dada Almanach,* 132.

51. Alfred Jarry, "Barnum," *Revue Blanche* 206, January 1, 1902, in *Oeuvres complètes,* 8:47–49. This is in line with Jarry's famous statement that 'pataphysics was the science of exceptions.

52. Filippo Tomasso Marinetti, "The Variety Theatre," trans. R. W. Flint, in Kirby, *Futurist Performance,* 179–86. See David F. Cheshire, "Futurism, Marinetti, and the Music Hall," *Theatre Quarterly* 1, no. 3 (1971): 54–58; and Giovanni Lista, "Esthétique du music-hall et mythologie urbaine chez Marinetti," in Amiard-Chevrel, *Du cirque au théâtre,* 48–64. In a monologue in the satiric puppet-play *Einfach klassich!* which opened the second Schall und Rauch cabaret in Berlin, Walter Mehring has Aegisthus

characterize a dadaist rebel as a cocaine addict who "Daily practices his gymnastic lessons. / 'My system,' for the improvement of muscle tone.'" *Schall und Rauch,* December 1919, 14.

53. Marinetti, "Meaning of Music Hall."

54. The Anglo-American presence in continental European popular entertainment at the fin de siècle was conspicuous, from the tours of Buffalo Bill Cody's Wild West and Barnum and Bailey's Circus to the great popularity in variety of Loie Fuller, Little Tich, Harry Fragson, and the Barrison Sisters.

55. Edmond de Goncourt, *Les Frères Zemganno,* definitive ed. (Paris: Flammarion & Fasquelle, 1922), 125. *Cf.* J.-K. Huysmans, who called them "lugubrious" and sinister" in his *Croquis parisiens. A Vau l'Eau. Un Dilemme* (Paris: P. V. Stock, 1905), 13. For the influence of the Hanlon-Lees on Zola, Banville, and E. de Goncourt see T. Walton, "'Entortilationists' (The Hanlon-Lees in literature and art)," *Life and Letters Today,* April–June 1914, 36; and Robert Storey, *Pierrots on the Stage of Desire: Nineteenth-Century French Literary Artists and the Comic Pantomime* (Princeton: Princeton University Press, 1985), 183–89. Most of the writing on the Hanlon-Lees in English (e.g., Richard Southern, John Towson) is riddled with errors and distortions.

56. The French caricature of the cold-blooded Englishman who enjoys watching public executions and feats of danger without moving a muscle may have its origin in the amusements of the eighteenth-century dilettante George Selwyn; a particularly striking example in a circus context appears in Eugène Sue's *Le Juif errant* (1845–46). The type was perpetuated in French music hall of the early twentieth century by Max Dearly.

57. Edmond de Goncourt, *Journal,* February 6, 1887, ed. Robert Ricatte (Paris: Robert Laffont, 1956), 3:12. Paul Margueritte, "Pierrot Mormon," in *Nos tréteaux* (Paris: Dorbon Aîné, 1910), 143–48. An American clown's more recent rejuvenation of European countercultural performance was engineered in the 1970s by Jango Edwards. See Barbara Held, ed., *Jango Edwards* (Flensburg: N. H. Matz, 1980).

58. Jeanne Lorang, "Cirque, champ de foire, cabaret, ou de Wedekind à Piscator et à Brecht," in Amiard-Chevrel, *Du cirque au théâtre,* 19–47; Laurence Senelick, "Wedekind at the Music-Hall," *New Theatre Quarterly* 4, no. 16 (1988): 32–69. Artur Kutscher suggests that the theme had come from Donald Wedekind, who had spent time in America (*Frank Wedekind: Leben und Werk* [Munich: G. Müller, 1922], 1:315).

59. Schumacher, *Jarry and Apollinaire.* This was meant for publication not in Paris, but in Milan as a statement of solidarity with Marinetti's movement.

60. Huelsenbeck, *Dada Almanach,* opp. 40. The reference is to the Soviet Russian constructivist artist Tatlin.

61. Quoted in Tikhvinskaya, *Kabare,* 90.

62. Kirk Varnedoe and Adam Gopnik, *High and Low: Modern Art and Popular Culture* (New York: Museum of Modern Art, 1991), 258–70.

63. Quoted in Chiara Valentini, "Karl Valentin," in *Enciclopedia del teatro '900,* ed. Antonio Attisani (Milan: Feltrinelli, 1980), 317.

64. Walter Mehring, "Wettrennen zwischen Nähmaschine und Schreibmaschine," in *Kleinkunststücke Band 2. Hoppla, wir beben. Kabarett einer gewissen Republik 1918–1933,* ed. Volker Kühn (Berlin: Quadriga, 1988), 25. The American language, as spoken on Tin Pan Alley and the Great White Way, also becomes part of avant-garde linguistic aggression. The macaronics of the dadaists and futurists were enriched by an ostensibly black *patois,* which, though filtered through the minstrel show and commer-

cial ragtime, had the allure of the untamed and exotic. Walter Mehring's "Niggersong," sung at the Schall und Rauch by Gussy Holl, is not untypical:

If the man in the moon
Were a coon und im Dunkeln liebten die girls,
Schenkten alle weisse ladys
Schwarze babies
Please, küss mich rein, lass mich rein
Schwarzen Kerls
Black boy, o my black boy
In the niggerparadies, in the niggerparadies

Brecht and Weill's "O moon of Alabama" is but a cakewalk step away.

65. Translations can be found in Senelick, *Cabaret Performance,* 197–200, 203.

66. Jean Cocteau, *Antigone. Les mariés de la Tour Eiffel* (Paris: Gallimard, 1928), 22.

67. Moholy-Nagy, "Theater, Zirkus, Varieté," in *Die Bühne in Bauhaus* (Mainz: Florian Kupferberg, 1965), 45–76. Also see Eric Michaud, "Au Bauhaus: Modèles populaires et rééducation des masses," in Amiard-Chevrel, *Du cirque au théâtre,* 123–31.

68. Wassily Kandinsky, *Über die Abstrakte Bühnensynthese* (Weimar-Munich: Bauhaus Verlag, 1923); it was originally published in Russian in "Sagi otdela izobrazitel'nykh iskusstv v mezhdunarodnoy khudozhestvennoy politike," *Khudozhestvennaya zhizn'* 3 (Moscow: Institut Khudozhestvennoi Kultury, 1919–20). Also see Peter Simhandl, "Kandinskys Theaterexperiment," program note for *Wassily Kandinsky: Bilder einer Ausstellung* (Berlin: Hochschule der Künste, 1983), n.p.; and P. Weiss, "Kandinsky: Symbolist Poetics and Theater in Munich," *Pantheon* 25 (1977), 209–18.

69. In 1923, the year that marks the introduction of radios into most homes, the Parisian newspaper *L'Éclair* noted that the literary cafés had been gradually disappearing and any new ones were ill-attended. "Fashion no longer cares much for those intimate meetings of poets, novelists, journalists, around a five-o-clock apéritif in which once a wit was squandered which is not current in today's streets." *L'Éclair,* August 12, 1923, quoted in Richard, *Cabaret, cabarets,* 329.

70. C. Carr, *On Edge: Performance at the End of the Twentieth Century* (Hanover, N.H.: University Press of New England, 1993), 105. *Cf.* Richard Schechner, who finds avant-garde an outdated category, with little meaning outside its historical context., "Introduction: The Five Avant Gardes or . . . [and] . . . . Or none?" in *The Future of Ritual: Writings on Culture and Performance* (London: Routledge, 1993), 5–21.

71. Fragerolle and Salis, quoted in Cate and Shaw, *The Spirit of Montmartre;* Bierbaum, "Manifesto for a Cabaret Theatre" from *Stilpe,* in Senelick, *Cabaret Performance,* 68; Huelsenbeck, *Dada Almanach,* 8.

David Graver

Antonin Artaud and the Authority of Text, Spectacle, and Performance

A cursory reading of Artaud can easily furnish citations that suggest he wishes to replace the authority of the text with the authority of theatrical performance. He states quite plainly that "it is essential to put an end to the subjugation of the theatre to the text,"[1] and then he calls for a subjugation of the audience to the performance that involves gripping the spectators with a "cruelty" that "is above all lucid, a kind of rigid control and submission to necessity."[2] Nevertheless, such a reading of his work would miss all of its distinctiveness and importance. First, he is not unique in calling for the creation of a theater freed from (literary) texts, and, second, the authority he wishes to see transferred to the theatrical event is, on close examination, a distinctly antiauthorial one. To understand what Artaud adds to the conceptual possibilities of theater, we need to understand how his notion of total theater differs from the calls for a total theater that precede him and to situate both within broader aesthetic currents. Artaud's theories of performance can best be understood as predicated on, but attempting to break with, late-nineteenth- and early-twentieth-century efforts to make theater less a social custom and more a work of art. The notion of the autonomous artwork, so much a part of bourgeois ideology since the late eighteenth century,[3] could not be easily applied to the practice of theater until the latter half of the nineteenth century. Earlier, the fully lighted auditorium, horseshoe arrangement of seats, late arrival of prominent patrons, and long, frequent intermissions put the activities of the audience on display as prominently as the activities of the actors, even after spectators were barred from sitting directly on the stage. Popular standards of taste, explicit laws of censorship, the exigencies of profit for large, capital-intensive theatrical enterprises, and the monopolistic control of certain audiences or types of productions by a few companies severely limited the forms and subject matter that could be articulated in plays. Thus, theater artists lacked the creative freedom that painters and poets were presumed to enjoy, and theatrical works lacked the commanding attention given to masterpieces of visual and literary art. Without creative freedom or authoritative display it was difficult for theater to lay claims to the autonomy assumed to belong to works of high aesthetic merit.

The distinction Michael Fried draws between "theatricality" and "absorption" testifies to an abiding faith in the autonomous, authoritative aura of great artworks and to an abiding denigration of the contingencies and circumstances of theatrical performance.[4] Fried praises those works that can dominate and monopolize the attention of the spectators by drawing them into its particular world of technical virtuosity and thematic poignancy, and he disparages those works that abdicate some of the authority of their presence in favor of drawing attention to the broader physical or social situation in which they exist.

Many of the major innovations in theater in the late nineteenth and early twentieth centuries aim at making theater less theatrical and more authoritatively autonomous in its aesthetic presence. With the advent of gas and then electricity, the lights in the auditorium were lowered and the lights on stage raised to give the performance a more commanding visibility. New theaters abandoned the horseshoe arrangement, which put the audience on display to itself, in favor of racked banks of seats with clear sight-lines directed only toward the stage. Small, private theaters were instituted to avoid censorship regulations and the need to accommodate popular tastes to turn a profit; to lend greater aesthetic freedom to the small company; and to create more intense performances through the closer proximity of actors and audience. One-act plays also became popular among theater innovators at this time because the elimination of intermissions enhanced the spectacle's ability to fully absorb the attention of the audience. Among these innovations two deserve closer examination: the rise of the director and the subjugation of theatrical performance to dramatic literature.

The Director, Realism, and Literature

The move from a theater dominated by actor-managers to one dominated by directors was a move from a performance-centered cultural event with a great deal of extraneous or incompletely integrated auxiliary points of interest to a spectacle-centered art in which all the elements formed an integrated whole. Scenery and supporting roles were no longer simply there to frame and support the performance of the lead actor. Instead, acting, set design, props, costumes, lighting, and all other elements worked together under the coordinating direction of the *metteur en scène* to produce a unified stage image.

Saxe-Meiningen, André Antoine, and Konstantin Stanislavsky were among the first to unite all the arts of the theater with ensemble acting designed to portray a particular scene rather than showcase particular acting talents.[5] This school of director-centered theater was advanced in France by Lugné-Poe, Jacques Copeau, and the Cartel des Quatre, with three of whom Artaud worked.[6] In contrast to Saxe-Meiningen, Antoine, and Stanislavsky, who relied upon various notions of realism or naturalism to provide a conceptual focus for the mise-en-scène and to distinguish their work from the mainstream theatrical conventions of the time, Lugné-Poe, Copeau, and the Cartel stressed the particularity of theatrical performance as the essence of their art. They did not pretend to make the stage more like the real world but, rather, sought to identify and refine the expressive particularities of the stage.

Copeau and the Cartel, while strengthening and refining the techniques of theatrical performance, also stressed the subjugation of theatrical performance to dramatic literature.[7] Rather than promote theatrical performance as an art form with its own autonomous aesthetic worth, they promoted it as a means of realizing the full potential of classic dramatic texts. They did not claim to be producing their own unique art but to be aiding in the production of the playwright's art. The stage was for them ideally an extension of a literary text. One can, perhaps, see in the reasoning of Copeau and the Cartel an attempt to deal with the theatrical prejudice that remained an abiding element in European culture despite the social prominence enjoyed by certain forms and institutions of theater. In rejecting realistic modes of performance (with their aura of scientific, documentary authority) in favor of more openly artificial, theatrical modes of performance, Copeau and the Cartel may have been anxious to distinguish what they were doing from other "lower" forms of nonrealistic theater that could lay no claims to aesthetic autonomy and contemplative authority. They created authority and legitimacy for their work by attaching it to the aesthetic realm of literature, whose legitimacy and authority was already well established in bourgeois culture.

The Primacy of Spectacle

Artaud distinguished himself from his mentors in the Cartel des Quatre by repudiating the subservience of the stage to dramatic literature, but he is not the first theorist and practitioner to defend the primacy of theatrical performance. Before he had begun to articulate his ideas, a uniquely theatrical art unattached to the scientific authority of realism or the aesthetic authority of literature had already been argued for and realized by, among others, Kokoschka, Kandinsky, Meyerhold, and Craig. A brief look at these four theatrical artists will help to clarify Artaud's unique particularities and his place in the broader developments of Western theater.

Of these four artists, Meyerhold remains closest to the authority of the text in that he still advocates performing works of dramatic literature, but for him the performance has an aesthetic power and integrity that takes precedence over the power and integrity of literature.[8] Indeed, he often abuses and violates the integrity of the literary text by cutting and rearranging its parts and adding elements never dreamed of, let alone intended, by the playwright. For him the literary text is nothing more than an easily modified superstructure upon which to build the theatrical performance with its elaborately layered and constantly unfolding series of visual images and physical feats. While Meyerhold clearly gives the director's aesthetic intentions precedence over those of the literary text, he is willing to leave room within his spectacles for the actors' unfettered display of their own performative skills. Thus, while minimizing the literary authority of the theatrical artwork (and denying the playwright any claim to authorship of the theatrical production), he allows space within his productions for the performers to assert their own autonomy and authority through set pieces that highlight their skills at clowning, acrobatics, and elocution.

Kandinsky advocated and Kokoschka realized a theatrical spectacle that was more purely focused on the talents of the designer/director. Their training and principal careers in painting lead both to a highly visual approach to theater in which the actors are reduced to images within a spectacle that develops through abstract alterations of sound, movement, and color rather than by virtue of the interplay of independent psyches within a particular objective situation.[9] Kandinsky's *The Yellow Sound* is completely emptied of dramatic conflict and portrayals of personality in order to more freely play with a heterogeneous array of visual images such as yellow giants, "vague creatures," and people in flowing robes.[10] Kokoschka allows the characters in his plays a significant amount of interior life and action in the world, but he ties this interiority and action to strong visual images that undermine the individual integrity of characters and make their feelings and strivings part of the general development and transformation of visual images on the stage.[11]

The first major promoter and theorist of a purely theatrical artwork controlled by a director was E. Gordon Craig.[12] Craig saw theater as primarily the manipulation of "action, scene, and voice," or, more abstractly, movement, imagery, and sound.[13] He saw most theater as corrupt and decadent but capable of powerful aesthetic effects once it realized its strengths and fundamental nature. He did not think theater could be improved by appeals to reality or literature but by tearing away all the layers of extraneous, irrelevant conventions and practices that stifle the possibility of true theatrical expression. He favored stylized sets with a minimum of detail and boldly composed shapes that evoke very particular moods.

Along with much of the scenographic practice of the early twentieth century Craig would have been happy to also eject the actor.

> Acting is not an art. . . . Art is the exact antithesis of pandemonium, and pandemonium is created by the tumbling together of many accidents. Art arrives only by design. Therefore in order to make any work of art it is clear we may only work in those materials with which we can calculate. Man is not one of these materials.[14]

To lend theater aesthetic authority (and to guarantee the undisputed authorship of the theatrical work to the director) he felt all its elements had to be under the control of one artist and all performances had to be as uniform as the copies of a book or prints from one lithograph. Clearly this kind of precision and predictability is impossible where actors are involved, particularly actors trained in the loose, improvisational methods of Western drama. Craig dreamed of a primordial "übermarionette" whose moves were not constrained by the limits of human bodies and could be repeated without variation when so desired. He imagined that this puppet (more religious idol than toy) gave birth to the notion of theater but that the intrinsic powers of theater were quickly vitiated by the loss of the übermarionette and its replacement with human actors. With human actors meddling in theater there is no guarantee that the director's aesthetic concepts will be as faithfully executed as paint dried upon a canvas executes the intentions of a master painter. Craig was keenly aware of the complexity of theater, of its conflicting centers of authority and expression, but rather than integrate these centers in some way he hoped that some day the poet and performer could be exiled from the stage leaving only the *metteur en scène* to work his or her will as desired with images, movement, and sound.

Theater as Plague

Artaud is heir to Craig's absolutist claims for the art of theater, but, significantly, he rejects Craig's desires for an artwork that displays only the expressive intentions of the director. Whereas Craig wants the theatrical artwork to preserve in perfect fidelity the creative ingenuity of the director, Artaud wants the theatrical work to exceed all possible conceptions of individual ingenuity. For Craig, the übermarionette represents the ideal form of theater; for Artaud, the ideal of theater is the plague. These two metaphors deserve closer comparison. Craig's übermarionette has no will of its own. Every movement is controlled by the director and can be programmed to repeat itself invariably. The artwork actualized by the übermarionette is cleansed of all contingencies and accidents, and all of its expressive powers and aesthetic innovations clearly flow from one ego, the director. The übermarionette provides a center and focus for a perfectly planned and ordered spectacle.

Artaud's concept of plague lacks center, focus, order, and control.[15] No human agency or even natural causes are responsible for it. It arises from malign and inscrutable divine powers and involves the disintegration of all values and competencies. It is characterized by random, unexpected, unnatural behavior. Whereas the übermarionette enjoys a calm immortality due to its unalterable inanimateness, the living participants/victims of the plague suffer in a frenzy from the awareness of their tenuous mortality and the workings of disease within their bodies.

> The dregs of the population, apparently immunized by their frenzied greed, enter the open houses and pillage riches they know will serve no purpose or profit. And at that moment the theater is born. The theater, i.e., an immediate gratuitousness provoking acts without use or profit.[16]

The plague metaphor is powerful and points out the kind of authority due to the loss of authorship that Artaud wants to bring to the theater. But how can this kind of soul-shaking chaos actually be created on the stage? To understand the ways in which Artaud's ideas are more than just a mad vision and actually rest upon a prescient understanding of the possibilities of theater, we need to understand what Artaud wants done with three distinct and in some ways inimical centers of authority in the theatrical performance.

In contrast to Craig, who wants to eliminate any authority within the theatrical performance that conflicts with or threatens to overshadow the director, Artaud cultivates multiple sources of authority as much as possible without dissipating the powers of the theatrical event. He agrees with Craig on the importance of the *metteur en scène* and the need to liberate theater from subservience to the literary text, some notion of realism, or the celebrity aura of a star actor, but he also wishes to undercut the authority of the spectacle (of action, scene, and voice) so precious to Craig with dissonant and demanding forms of textual and performative authority. Artaud is already unique among early-twentieth-century theater theorists in advocating a balanced combination of text, spectacle, and performance on the stage, but he pushes the borders of innovation further by arguing for the transformation of the text into a hieroglyph, the spectacle into cruelty, and performance into affective athleticism.

Hieroglyphic Text

For Copeau and the Cartel des Quatre the only text involved in a theatrical performance is the playwright's. The actions of the actors and the details of the scene have meaning only insofar as they corroborate and amplify the meaning of the dramatic literature being realized. Artaud does not banish the literary text's significance from the theatrical spectacle but suggests that the signs of the theater are superior to, rather than a supplement for, the written text. Describing theatrical signs as hieroglyphs obviously draws attention to their iconic qualities, that they (can) resemble what they signify and (sometimes) lack the arbitrary quality of linguistic signs, but Artaud uses this term to foreground qualities more particular to his vision of theater. Artaud sees theatrical signs as a kind of holy writing. The text they embody can be more than the text of a particular playwright. The significances they create point to a realm of forces beyond rational understanding. Holy texts not only signify, they also perform (blessings, curses, legal proclamations, prophesies), so the theater's hieroglyphic significance imbues it with the ritual efficacy of religion. The text does not just make sense; it conjures up spirits. It creates a world rather than just representing a world.

Attributing a hieroglyphic textuality to performance dangles the lure of readability before what might otherwise be taken as superficial physical play with no significance deeper than the display of physical skills at a sporting event. Sports have clear rules and explicit outcomes, but a text has shifting signifiers and unplumbable depths. A text demands interpretation that becomes an infinite conversation with a complex array of moveable meanings.[17] The apparent univocality of a literary text makes the endless task of interpretation not necessarily obvious. The status of literary meaning is, indeed, subtle enough to have generated considerable contentious debate.[18] The enticing but undecipherable meanings of a hieroglyphic theatricality are not missing from literary texts but are also not as apparent there.[19] One can see more easily, more unavoidably, in the daunting array of signs on the stage the inability to ever read them all accurately and completely. The holiness of theatrical hieroglyphs does not derive from an omnipotent, divine significance with which they are imbued and fixed, but from a semiotic aloofness and deferral that destroys meaning and order. Their sanctity is closer to the voice from the whirlwind in Job, which asks unanswerable questions, than to the God of Genesis 1, who systematically creates an ordered world in seven days. Theatrical hieroglyphs seek a connection with the gods that reigned before meaning set limits on the world.

Without a fixed meaning to be conveyed, a theatrical performance cannot be consumed. It can only be entered and experienced. Like a shamanistic trance, it is bigger than and beyond the responsibility of its participants. The hieroglyphic text is evoked or conjured up rather than created. Where Craig would have the significance of the text controlled by the director, Artaud wants the director to give the text of the performance over to powers greater than any of the human participants.

Although Artaud wants to strengthen theater with religious overtones, it would be a mistake to assume he wants to turn theatrical performance into religious ritual. The power of theater's hieroglyphic text arises in large part from its unsanctioned appropriation of the sacred. Where religious rituals generally try to bring order to invocations of the divine and hold the sacred within carefully set boundaries, Artaud's theater aims at a breakdown of such order and limits. He wants a theater attuned not only to the power of the sacred but also to the power of profanation.

It is instructive to take note of some of the themes and literary works around which Artaud declares that "we shall make attempts at direct staging": the fall of Jerusalem (including the metaphysical disputes of the prophets), the conquest of Mexico (again combining physical violence, metaphysical disputes, and cultural disintegration), the story of Bluebeard, a tale by the Marquis de Sade, *The Cenci,* and *Wozzeck.*[20] All these themes and texts deal with sacrilege more than with sacredness, but sacrilege, for Artaud, seems to be an essential part of the truly sacred. Theatrical hieroglyphs have a holiness so intense that their presence on the stage assumes profanation. Without a sense of sacrilegious outrage permeating the atmosphere of the theatrical event, one cannot be sure that one is really approaching a sacred realm.

Cruel Spectacles

Although Artaud uses "cruelty" to describe his theater in general, its array of concepts are most pertinent to the spectacle aspect of theatrical performance and mark sharply the differences between his concept of spectacle and Craig's. For Craig, spectacle is something to be seen. It is an animated visual composition created by a director and offered to an audience along clear, uniform sight-lines at a distance sufficient for calm, absorbed contemplation. The spectacle represents to the audience the acuity, ingenuity, and originality of the director. It embodies the director's creativity and offers the audience an entertaining diversion from daily life. Although Craig's theatrical ideal is much more abstract and aesthetically refined than conventional bourgeois theater (since it ideally does without a literary text and human actors), Artaud would probably include it with bourgeois theater as a form of "digestive theater," in that it is intended to nourish the visual appetites of the audience.

Artaud's spectacle, in contrast, does not permit a comfortable contemplation, nor does it reflect the genius of the director. The director does not display his talents in the theatrical image but, rather, uses his talents to encourage a display in the theatrical image of extraordinary spiritual and earthly powers. The manifestation of these powers upon the stage is not offered to the audience for contemplation and enjoyment but pressed upon the audience to overwhelm and disorient it. Although Artaud was keen to reassure his readers that "theater of cruelty" did not mean "theater of sadistic violence," the type of spectacular authority he conceives is akin to violence. It certainly does violence to the audience's expectations for the innocuous pleasures of aesthetic contemplation:

> [The spectator] will go to the theater the way he goes to the surgeon or the dentist. In the same state of mind—knowing, of course, that he will not die, but that it is a serious thing, and that he will not come out of it unscathed. . . . He must be totally convinced that we are capable of making him scream.[21]

Artaud advocates the creation of a spectacle that is more felt than seen. With this aim in mind he rejects the move toward clear, uniform sight-lines common to much theater innovation from the turn of the century on, in favor of a spectacle that surrounds the audience:

> We abolish the stage and the auditorium and replace them by a single site, without partition or barrier of any kind, which will become the theater of the action. A direct communication will be re-established between the spectator and the spectacle, between the actor and the spectator, from the fact that the spectator, placed in the middle of the action, is engulfed and physically affected by it.[22]

In being surrounded by the spectacle the spectators lose the implicit authority of their all-encompassing gaze. Whereas in traditional theater the spectators can engulf the image isolated on the stage with their eyes, in Artaud's theater the spectacle dominates and engulfs the spectators. "Communication" rather than display is established between audience and spectacle in that the invisible fourth wall (a convention established in the nineteenth century to strengthen the autonomy of the theatrical event) is opened so that audience and actors can mix together. The result is "cruel" in that now the actions in the spectacle have immediate consequences for the audience and cannot be enjoyed and dismissed as images contained in a separate (aesthetic) world. If the spectacle involves fire, the spectators can feel the heat. If dangers approach the characters from behind, the audience is just as likely to be unaware of and surprised by them because they are now vulnerable elements of the scene rather than invulnerable, omniscient eyes gazing comfortably upon events from a protective darkness.

Edmund Burke's distinction between the beautiful and the sublime is useful in elucidating the nature of Artaud's cruel spectacles.[23] Craig's idealized spectacle as well as the use of spectacle commonly made in conventional theater is basically "beautiful" in Burke's sense in that it offers up to the eye an ordered image whose enticing surfaces draw the spectator toward it. One can become absorbed in the beautiful because it is unthreatening and enticing. One can consume the beautiful because it exists only to be seen and enjoyed.[24] The sublime, in contrast, exceeds all human sense of order. It drives the spectator from it by its threatening powers. Its images invoke wonder and astonishment rather than pleasure, and they can never be viewed in their entirety. Their scope and dangers prevent full consumption by the spectator. The spectacle asserts an existence independent from and even sometimes inimical to human existence.[25]

Burke stresses that "terror is a passion which always produces delight when it does not press too close" and that this delight is even greater in the theater, where "the pleasure resulting from the effects of imitation" blends with both the stirrings of frightful scenes and the relief of being safely distanced from them.[26] But Artaud specifically wants to purge the theater of these delights. By bringing the audience closer to the spectacle he wants to take away their feeling of safety and their ability to savor the inconsequential energy of imitation. Burke notes, "We delight in seeing things, which so far from doing, our heartiest wishes would be to see redressed."[27] By mixing the audience with the spectacle Artaud means to confuse the distinction between seeing and doing. An ideally "cruel" spectacle would be one in which the spectator feels unwittingly implicated as both agent and victim. The theatrical nature of the event should provide some assurance that the extremities of the sublime—pain and death—are not a real threat, but the cruelty of the spectacle should make it difficult to identify any distance that can vouchsafe pleasure. The spectacle still attracts the spectators, but their desire to view is mixed with an uneasiness over becoming part of the scene. Artaud does not wish to terrorize the audience but to make them feel that their confrontation with the spectacle has consequences and is not entirely within their control or understanding. As he explains, cruelty is not so much the production of suffering as an awareness of constraint or powerlessness which cannot really be experienced from a distance:

> I employ the word "cruelty" in the sense of an appetite for life, a cosmic rigor and implacable necessity, in the gnostic sense of a living whirlwind that devours the darkness, in the sense of that pain apart from whose ineluctable necessity life could not continue.
>
> . . . creation and life itself are defined only by a kind of rigor, hence a fundamental cruelty, which leads things to their ineluctable end at whatever cost.[28]

Craig also speaks of necessity, but for him it means complete artistic control of the stage event. This sort of necessity is best viewed from an objectifying distance that clearly separates the spectacle from the spectator. Artaud, in contrast, is not interested in giving the spectators an image with a determined aesthetic form but rather a feeling for the necessity of life's events. For this he needs a spectacle that occupies a position of power greater than the spectator's eye.

Affective Athleticism

A subtle but important distinction to draw in discussing theater is the difference between spectacle and performance. The spectacle is the image created on the stage; the performance is the activity involved in the creation of that image. Not all performance arts consider the creation of an image of primary importance. Classical symphony orchestra concerts, for example, are very minimal, uniform, and conventional in their use of imagery. In theater the performance is intimately and inextricably involved in both the creation of visual images and the representation of the literary text, but its concerns need not stop there.

Performance in the theater has its own unique internal dynamics that are not exhausted by or entirely subject to its mandate to create images and represent texts. Performance involves a mastery and execution of specific bodily skills. It follows a rhythm dictated by a focused concentration on the course of an activity. When performance is combined with a firm expertise, it leads to what Victor Turner calls "flow": a focused concentration in which action and awareness merge and ego disappears, immersed in an activity in which the performer feels in complete control, knows exactly what to do, and is concerned with no goals other than the execution of the activity itself.[29] Whereas spectacle and textual representation are predominantly expressive in their being, performance is predominantly introspective. An image can hardly be said to exist unless it is seen, nor can a text unless it is read, but performances (i.e., nontheatrical performances) might very well take place in private.[30]

While Western theoretical discussions of drama and theater have, until the twentieth century, paid little attention to performance other than as a necessary appendage of dramatic literature, Asian traditions have often emphasized the dynamics of performance in the theatrical event more than the dynamics of representation or image.[31] Artaud's exposure to Cambodian dance theater in Marseilles in 1922 and to a Balinese theatrical troupe in Paris in 1931 may have helped impress upon him the intrinsic power and potential authority of performance in itself. Unlike any other Western theater critic before him, Artaud appreciated deeply the ways in which the intense somatic introspection of performance can work powerful effects upon an audience. He does not distinguish conceptually between the powers of the spectacle and of performance as I am doing here, but it is often not difficult to see that he appreciates some of the distinctions between spectacle and performance.

Artaud focuses predominantly on the intrinsic powers of performance in itself in his essay "An Affective Athleticism."[32] Here he stresses that emotion is generated in the performing body more than in the thinking mind:

> The important thing is to become aware of the localization of emotive thought. One means of recognition is effort or tension; and the same points which support physical effort are those which also support the emanation of emotive thought: they serve as a springboard for the emanation of a feeling.[33]

To most powerfully express emotion, one must cultivate an intense introspective concentration on the somatic vibrations from which emotion arises:

> To become conscious of physical obsession, of muscles quivering with affectivity, is equivalent, as in the play of breaths, to unleashing this affectivity in full force, giving it a mute but profound range and an extraordinary violence.[34]

The force of emotions grounded in the tensions and rhythms of the body results from the audience's emulation of the same tensions and rhythms in their own bodies:

> In order to reforge the chain, the chain of a rhythm in which the spectator used to see his own reality in the spectacle, the spectator must be allowed to identify himself with the spectacle, breath by breath and beat by beat. . . . To know in advance what points of the body to touch is the key to throwing the spectator into magical trances.[35]

Spectatorship always has its somatic consequences. The heartbeat and breathing pattern adjust subtly to be in harmony with the rhythms upon the stage. The more strongly absorbed in viewing the spectacle, the more fully one's muscles and nerves tingle with a ghostly double of the bodily movements and sensations on display. Zeami recognized this affective power of performance in the fourteenth century and recommended that actors pay close attention to it.[36] Artaud's study of shamanism and mysticism has lead him to a similar insight, although where Zeami's observations have a clarity based on years of practical experience in theatrical performance, Artaud's remarks are somewhat obscured by the metaphysical baggage of his sources and his own overwrought mind. Nevertheless, Artaud makes a tremendous contribution to Western theater theory in noting the authoritative powers of performance.

The authority of performance has, of course, always operated in at least a mild and atrophied way, usually to underscore the authority of the text or, in Craig, Kandinsky, Kokoschka, and Meyerhold, to underscore the authority of the spectacle. Artaud is less interested in subjugating the powers of performance to the authority of words or images than in liberating these powers from all constraints. He makes grand claims for the ability of performance to create trances, heal, or call down spiritual powers, but, even from a more restrained and skeptical point of view, we can see that a radical emphasis upon the authority of performance can lead to an extreme corporeal awareness, the spectators' bodies glowing with a sympathetic fatigue due to their resonance of the actors' efforts.

Authorities in Conflict

In Artaud's ideal theater, text, spectacle, and performance would all be strained to the utmost limits of expressive power. The text would become a hieroglyph glowing with a sanctity beyond understanding. The spectacle would expand from a picture to a place in which the spectator is too central to observe anything with equanimity. The performance would become a somatic communion between actors and audience in which both sink trance-like into the pulsing life of their muscles and nerves. Each facet of theater would exert an absolute and ineluctable authority over the spectators, but none of these authorities would heighten or define authorship. Rather than purify theater of its collective status, Artaud would heighten the chaos of this collectivity.

> The theater restores us all our dormant conflicts and their powers: and behold! before our eyes is fought a battle of symbols, one charging against another in an impossible melée; for there can be theater only from the moment when the impossible really begins and when the poetry which occurs on the stage sustains and superheats the realized symbols.[37]

Theatrical poetry is, for Artaud, not finely honed and organized symbols but symbols disintegrating in the incandescent heat of semiotic, spectacular, and somatic forces.

Ironically, Artaud does speak with a voice similar to that of an authorial *metteur en scène,* but rather than use this voice as an author to call into existence an artwork wholly his own, Artaud would use it as a shaman to call forth powers far beyond him and to initiate an event in which he is acted upon rather than initiating actions. He can lose his authorial authority by pushing text, spectacle, and performance each to their individual extremes to create a manifestation of powers without a rationalizing or focusing proclamation. Director, actors, and audience all become caught up in the activity and experience of theater to the exclusion of any message.

NOTES

1. *The Theater and Its Double,* trans. Mary Caroline Richards (New York: Grove Press, 1958), 89.

2. Ibid., 102.

3. See Peter Bürger and Christa Bürger, *The Institutions of Art,* trans. Loren Kruger (Lincoln: University of Nebraska Press, 1992), 77–83.

4. See Michael Fried, "Art and Objecthood," in *Minimal Art: A Critical Anthology,* ed. Gregory Battcock (New York: E. P. Dutton, 1968), 116–47.

5. The Meininger Company was active from the 1860s with influential tours in the last three decades of the century. Antoine founded his Théâtre Libre in 1887. Stanislavsky started the Moscow Art Theatre with Nemirovich-Danchenko in 1898.

6. Copeau founded his Théâtre du Vieux-Colombier in 1913. The Cartel des Quatre, formed in 1927, consisted of Gaston Baty, Charles Dullin, Georges Pitoëff, and Louis Jouvet. Artaud worked with Dullin (1921–24), Pitoëff (1922–23), and Jouvet (1931–32).

7. For a summary and comparison of stances on the relationship between text and performance taken by Copeau, Dullin, and Artaud, see Dominique Duvert, "From Jacques Copeau to Antonin Artaud: The Question of the Dramatic Text," in *Antonin Artaud and the Modern Theater,* ed. Gene A. Plunka (Rutherford, New Jersey: Associated University Presses, 1994), 66–79.

8. For a more detailed account of Meyerhold's approach to theater and his own pronouncements, see *Meyerhold on Theatre,* trans. Edward Braun (New York: Hill and Wang, 1969). His reworking of *The Government Inspector* is particularly noteworthy (209–30).

9. For a statement defending a pared-down theater of music, objects, and color, see Kandinsky's "On Stage Composition" (1912), in *The Blaue Reiter Almanac,* trans. Klaus Lankheit, ed. Wassily Kandinsky and Franz Marc (New York: Da Capo, 1989), 190–206.

10. See "The Yellow Sound: A Stage Composition" in Kandinsky and Marc, *The Blaue Reiter Almanac,* 207–25.

11. For more on Kokoschka see David Graver, *The Aesthetics of Disturbance* (Ann Arbor: University of Michigan Press, 1994), 65–92.

12. Before Craig, Wagner had important things to say about the authority and unity of the theatrical work of art, but where Wagner saw the theater as a *Gesamtkunstwerk,* i.e., a work that draws into one totality the distinct spheres of music, poetry, and visual imagery, Craig saw theater as a particular artistic medium that should be purged of extraneous factors such as acting and poetry.

13. See Craig's "The Art of the Theatre (First Dialogue)" (1905), in *On the Art of the Theatre* (New York: Theatre Arts Books, 1956), 137–81.

14. "The Actor and the Übermarionette" (1907), in Craig, *Art of the Theatre,* 55–56.

15. For an extended discussion of Artaud's concept of the plague and its pertinence to theater, see Jane Goodall, "The Plague and Its Powers in Artaudian Theatre," *Modern Drama* 33, no. 4 (1990): 529–42.

16. Artaud, *Theater and Its Double,* 24. For the original see *Oeuvres complètes* (Paris: Gallimard, 1978), 4:23.

17. For a discussion of the complexities of reading see Maurice Blanchot, "Parler, ce n'est pas voir," in *L'Entretien infini* (Paris: Gallimard, 1969), 35–45.

18. Hermeneutic, Marxist, and poststructuralist theorists have made a considerable variety of observations on the multivalent ambiguities of the literary text. See, for example, Hans-Georg Gadamer, *Truth and Method,* trans. Garrett Barden and John Cumming (New York: Continuum, 1975); Theodor W. Adorno, *Ästhetische Theorie* (Frankfurt am Main: Suhrkamp, 1970); and Jacques Derrida, *Writing and Difference,* trans. Alan Bass (Chicago: University of Chicago Press, 1978).

19. Derrida argues that Artaud's proposed theater of cruelty wants to make apparent the absence and deferral that underlies all language but is denied by logocentric ideology. See "La Parole soufflée" and "The Theater of Cruelty and the Closure of Representation," in *Writing and Difference,* 169–95 and 232–50.

20. Artaud, *Theater and Its Double,* 99.

21. Antonin Artaud, *Selected Writings,* ed. Susan Sontag, trans. Helen Weaver (New York: Farrar, Straus and Giroux, 1976), 157, *Oeuvres complètes,* 2:17.

22. Artaud, *Theater and Its Double,* 96.

23. See Edmund Burke, *A Philosophical Enquiry into the Origin of Our Ideas of the Sublime and Beautiful* (1757) (Oxford: Oxford University Press, 1990).

24. Burke associates the beautiful with the attractions of sex (ibid., 39).

25. The power of the sublime Burke associates with the threat of pain and death (ibid., 36).

26. Ibid., 42, 43.

27. Ibid., 44.

28. Artaud, *Theater and Its Double,* 102, 103.

29. See Victor Turner, *From Ritual to Theatre: The Human Seriousness of Play* (New York: Performing Arts Journal Publications, 1982), 55–58.

30. Many performance artists made this point in various ways in the 1970s and 1980s. An arduous performance by Tehching Hsieh involved living in a cage in his studio for a year without reading or speaking to anyone (1978–79). One Chris Burden performance simply involved disappearing for three days without telling anyone where he had gone (December 22–24, 1971), described in *Chris Burden, 71–73* (Los Angeles: Chris Burden, 1974), 34.

31. For a sophisticated example of the Asian emphasis on performance, see Zeami, *On the Art of the No Drama: The Major Treatises of Zeami,* trans. J. Thomas Rimer and Yamazaki Masakazu (Princeton: Princeton University Press, 1984). For a discussion of the theoretical implications of Asian theater, particularly *kathakali,* and its use in twentieth-century Western theater, see Larry Tremblay, *Le Crâne des théâtres: Essais sur les corps de l'acteur* (Montreal: Leméac, 1993).

32. Artaud, *Theater and Its Double,* 133–41.

33. Ibid., 138.

34. Ibid., 139. I have modified the translation. For the original see *Oeuvres complètes,* 4:130.

35. Ibid., 140.

36. Zeami, *Art of No Drama,* 82–87.

37. Artaud, *Theater and Its Double,* 27–28.

Christopher Innes

Text/Pre-Text/Pretext: The Language of Avant-Garde Experiment

In hindsight the search for a new form of theater language can be seen as one of the defining elements for the theatrical avant-garde as a whole. Indeed even the earliest practitioners were preoccupied by the problematic nature of spoken words on the stage; and this can be traced to some of the basic modernist principles. The assertion of art as autonomous, aspiring to pure form, which led T. S. Eliot to reject "narrative method" in poetry and Kandinsky to declare that "the literary element, 'story-telling' or 'anecdote' must be abandoned" in painting, led to calls for an "Anti-Psychological Abstract Theatre of Pure Forms and Tactilism" (the title of Marinetti's 1924 futurist manifesto).[1]

For Marinetti, of course, abstraction (i.e., the denial of copying external, materialistic appearances on the stage) and antipsychology represented the opposite of naturalistic drama—and to some degree the whole avant-garde movement from the early dadaists in Zurich during World War I, to Spalding Gray or Karen Finley in the contemporary United States, is motivated by opposition to mainstream/traditional theater. But the psychology that Marinetti was attacking, or even the individuality of a dramatic character, is expressed primarily through dialogue; and the socially sanctified, hence inherently conservative mainstream is always encoded in literary language. The target may change for each generation of avant-garde artists. For Jarry in the 1890s "traditional" meant Shakespeare; for Marinetti in the 1920s it was represented by Ibsen; for Brook in the 1960s it was the "deadly" commercial theater of the West End. Yet in each case the dominance of the word—theater as text—is the key common element that focuses avant-garde opposition. In one sense this verbal dominance is simply a by-product of any performance piece becoming part of the standard repertoire: almost by definition, mainstream drama has multiple productions, achieving traditional status by being restaged over decades (if not centuries); and to be reproducible there must be a core text. The play itself is then identified with this script. At the same time, conventional playwrights, even when writing in prose, have called themselves "poets" (as indeed Ibsen also did), thus stressing the literary quality of their work, and giving grounds for the rejection of text as the basis for performance.

This has been expressed in a wide variety of experiments with nonverbal performance throughout the century. Perhaps the most extreme was Gordon Craig's vision of a purely abstract theater created by the interplay of changing light and moving masses. His starting point was the rejection of the kind of drama represented by Bernard Shaw (the most relentlessly verbal of all twentieth-century playwrights) in preparing designs for a 1905 production of *Caesar and Cleopatra;* and in many ways his procedure anticipates the ideal of physical theater that characterized the avant-garde performance groups of the 1960s. First Craig cut

> the author's stage directions. . . . And as I read the words I wanted to omit these too. . . . When I had got the words out of my head I looked to see what was left of the First Scene and I found this First Scene to be like a great rat trap in which figures were scurrying to and fro like so many squeaking animals.[2]

The only dialogue remaining would be a chanted sound—repeated variations on the name "Ftatateeta"—again anticipating some of the 1960s experiments. But as his ideas developed, Craig went on to cut the actor along with the text, replacing human performers with mobile architecture: transforming the stage floor and flies into series of square columns that would rise and descend in continual progression and variety, accompanied by modulating flows of light. This "Scene," which Craig experimented with in model form, was never realized; and in its abstraction, as well as the total autocracy of the director that it represents, his extreme of nonverbal theater denies the animating principles of avant-garde performance groups.

However, other early experiments in creating physical theater were far more productive; and the most influential of these was Antonin Artaud's "Theater of Cruelty." One of his essays from the early 1930s famously declared NO MORE MASTERPIECES in demolishing the whole tradition of Western drama (and indeed attacking canon-formation in a way that still reverberates in today's academic arguments) as "one of the aspects of bourgeois conformism." In addition to dismissing written texts as a basis for theatrical performance, Artaud argues

> that an expression does not have the same value twice, does not live two lives; that all words, once spoken, are dead and function only at the moment they are uttered, that a form, once it has served, cannot be used again and . . . that the theatre is the only place in the world where a gesture, once made, can never be made the same way twice.[3]

Though overtly aimed at "the idolatry of fixed masterpieces" (Sophocles, Shakespeare), this emphasis on the uniqueness of each theater-event also provides the basis for valuing process at the expense of product in any performance. And picking up on the futurists' rejection of naturalistic illusionism and "storytelling psychology"—which are diagnosed as "the cause of the theater's abasement and its fearful loss of energy"[4]—the essay goes on to outline an experimental type of performance that effectively served as an embryonic manifesto for later avant-garde performance groups.

Specifically, the aspects of Artaud's Theater of Cruelty that came to resonate most powerfully in the 1960s were concerned with physicality, the concept of theater as a primal force, and primitivism. The essay proposed the ideal of a performance that would act on the spectator like Chinese acupuncture, directly affecting the central nervous system through the body (as opposed to communicating intellectually/verbally through the mind), returning "theater to . . . the physical knowledge of images and the means of inducing trances." The means were to be a "dynamism of action . . . in which violent physical images crush and hypnotize the sensibility of the spectator seized by the theater as by a whirlwind of higher forces." And the effect would be analogous to the psychoanalytic treatment of making a patient "assume the apparent and exterior attitudes of the desired condition," which Artaud declared went back to an "elementary magical idea." This nonverbal "religious idea of the theater" was also literally pretextual in seeking to return to the "poetry-through-theater which underlies the myths told by the great tragedians"—and it was grounded in Artaud's belief

> that the theater, utilized in the highest and most difficult sense possible, has the power to influence the aspect and formation of things: and the encounter upon the stage of two passionate manifestations, two living centers, two nervous magnetisms is something as entire, true, even decisive, as, in life, the encounter of one epidermis with another in a timeless debauchery.[5]

This essay was published in 1938 as part of *The Theater and Its Double*—a seminal book of theory that was almost completely ignored by the English-speaking world until a translation appeared in 1958. Twenty years later, and over a decade after Artaud's death, this slim volume became a revolutionary catalyst that motivated the formation of counterculture performance groups in America and England. Passionate (if frequently obscure—which added to their attraction) Artaud's incendiary writings were the bible of the 1960s avant-garde, many of whom shared his belief in the mystical efficacy of hallucinatory drugs, as well as his faith in theater as means of destabilizing and purifying an alienating and materialistic society. Among the other ideas that they adopted were Artaud's "Total Theater," in which all the barriers between audience and actor were broken down, surrounding the spectator with the action (later elaborated into "Environmental Theater"); and the search for a "concrete language, intended for the sense and independent of speech" through which actors would "signal through the flames," having achieved "the automism of the liberated unconscious."[6] Above all the avant-garde performance groups were influenced by Artaud's use of Balinese dance-drama as a model for his ideal of theater.

Artaud had been deeply impressed by a Barong performance, involving a grotesque witch, a mythical beast, and trance states—presented, ironically, at a 1927 Colonial Exposition—and hailed these Balinese "ceremonies of indubitable age and well-tried efficacy."[7] How much of the "magical" effect was real in that touristic context is hard to say, although at a similar performance filmed in Bali by Margaret Mead the dancers, once in their trance, indeed become invulnerable to the swords they turn against their naked chests. At any rate this Balinese "spectacle," with its archaic incantation and hieratic gestures, leading to mass hypnosis through contagious delirium, seemed to offer a practical realization of Artaud's ideas. In particular, he saw in it a form of theater that not only *"eliminates words"* (Artaud's italics), but expressed "a state prior to language" in presenting "a secret psychic impulse which is Speech before words." Instead, communicating through "the visual and plastic" mise-en-scène, "The Balinese theatre has revealed to us a physical and non-verbal idea of the theater . . . independently of the written text, whereas the theater as we conceive it in the Occident has declared its alliance with the text, and finds itself limited by it."[8] It was this—together with the sacred nature of the origins of theater, still retained in the Balinese drama—that motivated the recourse by 1960s performance groups to archaic, non-Western forms of religious theater. Indeed it even gave a rationale for the communal nature of those groups, since Artaud had stressed the unifying effect of this kind of performance: both in the holistic assimilation of individual performers, and in the spiritual "oneness" with nature.

In addition, Artaud was hypersensitive to the destabilizing effect of modern conditions, of being faced with a period "when the world . . . sees its old values crumble. Our calcined life is dissolving at its base." This certainly echoed the perception of 1960s radicals in America. His theater was both a response, and a reflection in being designed to function metaphorically like "the plague" that ushers in "spiritual freedom" by causing "all social forms to disintegrate"—and it is hardly surprising that one of the first attempts to incorporate Artaud's work was the Living Theatre's staging of "the Plague" in their 1964 *Mysteries* as "the very embodiment of his theatrical philosophy."[9] It was also in the same year that Brook staged one of Artaud's short plays, *The Jet of Blood,* as part of his experimental "Theatre of Cruelty" workshop in London.

The Living Theatre, which established itself off-off-Broadway in 1959, became the model for many of the American performance groups. Joe Chaikin, together with several of his actors in the Open Theatre, had performed with them; others became part of Richard Schechner's Performance Group or formed their own groups. Up to that point, Judith Malina and her husband Julian Beck had run a fairly conventional "little theater" company, whose reputation for innovation was founded on European imports—Cocteau, Strindberg, Picasso, even classics like medieval mystery plays and Racine—and poetic pieces by William Carlos Williams or Gertrude Stein. These were all text-based, even highly literary, although much of the surrealist drama dispensed with individualized characters and standard plot structures. Exposure to Artaud initially meant integrating their communal ethos and anarchist politics with their productions, selecting political works to radicalize their audiences, as with *The Connection* (an intensely realistic portrayal of drug addicts by Jack Gelber) or *The Brig* (Kenneth Brown's brutal depiction of life in marine prison).

These too were scripted plays, defined by written dialogue. However, their documentary quality encouraged an extreme degree of actuality in performance—corresponding on one level to Artaud's principles, but by intensifying the naturalistic illusionism that he had rejected. The police broke up one performance of *The Connection,* believing that cocaine was in reality being trafficked and injected on the stage, while the actors in *The Brig* were required to live by the prison rules for extended periods as part of the rehearsal process. More to the point, the realism combined with the squalor of street life or the deadening simplifications of prison routine, led to extensive verbal improvisation. The words on the page, though defining the situations, characters and relationships between figures for rehearsal, became a general score for performance; and mimicking the yelled army orders in *The Brig* transformed the words of command into nonverbal sound-language. In addition, the dominant element of these productions became the gestures and movements of the actors, and (particularly in *The Brig*) the rhythms of the performance. Although still containing texts, these productions were already in essence physical theater, with the core meaning carried by the mise-en-scène, which expanded to envelop the whole theatrical event. In *The Connection,* for example, the actors stayed in character as addicts during the intermission, panhandling members of the audience; and this blurring of pretence and reality, together with the self-expression allowed by improvising, meant that "the actors began *to play themselves*," which Judith Malina described as "a very important advance."[10]

The next phase in the group's development came with the adoption of Artaud's ideal of sacred theater functioning on a spiritual level. Merging with the 1960s counterculture search for alternative religious experience, they borrowed from an eclectic range of non-European traditions to turn performances into "an absolute communion" with the audience. The aim was therapeutic—both for the actors, who would be enabled to transcend physical limits of performance by breaking through their own psychological inhibitions, and by extension for society as a whole through liberating audiences from socially imposed repressions—thus effecting "the transformation of the demonic forces into the celestial."[11] The fullest expression of this came in *Paradise Now,* first performed in 1968 and elaborated over the next two years on tour in Europe and across the United States, which included sequences of action first evolved for such earlier Living Theatre performance pieces as *Mysteries* (1964) and *Frankenstein* (1965).

This element of repetition in their work is characteristic of most performance groups who have rejected verbal texts for physical language. Specific combinations of movement and gestures, generally arrived at in rehearsal exercises, become fixed images that appear as identifying "trademarks." Encapsulating a particular vision—of political repression, personal liberation, group solidarity, and so forth—they are felt to express the essential nature of those performance groups. In the case of the Living Theatre, perhaps the most representative "physical nexus" of this sort was a sequence of "flying." A culminating moment in *Paradise Now,* this was a simple acrobatic display: each of the actors in turn launching themselves off a platform some fifteen feet above the stage, as if diving upward, to fall safely into the interlaced arms of the rest of the group lined up below. As well as both a demonstration of individual trust and the strength of community, it signified a visionary "expansion of human potential. This could lead to flying . . . freed from the constraint and injury brought down on us by the errors of past civilisation, we will be free to expand and alter the nature of our being."[12] Members of the audience were also invited to participate, to experience a foretaste of this liberated transcendence and as a sign of willingness to join the group whom they relied on to catch them. This deliberate bridging of the barrier between actor and spectator—which worked both ways in Living Theatre productions, with the group moving out into the audience to act as cheerleaders or provocateurs, as well as the audience invading the stage at various points during the action, in particular to join the copulation of "Universal Intercourse," when all distinction between the actors and spectators was obliterated—is also integral to many performance groups.

The symbolic associations of "flying" were immediately apparent, even to the uninitiated; but however effective, the range of meanings such an action contained were necessarily very general. The political aims of *Paradise Now* required a more detailed level of communication to portray sequences such as the following:

> BOLIVIA: A GROUP OF REVOLUTIONARIES PLOT THEIR STRATEGY . . . THE REVOLUTION OF REVELATION / THE DESTINATION MUST BE MADE CLEAR . . .
>
> PARIS: TIME FUTURE: THE NON-VIOLENT ANARCHIST REVOLUTION . . . THE VISION OF THE LANDING ON MARS.[13]

One solution was to model groupings and postures on preexisting cultural symbols—Icarus or the Minotaur from Greek mythology, Amerindian totem poles, the crucifixion and Michelangelo's *Piéta*. Another was to copy images from the news media, the most successful of these being Edward Adams's 1968 award-winning photo of the Saigon police chief shooting a Vietcong prisoner in the head. Paired off actors took up the same positions in a line across the stage, and "in unison . . . the executioners fire, the victims fall. This is repeated twenty times." In each case the visual impact was determined by the shared connotations with which it was already loaded. In a sense this corresponded to the physical language of "precise and immediately readable symbols" that Artaud had envisaged.[14] However, almost all these images could only be "read" in the form of tableaus, requiring stasis, and were limited to a sort of cultural lowest common denominator in depending on the widest possible public familiarity for understanding.

There was also a degree of literalness in many of the Living Theatre scenes, where the actors' bodies were not so much Artaudian hieroglyphs communicating in a preverbal mode, as substitutes for missing speech. At times this was even explicit, as when the group took up positions for the letters to visually spell out the word *Anarchism,* which then was transformed with a shout of "Now!" into the word *Paradise.* In short, despite the ideological value placed on pretextual, physical theater, the performance of *Paradise Now* was still linguistically determined—reduced in fact to the level of visual slogans, which corresponded to the type of dialogue that remained. Much of this was not so much speeches as spoken stage directions, either interpretative glosses on what the actors were portraying:

> Be the heart. Act. Find the pain. Feel it. Make the sound of it.
>
> The heart of Africa

or cues for action by the spectators:

> Free theater. The theater is yours. Act. Speak. Do whatever you want.
>
> Free theater. Because in the society we envisage, everyone is free.
>
> Free theater. Free being. Free life. Do anything. Do nothing. Be.
>
> Breathe.
>
> Expand consciousness.[15]

The physical basis of performance was thus retained, but codified in a way that led back to text. And ironically, given the Living Theatre's reliance on improvisation and their belief in performance as ongoing process that denied any validity to theater as a fixed product, after the group split up in 1970 Malina and Beck indeed published a printed text of *Paradise Now.*

This text is hardly a conventional dramatic "script," since it reveals that less than a quarter of the performance time was actually scripted, to allow spontaneous actions (either by members of the group, or by the audience) to be incorporated. In addition, over 20 percent of the pages are taken up by photographs, which give visual definition to each of the scenes except two: an omission explained by a note that "no photographs are available for The Rite of New Possibilities and The Vision of Landing on Mars (Rung VII) since they are performed in total darkness." Scene designations like "Rite" and "Rung" point to the complex philosophical, even religious structure that underlay the action of *Paradise Now.* The description for each of the eight "rungs"—the overall image for the piece being a ladder signifying "a vertical ascent toward Permanent Revolution"—contains a section of political commentary, combined with hexagrams from the I Ching (each with elaborate explication), lengthy quotations from the Hasidim and/or the cabala, as well as a number of yoga exercises (with rationales for those selected). Specifically intended as "preparation" for the actors, or cues for the emotional states to be created at each point in the structure, there is no discernable link between these "texts" and anything physically performed on the stage. Yet they take up over a third of the script and are given a central function of embodying the "individual spiritual change" that is seen as the prerequisite for "exterior political change."[16]

The book is clearly designed as a documentation—with the photos recording moments from many different performances—but it is also intended as a script to be reproduced on the stage and contains an announcement on the copyright page that "*Paradise Now*. . . is free: for any community that wants to play it." In addition, the visual material relates to the printed words in much the same way as conventional illustrations; and the description makes clear that the physical presentation was structured by spoken language, with variations on the verbal "free theater" exhortation being reiterated at the end of all eight sequences of action that made up the complete (but in practice often truncated) performance. As a result the printed piece is open to standard literary analysis. Ultimately the Living Theatre never managed to free themselves from text. Their abandonment of *Paradise Now,* the vehicle for theatrical renewal as well as political revolution, signals their failure to achieve a purely physical theater—although their European exile, where the group was intentionally performing for non-English-speaking audiences, had been designed specifically "to find a way of communicating our feelings and our ideas through signs and being."[17]

That was also precisely Peter Brook's aim, when he took a performance group to Africa. His 1964 "Theatre of Cruelty" season was an exploration of the potential in physical modes of communication. But, being designed as preparation for a production of Genet's *The Screens,* it had been text based; and these aims clearly conflicted. Even with *Jet of Blood* there was an all too obvious contradiction between Artaud's hallucinatory visions—which depended on cinematic techniques and had analogies to surrealist films such as *Un Chien Andalou*—and the focus on movement and gesture that was achieved by removing all illusionistic elements: facial expression (the actors' heads being covered with white paper bags) as well as scenery, costuming, and stage props.[18] A transitional period when Brook tried out different combinations of physical theater and text in a series of brilliant productions, ranging from the violent insanity of *The Marat-Sade* by Peter Weiss to circus acrobatics in Shakespeare's *Midsummer Night's Dream,* culminated in an experiment with a language of pure sound in the 1971 production of *Orghast.*

This still had a text (written by the poet Ted Hughes), but the "words" were musical vocalizations, designed to have the same quality as physical action and intended to communicate solely on a subliminal level. Indeed, meanings for different basic sounds were derived from common physiology (thus "GR" for "eat," "ULL" for "swallow") in order to create a universal language: one that communicated "*below* the levels where differences appear, close to the inner life of what we've chosen as our material, but expressive to all people, powerfully, truly, precisely." The aim was to discover the roots of language—an "Ur-Sprache" that would transcend cultural diversity—and this emphasis on universality also determined the content of *Orghast,* which the program defined as stemming

> from certain basic myths—the gift of fire, the massacre of the innocents, the imprisonment of the son by the father, the search for liberation

> through revenge . . . as reflected in the hymns of Zoroaster, the stories of Prometheus and Hercules, Calderón's *Life's a Dream,* Persian legends, and other parallel sources.[19]

And it was this intercultural dissolving of boundaries that took Brook and his acting group to Africa in 1972.

In order to communicate with audiences who had no concept of theater or even acting, all culture-specific conventions and symbols had to be discarded; and the group's performances in villages, as they traveled through Dahomey or Mali, were exercises in returning to the basics. Improvisations developed around the simplest of objects—shoes, bread, a flute—were used to explore the expressive capacities of the body, as the only "common ground" between the actors and the native spectators. A repertoire of actions, gestures, and sounds, gathered in this way, became elaborated into a performance piece loosely based on a twelfth-century Persian poem: *The Conference of the Birds.* Presented in Nigeria as a series of improvised actions that could be varied at will, or in response to audience reaction, this was staged at a weeklong performance workshop in New York following their African tour to demonstrate Brook's principles of physical theater:

> Our work is based on the fact that some of the deepest aspects of human experience can reveal themselves through the sounds and movements of the human body in a way that strikes a chord in any observer, whatever his cultural and racial conditioning. And therefore one can work without roots, because the body, as such, becomes a working source.[20]

This was indeed theater for an "Empty Space" (as Brook had titled his performance ideal), with plain white, nonrepresentative costumes and the acting area defined solely by a carpet. But in practice the physical language displayed in *The Conference of the Birds* was largely anthropomorphic, with actors miming peacocks, falcons, and mythical avian creatures; and speech was gradually reintroduced, with a full play-text being created for the 1979 Avignon Festival—where the performance was coded through a whole range of exotic theatrical symbols: Oriental masks, Balinese puppets, Indonesian shadow play.

Another piece that also derived from their African experience exposes the limits of purely physical communication. The material for *The Ik* was based on an anthropological study of a displaced African tribe, where even the most fundamental human relationships had broken down under extreme pressures of famine and exile. It thus had a written text as its basis, *The Mountain People* by Colin Turnbull; and this was foregrounded in performance, with actors stepping out of role to read passages from Turnbull's book, and with Turnbull as a character/commentator. However, the Ik themselves were presented solely through bodily expression. As tribesmen, the actors were restricted to nonverbal vocalization of gutturals, clicks, and cries. Wearing standard European clothes and without makeup, their status, race, and cultural background was communicated through posture, the way they moved, and gesture alone. These poses and physical attitudes were imitated from photographs of the original natives; and the external reproduction of actuality was accompanied by a search for inner authenticity. The group built a replica of the Ik stockade, in which they lived during the rehearsals, to experience the same conditions as the tribe and thus share the essential "being" of a people on the verge of extinction.

Such emphasis on authenticity, where the role performed is inseparable from the psychology of the performer, is a defining element in avant-garde performance group work. Indeed it underlies the rejection of professionalism and their foregrounding of the amateur—natural expressiveness being seen as connecting to an inner truth that actor training, with its standardized conventions of communication, implicitly negated. Apparent amateurism in presentation was also a prerequisite for the merging of audiences into the performance, since any display of special skills would inhibit participation by untrained spectators. As such, however, this overt amateurism was itself a conscious technique; and Brook's work brings out (unintentionally) some of the inherent contradictions in the dominant value placed on authenticity by the avant-garde. The rehearsal process for *The Ik* exactly parallels the use of prison regulations and military power relationships in the Living Theater's preparation for *The Brig* twelve years earlier. Yet while one might accept the potential for sadism or submission as part of anyone's psychology, Brook's multinational group were embodying racial characteristics and externally determined circumstances that were—almost by definition—outside their personal experience. The element of pretence is underlined by their copying of recorded visual images to communicate a specific ethnicity; and the printed regulations used for *The Brig* have a comparable documentary status. Although the imaginative projection required for the Living Theatre production was less obvious, the artifice is the same.

In the same way, *The Ik* exposes the overlap between avant-garde performance and conventional theater in other areas. As typical for most performance group work, Brook's stage was bare, with no scenery and the only stage properties being the most basic objects: earth thinly scattered over the acting area, a few stones and sticks, one or two empty tin cans. Yet this paucity was itself a signifier, with the thinness of the soil representing the tribe's inability to grow crops, the empty tins their starvation, and the lack of any other surroundings standing for the loss of all hope or the cultural void that produced the breakdown of all social structures witnessed in the vignettes of their daily life, which formed the action of the piece. The absence of setting became a scenic statement; and this applies to almost all "empty space" theater, even if the bare stage seldom has such specific thematic relationship to the dramatic material.

Above all *The Ik* provides an example of the tension between physical expression and verbal communication. Wherever comprehension of a specific meaning was required, the vocalizations of the natives was accompanied by voice-over from the Turnbull character. In a different context this might have represented the opposition between European intellectualism (false values) and a holistic apprehension of reality. But the point of this production was to present the disintegration of communal standards and personal relations in the tribe as an extremity that awaited modern Western society, with its materialism, industrialization, and consequent moral deterioration. While the European clothing of the actors established the parallel, the implications were spelt out in the commentary. Thus the effect of the voice-over demonstrated that body language, precisely because of its universality, incorporated a limited register of experience. It might convey existential states, emotional being, even (as with Grotowski-trained actors) spiritual essence. However, any political, social, or moral statement requires words. The twin-track separation of text and performance that marked this production points to the problematic nature of the principles on which performance group work is based; and even if the body remains "a working source," all Brook's subsequent pieces have not only been derived from preexisting texts (whether Oliver Sacks's *The Man Who Mistook His Wife for a Hat* or *The Mahabharata*), but also based on conventional scripts.

Working in Paris, at the government-funded Centre for International Theatre Research, Brook's group is in many ways atypical. From *Orghast* to *The Mahabharata* Brook has tended toward productions on an epic scale, staged (as these pieces originally were) on mountain-tops or in rock quarries, in which individual performers become subsumed in a large-scale picture, requiring carefully rehearsed, choreographed movement. In such a context improvisation and the (deliberately) amateur quality that characterizes most of the other performance groups of the 1960s and 1970s is ruled out; and indeed the sheer space of the performing area requires an autocratic director, which is the opposite of the communal values on which such performance groups were founded. However, Brook's stripping down of the stage to an "empty space" was highly influential; and his search for universal modes of communication in the traditions and rituals of non-Western or prehistoric societies, as well as his emphasis on the body as a "working source," was paralleled by various groups, most notably Schechner's Performance Group and Joe Chaikin's Open Theatre.

At first glance Richard Schechner also appears atypical since his background was academic, which implies an intellectual approach—the very thing Artaud rejected, and the opposite of all that performance group work represented. However, in America it was largely an academic journal (the *Drama Review,* under Schechner's editorship) that promoted the exploration of nonverbal theater-language, and linked this with the religious rituals surviving in non-Western and still preindustrial cultures. In addition, it was the student revolution, fueled by opposition to the Vietnam War, that provided the broader social context for counterculture theater; and the majority of the Living Theatre performances after the midsixties took place on university campuses. It was also Schechner, in calling his team of actors the Performance Group, who coined the term for all such avant-garde work.

Both Schechner and Chaikin incorporated ritualized action and mythic material into the pieces that defined the work of their groups: *Dionysus in 69,* first performed in 1968 (the same year as *Paradise Now*) and *The Serpent,* developed between 1967 and 1968. Schechner was explicitly attempting to return theater to its original status of "shamanism or initiation rituals, or a combination of the two"; and *Dionysus in 69* was structured as an initiation rite, with the opening imitating African ceremonial practices described by the anthropologist Van Gennep in *Rites of Passage,* followed by "the birth ritual—adapted from the Asmats of New Guinea."[21] Rather than searching out ritual sources, the acting exercises out of which Chaikin's Open Theater pieces grew were direct explorations in nonverbal expression of somatic experience, based on Viola Spolin's physical "theater games" or derived from Chinese theater. Yet in developing material for these performance pieces they enacted ceremonies from various cultures—rites of mourning, excommunication rituals (specifically the excommunications of Spinoza and a Buddhist monk)—or invented ritual activities; and the movements and poses of one sequence in *The Serpent,* the "Begatting," were almost identical to the birth ritual in the Performance Group's *Dionysus in 69.*

From the beginning Schechner's performances had always incorporated scripts; and indeed several were based on pre-texts, with adaptations of Euripides *(Dionysus in 69)* or Shakespeare *(Makbeth).* In both of these some of the original words were retained, reminding the audience of this pre-text, as in the invocation to *Dionysus in 69,* which gave Euripides the status of an archetype. However, the dramatic situations of *The Bacchae* were retained only as a general frame for the action: a source of "scenarios" for improvisation. As in Brook's work, or the Living Theater, authenticity was the basis for the Performance Group's acting—but in a more overt (and superficial) way, with the performers announcing their own names and life histories before being "born" as the characters, and continuing to address each other by their real names during the performance. The aim throughout was to bring the audience into the action, indeed one of the premises of the performance was that their involvement could change the outcome (saving Pentheus from sacrifice), although this only happened during a single performance. The speeches at specific points could be varied according to the spectators' reactions, or to take account of current political events; and the words of key speeches also differed, depending on which actor was performing any given role. However, even if the colloquial tone gave a spontaneous effect, all the variants were fixed—indeed the dependence of the Performance Group on the script was demonstrated by the one occasion when a girl in the audience bonded with the actor playing Pentheus, and they left the performance space. The rest of the group were unable to continue, since no alternative had been rehearsed.

Like *Paradise Now,* a text of *Dionysus in 69* was subsequently published (as were texts for all the other Performance Group pieces). This contained both a "standard" version and selected variations, as well as explanations of the Group's intentions by Schechner and commentary on motivation, or poetic evocations of mood by the lead actors. Significantly more emphasis was placed on physical action, with the photographs far outweighing the verbal text, sometimes recording moments beat-by-beat. For instance in the culminating sequence (where the birth ritual of the opening was reversed, with the tunnel of naked bodies becoming "a vagina dentata and those teeth tear [Pentheus] to pieces") over a hundred photos accompany twenty-eight pages of script; and of this text only about two-thirds are words spoken by the actors.[22] The rest includes verbal description of what happened on stage and recollections of significant incidents or interactions with spectators in various performances—the equivalent of stage directions—as well as comparison with Euripides and commentary. However, the overwhelming visual emphasis served to codify the gestures and movement; and like the Living Theatre texts, this was not only a documentary record, but intended as a preset piece for others to perform—although in contrast to the script of *Paradise Now* (as with all the other Performance Group pieces) "professionals and amateurs" were "warned that *Dionysus in 69,* being fully protected under the copyright laws . . . is subject to royalty. All rights . . . are strictly preserved."

This standard injunction indicates the degree to which performance pieces such as *Dionysus in 69* were conventional plays; and from 1972 until 1980, when the Performance Group disbanded, Schechner's productions were all modern classics. Artaud had argued that any preestablished dramatic "situations are only a pretext" for performance—indeed that "everything that is a conception of the mind is only a pretext"[23]—and working from "finished texts" undermines the premises of physical theater, although Schechner presented this contradiction as an advance:

> Several years ago I argued forcibly that play texts were mere pretexts out of which the performance is made; material to be used dismembered, distorted, reassembled. . . . We have moved beyond the point when actors acted with their faces, hands and voices. The rebirth of the whole performer demands the reintegration of the writer into the theater.

And the piece selected for their first text-based performance, *Tooth of Crime,* was (for all its experimental nature) irreconcilable with a physical approach. As Sam Shepard pointed out, the play is "very preconceived. I got exact diagrams and pictures in my head about how it should be done."[24] Despite unconventional aspects, such as Shepard's use of music to communicate "the emotional line" in the action, the speeches are highly structured, interwoven, and intensely verbal.

By contrast with Schechner, who either developed fixed texts out of improvised group work around classical "pre-texts" or used preexisting, published texts, Chaikin collaborated closely with playwrights as an integral part of the Open Theatre creative process. He also continued a career as an actor in conventional theater (for instance at the Writer's Stage Company), even specializing in Beckett, an author noted for insisting on exact reproductions of his scripts.[25]

Even though the Open Theatre was initially a workshop devoted exclusively to investigating nonverbal physical expression, when they began public performances to showcase their explorations, Jean-Claude van Itallie was brought in to create scripts. At first these were "scenarios" built around specific acting exercises, although they also performed *America Hurrah,* which van Itallie had written for the group. But with their first full-length piece, *The Serpent,* a full verbal text was evolved, using a team of writers: Megan Terry, Patricia Cooper, as well as van Itallie. There was also a (specifically archetypal) literary pre-text, the Bible and in particular the Book of Genesis, from which they developed physical images through improvisation. These included the striking embodiment of the serpent itself as the Tree of Life—five intertwined actors, with flickering tongues and sinuous arms, offering apples in their hands—animals in the Garden of Eden, or the assassination of President Kennedy (based on frames from the Zapruder film of the actual event). While the physical images were the most immediately striking element of the performance, the piece was structured by the words, with a chorus of women providing narration that orchestrated the changing tone and linked the different segments.

As with all Chaikin's Open Theatre work, the scripts for the scenes of *The Serpent* that the various writers contributed were in a continuous process of change and rewriting up until the last moment before the first performance. On shows such as *Terminal* (which developed out of *The Serpent*) and

Nightwalk (1973), none of the several authors writing for the group had a picture of the overall shape, or even the main thrust of the piece. Susan Yankowitz, for instance, commented on the difficulty of writing *Terminal* "without having a sense of the whole; and yet the discovery of the whole was the process that occasioned the writing," while Shepard was sending material for *Nightwalk* from London.[26] Even *The Mutation Show*—the only real ensemble piece, for which all the dialogue was created through improvisation by the actors—credited writers in the program; and Chaikin's commitment to verbal language can be illustrated by *Tongues*. A piece for solo voice and percussion, cowritten by Chaikin and Shepard, this monologue was performed by Chaikin, seated facing front and motionless, with Shepard hidden behind his chair providing the musical accompaniment. Although a major theme in the speeches is the inadequacy of words, the performance was a demonstration of the communicative power of verbal and facial expression. Indeed, for all its experimental quality, the Open Theatre was far more mainstream than most avant-garde performance group work, as the number of Obie and Drama Desk awards indicate. For example, although like *Paradise Now, The Serpent* was first presented on a European tour (in many of the same venues as the Living Theatre), when remounted in New York it won an Obie and a Vernon Rice award for "outstanding contributions" to the theater.

The comparison between the reenactment of Kennedy's death in *The Serpent* and the *Paradise Now* replay of the Saigon police chief shooting the Vietcong prisoner, both reproducing hauntingly familiar documentary photographs, underlines the differences between the Living Theatre and Chaikin's work. Instead of a single image multiplied to present an emotive slogan (the evil violence of Western politics), the Kennedy scene was a complex sequence—extended to include the assassination of Martin Luther King and focusing on the watching crowd: "I was not involved . . . / I stay alive"[27]—which contained a whole range of subliminal meanings. It became a contemporary version of the expulsion-from-Eden myth, echoing the loss of innocence, as well as paralleling Cain's murder of Abel and representing the mistaken attempts of Adam and Eve's contemporary children to regain Paradise though human sacrifice. As such it was a highly intellectual form of theater; with the physical images being created out of disciplined acting exercises, and accompanied by a text that conditioned the reception of the images.[28]

The productions mounted by the Performance Group following *Tooth of Crime,* such as Brecht's *Mother Courage,* were all "literary"; and Schechner's focus reverted to the type of audience participation that he had first tried out with *Victims of Duty* in 1967 (before moving to New York and founding the Performance Group). The whole studio in which Ionesco's play was staged had been laid out as the Choubert's living room, with the spectators seated between the sofas and chairs, even at the table where the characters sat eating a meal. In the same way the whole Performance Garage became Mother Courage's wagon, with the audience as her "customers"; and her haggling continued outside on the pavement. This type of performance, where the audience are surrounded by the action, indeed part of the play's environment, and where the action extends into the world outside, Schechner labeled "Environmental Theater." As a new variant of Total Theatre, it is perhaps the one important contribution made by the Performance Group.

Similarly, Chaikin, whose Open Theatre was followed by a more restricted "Winter Project" that lasted until the mideighties, devoted more of his time to conventional texts, ranging from van Itallie's *A Fable Telling about a Journey,* through his adaptation of *The Seagull,* to *The Dybbuk.* And the group also created a radio piece, *Night Voices,* which necessarily relied totally on words and the voice. At the same time the workshop continued to explore fundamental elements of theatrical expression, and the nature of the actor-audience relationship. And it is these "preparatory" exercises that have carried through into the work of contemporary performance artists.

In a sense, then, the avant-garde performance groups of the sixties and seventies mark the limitations of purely physical theater. Inspired by Artaud, they experimented in various degrees with a purely physical, participatory mode of communication. But like Artaud himself, whose performances were all based on scripts, even their most unconventional work were codified as texts, and both Schechner and Chaikin reverted to productions of preexisting plays. Even so, their experiments effected a fundamental change in American theater. Their nonnaturalistic approach is now widely accepted, expanding the acting and staging vocabulary even of Broadway; and their work directly influenced contemporary performance artists. Spalding Gray, for instance, was one of the key actors in the Performance Group, while Chaikin has exerted a more indirect, but possibly more significant influence on some of the major figures on the contemporary scene, including Joanne Akalaitis, Lee Breuer, and Andrei Serban.

NOTES

1. T. S. Eliot, "Ulysses, Order, and Myth," *Dial,* November 1923, 483; Wassily Kandinsky, *Concerning the Spiritual in Art,* trans. M. T. H. Sadler (1912) (New York, 1977), 71.

2. Gordon Craig, *Towards a New Theatre* (London: J. M. Dent, 1913), 51.

3. Antonin Artaud, *The Theater and Its Double,* trans. Mary Caroline Richards (New York: Grove Press, 1958), 76, 75. All quotations are taken from this source because of its specific relevance to avant-garde performance groups.

4. Ibid., 76, 77.

5. Ibid., 80, 82–83, 79.

6. Ibid., 87, 13, 54.

7. Ibid., 53. For a fuller discussion of the nature of this Balinese performance, and the influence of non-Western models, see chapter 1 of my *Avant-Garde Theatre: 1892–1992* (London: Routledge, 1993).

8. Ibid., 53–54, 62, 60, 69, 68.

9. Ibid., 115, 23; Julian Beck, in *We, the Living Theater,* ed. Aldo Rostagno (New York: Ballantine Books, 1970), 81.

10. Cited by Jan Kott, *Drama Review* 14, no. 1 (1970): 23.

11. Rostagno, *We, the Living Theater,* 24; Judith Malina and Julian Beck, *Paradise Now* (New York: Random House, 1971), 77.

12. Malina and Beck, *Paradise Now,* 127.

13. Scenes designated in the chart outlining the structure of the performance, program for *Paradise Now,* 1968.

14. Malina and Beck, *Paradise Now,* 75; Artaud, *Theater and Its Double,* 94.

15. Malina and Beck, *Paradise Now,* 27, 63, 111.

16. Ibid., 152, 5, 7.

17. Julian Beck, "Containment is The Enemy," *Drama Review* 13, no. 3 (1969): 42.

18. For fuller descriptions of Brook's *Jet of Blood* production and his other work in the 1960s, see Albert Hunt and Geoffrey Reeves, *Peter Brook* (Cambridge: Cambridge University Press, 1995), 65f., or my *Avant Garde Theatre,* 125f.

19. Ted Hughes, *Times Literary Supplement,* October 1, 1971 (emphasis added); program note (1971), cited by A. C. H. Smith, *Orghast at Persepolis* (London: Eyre Methuen, 1972), 50.

20. Brook, in *Drama Review* 17, no. 3 (1973): 50.

21. Richard Schechner, *Environmental Theater* (New York: Hawthorn Books, 1973), 189. Compare the Performance Group, *Dionysus in 69* (New York: Farrar, Straus and Giroux, 1970), "Opening Ceremonies," n.p.; and Arnold Van Gennep, *Rites of Passage,* trans. Monika B. Vizedom and Gabrielle L. Caffe (London: Routledge and Paul, 1960), 185; *Dionysus in 69,* scene 1.

22. *Dionysus in 69,* "I'm the Messenger" sequence (n.p.).

23. Artaud, *Theater and Its Double,* 53, 63.

24. Schechner, *Environmental Theater,* 242; and Sam Shepard, cited by Schechner, 235.

25. For a full analysis of Chaikin's work, see Eileen Blumenthal, *Joseph Chaikin* (Cambridge: Cambridge University Press, 1984).

26. Cited in ibid., 145.

27. The van Itallie poem is cited ibid., 131.

28. This intellectual quality was recognized by the reviewers, with Walter Kerr commenting that "*The Serpent* starts the mind off on tangents that keep extending themselves" (*New York Times,* May 24, 1970, sec. 2, p. 3).

II. Theorizing Antitext and Beyond

Erika Fischer-Lichte
Translated by James Harding

The Avant-Garde and the Semiotics of the Antitextual Gesture

A New Definition of the Theater

The closer the last century neared its end, the louder became the voices announcing a fundamental cultural paradigm shift. The long-enduring conception of the "World as Text" is increasingly and radically giving way to a conception of the "World as Performance," as the ethnologist Dwight Conquergood noted at the beginning of the nineties.[1] But such a shift in emphasis did not first begin with the development of performance culture and performance art in the sixties. On the contrary, it can be traced back to the turn of the previous century, indeed back to Nietzsche. What today is regarded as the dominant paradigm had its point of departure there.

This is especially evident in the example of the theatrical avant-garde. The radical redefinition of the theater, which the avant-garde began at the turn of the century, fundamentally transformed the two categories "text" and "performance" and thereby produced a new, highly charged dynamic between them.

The redirection of the theater occurred on two levels—one with regard to the theater as an art form and the other with regard to the relation of theater and life. In the nineteenth century, the theater had the status of art only insofar as it served the dissemination of literature. Its artistic character was primarily granted and guaranteed by the artistic character of drama as a work of literature. But already in the nineteenth century, isolated voices were rising that wanted to characterize and identify theater production as art. In his 1798 discussion *Über Wahrheit und Wahrsheinlichkeit der Kunstwerte* Goethe, citing the example of operatic production, had already tried to establish the autonomy of the theater as art. For "when opera is good, it certainly makes a little world for itself, in which everything wants to be judged according to specific laws, experienced according to its own characteristics."[2] Richard Wagner was one of the few who in the nineteenth century continued and developed this idea. In his 1849 piece "The Artwork of the Future," he characterized the production of music drama as the only worthy and conceivable art of the future: "The great *Gesammtkunstwerk* that has to embrace all forms of art in order, as it were, to exhaust each individual form as a means, to destroy in favor of the realization of the common goal of all, namely, the unconditional, immediate representation of perfected human nature."[3] This representation seemed possible to him only through a singing and dancing performer.

Even though Goethe and Wagner considered performance itself a work of art, for the overwhelming majority of nineteenth-century contemporaries the artistic character of performance was primarily affirmed through the performance of literature, through the dramatic literary text that was supposed to steer and control performance. As late as 1918, the theater critic Alfred Klaar was writing—and writing specifically as a polemic against the newly emerging discipline of theater studies, whose focus was supposed to be performance—that "the stage can only claim to have its full worth if literature provides it with the content."[4]

At the beginning of the twentieth century, a programmatically expressive avant-garde theater reacted sharply against this widely disseminated and dominant view. In his essay *The Art of the Theatre* (1905), Edward Gordon Craig maintained that

> The Art of the Theatre is neither acting nor the play, it is not scene nor dance, but it consists of all the elements of which these things are composed: action, which is the very spirit of acting; words, which are the body of the play; line and colour, which are the very heart of the scene; rhythm, which is very essence of dance.[5]

Corresponding formulations can be found in the writings of Vsevolod E. Meyerhold (1907), Wassily Kandinsky (1912), Lothar Schreyer (1916), Alexander Tairov (1915–20) among others. Contemporary theater was criticized for its willingness to be content with its role as a "maid to literature." As art, theater, on the other hand, demanded that a theater-specific language be created. For, as Kandinsky observes, "every art has an independent language, i.e., a means unique to itself."[6] Only when performance is conceived and received as an autonomous work of art can the theater live up to its future task—what, for Craig, means a theater of movement, a theater that makes the "invisible force" of movement visible and facilitates its representation. Theater is thereby declared the performative art par excellence.

The conception of performance as an autonomous work of art fundamentally redefines the dynamic between the literary dramatic text and performance. No longer does the text steer, control, and legitimize performance. Rather, the text becomes one material among other materials—like the body of the actor, sounds, objects, et cetera—each of which the performance manipulates or adapts, thereby constituting itself as art.

The second important redirection of the theater added to the dynamic between performers and audience and concerned the relation of theater and life. The avant-garde faulted bourgeois theater for maintaining a strict separation between the performers and observers through the proscenium stage and for thus having reduced the process of theatrical interaction to a form of one-way communication that corresponded to bourgeois ideology. The avant-garde, on the other hand, postulated a principal unity between performers and audience, which they considered to be the indispensable prerequisite for moving the audience to action and for its thus becoming performers.

This action, however, was always conceived differently. The conservative, nationalistic Nietzschean Georg Fuchs as well as the social democratic producers of the *Leipziger Massenspiele* (in the twenties) understood the uniting of performers and audience as a "community of experience" or a "communal experience." Dadaists and futurists planned the action as furious attacks and the aggressive reactions of the (bourgeois) public, which was irritated by calculated provocations against its customary manner of reception. Piscator and the communist proletarian-cult movement expected the action of the public to be a partisanship on behalf of the proletariat as well as an expression of commitment to class struggle.

Corresponding to the divergent conceptions of public action, the avant-garde—in manifestos and programmatic pamphlets as well as in their own productions and other types of organized events like the transformations of a worship service in the Berlin Cathedral in 1918 and a parliamentary session in Weimar in 1919 by the "Oberdada" Johannes Baader or the tour of cultural memorials by the surrealists—announced a transformation of theater into many different forms of cultural performances: into a festival (e.g., Peter Behrens, Adolphe Appia, Emile Jaques-Dalcroze, Max Reinhardt, Nikolai Evreinov), ritual (e.g., Georg Fuchs, Antonin Artaud), a circus or variety show (Filippo Tommasso Marinetti, Boris Arvatov, Sergei Eisenstein), a pubic meeting (e.g., Vsevolod Meyerhold, Platon Keržencev, Erwin Piscator), happenings (dadaists, futurists, surrealists). With the postulated transformation, the concept of theater was fundamentally redefined. For one, emphasis was placed on the unity of performers and audience, on the realization of action through both groups, and on the effect of participation in the production on the "audience." That unambiguously focused the performative function of the theater.

Theater always fulfills a referential and a performative function.[7] While the referential function deals with the representation of figures, actions, relationships, situations, and so forth, the performative deals with the realization of actions—through performers and through the audience—and in this sense, with the "eventness" of the theater. The history of European theater can be understood as a record of the shifting dominance and corresponding restructuring of the relations between these two functions. Toward the end of the nineteenth century, the theater's referential function dominated the playhouse—to such a degree that its performative function was almost completely eclipsed. The goal of performance was to convey the sense and meaning of the literary text; the task of the audience was to understand it. The transformation of the theater into a ritual, a festival, and other genres of cultural performances shifted the dominance from the referential to the performative function. Thus the center of interest pivoted on the action of the audience, that is, its transformation into participants, into performers. In order for this transformation to occur, the postulated unity of performers and audience, as previously stated, represented a fundamental condition. In this sense, a unity existed among the different representatives of the avant-garde. Significant differences existed, however, with regard to the more precise determination of this unity (e.g., as cult-religious community, political rally, folk community), as well as the ways and means through which it should be reached (e.g., shock, intoxication, trance, alienation). As always, in each case, emphasis shifted to the performative function of theater and thus from text to performance.

This implied, at the same time, a change in attitude toward the human body. Boris Arvatov, the theorist of the proletarian-cult movement in the new Soviet Union, unequivocally pointed to the change with his comparison of theater and circus performance: "While in the theater the actor only creates the appearance that he is bold, adroit, astute, resourceful, brave, etc., . . . [in the circus] he actually is."[8] Naturally, actors in the nineteenth-century theater also performed physical acts: they had entrances, reclined in chairs, picked up letters, et cetera. Yet the focus of the audience was not supposed to be on the actions but rather on that which they were supposed to mean. The body of the actor was considered primarily to be a carrier of signs. With the shift in dominance toward the performative function, attention also shifted to the body itself and its acts: to the moving body. The connections with the *Körperkulturbewegung* as well as with the emergence of rhythmic gymnastics or free dance are obvious.

The transformation of theater into many different genres of cultural performances not only fundamentally altered the traditional conception of the theater, but consequently also altered the relation of theater and life. Correspondingly, Arvatov continues in his comparison of theater and circus performance: "And when Eisenstein, Meyerhold, Radlov, Foregger, and others advocate, each in his own way, the usefulness of circus and cabaret in theatre, they actually fulfill one and the same task: they bring life into the theater."[9]

These ideas indicate that the issue for the avant-garde in the early decades of this century was not merely a new theater but a new culture. The new theater was so conceived that it could emerge as a culture-creating factor—so that it opened the way into, and itself represented, a new performative culture. The revolution in the theater was conceptualized as a cultural revolution.

It may consequently appear at first glance as if both new theater concepts—performance as an artwork and performance as a realization of another form of cultural performance—would contradict each other. But this appearance is deceptive. As I hope to show over the longer course of my essay, they are rather in multiple ways mutually dependant, that is, mutually referential. This above all results from the fact that both concepts redefine the relation of "text" and "performance": absolute priority is granted to performance.

New Spaces as Sites of Transformation

The demand to transform theater into other forms of cultural performances and thus to unify performers and audience (i.e., to move the audience to action) rendered the traditional form of the proscenium stage counterproductive and obsolete. A search for new theatrical spaces began.[10] Max Reinhardt—who believed the "true destiny" of the theater was its realization as "festive play,"[11] and thus postulated the transformation of theater into festival—experimented not only with steps connecting stage and auditorium (after 1901) or with the *hanamichi* borrowed from Japanese Kabuki theater (after 1910). Beyond that, he developed a nearly inexhaustible imagination for discovering and developing new spaces for the theater. Performances took place in exhibition and festival halls, in the circus and marketplace, in churches, in city squares and streets, in gardens, parks, and forests. Shakespeare's *Midsummer Night's Dream,* which Reinhardt had first produced in 1905 with a spectacular utilization of the recently installed revolving stage, he relocated in subsequent years to actual forests: in 1910, he had it performed in a pine forest in Berlin-Nikolasee and later the same year in Murnau's Seidl-Park, where he created a "theater environment" out of hills, birch trees, and ponds. In the summer of the same year, he produced Sophocles' *Oedipus the King* (Hugo von Hofmannsthal's adaptation) in the Munich Festival hall, which he had transformed into an arena. Then in November of the same year, he assumed production in the Berlin Schumann Circus. There Reinhardt produced Aeschylus's *Oresteia* (Karl Vollmoeller's adaptation) and Hugo von Hofmannsthal's *Jedermann.* Likewise, in 1911 he directed his stage builder Ernst Stern to redesign the London Olympia Hall into an arched gothic cathedral that united the audience and performers for the production of Vollmoeller's *Mirakel.* In the twenties, Reinhardt staged *Jedermann* atop wooden scaffolding in front of the Salzburg Cathedral (1920) and Hofmannsthal's *Salzburger Großes Welttheater* (1923) in the Salzburg Kollegienkirche. In all of these projects, Reinhardt attempted to create and to guarantee the unity between players and public by relocating the performance in spaces that stood in a direct relation to the life of the audience and, simultaneously, to the festive tone of the theater emphasized by Reinhardt.[12]

The proletarian-cult movement evinced a similar imaginativeness in the search for new spaces. On the one hand, they were supposed to be so composed that they in themselves allowed the theater to be connected with the working reality of a proletarian audience. To this end, Eisenstein, for example, moved his production of Tretyakov's *Gas Masks* (1923) to a gas factory. On the other hand, the new spaces were supposed to be suitable as a fairground for a large festival. For this, only city streets and squares were suitable. On May 1, 1920 the proletarian-cult organized, as part of a festival, the first mass spectacle in the Soviet Union. It took place in the colonnades of the former bond market in Petrograd. Among the subsequent outdoor mass spectacles, *The Storming of the Winter Palace* (1920) became especially famous, having been performed in Petrograd, under the direction of Nikolai Evreinov, on the anniversary of the October Revolution. The drama took place on the "original site." Among the approximately ten thousand participants who played a part in the production were people who actually had been involved in the coup d'état of 1917. The audience stood on the former Alexander Square between the Winter Palace and the general staff. Next to the general staff two terraces were built, the right one white and the left one red. They were joined by a bridge where certain scenes took place as well. In the first part, the action took place in the square, toward the end of the second part behind the illuminated windows of the Winter Palace. And, as at the time of the October Revolution, the warship *Aurora* was also stationed on the Neva, participating—as previously in the historical events—with cannon fire.

The selection of scene was in all these cases highly significant. With the selection of the Schumann Circus for his production of *Oedipus* and *Oresteia,* for example, Reinhardt in one sense followed the form of Greek theater that Wagner recalled in his festival theater in Bayreuth. He thereby advocated his theater of five thousand, a *Volkstheater,* in which the public "became the people, were drawn into, and themselves became part of the action."[13] On the other hand, he emphasized throughout that the production took place in a circus, a place of physically oriented mass entertainment. Corresponding to the masses in the viewing stands were the masses in the chorus, which extended to the whole people and which—comprised of more than one hundred members (some even suggest a chorus of between five hundred and a thousand members)—repeatedly poured out into the public and thus brought the drama out into the audience. With this expressed reference to the circus arena, Reinhardt unmistakably shifted dominance from the referential to the performative function.

It was precisely there that theater critics took offense. They complained: "How barbaric the entrance of Agamemnon was with tubas and cymbals and four genuine snorting and stamping steeds, how circus-like in the crudest sense."[14] The critics also reacted with anger and repulsion to the physically oriented acting: "In the middle . . . a monstrous example of the thrilling entertainment of mass audiences who grew up at the bullfights. When Orestes wants to kill his mother, it more than suffices that he storms after her out the palace door, holds her firmly against the door, and, after a battle of words, shoves her back into the palace. Here he pursues her down the stairs into the arena, there he struggles around with her and then all too slowly drags her up the stairs again. It is atrocious."[15] And the physical closeness, with which the unity between performers and audience was supposed to be established, aroused disgust among some critics. Monty Jacobs, for example, asked himself whether communal feelings could "really only [be] cultivated" "by reaching over the forestage? Certainly, physical contact is not necessary. In fact it inhibits. . . . The actor next to me, whom I hear breathing, distracts rather than convokes, and only nervousness increases, rather than the desired effect, when the voices ring from the gallery. Outwardly, physically the unification of those with and without makeup was amazingly successful. But the *Unio mystica,* the marriage of the souls, failed to materialize."[16]

Even as these critics, relying on the nineteenth-century conception of culture, spoke out against the arena theater, it was spontaneously accepted by the larger public. The performances in the Schumann Circus continuously proved to be big public successes. This development confirmed the assumptions of the theorists and practitioners, for whom the new conception of the arena theater appeared to be the ideal symbolic space for a community-building theater, indeed almost the prerequisite for its possibility. In the work *Das Große Schauspielhaus* (1919)—published by the Deutsches Theater in honor of the opening of the *Großes Schauspielhaus* into which Hans Poelzig had rebuilt the Schumann Circus—Reinhardt's colleagues and combatants summarized the most important arguments that since 1910 had been exchanged in this discussion. Reinhardt's dramaturgist Heinz Herald emphasized that in the arena theater, theater transformed "again from a occupation of the few into an occupation of the many" since "a receptive, unspoiled, eavesdropping public assembled here, which for that reason [was] an active—absorbent and radiant—public," a public "that came out of all classes" and could "absorb the masses" that "heretofore had been foreign to theater."[17] Carl Vollmoeller lauded the arena theater as "the people's assembly from today. . . . What the depoliticization during fifty years of imperial regime hindered is possible today: the concentration of the theatrical space of thousands into a community of co-acting, co-traveling, and cooperating citizens and national comrades [*mithandelnden, mitgerissenen und mitreißenden Bürgern und Volksgenossen*]."[18] And Kurt Pinthus celebrated the arena theater as the only truly possible path not only to "the future *Volkstheater*" but also to "the future of humanity."[19] For

> up to now the theater remained far behind the development of humanity because the entertainment and representation structures of a long-departed view of society had been maintained. Now its podium will be an exhilarating springboard for forward-striving generations, a trampoline from which unbridled man in his richest depths and forms springs upward. The *Volkstheater* will have the immense task of keeping the people awake and strong amid the wearing down of chaos and of giving them belief and strength for its purpose and future. The theater again has the meaning that the *Volk* always attributed to it. In it, art, faith, politics blend together. It is: theater for everyone![20]

The dominance of the performative, which here justifies attributing the function of a kind of civil religion to theater, is clearly connected to the specific conditions of space in which the production occurs. It is the space that transforms the individual into a member of a community, into a communal being and thus evokes specific actions from him.

A similar conclusion can be made with regard to the mass spectacle *The Storming of the Winter Palace.* The drama began around ten o'clock at night—in other words late at night in darkness. It ended shortly before midnight with fireworks. The repetition of the "mythical" founding events—with which first the tsarist and then bourgeois regimes were extinguished and the light of the revolution emerged—on the third anniversary at the original site of events allowed the observer to become participant and partner in the events. At a point in time when one still always had to take into account the danger of a counterrevolution, the production served the function of welding together performers and audience in a revolutionary community and of activating them in defense of the revolution. Simultaneously, it conjured up the "magical" powers of the place and projected them onto the bodies of the audience: the direct contact with the original site of events was supposed to "infect" the performers and audience with a revolutionary power of action.

In both cases, with the productions in Reinhardt's Theatre of Five Thousand and with Evreinov's mass spectacles, the theater generated community-building power not through an appeal to a specific text but through the performance, which in the use of bodies, voices, music, sounds, lights, et cetera, attempted to directly affect the senses of the audience and which occurred at a very specific place. The transformation of the audience, when they then entered, took place via the direct physical effects in this space, and through this space the performative aesthetic of the transformation, as it here evolved, was made possible by the specific conditions of each space.

Sparagmos of the Text's Body

The transformation of theater into a festival, a circus performance, a political rally, et cetera, implies that the literary text of a drama, insofar as it was used in a production, obtained a wholly new function in the production. During the 1860s and 1870s, the Meiningers expressed the demand for "faithfulness to the text." The texts of the classics, which, without fuss or problem, had been adapted according to the prevailing stage conventions and current moral norms and standards of behavior, remained unchanged by them or were only minutely cut. Consequently, they brought the theater a new function: that of being the conscience of its culture—a culture that was materialized and embodied in specific canonized texts. This function recalled a relation that, according to Roland Barthes, originally existed between theater and memory of the cult of the dead: "the first actors distinguished themselves from the rest of the community in that they assumed the role of the DEAD: to make oneself up meant to identify oneself simultaneously as a living and dead body."[21] This relationship was recalled in the classical productions of the Meiningers (and after them in many classical productions up to today). With these productions, the theater carried out its new task—first formulated by Goethe in his proclamation of a world-theater repertoire—to be a place for conveying the past to the present. The physical presence of the actor thus attained a specific historical signature. For when dramas out of the Western tradition from Aeschylus to Hebbel were produced, figures appeared on the stage whose history was a part of the collective memories of the educated classes. But they appeared not as when read or as in dreams, memories, or fantasies. Rather, they entered *in corpore*—the performance occurred as a daily evening resurrection of the dead who, before the eyes of the audience, once again "relived" the life that the dramatic text formed for them and in which it had them spellbound.

The transformation of the theater into other genres of cultural performances let this type of classical production become functionless. Classical texts, which found application as material for such productions, were now consulted and examined for specific potential effects that they were capable of developing. They were correspondingly shortened, rearranged, combined with other texts, rewritten.

For Eisenstein's production of Ostrovsky's comedy *The Wise Man* (1922), Sergei M. Tretyakovsky did the textual adaptation. He took approximately 25 percent of the textual material directly from Ostrovsky's text and altered, that is, supplemented the rest rather heavy-handedly. As a fundamental change, he transposed the story, which in Ostrovsky takes place in the Russian commercial milieu of the nineteenth century, into the Paris immigrant milieu of the twenties. Each actor had to play three roles at the same time: the one conceived by Ostrovsky, the role of a contemporary politician of the Entente, and a circus role like a clown, juggler, trapeze artist, or tightrope walker, et cetera. Each time, the circus roles provided basic models for the movement of the actor. Correspondingly, the staging was built upon the physical feats of acrobatics: "the gestus pivots on acrobatics, rage is represented in an acrobatic leap, excitement in a death-defying somersault, and the lyrical in an ascent up the 'death mast.' . . . The eccentric, grotesque style of this staging made possible the jumping from one form of expression to another as well as the highly uncommon combinations of these two."[22]

The individual scenes of Ostrovsky's comedy that were kept gained a strong parodic element through these specific alterations in the characters, which was further strengthened through new textual material as well as through the unique gestures. At the same time, they appeared throughout in a different sequence than in Ostrovsky's comedy (which the audience naturally noticed, since this text was one of the most famous and popular in Russian literature). In Ostrovsky, numerous moments of intrigue are linked one after another with each other. Thus in one scene, Mamaev demands rather unambiguously of his relative Glumov that Glumov court Mamaev's wife because he wants to have a little rest from her. When in a later scene Glumov acts upon this demand, he goes so far beyond the directions of his uncle and courts his aunt so passionately that she believes his flirtations to be genuine.

Eisenstein so interwove these scenes that they ran simultaneously. The scene between Mamaev and Glumov was performed in the arena and the scene between Glumov and Mamaeva on a small pedestal in the background. In place of a fluidly changing entrance, Glumov now flew constantly back and forth between Mamaev and his wife: "He has a dialogue with Mamaeva, then breaks it off in order to pursue it further with Mamaev. The concluding statements of one fragmentary exchange overlapped with the beginning of the next, where they received a new meaning and from time to time became a game of puns."[23] With the simultaneous montage as well as with the successive montage, music had an important function.

The text of Ostrovsky's drama was also completely dissected; individual sections were fused with other elements—other texts, movements, objects, film clips, music—and thus became components of an event: the Performance.

Leopold Jeßner proceeded similarly with his classical productions. In his production of *Don Carlos,* for example, which had its premiere February 13, 1922, in the Staatstheater Berlin, he shortened the text to a degree that was hitherto completely unknown on German stages. As the critic Emil Faktor observed, "one of the shortest-ever *Don Carlos* productions" thus came into existence.[24] "A driving tempo, a leaving out and a cutting out, even of scenes that are central to the structure of the tragedy, gives the big scenes, on which Jeßner . . . depended, room to let themselves unfold."[25] The Carlos-Posa plot was radically edited so that the conspiracy among Alba, Domingo, and Eboli stepped strongly into the foreground. The concluding scene fell out. The performance ended with the grand inquisitor scene, to which Philipp's closing statement was added: "Cardinal, I have done my part, do yours."

The stage (Otto Strand) consisted of three steps that extended "from the forestage to the horizon [*Lufthorizont*]"[26] and were equipped with hollowed-out segments that made "two engulfing entrances" possible. In the middle was "a relatively small platform upon which the figures could only move when absolutely necessary."[27] These foundational structures were interspersed in the different scenes with columns that "lowered the space,"[28] curtains and decorative pieces like Ebolis's sofa or Philipp's bed. It was thus the space that dominated and that opened specific possibilities for the movements of the actors, as, for example, with the entrance of the king and his court: "one did not yet see it as effectively festive. High above on the arch to the stairs, which touched the horizon, the Spanish King Philipp II climbed up. It is black with grandees, black with habits. The left stares in silent etiquette, to the right the sky turns dark with gloomy father confessors. In the middle walks the lonely ruler of the gigantic kingdom. The stairs helps the production achieve an uncommon intensification of the symbolic."[29] In its symbolism, this changing relationship between the stairs and the choreography are characteristic for the entire performance. "Lovely details, when Posa, in a speech before Philipp, stands under the cross so that the golden rays like distant halos surround his head, or when through dark doors on both sides of the king, Alba and Carlos woo his soul, and Alba disappears into the evening background only to shine forth again gray and victorious."[30] This principle is intensified one final time in the closing scene. Here "in the front the king kneels down and in the back on two elevated pedestals the blind Grand Inquisitor atop two silent monks (burning red flanked by darkness) breathed forth his tyrannical convictions like an oracle from an empire of flames."[31]

The processes of constructing meaning that could be realized here essentially referred to the dynamic between spatial form and proxemic signs (choreography). In this, the literary text of the drama had no immediate part.

This manner of dealing with classical text was taken up again in the sixties and seventies by Grotowski, Schechner, Zadek, Peymann, and others.

What happened in each of these instances can perhaps be described as *Sparagmos:* tearing apart and incorporation of textual bodies in which we symbolize our cultural traditions, indeed in which we see our culture embodied. With *Sparagmos,* which in such productions was realized, the textual body supplanted the totem, that is, the sacrificial victim. The process unfolded exactly like a Greek sacrificial meal—such as that which Walter Burkert had described in his anthropology of religious sacrifice, *Homo Necans* (1972). The sections that the director deemed "eatable" were enthusiastically incorporated into the production; what appeared to him as "bones," unappetizing "innards," or as "fat" would be left to "the gods." In the performance, the cultural tradition incorporated in and handed down by the text was thus questioned and examined for validity by the performers and audience on—or rather through—their own bodies. It is not unreasonable to postulate the thesis that this manner of dealing with classical texts transformed the production into a different genre of cultural performance: into a totem-meal, that is, a sacrificial ritual. With and in the texts of the classics a symbolic order was constituted that the historical avant-garde at the beginning of our century and the neo-avant-garde of the sixties and seventies both viewed as a form of power. Performance as *Sparagmos* of the textual body carried out—at least in a symbolic sense—in the same performative act a dismembering of the text as a negation that simultaneously was aimed at the symbolic order codified with the text and at its resurrection in bodily appropriation, that is, in the new construction by director, actor, and audience. The literary text of the drama did not survive as a driving or controlling force for a performance, rather solely through the performance that incorporated it in with diverse performative acts.

While in the classic productions of the nineteenth century the texts of the past haunted the theater, in a manner of speaking, like ghosts or wandering spirits and made it place for the cult of the dead, in *Sparagmos* they were redeemed for a new, fleeting, ephemeral, and in this sense livelier present.

Performance as a Fabric of Floating Signifiers (Text)

As becomes evident in the previously discussed examples, the avant-garde directed its antitextual gesture not against texts in general but against a very specific conception of the text: against the idea that in texts fixed meanings are established once and for all, meanings that steer, control, and indeed legitimate further cultural productions, for example, those of performance. It was not only the transformation of performance into other genres of cultural performances—for example, into a wake or sacrificial ritual—that led to a change in the relations between performance and text and thus to a change of the concepts of performance and text, but also the demand for development of a uniquely theatrical language.

With this demand, the avant-garde was in fact following Wagner, but with a specific modification. While Wagner designed his concept of the *Gesamtkunstwerk* for the development of a unique theatrical language, Craig's definition offered a critique of precisely this concept: "How can all arts unify and produce a single art? That will produce a joke."[32] Craig argued on the contrary that each art form defined itself through the uniqueness of its material. For this reason, the elements that constitute theater cannot also determine the individual arts involved. They can only be determined by breaking the "individual arts" down into their smallest constitutive elements: movement, word, line, color, and rhythm. They function, according to Craig, as the elementary material constituting theater.

Other members of the avant-garde proceeded similarly. Kandinsky, for example, identifies three elements: "the musical tone and its movement," the "material-spiritual sound and its movement expressed through humans and objects," and the "shaded tone and its movement."[33] Lothar Schreyer, on the other hand, postulates four types of elements: the "elementary forms" (mathematical bodies and planes), the "elementary colors" (black, blue, green, red, yellow, white), the "elementary movements" (horizontal and vertical, ascending and descending movement, the opening and closing movement) and the "basic tones" (pure tones).[34] A performance results thus not from the unification of different arts; it is rather created through a selection and combination of such basic constitutive elements. The director undertakes both processes and as "an artist" masters the uses of "action, words, line, colour, and rhythm."[35]

Thus the avant-garde saw itself confronted with a semiotic problem: according to what criteria ought the corresponding theatrical signs be developed out of the identified basic elements? Which principles ought to govern the combination of such developed theatrical signs? And which meanings under which conditions can be attributed to these signs, that is, which effects under what conditions are they able to trigger?

The most important criterion through which they oriented themselves in the process of constructing signs was that of functionality. Immediately, inquiries were made regarding the function that the corresponding signs were supposed to serve. This is the way that Appia proceeded, for example, when devising his "rhythmic spaces" for Dalcroze, when developing his biomechanics for Meyerhold, or when choreographing his different Bauhaus dances for Oskar Schlemmer.

The consequence of the principle of functionality was that no established repertoire of signs could be developed that could be referred to in each production—such as was the case in other anti-illusionist theaters like the Chinese and Japanese traditional theaters to which the avant-garde enthusiastically appealed, albeit for other reasons. Indeed, new theatrical signs were constantly introduced corresponding to each respective function. That also means that any element of any other cultural system can be appropriated and used as a theatrical sign if it is able to fulfill the corresponding function.

The combination of theatrical signs cultivated or "invented" according to their respective function was supposed to follow rhythmic principles. Though it is not always clear from their comments what the avant-garde meant by the term *rhythm,* they were clearly unanimous in their conviction that with the help of rhythm *space, time,* and *body* could be related with each other: "rhythmic space" was coordinated with the "rhythmic movement" of the performers, objects and lights, with rhythmic language, rhythmic sounds and with music. It is thus of little wonder that in many productions music functioned as a dominant form.

Since the theatrical signs and the principles of their combinations are "abstract," that is, semantically neutral, or since they, when appropriated from other cultural systems, lose their "original" meanings through specific application, their reception can in no way be performed as a reaffirmation of the familiar and an ordering into an accepted context. The audience is not in a position to randomly assign them a meaning. In order to be in a position to perform the process of assigning meaning, the audience must in fact commit itself to an active and creative relation to the production. The specific *modus* of the application of signs moves the audience, accordingly, into permanent action and elicits its corresponding participation.

Here the connection that exists between the postulated cultural revolutionary function of the theater and the demand for performance as a autonomous work of art becomes evident. For only when the performance as an artwork in the manner described above is conceived and realized—that is, according to the principles of functionality and rhythm—does the syntactic and above all the pragmatic dimension dominate the semantic. The theatrical signs unfold their potential for meaning and effect on the basis of their specific selection and combination initially in the process of reception. The new spatial ordering of performers and audience, the new spaces for play, create the necessary preconditions in that they establish the conditional frameworks that favor a direct influence on the audience. The revolution of the theater thus can only occur as cultural revolution if it succeeds in developing a "language of the theater" with which not messages are formulated but rather reactions evoked or provoked—in other words, in which not the semantic but rather the pragmatic dimension dominates.

As stated, three features characterize his new theatrical language:

> 1. It lacks a stable repertoire of signs.
>
> 2. The combination of elements used as signs results from rhythmic principles.
>
> 3. The elements that are used as theatrical signs lack an independent semantic dimension, that is, they bring no previously established meaning into the production. They are in a sense floating signifiers, to which signifieds can be attributed according to—internal or external—contextualization.

The production can thus be understood as a unique web of floating signifiers—or more generally stated: as a context of theatrical signs. Inasmuch as semiotics conceptualizes text as the connection between signs, the production, semiotically speaking, is concerned with a theatrical text.

This theatrical text cannot be subsumed beneath the concept of text against which the avant-garde crusaded. First of all, as previously stated, no stable meaning can be attributed to this text or its individual elements or signs. And secondly, the issue here is a text whose individual elements can never be fixed—as actions, tones, sounds they represent fleeting, ephemeral signs that as such resist stability and being fixed. That means the text itself appears as a moving, ever-changing creation that is constantly in flux. That is to say: to determine the performance as a theatrical text means to redefine the concept of text anew.

Consequently, "text" and "performance" enter into a new relationship: While the concept of "performance" focuses on the eventful, on the character of occurrence, on the fleeting and the ephemeral, the concept of "text" takes up the possibilities of establishing relations between individual elements and of being able to provide them changing meanings. So applied, the concepts of text and performance are concerned not with different phenomena and processes but rather with the different aspects of one and the same phenomenon or process. That means that each marks the end of a wide spectrum, in which ever-changing focal points can be taken.

Such an instability in the relationship of text and performance is thoroughly implied by the two new theater concepts of the avant-garde. But it is rather obscured by their explicit antitextual gestures. From today's perspective this specific instability appears as pathbreaking.

Craig identified the director as the author of the theatrical text that is created as an autonomous work of art for the stage. Interestingly, this authorship led to the development of a new genre of literary text: the director's manual.

The director's manual holds a curious oscillating status with regard to the production. One could describe it as a notation book. In it, the director keeps track, on the one hand, of his thoughts, concepts, and ideas—in short, the first design for production—as a kind of memory aide. In this sense, the director's manual functions as a steering mechanism in the rehearsals. But on the other hand, the thoughts, concepts, and ideas that the actors, for example, develop during rehearsals are noted in the director's manual. It thus keeps track of the results of the rehearsal process and for further work can take over as a type of memory—and in this sense a kind of control function. It represents a text that from rehearsal to rehearsal, indeed partly from performance to performance, is further written and revised. As an aid to a work in progress, it can function as an instance of memory, steering, and control.

Following the removal of the production from the program the director's manual obtains the status of a documentation of the work of the director, as one can observe in the director's manuals of Stanislavsky, Reinhardt, Jeßner, or Piscator. It simultaneously becomes a document of the tense relations between text and performance, in which process, the fleeting, the ephemeral, and the changeable receive absolute priority over the fixed, stable, enduring, and unchangeable. It may sound paradoxical, but with the emergence of the director's manual by Reinhardt and Stanislavsky a paradigm shift—in other words a kind of undercurrent—announces itself, which in the course of our century has led from text to performance as the dominant cultural model.

NOTES

1. Dwight Conquergood, "Rethinking Ethnography: Toward a Critical Cultural Politics," *Communications Monograph* 58 (1991): 190. For more recent considerations of this shift, see *Performance and Cultural Politics,* ed. Elin Diamond (New York: Routledge, 1996).

2. Johann Wolfgang von Goethe, *Werke,* vol. 47 (Weimar: Weimar Ausgabe, 1909), 61.

3. Richard Wagner, *Gesammelte Schriften und Dichtungen,* vol. 3 (Leipzig, 1887–88), 60.

4. Alfred Klaar, "Bühne und Drama," *Vossische Zeitung,* July 30, 1918.

5. Edward Gordon Craig, "The Art of the Theatre: The First Dialogue," in *On the Art of the Theatre* (London: Heinemann, 1911), 138.

6. Wassily Kandinsky, "Über Bühnenkomposition," in *Der blaue Reiter,* ed. Kandinsky and Franz Marc (Munich: K. Lankheit, 1967), 207.

7. See Jean Alter, *A Socio-semiotic Theory of Theatre* (Philadelphia: Temple University Press, 1990).

8. Boris Aravtov, *Kunst und Production* (Munich: Carl Hanser Verlag, 1972), 91.

9. Ibid.

10. See Erika Fischer-Lichte, *Kurze Geschichte des deutschen Theatres* (Tübigen: Francke, 1993), 263–72.

11. Cited in Arthur Kahane, *Aus dem Tagebuch des Dramaturgen* (Berlin: Bruno Cassirer Verlag, 1928), 119.

12. See also Heinrich Huesmann, *Welttheater Reinhardt: Bauten, Spielstätten, Inszenierungen* (Munich, 1983).

13. Cited in Kahane, *Aus dem Tagebuch,* 119.

14. Siegfried Jacobson, *Das Jahr der Bühne,* vol. 1 (Berlin: Osterheld, 1912), 129.

15. Cited in Heinrich Braulich, *Max Reinhard: Theater zwischen Traum und Wirklichkeit* (Berlin: Henschelverlag, 1969), 129.

16. Cited in ibid., 167.

17. *Das große Schauspielhaus* (Berlin: Deutschen Theater), 11.

18. Ibid., 21.

19. Ibid., 46.

20. Ibid., 54.

21. Roland Barthes, *Die helle Kammer,* trans. Dietrich Leube (Frankfurt am Main: Suhrkamp, 1989), 41.

22. Sergei Eisenstein, *Schriften,* ed. Han Joachim Schlegel, vol. 1 (Munich: Hanzer, 1974), 249.

23. Ibid., 256.

24. *Berliner Börsen-Courir,* February 14, 1922.

25. Rolf Brandt, undated review of unknown origin, Archiv des Theatermuseums Köln.

26. Heiner Kienzel, undated review from unknown source, Archiv des Theatermuseums Köln.

27. Alfred Klaar, Undated review from unknown source, Archiv des Theatermuseums Köln.

28. Emil Faktor, Undated review from unknown source, Archiv des Theatermuseums Köln.

29. Faktor, review.

30. Brandt, review.

31. Faktor, review.

32. Craig, *On the Art of the Theatre,* 60.

33. Kandinsky, "Über Bühnenkompositionen," 207.

34. Lothar Schreyer, *Expressionistisches Theater: Aus meinen Erinnerungen* (Hamburg: J. P. Toth, 1948), 173.

35. Craig, *On the Art of the Theatre,*140.

Patrice Pavis
Translated by David Williams

Which Theories for Which Mise-en-Scènes?

Limits of Analysis, Limits of Theory

Reevaluation of Theory

Criticism of the Sign

A frequent argument employed to put one on one's guard against the difficulty of interpreting theater performance consists of stressing the impossibility of knowing whether a particular element of the acting or of the decor is (or is not) the sign of an intention expressed by the director. As soon as one adopts the point of view of an analysis of a performance, one chooses the perspective of its reception (and not of its production). Indeed it is always up to the spectators to make up their minds on this in terms of the overall performance. Not everything in the performance is reducible to a sign; there remain authentic moments, unforeseeable and unrepeatable events. How can one know whether the whiskey drunk by an actor is actually whiskey after all, or whether the plaster cast covers a leg that is really broken? Therefore, if everything can be a sign, and if nothing is absolutely certain, is it still useful to secure the services of semiology? Broadly speaking, this is Lyotard's argument: "The modernity of this fin de siècle consists of this: there is nothing to replace, no *lieutenance* [place taking/taking place] is legitimate, or all of them are; replacement, and consequently meaning, is itself only a substitute for displacement."[1] Lyotard's thesis is valid for a unique, aleatory performance, such as a Cage event or a happening, but it is inapplicable as soon as a performance is given at least a second time, and its repetition necessitates foreshadowing the effects. Nevertheless his argument has the merit of leaving mise-en-scène open as a reserve of materials and signs, as matter and spirit, signifier ready to signify. Moreover, it is not a new argument, for Copeau had previously made it the touchstone of his aesthetic: "We reject the empty old distinction, in an intellectual work, between what belongs to matter and what depends on spirit, between form and content. Similarly, we refuse to conceive of a factitious dissociation between art and professional craft."[2]

Criticism of Representation

Criticism of the sign leads to criticism of representation: Derrida, for example, rereading Artaud, directs such criticism at theater that continues to represent, instead of being, life itself: "The theater of cruelty is not representation. It is what is unrepresentable in life itself."[3] This refusal to represent is sometimes claimed by actors (or more exactly *performers*) who do not perform any role (not even their own), yet remains present on stage, their performance no longer referring to anything other than itself.

The aesthetic of representation, which requires a community of themes or interests, gives way to an aesthetic of reception and of individual perception: receivers become the principle authority making judgments in terms of their tastes, life, and personal experience. In place of the represented work, they endeavor to substitute an erotics of art, an experience of sensoriality, in which everything is appreciated according to the pleasure taken in contemplation of the work. This "pre-expressive" manner (as Barba would say) of enjoying theater distances us from signs and meaning, and pitches us into sensations of presence and of balance, which attempt to neutralize any intellectual aspect of theater experience. What emerges is an "energetic" criticism of semiology.

Energetic Criticism of Semiology

Criticism from the perspective of an "energetic theater" attempts to substitute the network of signs with the flux of impulses, the force of presence, the immediacy of the signifier and of scenic materiality.[4] An energetic circuit is supposed to provoke displacements of affect and impulsive flux.

Instead of a static network of signs, we have suggested imagining a circuit in which meaning appears and is displaced in accordance with a "semiotization of desire" or "vectorization." This model reconciles a semiology of the perceptible with an energetics of displacements that are not visible. For example, we do not define space only in a representative manner—as a space already framed and put in perspective, a space to be filled—but rather as an energetic vector connected to its users, to their spatiotemporal coordinates, presence, energy, movements and route through it. It is a question of holding to the oxymoronic notion of a "semiotization of desire"—of describing actor and spectator as objects inhabiting the space between semiotization and desemiotization, by keeping the energetic erotics of signifiers present for as long as possible. The attention we bring to bear on scenic materiality is reinforced by a denial that reminds us incessantly that we are at the theater and that we perceive only forms and matter.

So the semiological model of the theatrical object caught in a network of signs with its own systems, connections, and regularities operates in relay with the vectorial model, a model that straddles a visual semiology and an energetics. Then, and only then, is there meaning in talking of an "energetic charge," for the work as much as for its receiver, and one can reference this charge in one as much as in the other. "In the work of art is inscribed an energetic charge, which arises from the creator's engagement; it is connected to their personal history, in the face of the society in which they are immersed and of their collective unconscious."[5] In order for spectators to feel a similar shock, a similar discharge, this shock must be prepared by what they perceive; the spectators must also understand these impulses as signs and vectors, and not only as shock waves. Such is the aim of the "integrated semiology" we are proposing.

Reference Points for Integrated Semiology

Such recurrent criticisms of the sign, representation, semiology are not without interest. They enable us to reevaluate a theory that is too statically modeled on a survey of abstract signs. We can propose central axes of reference in our approach to mise-en-scène, and work theatrical representation as one works dreams: starting from major structural and structuring processes.

Let us consider the model of vectors inspired by Freud's *Interpretation of Dreams,* further developed by Jakobson and Lacan, adapted to the primary working processes of theatrical representation. Let us clarify the nature of its two main axes:

> The axis of *displacement,* or of *metonymy,* which replaces one element with another ("connector"), or breaks the chain's links so as to move on to something quite different ("cutter"): the axis of an aesthetic that is somewhat mimetic, realist, prosaic, linear, in which the stage is hewn from the external world with which it is consubstantial.
>
> The axis of *condensation,* or of *metaphor,* which accumulates and mixes elements (through "accumulators") or creates access to a quite different sphere (through "shifters"): the axis of an aesthetic that is somewhat nonrealist, symbolist, poetic, circular, and tabular, in which the stage tends toward autonomy, condensing the world in a new reality closed in on itself.

Within this very general framework, one can examine the major axes according to which mise-en-scène works, and one can reference vectorial points of departure and outcomes, without necessarily deciding on the energetic forces that interconnect them. Vectorization remains open: not only does identification of the dominant vector at any particular moment remain difficult; what is more, the link between connection, accumulation, rupture, and shifting remains to be established, and this is the very object of analysis and interpretation. Therefore at best this framework provides the conditions for all subsequent analysis. We have been able to verify this with our analysis of "cultural legibility" in the *Teatrum mundi*.

Conditions for Analysis

Dimensions

In the era of the video camera, remote control, and slow motion, the problem is no longer the ephemerality of performance, nor the exhaustive surveying and recording of all signs. Instead it is the choice of which signs to deem pertinent and noteworthy, and their hierarchization and vectorization. Nowadays one can find exhaustive critical works devoted to one mise-en-scène, even a second-rate one. The mass of informational and relentless technological detail might be intimidating to exegetes and nonspecialist spectators, all the more so given that recording technologies (video, computer, and so on) are certainly capable of digitally encoding every aspect, but on condition that they take no interpretative risk.

Acceleration or Braking

Therefore instead of accumulating and quantifying informational detail, we propose not only to articulate hypotheses on their vectorization, but also to concentrate on some aspects and to use a sort of mental remote control for acceleration, in order to perceive a mise-en-scène's lines of force. Acceleration (fast forward) can prevent the blocking of meaning, repair fragmentation, and release the lines of force. Deceleration (slow motion) can lead the spectator to a sort of illumination, a flash in which one is able to bring into relief all the pertinent factors in a series and to localize moments of recapitulative synthesis—moments variously called satori or *To* (Korean Tao), propitious moment (Zeami), pregnant moment (Lessing), gestus (Brecht), or psychological gesture (Michael Chekhov).

These new conditions for analysis are not necessarily perceived as facilitating theory, but often on the contrary as an incitement to abandon theoretical debate, relativizing, even depreciating all analytical methods, calling into question the very possibility of theorizing stage work, and particularly so-called postmodern mise-en-scène. But need one be so hasty to exclude theory?

Against Postmodern Relativism

Difficulties of Description

Artists often reject theory, reproaching it for its inability to account for theatrical performance that is either unique and unrepeatable, or asemantic and closed in on itself. Barry Edwards and Geoffrey Smith, from the group Optik, for example, describe their performance *Tank* as an event that can be neither described nor foreseen: "The performance event obviously cannot be 'described,' it's not a metaphor for 'something else'; each performance generates its own evidence, its own history; but each performance is totally new."[6] Even if each performance by Optik is indeed unique, in the same way as a happening or a ceremony that takes place only once, nothing prohibits describing and interpreting the event produced on that particular evening; ultimately it will still create meaning, even if it is in spite of itself, or as if fortuitously. Space, time, and action on stage necessarily inscribe themselves into history, our own history, once they are deployed to the knowledge of an audience. On the other hand, one cannot interpret the event as the response to a preordained text or intention. But who would still dream of doing that?

In the same way, nowadays who would dream of *decoding* a performance of this kind? Clearly a semiology of communication is of no usefulness in this context; given this, therefore, is it adequate to talk of *deconstructing* the performance? Now is an appropriate time to agree on some mutual understanding of this frequently employed word in postmodern criticism.

Limits of the Concept of Deconstruction

In the banal sense of the term, one talks of deconstruction when a mise-en-scène presents itself in a fragmented form, with no possibility of fixing a stable meaning, each fragment apparently in opposition with the others. When a mise-en-scène starts from a text, it can also deconstruct this text by opening it up to a multiplicity of contradictory meanings, proving the impossibility of a single correct reading being concretized in the performance.

In the technical sense of the term, that of Derrida and deconstructionism in philosophy, deconstruction applied to mise-en-scène could consist of finding a playful and interpretative disposition that "demonstrates" the impossibility of reading mise-en-scène by reducing it to one meaning, and that invents false trails and an entire strategy for unsettling and dismantling its own mechanisms, for quoting and parodying itself. Certain groups, such as the Needcompany[7] or the Wooster Group,[8] have specialized in deconstructing their own aesthetics. There is always a moment at which the performance indicates how it is constructed (and therefore deconstructed), an element that at the same time discourages any referential allusion to the outside world. So it is not only the text that is deconstructed by the mise-en-scène (as is always the case to some degree, particularly when the actor critiques textual meaning in action); the entire mise-en-scène is contradicted and deconstructed by this very strategy.

In its banal version, deconstruction of the mise-en-scène can be constantly recycled: indeed the signification of the performance is never established, it is no more than a hypothesis at any particular moment—at best the least unsatisfactory hypothesis continuously undone by new indices or as yet unexplored avenues.

Therefore any act of deconstruction is only provisional, in anticipation of those that will follow; and it is the spectator who decides in the final analysis on their succession. Consider for example the relationship between text and stage: even if the mise-en-scène attempts to contrive a space of neutrality between the dramatic text and the scenic configuration, the practice of the mise-en-scène soon fills this space in an "author-itarian" way; for it is the mise-en-scène as scenic writing and subject of the enunciation that decides, that creates meaning at the same time in the configuration and the dramatic text. Even if the director pretends not to want to assume a stable position with regard to the text, the mise-en-scène will suggest a connection between text and scenic configuration; if this connection manages to remain open, then the spectator will make a hypothesis of this openness and will assume that this connection is metaphoric, scenographic, or eventlike (to take up Lehmann's categories). Therefore there will necessarily be deconstruction of the text by the stage (or if there is no text, of one scenic system by the other). In more general terms, the fundamental instability of mise-en-scène will readily produce the impression of self-deconstruction. Deconstruction occurs en bloc, so to speak, and not in the detail of analyses, nor in the plurality of its methods.

Methodological Pluralism, Rather Than Eclecticism

For postmodern criticism resorts to an eclecticism (rather than a plurality) in the choice of its analytical methods; it prefers lucky dips to toolboxes. But what tools should be taken from the box? It would be tempting to reply: any of them, provided that they are used systematically and not tossed around while they are in use! For example, we have already come across the following tools en route:

> *Structuralism* and *functionalism* offered us a semiology of scenic systems, which remains an indispensable basis for all investigations. Let us remember that a semiology of mise-en-scène is not a matter of translating a performance's signifiers into linguistic signifieds (in other words, of verbalizing them). Rather the tendency is to base descriptions on the materiality of a performance, avoiding cutting it up according to the traditional categories and codes of bourgeois theater, thereby reestablishing these categories and codes.

Hermeneutics have been reintroduced (although semiology arose in the 1960s as a means of moving beyond a subjective, raw art of interpretation). At present we encourage a hermeneutically controlled utilization of semiological instruments. This can clarify the constitutive processes of units, ensembles, syntax, itineraries, and (as we shall see later on) vectorizations between signs.

The *historicity* of production and of reception have been brought into confrontation in order to lay the foundations for an aesthetics of reception.

Criticism of the sign and of semiology, particularly Lyotard's, whether it results in an energetic theater or not, has the merit at least of sensitizing one to a fluctuation of energies and of lines of force in mise-en-scène. It enables access to the compromise of our "vectorization of desire," which in turn opens the way for a series of *theoretical oxymorons,* such as: chaos theory, analysis of syntheses, blocks of isolated events, scenic chronotopes. The tension of these oxymorons protects us from an omnidirectional use of the most contradictory of theories; it is the guarantor of a necessary methodological plurality.

Paradigm Shift

A plurality of methods, nowadays widely accepted in performance analysis, seems to be on a par with a broadening of the favored paradigm of representation—visuality—toward paradigms of auditory perception, rhythm, and kinesthesia.

Through a reaction against literature and a literary conception of theater, performance semiology was founded on visuality, defining its units as signs of the visible made legible by means of a language of the stage.

In the wake of Vinaver's thoughts on mise-en-scène as "mise en trop," one is much more attentive to the rhythm of the text and to the orientations of auditive memory.[9]

Furthermore, visuality and the auditory are not the only systems actively perceptive in the reception of a performance. In a way they are dependent upon the "entire muscular apparatus," as Jaques-Dalcroze demonstrated so effectively in his studies of rhythmics: "Authentic perception of movement is not of a visual nature, it's of a muscular nature, and the living symphony of steps, gestures, and attitudes linked together is created and regulated not by the instrument of appreciation that is the eye, but by the instrument of creation that is the entire muscular apparatus."[10] An analysis sensitive to muscular meaning describes the *kinesthetic* value (perception of movement), and more generally the *aesthetic* value, of a performance.

Sensitized in this way to the corporeality of performance, analysis draws considerably closer to a practice of sense and of the senses; one can then envisage theory and analysis from the point of view of the director's know-how.

Theory and Analysis from the Point of View of Practice

Distancing

In the course of rehearsals, the director tends to dissociate himself increasingly from the group (within) which his actors and collaborators negotiate, in order to place himself at a distance and direct from the auditorium; in this way he prefigures his future audience and endows it with his perspective on the developing performance. Evidently all decisions on the mise-en-scène are influenced by his gaze, and by the analysis it presupposes: analysis determined by the signifying systems artists put in place (thus transversal analysis of the performance at a given moment), and analysis in terms of the rhythmic organization of time, and thus of the performance's articulation, into different moments (longitudinal analysis). In elaborating a performance, the director has a sense of the division of work (between different trade groups) and of the segmentation of the performance. He knows how to articulate a scene in order for it to be legible, how to place key moments, rhythmic and dramaturgical turning points, how to prescribe breaks and pauses. In this way progressively the score and, for the actors, the subscore of the performance are set in place. This analytical structuration of the performance, these traces of its genesis, are still perceptible and able to be referenced in the finished product, like scars from former operations, or like the work's respiration. Some knowledge of practice is useful, even indispensable, to performance analysts; taking the end result as starting point, they can imagine what the preparatory dramaturgical work could have been, the decisions and chance occurrences that led to this end result. In turn, practice itself cannot dispense, if only as a first indication, with a theory for these various processes. One could even define mise-en-scène, as Juan Antonio Hormigón does, as "the coordinated articulation of dramaturgical work and technical-craft practice."[11] There is necessarily an element of dramaturgical work (even if it denies its own existence); it comprises the systematizing of practical actions realized in concrete terms by a "technical-craft practice."

Logic of Process, Logic of Result

Like practitioners, theorists are aware that performance analysis does not begin and end with one evening's show, that it must be interested in its preparation as well as its reception by the spectator. Carlos Tindemans perfectly encompasses the range of epistemological problems that confront analysis: "The notion of performance analysis cannot limit itself to a phenomenological image of the scenic process; it must also cover the intentionality of the theater practitioners and the effect on spectators."[12] We will leave the notion of intentionality to one side, for it is unknowable, and it does not prejudge the end result; instead we will distinguish three successive moments in the elaboration of a mise-en-scène.

(1)	(2)	(3)
Preparation of the performance	Phenomenological image of the scenic process (image of the preparatory process in the final performance)	Effects on spectators

However this chronological succession is only apparent; it is an extreme simplification of the mechanisms in play at each moment and in each instance, artificially separating what should not really be separated.

Knowledge of a performance's preparatory process (1) has no interest, at least for analysis, unless it illuminates the phenomenon produced: the mise-en-scène (2).

The mise-en-scène will only be understood if one is able to adjudge the ways in which it touches and influences the spectator (3).

So the imbrication of all three moments and instances is at the crux of the problem. Description of one is of little interest without description of the other two. We locate ourselves in (3), we perceive (2), but in order to grasp it we must develop an idea of (1).

The difficulty is in dealing with the preparatory phase of a performance and at the same time the end result; the problem is one of knowing, to borrow Barba's terms again, the logic of the process and the logic of the result.[13] Evidently one should not confuse the perspectives of production and reception; but neither can one ignore the other side of the barricade. These two perspectives are those required by training institutions, in a clear-cut way: at universities, what is sought is the model, ideal spectator, excessively cultured and intelligent, knowing how to receive the finished performance; in drama schools, the perspective is that of future artists learning their craft, and thus concerned with technique and know-how, en route to producing their own performances and therefore engaged in creative process. This institutional opposition is baleful, and it blocks research that is both theoretical and practical.

Systemic Approach
Nevertheless certain artists, such as Le Théâtre REPÈRE,[14] cover the entire cycle of production and reception. This group has elaborated a working method that enables the passage from rehearsals to performances without difficulty or rupture, and recycles performances by using them as starting point and raw material for further work.

	Resources	
REprésentation (performance)		**P**artition (score)
	Evaluation	

Resources are the starting point for research: spare material, scenes that have already been worked, particularly those that are triggers generating themes and ideas. These resources are organized in the form of preestablished dispositions and an exploratory score that "allows the unconscious to access the conscious."[15] Evaluation authorizes critical reflection on the score; it reconstitutes a scenic metatext in which the principle options are already suggested. It leads to performance *(REprésentation)* that in turn could become material for a new cycle. So the "autocorrective dynamic of creative systems" has been reconstituted by examining what options have been taken and when, what redundant material has been maintained, and what ambiguities (voluntary as well as involuntary) have been introduced.

This kind of cyclical orientation takes performance and its analysis out of their isolation, by showing the interaction and interdependence of process and end result. Analysis is no longer fixed at an ideal moment (that at which the spectators would purportedly understand everything); it is extended in duration and bases itself on data until now reserved for the creators and their taste for the secretive.

In the same way, theatrical documentation is no longer exclusively the material trace of a performance, delivered after the event, constituting archival documents arising from the performance. It also includes preparatory materials, further enriching itself with knowledge of resources, intermediary scores, statements by those artists involved in the performance.

Evidently, when applied to contemporary mise-en-scène, theory and analysis have serious limitations; sometimes they give the impression of being impotent and mute in the face of the complex constructions of the postmodern. Nevertheless a pluralism of methods does not relativize the possibility of dealing with contemporary works. Far from surrendering before the complexity and sophistication of mise-en-scènes, theory can extend its domain into a sphere that seemed to reserved for artists alone: that of practice. The separation between doing and saying now finds itself challenged again, to the great joy of theorists. This major concession by practitioners to their less fortunate colleagues—theorists—opens up new research perspectives. If the hope of resolving the question of analysis quickly and definitively seems to grow ever fainter, on the other hand the prospect of a greater overall understanding of the creative processes of theater is perhaps no longer an empty mirage. In this respect, semiology—let us call it *integrated semiology,* locating itself at the intersection of theories and practices—can play a core role.

Integrated Semiology: At the Crossroad of Theories and Practices

A Theoretical Oxymoron for an Unlimited Scenic Production

In the preceding pages, we have seen what semiology has borrowed and learned from poststructuralist theories (and the latter also owe a great deal to semiology). Preferring confrontation to compromise, we have chosen to connect contrary notions and thereby create oxymorons, as a site for productive contradiction.

> Sign and energy
>
> Semiology and energetics
>
> Vector and desire
>
> Semiotization and desemiotization, etc.

Such oxymorons interrogate and destabilize the classical working methods of semiology, such as the location and reading of signs, the translation into signifieds, and so on. They suggest a movement beyond, or at least a reexamination, of other oppositions.

That of diachrony and synchrony, for example, and not only through the performance being perceived as both process *and* end result. Performance analyses can also examine the ways in which a mise-en-scène is inscribed in history and history is inscribed in it, through successive layers or juxtaposed details. They can determine what stratifications history has already deposited on what seems a wholly present and actual contemporary object. Foucault's archaeology of knowledge, and the reevaluation it is currently undergoing, help us reference knowledges and discourses circulating in the detailed marquetry of a mise-en-scène.

The opposition between surface and depth, between discursive and actantial structures (in Greimas's terminology), is also contested: if only in the score/subscore coupling, which is based more on the difference between the visible and the invisible, the shown and the hidden, than on the notion of depth. In place of a binary model (depth/surface), we prefer a progressive ternary division for analysis, in the manner of Zeami:[16] skin, flesh, and bone, which correspond to "the three faculties of perception, the knowledge that comes from sight, from hearing, from the heart or spirit: sight corresponds with *skin,* hearing with *flesh,* and spirit with *bone.*"[17] In terms of voice, according to Zeami, vocal emission would be the *skin,* melodic modulations the *flesh,* and breath the *bone.* In terms of gesture and movement: "the general appearance is the *skin,* the patterned movements of dance are the *flesh,* the spirit of the dance is the *bone.*" These metaphors remind us that psychology and contemporary linguistics also endeavor to bring together cognition and aesthetic perception; they assert that, in order to think of the most abstract things, we must have recourse to the imagination, we must find a way of impregnating spirit with body, in Mark Johnson's sense in his book *The Body in the Mind.* As average rather than model spectators, we apprehend a performance with the body as much as the head, providing that we remain attentive to its materiality, and that we do not immediately translate sense perceptions into words or concepts.

This kind of oxymoron is particularly appropriate for avant-garde performances, which seem to go to great lengths to avoid linguistic or conceptual meaning; they immerse the spectator in a flood of sensations and perceptual impressions that unsettle and delight him, making him forget all desire to translate what is perceived into words or signifieds. Nevertheless the necessity of maintaining a direction and vectorization means that one can never fully leave the domain of semiology, even if the performances of actors nowadays defy any controlling element in the mise-en-scène.

In fact it is as if the stranglehold of mise-en-scène has released its grip on the systems of signs, thereby losing all reason for its existence, becoming "performance," for instance: a "signifying practice" in which signs drift unmoored, as if an actor's performance resists the director's working strategies: "If mise-en-scène is *mise en signe* [transposition into signs], then performing is displacing signs, instituting the movement of those signs, even their drift, in a defined space and time."[18]

Performing becomes a subversive activity displacing the certainty of a mise-en-scène's realized configuration and fixed metatext, notably its visual representation. Music emerges as the dominant analytical model, since it is a matter of evaluating rhythm, tempo, temporality, and the routes of vectors, both underlying and visible. Already perceptible in the work of many directors (Stanislavsky, Meyerhold, Pitoëff), reference to music becomes the dominant metaphor in the analysis of the progression of vectors (the actors' performance, forms, colors). Jaques-Dalcroze's rhythmics can be used once more, but as theoretical simulation rather than as aesthetic; for it applies not only to music, but also to gestural systems, space, and diction. Nevertheless the problem remains one of representing and describing this experience. We need to find a discipline capable of relating the experience without schematizing it, especially as there are several enunciators in play, each complying with different logics.

To Conclude?

So which theories for which mise-en-scènes? Should one hope for a global model, a miraculous recipe that gathers up all the stakes and adapts itself to all kinds of performance? Evidently not!

And what about the performance analysis itself? Who will say whether it "works" or not? Perhaps quite simply it will succeed if an encounter between performance and spectator has occurred. Vinaver's words on textual analysis are also valid for performance analysis: "An analysis is successful, which makes it transmissible and thus useful, only to the degree that its author, combining affectivity and intelligence, has been engaged in his contact with the work; also to the degree that the writing of the commentary bears the mark of the event that the particular encounter between a reader and a text constitutes."[19]

Theories have followed the tendency to differentiate between performances, but nevertheless there remain certain core instances. There is always a time-lapse between theater practice and its theoretical articulation, as if theory takes some time to adapt to a new demand; the time-lapse is often about a decade. Brechtian theory, for example, still new and scandalous in the 1950s and 1960s, greatly inspired the semiology of the 1970s, but is no longer appropriate for the decentered productions of the 1980s and 1990s. Or French theory (referred to as "poststructuralist" in Anglo-Saxon contexts), inspired by the work of Barthes, Derrida, Foucault, and Lacan; although there are few pertinent examples in French or European performance, poststructuralism is applicable to the American avant-garde ten years on: Robert Wilson, Richard Foreman, Robert Ashley, Merce Cunningham, Laurie Anderson. When theory comes back to France in the early 1990s, theater production has entered another phase: a time for restoration of the text and antitheoretical empiricism. A moment at which, in order to resist the immaterialism of scenic language (what Vinaver called "la mise en trop"), although already outmoded, mise-en-scène reintroduces the text; but now it postulates the text's irreducibility, its resistance to all *messe en scène* [High Mass on stage], hoping (naively) that it will hold its own on the stage and will not be metaphorized by it.

However, these successive waves of theory, desperately pursuing theatrical methods, should not sweep us away into listless skepticism or a free-floating postmodern relativism. In opposition to this drift, we prefer the apparent blockage of a paradoxical response, a theoretical oxymoron along the same lines as that of a SEMIOTIZATION OF DESIRE, the operative power of which we have been able to adjudge here.

In calling for new theories, more appropriate to the task and continually updated, performance practice also takes theory forward; and in return theory contributes to an improvement in the understanding we have of practice. In this way they feed (off) each other; out of this ongoing and generalized "intercannibalism" arises a revolution that is nowhere near its end.

As well as a permanent revolution in our performance analyses.

NOTES

1. Jean-François Lyotard, "La Dent, la paume," in *Des dispositifs pulsionnels* (Paris: UGE, 1973), 95.

2. Jacques Copeau, "Un Essai de renovation dramatique" (1913), in *Appels, registres,* vol. 1 (Paris: Gallimard, 1974), 2.

3. Jacques Derrida, *L'Écriture et la différence* (Paris: Seuil, 1967), 343.

4. The expression is Lyotard's ("La Dent, la paume"). See also Hubert Godard, "Le Déséquilibre fondateur," *Art Press,* special edition, October 1992; English translation, "Singular, Moving Geographies," *Writings on Dance* 15 (1996).

5. Pierre Gaudibert, "Conversation sur l'oeuvre d'art," in *Peuples et cultures* (Paris: Grenoble, 1982), 11.

6. Barry Edwards and Geoffrey Smith, "Theatre Statement," program for Diskurs, European festival of student theater, Giessen, 1993, 90–100.

7. A Dutch group that likes to deconstruct universal classics.

8. An American group that grew out of Richard Schechner's Performance Garage; inspired by intercultural deconstruction.

9. Michel Vinaver, "La mise en trop," *Théâtre/Public* 82–83 (1988). [Translator's note: Vinaver's expression "mise en trop," which critiques certain mise-en-scènes as excessive and redundantly illustrative, puns on the title of Molière's *Le Misanthrope*].

10. Émile Jaques-Dalcroze, *Le Rhythme, la musique et l'éducation* (Lausanne: Foetisch Frères, 1919), 140.

11. Juan Antonio Hormigón, *Trabajo dramaturgico y puesta en escena* (Publicaciones de la Asociación de directores de escena en España, 1991), 63.

12. Carlos Tindemans, "L'Analyse de la représentation théâtrale: Quelques réflexions méthodologiques," in *Théâtre de toujours, d'Aristote à Kalisky: Hommages à Paul Delsemme* (Brussels: Editions de l'Université de Bruxelles, 1983), 45.

13. Eugenio Barba, *Le Canoë de papier* (Lectoure: Editions Bouffonneries, 1993), 57.

14. Irène Roy, "Schématisation du parcours créateur au théâtre," *Protée* 21, no. 2 (1993): 87.

15. Ibid.

16. Zeami, *La Tradition secrète du Nô* (Paris: Gallimard, 1960), 146.

17. Ibid., 147.

18. Bernard Dort, *La Représentation émancipée* (Arles: Actes Sud, 1988), 182.

19. Michel Vinaver, *Écritures dramatiques* (Arles: Actes Sud, 1993), 11.

Philip Auslander

Fluxus Art-Amusement: The Music of the Future?

In his provocative and eccentric book *Noise: The Political Economy of Music,* originally published in 1977, French economist Jacques Attali presents a utopian vision of the music of the future. He suggests that the future production of music will take place under the rubric of "Composition," by which he means that listeners, who now are only consumers of music, will become its producers as well. In Attali's view, although music once served important social functions as symbolic ritual, music is now completely subordinated to its status as a mass-produced, recorded commodity: "[W]hat was an element in the social whole appears as a work of art to be consumed."[1] The future music he envisions would completely reject commodification: it would exist purely as an end in itself rather than a means to profit. Attali does not envision Composition as a nostalgic return to a time before commodification when music enjoyed a more important social position. "Make no mistake. This is not a return to ritual," he declares: "Nor to the spectacle. Both are impossible, after the formidable pulverizing effected by the political economy over the past two centuries. No. It is the advent of a radically new form of the insertion of music into communication."[2]

For this to be the case, individuals would have to create their own idiosyncratic music entirely for their own pleasure, without regard for whether or not anyone else would (or could) appreciate it. The division of labor that currently defines music production would be completely eliminated. There would be no distinctions between musicians and audiences or, for that matter, between musicians and nonmusicians. Conventional musical training and skills would no longer be required: everyone would be able to produce something they could call and enjoy as "music." Inasmuch as Attali implies that the perfect instrument for creating this kind of music is the video camera, which he quaintly calls an "image recorder," it is apparent that he aims to shatter conventional definitions of music completely. Even avant-garde composer John Cage's definition of music as "organization of sound"[3] is not broad enough for Attali, who suggests that music need not even be defined as sound—the distinctive visions rendered by each person with an image recorder would constitute their "music."[4] It is worth observing that Attali himself describes Composition as "an abstract utopia," a theoretical social model not necessarily to be taken as a real possibility.[5]

Musicologist Susan McClary, writing in 1985, identifies musical phenomena that she considers to be harbingers of Composition, including the do-it-yourself aesthetic and anticapitalist stance of early punk rock (which she calls New Wave), as well as the emphasis on live, multimedia, sometimes participatory performances that resist the definition of music as recordable sound to be found in the work of such composers as Pauline Oliveros.[6] To update McClary's account a bit, I would note that Attali's discussion of the image recorder anticipates the dominance of music video and its role in making the experience of popular music as much visual as aural. I will also suggest that such practices as rapping, scratching, and sampling can be seen in relation to Composition.[7] Each of these practices has enabled people with no formal musical training to make music using immediately available means: voices, turntables, old records. They have also helped to redefine what "music" is for the late twentieth century. Rapping is a way of making "music" out of words that are organized in terms of rhythm and rhyme rather than melody. Scratching and sampling have expanded the definition of music to include pieces constructed out of existing recordings by mechanical or electronic means. Neither is unprecedented, of course: rap is a form of oral poetry, and the concept of producing new music from previously existing recordings was pioneered by practitioners of musique concrète in the 1950s. Although the music produced by rapping, scratching, and sampling has proved itself only too readily commodifiable, as had punk before it, the impulses behind these practices suggest an affinity with Composition as defined by Attali.

Although these recent and current musical practices illustrate important aspects of Composition, even better examples can be found in the work of a segment of the New York avant-garde of the early 1960s, the Fluxus group. The ideas underlying Fluxus resonate in many ways with Attali's concept of Composition, and it is certainly the case that Fluxus "music" has never been commodified in the conventional economic sense (though Fluxus has entered the canon of the avant-garde through scholarly studies, museum retrospectives, and the other forms of symbolic commodification prevalent in the art world). In the remainder of this essay, I will offer a brief history of Fluxus, review some of its philosophical bases, and identify some of the performance practices in which it engaged and the relationship of those practices to Composition. I will conclude by suggesting some speculative connections between Fluxus and two other musical phenomena of the 1960s: a piece by the American avant-garde composer Ben Johnston on the one hand, and the destruction of musical instruments by rock musicians on the other.

Fluxus has a complex relationship to the concept of textuality this volume addresses. Although its avant-garde credentials are beyond dispute, Fluxus was not antitextual. Far from it—Fluxus artists embraced textuality in a way that their contemporaries who made happenings did not. Fluxus performances were conceived as music and were based on the textual model that informs classical music and musicology. Each Fluxus performance was the interpretation of a text, a score identified as the work of a particular composer. Fluxus did not privilege performance over text or consider performance an autonomous entity separate from text. Rather, Fluxus emphasized a text/performance relationship considered anathema to, for instance, theatrical avant-gardes that have reacted against the dominance of the playwright.

The relationship between score and performance may be seen in two different ways, depending on whether one is looking at musicology or music itself. Classical musicology considers the scored work an urtext that gives rise to "a variety of subordinate and derivative texts."[8] In this respect, the musicological view is not significantly different from a literary perspective that sees theatrical performances as mere adjuncts to dramatic texts. Looking at the nature of musical works themselves, however, Stan Godlovitch argues that musical scores of all historical eras are "intrinsically undetermined, skeletal and incomplete" works that do not determine performances in any strong way. Far from imposing textual authority, musical scores invite "a collaboration between the scored work and the performer."[9] Fluxus can be seen as addressing both of these aspects of music as a scored work. Fluxus's undercutting of the self-conscious "seriousness," pomposity, and elitism that characterize the culture of classical music mocks the worshipful attitude toward the score displayed in musicology. Yet by refusing to dismantle the basic textual structures of classical music (i.e., composer, score, audience) and their canonical relationships to one another, Fluxus emphasized the potential for freedom and collaboration that Godlovitch considers intrinsic to the particular textual conformation of the musical work and its relationship to performance.

Fluxus: A Little History

The origins of Fluxus are traceable to a course in music composition taught by John Cage at the New School for Social Research in New York City in 1958. The membership of this class included Dick Higgins and George Brecht, who would become two of the principal Fluxus artists. Also in attendance were Allan Kaprow, who is usually credited with inventing the performance art genre of the happening; Al Hansen, who authored many happenings in his own right; and others. As Fluxus historian Peter Frank has observed, "Arguably, the whole American school of Happenings came out of this class. Inarguably, the seeds of the Fluxus sensibility were sown in this class."[10] Although Fluxus events are often discussed as performance art or as a relative of happenings, the artists who made them called them music, and it is in that light that I shall discuss them here.[11] Whereas Kaprow and other artists who participated in Cage's class considered the happening to be a new art form, Higgins, Brecht, and other Fluxus artists presented performance work under the traditional rubric of music, though the concept of music they received from Cage was hardly traditional.

The Fluxus group was organized by George Maciunas, a Lithuanian immigrant art dealer who undertook a series of concerts and lectures focusing on experimental music at his gallery in 1961. Maciunas also designed the publication of a collection of experimental music scores and writings entitled *An Anthology of Chance Operations,* which he hoped to continue as *Fluxus* magazine. The magazine never appeared; late in 1961, Maciunas closed his gallery and fled to Europe to avoid his creditors, taking with him the materials that would eventually be published in the *Anthology.* He continued his activities in Europe. By September 1962, Maciunas had assembled an international group of artists and was ready to launch the first Fluxus event, the Fluxus Internationale Festspiele Neuester Musik (Fluxus International Festival of the Newest Music) at Wiesbaden, Germany. Other Fluxus events followed in Amsterdam, Copenhagen, Paris, and Nice.[12]

These European Fluxus manifestations indicated that Fluxus had metamorphosed from a publishing project into a performance organization operating in the context of music. When Maciunas left New York, Fluxus did not exist; when he returned in 1963, it was a fledgling international art and music movement. Within four months of his return from Europe, Maciunas put together a working Fluxus apparatus in New York. But whereas Fluxus in Europe had emphasized performance, New York Fluxus once again emphasized publication. The *Anthology* finally appeared; *V TRE* (or *CC V TRE*), a broadside begun independently by George Brecht, became the official Fluxus organ, carrying advertisements for performances, sample performance scores, articles, and photographs of Fluxus events. Maciunas also began publishing editions of books and objects by Fluxus artists. In the spring of 1964, Maciunas opened the Fluxhall, a loft on Canal Street, which served as his residence, a shop where Fluxus editions and publications were offered for sale, and a performance space. Despite Maciunas's authoritarian tendencies and desire to control the membership of Fluxus, Fluxus functioned successfully for a brief period as an artists' collective. Intense Fluxus activity began to drop off as early as 1965, when George Brecht went to live in Germany. The artists associated with Fluxus dispersed (some were excommunicated by Maciunas), sometimes carrying the Fluxus name with them, with or without Maciunas's permission. But most of the energy drained out of Fluxus during the second half of the 1960s.

The Fluxus Sensibility

Given the diversity of the artists who worked under the Fluxus banner, it would be wrong to characterize the Fluxus sensibility in any monolithic way. Nevertheless, it is worth taking a look at some of the founding ideas that informed Fluxus. Cage, who exposed the members of his class at the New School to concepts of art originating with avant-garde movements from earlier in the twentieth century, was certainly a major influence. Cage's definition of music as "organized sound" is a sympathetic echo of the Italian futurists, who argued both that noise could be music and that the sounds of nature as well as those of urban, mechanized society should become the raw material of composition.[13] Whereas the futurists were content to create noise as music and to re-create natural and industrial noises using special instruments, Cage sought to frame the sounds of life itself as music, thus achieving an identity of art and life to which the futurists did not aspire. "I think daily life is excellent," he writes, "and that art introduces us to it and its excellence the more it begins to be like it."[14] He talks of using art, of consuming it: "We should be able to consume it in relation to the other things in our lives which we consume."[15] In this regard, Cage's ideas are similar to those of dada, particularly those of Marcel Duchamp, whose earlier concept of the "ready-made" implied that objects from daily life, consumer objects in particular, could be reframed as "art" by the artist's act of designating them as such.[16] Ultimately, in both art and life, Cage sees individual perception as the only valid ordering principle: "We are concerned with the coexistence of dissimilars and the central points where the fusion occurs are many: the ears of the listeners, wherever they are."[17] Beginning in 1950, Cage advocated expanding musical practice in the direction of theater, arguing on perceptual grounds that that "art form more than music resembles nature. We have eyes as well as ears, and it is our business while we're alive to use them."[18] In keeping with his desire to unify life and art, Cage's definition of theater is as expansive as his definition of music: "I would simply say that theater is something which engages both the eye and the ear. [T]he reason I want to make my definition of theater that simple is so one could view every-day life itself as theater."[19] In Duchampian terms, Cage saw daily life as ready-made theater. Cage's emphasis on performance that goes beyond the conventional bounds of music and his concepts of unifying art and life, of constructing art forms that we experience in the same ways as the rest of life, and of transforming life itself into art resonate with the legacy of the historical avant-garde and proved of crucial importance to Fluxus.

But Fluxus was not simply derivative of Cage. *An Anthology of Chance Operations,* to which Cage himself contributed, contains writings indicative of other avant-garde aesthetics of the early 1960s, the context in which Fluxus arose. Among them is conceptual artist Walter DeMaria's brief essay "Meaningless Work" (dated 1960). Although DeMaria was not a Fluxus artist, the proposal he makes in this essay reflects exactly the kind of thinking that animated Fluxus.

> Meaningless work is obviously the most important and significant art form today. The aesthetic feeling given by meaningless work can not be described exactly because it varies with each individual doing the work. . . . Meaningless work can not be sold in art galleries or win prizes in museums. . . . By meaningless work I simply mean work which does not make you money or accomplish a conventional purpose. For instance putting wooden blocks from one box to another, then putting the blocks back to the original box, back and forth, back and forth, etc., is a fine example of meaningless work.[20]

DeMaria clearly shares with Cage and the historical avant-garde the idea that everyday activity can be understood as art. But there are also crucial differences in their respective formulations. Whereas Cage argues that art can produce a form of attention through which everyday life can be perceived as art, DeMaria suggests that everyday activity must be divorced from its quotidian context to function as art—it must be rendered "meaningless." DeMaria's explicit stance against the commodification of the artwork differs from Cage's comment that we should consume art in the same ways as we consume everything else. There is also an element of gratuitousness in DeMaria's conception of "meaningless work" that is absent from Cage but present in Fluxus. While Cage's notion that any sound can be music may seem gratuitous by comparison with more traditional definitions, his formulation is in service to a concept of realism. The arbitrary elements in his music make it, in his view, a more faithful representation of the arbitrariness of real experience. As his use of the word *meaningless* suggests, DeMaria does not invoke such high-minded principles. Finally, and most important, Cage's ideas are based on essentially conventional assumptions about the relationship between the composer (and performer) and the audience. For Cage, the audience makes the ultimate synthesis of the materials offered to it by the composer and performer, but does not participate in the production of the work itself, only in its reception. In this respect, Cage is at odds with the avant-garde tendency toward decentralizing authorship by creating performances based on collaboration between performers and audience members or by breaking down that distinction. By contrast, DeMaria does assault the performer/audience distinction: "meaningless work" is something you perform for yourself. You perform the work and are also the sole audience for that performance; you are simultaneously the only producer and the only consumer of the performance.

A manifesto-like statement by George Maciunas, circa 1964, gives a sense of the Fluxus synthesis of these ideas. Opposing art to Fluxus art-amusement, Maciunas proclaims that

> To establish the artist's nonprofessional status in society, he must demonstrate the artist's dispensability and inclusiveness, he must demonstrate the selfsufficiency of the audience, he must demonstrate that anything can be art and anyone can do it.
>
> Therefore, art-amusement must be simple, amusing, unpretentious, concerned with insignificance, require no skill or countless rehearsals, have no commodity or institutional value.
>
> The value of art-amusement must be lowered by making it unlimited, massproduced, obtainable by all and eventually produced by all.[21]

The idea that "anything can be art" comes from Cage and Duchamp, of course; Maciunas also retains Cage's idea that the artist has a specific function, which can be distinguished from that of the audience—at least until everyone becomes an artist. Maciunas's opposition to commodity and institutional value in art clearly resonates with DeMaria, as does his idea that art-amusement dwells on insignificance. The term *art-amusement* itself points to an aspect of Fluxus that is not foregrounded by either Cage or Demaria: a robust sense of humor. Although Fluxus was very much a product of the kind of ruminations on the nature and limits of art in which Cage and DeMaria were both engaged, it inflected those ruminations with an antic sense of humor that was frequently manifest in the rowdiness of Fluxus performances. Placing Fluxus at the juncture of high-art avant-gardism and more explicitly comic or ludic traditions, Maciunas concludes that "it is the fusion of Spikes [*sic*] Jones, vaudeville, gag, children's games and Duchamp."

It is worth noting that Maciunas took very seriously the populist, democratic ideology of Fluxus he alludes to when he talks about mass production and mass accessibility. That kind of mass production was what Maciunas strove for in the Fluxus program of publishing books and multiples. Like André Breton, the "pope" of surrealism, Flux pope Maciunas tried to align his group with a leftist ideology. Ultimately, Maciunas was no more successful in imposing that ideology on Fluxus than Breton had been with the surrealists.

Fluxus "Music"

I have already referred to Fluxus productions as "performances" and mentioned that they often have been grouped with other forms of performance art of the 1960s and 1970s, to which they certainly bear a family resemblance. It is crucial to keep in mind, however, that unlike the makers of happenings and other forms of performance art, Fluxus artists generally defined and presented their performances as *music,* often at music festivals and venues such as the Carnegie Recital Hall. Like classical music, Fluxus performances were generated from scores. Unlike traditional classical music notations, these scores are usually verbal, though some involve graphics. By preserving the basic textual structure of classical music, Fluxus was able both to mount a critique of the cultural pretension surrounding classical music and to avail itself of the indeterminate, collaborative aspects of the musical score as a textual form. Rather than presenting an exhaustive account of the performances done under the Fluxus banner or attempting to address the work of all participants, I will focus here on two types of pieces: satirical, sometimes violent, commentaries on the conventions of musical performance, including the uses of musical instruments, and gentler, more contemplative works.

One of the least violent of Fluxus compositions that nevertheless involves the abuse of a musical instrument is Benjamin Patterson's *Variations for Double Bass,*[22] an instrument Patterson himself plays. The score reads, "17 variations are performed, such as locating pin of bass over location of performance on map, attaching clothespins on strings and rattling them, agitating strings with comb, corrugated board, feather duster or chain, eating edibles from peg box, posting a letter through the *f* hole, etc., etc., etc."[23] Through the indignities to which he subjects an instrument important to both classical music and jazz, Patterson pokes fun at the status of musical instruments as sacred objects. He even makes light of the avant-garde's own mockery of that sacred status. Placing clothespins on the bass's strings is reminiscent of the kinds of "preparations" Cage made in his pieces for "prepared piano," such as the *Concerto for Prepared Piano and Orchestra* (1951), for which the piano is altered by the insertion of various wooden and metal objects into the strings. Cage was concerned in those pieces to widen the piano's timbral range and to introduce an element of chance into piano playing, since the exact behavior of the elements placed on the strings cannot be predicted. Patterson's piece can be seen as satirical of Cage's intentions. The musician seems to be preparing the bass, but never playing it. Some of the "preparations," such as posting a letter through the hole, are comic bits with no specifically musical significance. Patterson emphasizes the performative (visual) side of Cage's approach at the expense of its musical (aural) aspect. In this way, the Fluxus definition of music was even more radical than Cage's. Whereas Cage posited that any sound could be musical but defined the realm of the gestural as theater, Fluxus asserted that music need not produce sounds but could consist solely of performed actions.

Patterson's misuse of his bass and mockery of musical conventions are mild in comparison with the humiliations suffered by music and its instruments at the hands of Nam June Paik, the well-known video artist who was a Fluxus mainstay in the 1960s. Paik's pieces are often sensationalistic and overtly aggressive. At the Dusseldorf "Neo-Dada in der Musik" concert in 1962, Paik performed his most notorious piece, *One for Solo Violin,* by raising a violin very slowly over his head, then bringing it crashing down on a table. Whereas Patterson's assault on his bass is essentially good-humored, Paik's performances were often perceived as expressionistic and fueled by strong, negative emotion on his part. Dance and performance art critic Jill Johnston, writing in the *Village Voice,* noted in her review of the 1964 Fluxus concert at the Carnegie Recital Hall that whereas Paik had previously performed *One* in a detached manner, on this occasion he seemed genuinely enraged.[24]

In his *Suite for Transistor Radio,* Paik suggests disrupting a symphony concert by playing a portable radio between movements, adding, "I love quite much the distorted twist coming loudly from the cheap transistor radio of a teenager."[25] In this score, Paik takes on the role of the boor present in every symphony audience who exhibits a lack of understanding of the conventions of symphony audience behavior by applauding between movements and exaggerates it through an even less acceptable piece of behavior. By implying that the radio should be playing popular music, Paik also proposes a challenge to the distinction between the symphony as high art and the twist as popular culture. To play the twist between movements of a symphony is to create a musical work incorporating both.[26] It is worth comparing Paik's radio piece with Cage's *Imaginary Landscape No. 4* (1951) "for twelve radio sets playing twelve different programmes simultaneously, with their tuning, dynamics and durations (whether of sound or silence) all determined by chance."[27] In Cage's piece, the random noise produced by the radios under Cage's arbitrary manipulations becomes music; for Paik's piece to have its disruptive effect, the radio must be perceived as producing noise that is unacceptable within the context of symphonic music. After all, if the audience is really open to hearing all random sounds indiscriminately as music, it would not be upset at Paik's playing a radio during the symphony, and his gesture would not be provocative. Whereas Cage uses radio noise to expand the definition of musical sound, Paik reifies the existing, conventional definitions against which his piece is an aggressive provocation.

Paik's *Étude Platonique I,* like Patterson's *Variations,* satirizes classical and contemporary music simultaneously. The score reads, in part: "play Beethiven's [*sic*] Krutzer [*sic*] Sonata very sincerely with violin woithput srtring [*sic*] and piano without hammer." This silent *Étude* clearly evokes Cage's well-known *4' 33"* (1952), a piano piece whose score is blank. The idea of Cage's piece is that all sounds occurring in the performance space during the stated duration of the performance constitute music. Cage's piece is expansive in spirit, inviting the audience to embrace the broadest possible definition of music. By contrast, Paik's *Étude,* like his *Suite for Transistor Radio,* is an act of aggression against the limited definition of music implicit in the classical tradition. While *Suite* interpolates foreign musical sounds into a symphony, thus sullying its purity, *Étude* is an assault on one of the icons of classical music. Whereas Cage's *4' 33"* implies that a new form of perception can be achieved within the musical, performative, and cultural conventions of classical music, Paik takes those conventions to be rigid ideological structures, then attacks them. Cage seeks to create a new paradigm for music; Paik limits himself to criticizing the existing paradigm. Paik attacks Beethoven by reducing one of his best-known compositions to silence. Rather than using that silence to focus attention on the nonmusical sounds the audience is hearing and proposing they be heard as music, in Cage's fashion, Paik draws attention to the musical sounds the audience is *not* hearing—the silenced *Kreutzer Sonata*—and on Paik's ability to render mute the great Beethoven. Like Patterson, Paik also draws attention to the performance conventions of classical music: with Beethoven silenced, the musicians' gestures as they mime the effort of playing Beethoven "very sincerely" become the performance. Music as an audible phenomenon is replaced once again by music as a visual phenomenon.

George Maciunas, too, attacked musical conventions in his work. Like Paik's *One for Solo Violin,* Maciunas's destructive pieces are acts of violence against musical instruments. *Carpenter's Piano Piece* consists of nailing down each key of a piano, from lowest to highest (in a photograph, Maciunas is seen performing the piece on what appears to be a derelict instrument). His *Solo for Violin* (1962) is related to Paik's violin piece: "Old classic is performed on a violin. Where pauses are called for, violin is mistreated."[28] The strings are scraped and broken, pebbles placed inside and shaken, the violin is sawed, drilled, and hammered upon, dropped, bitten, ripped apart, and finally thrown to the audience in pieces. The affinity with Patterson's *Variations* is also apparent. But whereas Patterson's abuses of the bass are whimsical and essentially nondestructive, Maciunas's are violent and polemically anti–high art. Like Patterson and Paik, Maciunas parodied both classical music and the avant-garde in these destructive pieces.

He also composed several pieces intended to be performed in relation to another composer's work. His *Homage to Richard Maxfield* (1962), for instance, to be performed after playing one of Maxfield's taped electronic compositions, consists in erasing the master tape while rewinding it, thus destroying Maxfield's work.[29] Maciunas's composition is the musical equivalent of Robert Rauschenberg's *Erased de Kooning Drawing* (1953)—in both cases, a new work is produced when one artist destroys another's existing work. A key distinction is that Rauschenberg had acquired the drawing and had de Kooning's permission to erase it—but there is no indication in Maciunas's score that Maxfield would agree to its performance.[30] This piece reverses the polarity of the others discussed here. In Fluxus pieces involving violence to classical instruments, the "music" comes into being by destroying the instruments. Maciunas's "homage" to Maxfield suggests that the instrument (in this case, the tape recorder) can destroy the music. An electronic composition that exists only as a tape recording can be destroyed by the very same equipment on which its existence depends. (I will return to the issue of violence against the classical music tradition and musical instruments in the last section of this essay.)

The quieter side of Fluxus is best represented by George Brecht, one of the participants in Cage's class at the New School. Brecht's scores were performed at the initial Fluxus concerts in Europe, though he remained in the United States. The scores he had been writing since the mid-1950s were collected and published for the first time in 1963 as *Water Yam,* a box containing each score on a separate card.[31] The Brecht pieces most often performed at Fluxus concerts both in Europe and New York were his "instrumental" compositions. These fall into two categories: those that call for a task to be performed during a concert and those that are more open to interpretation. Of the former, his *String Quartet* (1962): "shaking hands"; *Flute Solo* (1962): "disassembling, assembling"; and *Solo for Violin, Viola, Cello, or Contrabass* (1962): "polishing" were among the most frequently performed. The performance of each consisted of the action described in the score: four musicians shook hands; a performer took a flute apart, then put it back together; a stringed instrument was polished. These clearly constitute a musical equivalent of "meaningless work" in the sense that performance conventions and routines associated with the maintenance of instruments are performed for their own sake, divorced from their utilitarian contexts.

Brecht's more loosely interpretable instrumental compositions include *Saxophone Solo* (1962): "Trumpet"; *Organ Piece:* "Organ"; *Concerto for Clarinet* (1962): "Nearby"; *Piano Piece:* "Center"; and *Piano Piece (1962):* "A vase of flowers on(to) a piano." The point of these pieces is the multiplicity of interpretations to which they can give rise. Unlike Paik's or Maciunas's destructive pieces, which make their provocative points only if performed for an audience, many of Brecht's pieces can be performed privately; some even can be realized purely conceptually. *Piano Piece (1962)* has been performed publicly by placing a vase of flowers on a piano. Doing the same thing privately is just as much a realization of the score. The notion that one can perform the piece for oneself allies Brecht's score with DeMaria's concept of "meaningless work." It also challenges a theatrical model of performance that demands the presence of an audience.[32] In musical terms, however, Brecht's gesture is arguably less radical. Playing a musical composition by and for oneself is no less a performance of the score than playing the same piece for an audience. However, Brecht takes the issue of textual interpretation into conceptual realms that challenge both the theatrical and the musical models of performance. Because of the diction used in the instruction ("on(to)"), simply noticing a vase of flowers already on a piano is also a realization. *Piano Piece* ("center") has been performed by centering a piano within the performance space. Brecht also made a painting with the words "Piano Piece" along the bottom left edge and a pencilled *x* at the center of the canvas, showing that the score can be realized equally well as a performance and an art object. Brecht's refusal to distinguish between objects and performances reflects his background as a research scientist. He points out that since matter is made up of moving particles, every "object is becoming an event and . . . every event is an object."[33]

Others of Brecht's scores have no musical referent and emphasize the idea of private, conceptual performance. *Two Exercises* (1961) can be realized as a physical activity (public or private) or as thought:

> Consider an object. Call what is not the object "other."
>
> EXERCISE: Add to the object, from the "other," another object, to form a new object and a new "other." Repeat until there is no more "other."
>
> EXERCISE: Take a part from the object and add it to the "other" to form a new object and a new "other." Repeat until there is no more object.

It is virtually impossible not to realize the score for at least one of Brecht's *Three Telephone Events* (1961) in the course of daily life:

> When the telephone rings, it is allowed to continue ringing, until it stops.

> When the telephone rings, the receiver is lifted, then replaced.
>
> When the telephone rings, it is answered.

Awareness of Brecht's scores can lead to self-consciousness about daily tasks and activities: every chore becomes the execution of a score and, therefore, a piece of music and a performance. With Cage, Brecht seems to say that every part of life, no matter how ordinary (a telephone call, a vase of flowers) takes on an aesthetic quality when framed as music and treated with concentration. In this respect, Brecht's work can also be seen as proposing a radical approach to textuality that is exactly opposite to the theatrical avant-garde's rejection of textuality. By becoming the execution of musical scores, events from daily life are textualized, framed, and given added meaning by their relations to the scores.

Other Fluxus artists who share Brecht's attitude toward life and art include Alison Knowles and also Takehisa Kosugi and Mieko Shiomi, two Japanese artists who joined Fluxus in its later period. Knowles often designates a specific life-activity as a public performance. The score for her *Proposition* (1962) reads: "Make a salad." *Nivea Cream Piece* (1962) has performers rub cold cream on their hands; the score for *Braid* (1964) reads: "The performers, usually two, find something to braid, hair, yarn, etc., and do so."[34] Kosugi's pieces (published by Fluxus in 1964) concentrate more on sensory experience than on the material circumstances of life. The score for his *Organic Music,* performed at the Carnegie Recital Hall concert by having performers breathe through large tubes, states:

> Breathe by oneself or have something breathed for the number of times which you have decided at the performance.
>
> Each number must contain breath-in-hold-out.
>
> Instruments may be used incidentally.

Shiomi's pieces are similar to Kosugi's in their focus on the senses, but seem more spiritual in intent. *Music for Two Players II* (1963): "In a closed room / pass over 2 hours / in silence / (They may do anything but speak)." Her *Passing Music for a Tree* (1964) reads: "Pass by a tree / or let some object pass by a tree / but each time differently."[35]

As music, these Fluxus performances can be analyzed fruitfully in terms of Attali's concept of Composition. Overtly satirical and violent Fluxus pieces like those of Patterson, Paik, and Maciunas meet only some of the requirements of Composition. They require no musical skill, can be performed by anyone, and are primarily visual in nature. I have argued here, however, that they depend on the presence of an audience for their satirical or polemical effect. In that sense, they do not effect the breakdown in the crucial distinction between producers and consumers of music that Attali sees as the hallmark of Composition. These pieces are violent attacks on conventional notions of music and how it is performed, but they do not ultimately present an alternative way of conceptualizing and making music. Violent Fluxus compositions are perhaps best described in the terms Attali uses in a discussion of Cage: "They are not the new mode of musical production but the liquidation of the old."[36]

The gentler side of Fluxus, represented here primarily by George Brecht, fulfills Attali's vision of Composition more completely. His pieces also require no musical skill to perform and are primarily visual in nature. Additionally, they do not require an audience—Brecht's scores are realized as effectively as private action or thought as they are as public performance. This is a crucial point, for it allows Brecht's pieces to constitute the kind of wholly idiosyncratic activity that Attali envisions, activity that in no way depends on the presence or approval of others, occurs solely for the pleasure and satisfaction of the performer, and thus completely avoids commodification. Since the performer is also the audience, that distinction is broken down in Brecht's work in the way that is central to Attali's vision of Composition.

The one respect in which neither the more violent Fluxus pieces nor Brecht's meet Attali's requirements for Composition is that they all retain the traditional relationship between composer and performer. Whereas Attali envisions a world in which each person defines what music is for him- or herself, creates it, performs it, and serves as the audience for it, Fluxus retains the conventional relationship in which the definition of music and the parameters for its performance are determined by composers who express them to performers by means of scores. I have suggested here that Fluxus did not see this form of textuality as oppressive; rather, Fluxus exploited the undetermined, collaborative nature of the musical score as a textual form. However, the Fluxus version of the composer/performer relationship is a parody of the truly conventional version, since Fluxus scores bear little resemblance to traditional musical notation and often invite idiosyncratic interpretation to a degree traditionally scored music does not. In fact, many of the scores are so widely open to interpretation that it becomes difficult to say that the composer has done anything more than create an opportunity for the performer to select a thought or action and conceive of it as music. It is implicit in Fluxus music not only that anyone can perform it but that anyone can compose it, since Fluxus music requires no more musical training or skill to invent than to perform. Once one becomes familiar with the kinds of possibilities that Fluxus opens up, it is not at all difficult to start creating one's own Fluxus pieces. Even this possibility is not truly what Attali has in mind, since to compose one's own Fluxus pieces is to remain within a particular historical framework, rather than inventing a version of what "music" is that is purely one's own. Nevertheless, the dizzyingly broad definition of what can constitute music and how it can be created proposed by Fluxus represents a large step toward the kinds of freedoms Attali envisions.

In Conclusion: Two Tangents

The question of whether or not Fluxus had a lasting influence is a tricky one.[37] Peter Frank has argued that in the 1970s, the artists associated with Fluxus took up teaching positions and exerted an influence on a younger generation of artists.[38] It is also the case that certain art forms, including artist's books, nontraditional multiples, and fringe activities like mail art all gained momentum from the participation of Fluxus. But these developments belong to the world of the visual arts—it is far less clear that Fluxus had a direct and lasting influence on music.

Rather than try to argue that point one way or another, I will conclude this essay by discussing two musical phenomena from two different cultural strata—a piece by the American avant-garde composer Ben Johnston and the destruction of musical instruments in rock—that resonate in some way with the Fluxus conception of music. I am not arguing that these examples illustrate the influence of Fluxus, only that Fluxus provides a useful point of reference for thinking about them.

Casta * (the asterisk signifies that the performer is to insert one of his or her names into the title) is one of Ben Johnston's three *Do-It-Yourself Pieces* (1969). It can be played on any instrument; the score is a set of written instructions for constructing the piece by means of both recording technology and live performance. Part of the score reads:

> Prepare sound and score components: (1) 4 segments, 45 seconds each, of vocal and instrumental noises, at least 1/3 vocal, many scatological; (2) a list of these noises clearly identifying each; (3) 25 standard repertory excerpts, from very brief to a phrase or two in length, many virtuosic.[39]

In the first phase of performing the piece, the musician records a complex series of tape loops combining the noise segments with each other. In the second part, the musician is instructed to "go to [a] typewriter. . . . Type on file cards 25 of the sounds listed, while humming, whistling and otherwise travestying your repertory excerpts." The last part of the piece brings the recorded material together with the live performance of the repertory excerpts. The musician shuffles the file cards. "Perform repertory excerpts one by one. After each, perform noise on top file card, throwing card into audience."

Casta ★ is unlike a Fluxus piece in that it is written for a trained, even virtuosic, musician. In fact, since the piece's full impact depends on the performance of the repertory excerpts, it is imperative that the musician be highly skilled. It also exhibits none of the democratic impulse that informs Composition: the frame of reference of *Casta* ★ is the repertory and culture of classical music, and the piece is most meaningful to those familiar with that context. Johnston's piece *is* like a Fluxus composition, however, in several other respects. The score is a verbal recipe for the construction of a piece out of materials chosen by the performer rather than a specific set of musical sounds to be performed. It is highly open to idiosyncratic interpretation—Johnston's desire that the performer personalize the piece by inserting one of his or her own names into the title indicates as much. *Casta* ★ is like some of Brecht's scores in that it incorporates preparations for the performance of the piece into the piece itself. Just as Brecht transforms the maintenance of musical instruments and the social conventions that precede performance ("shaking hands") themselves into music, so the recording of tape loops and the typing of cards necessary to perform the climactic final section of Johnston's piece are incorporated into it.

Although *Casta* ★ does not call for any violence toward musical instruments, it does exhibit a disrespectful—if not openly antagonistic—attitude toward the classical repertory reminiscent of Maciunas's *Solo for Violin*. The musician is specifically instructed to travesty the repertory selections he or she has chosen. The third section brings together those selections with noises chosen by the musician, some of which are specified to be "scatological." That the classical repertory excerpts occupy no privileged position in this mix is clearly indicated by Johnston's specification that the twenty-five excerpts are equally matched by twenty-five noises. The repertory is treated with an insolent levity that is certainly congruent with the spirit of Fluxus. Johnston's penultimate instruction even bears a resemblance to the vaudevillian, comic spirit evoked by Maciunas's reference to Spike Jones: "[Recording] Technician escorts performer, still playing excerpt 25, from stage." A far cry from the dignity with which classical music performances are usually associated!

Finally, I return to musical performances that do involve the abuse and destruction of musical instruments. Rock musicians more or less contemporaneous with Fluxus also subjected their instruments to violence. Beginning in late 1964, the British band the Who developed a reputation for smashing guitars, drum kits, and amplifiers to climax their performances. In 1967, Jimi Hendrix gained instant notoriety at the Monterey Pop Festival, where the Who also appeared, in part by burning and smashing his guitar.

Although what Hendrix did in burning his guitar is finally quite different from what Paik did in smashing a violin, there is at least one parallel to be drawn between Fluxus and Hendrix. Robert Palmer distinguishes Hendrix's destruction of his guitar at Monterey from the Who's attacks on their instruments in the following terms: "Hendrix smashed and burned his guitar, and kept his amps on full-throttle. The sound of guitar strings vibrating and uncoiling as the instrument crumpled and went up in flames wasn't just showmanship, as in the Who's instrument-smashing rampages; it was *music*."[40] For both Hendrix and Fluxus, then, the destruction of musical instruments was ironically a means of producing music, understood in Cage's expanded sense of music as incorporating both sound and theatrical spectacle. Any resemblance ends there, of course, for Hendrix's gesture cannot in any sense be understood as representing the kind of aggression against a certain musical or aesthetic tradition apparent in Maciunas's *Solo for Violin,* in which the instrument is destroyed during pauses as it is used specifically to play an "old classic." Hendrix's destruction of his guitar does not imply any antipathy toward the rock and blues he played on it that would parallel Maciunas's antagonism toward high art and the classical tradition.

Hendrix's immolation of his guitar was a curious and complex gesture. He explained to the audience at Monterey that he wanted to sacrifice something he loved to them to thank them for the favorable reception he had received at his first important performance in the United States after returning from England, where his British manager had created a group, the Jimi Hendrix Experience, around him. Burning the guitar was, then, both a personal and a spiritual ritual, a gesture of gratitude with Dionysian overtones of self-sacrifice, as if by burning his guitar, which he identified with himself as something he loved, Hendrix were allowing his audience symbolically to devour him. The Who's smashing of their equipment and Paik's and Maciunas's respective violence against classical instruments can also be seen as ritual, but each of these examples constitutes a different kind of ritual: I would describe The Who's violence as *social* ritual and the Fluxus destruction of instruments as *cultural* ritual. Palmer's dismissal of the Who's practices as mere showmanship notwithstanding, the Who's audiences saw the group's destructiveness as representing a generalized social antipathy with which they could identify. "Some fans experienced a vicarious thrill, the symbolic act of rage and rebellion carried out by their surrogates on stage."[41] If the Who's performances provided a symbolic outlet for their audiences' antisocial anger, their music performed something of the social function Attali attributes to music in general. Attali analogizes music with scapegoat rituals to argue that all music, not just violently performed music, symbolically channels the violence inherent in society, thus providing an outlet for it and making society itself possible. As ritual, Fluxus music does not have this broad a social function. Rather, I would describe Fluxus violence against violins and pianos as a specifically cultural ritual, the object of which is to desecrate an aesthetic order—that of high art—by smashing its sacred artifacts in its own sacred spaces.

NOTES

A shorter version of this essay was commissioned for *Art Papers* 23, no. 2 (1999): 30–35.

1. Jacques Attali, *Noise: The Political Economy of Music,* trans. Brian Massumi (Minneapolis: University of Minnesota Press, 1985), 134.

2. Ibid.

3. John Cage, *Silence* (Middletown, Conn.: Wesleyan University Press, 1961), 3.

4. It is worth noting that although Attali certainly envisions this future music as highly personal, he does not limit its production and consumption to individuals. "Any noise, when two people decide to invest their imaginary and their desire in it, becomes a potential relationship, future order" (*Noise,* 143). In Attali's terms, it would be crucial that this order not freeze into a standardized musical vocabulary that could be performed for the pleasure of audiences, rather than solely that of its producers, for that would lead directly back to the kind of commodified music that Attali's proposal is meant to eliminate.

5. Ibid., 145.

6. Susan McClary, "The Politics of Silence and Sound," in Attali, *Noise,* 157–58.

7. For a critique of Attali in terms of current African American musical practices, see Russell A. Potter, "Not the Same: Race, Repetition, and Difference in Hip-Hop and Dance Music," in *Mapping the Beat,* ed. Thomas Swiss, John Sloop, and Andrew Herman (Malden, Mass.: Blackwell, 1998), esp. 42–45.

8. Nicholas Cook, "Music Minus One: Rock, Theory and Performance," *New Formations* 27 (1995–96): 39.

9. Stan Godlovitch, *Musical Performance: A Philosophical Study* (London: Routledge, 1998), 88, 91.

10. Peter Frank, "Fluxus in New York," *Lightworks,* fall 1979, 29.

11. In my M.A. thesis on Fluxus performance (Hunter College, CUNY, 1980), I followed this path by seeking to place Fluxus in the contexts of avant-garde theater and performance art. Here, I prefer to explore the possibilities of thinking of Fluxus performance as music, the art form with which Fluxus artists themselves identified their performance work.

12. It is my belief that Fluxus found fertile ground for its parodistic approach to the classical music tradition in Europe in part because that tradition has more cultural presence and its historic roots run so much deeper there than in the New World.

13. For a useful discussion of Italian futurist music, see Michael Kirby, ed., *Futurist Performance* (New York: Dutton, 1971), 33–40. It is noteworthy that the most innovative futurist musician, Luigi Russolo, who invented a number of new instruments, was ultimately opposed to using them merely to re-create the sounds of nature and the city. He wanted noise to be appreciated for its own abstract qualities rather than as representation. Russolo's commitment to the idea that music must be produced by musical instruments is quite different from Cage's notion that real-world noise can be framed as music, a concept I discuss immediately below.

14. Michael Kirby and Richard Schechner, "An Interview with John Cage," *Drama Review* 10 (winter 1965): 55.

15. Cage, quoted by Richard Kostelanetz, *The Theater of Mixed Means* (New York: Dial Press, 1965), 54.

16. See Wilfrid Mellers, *Music in a Newfound Land* (New York: Hillstone, 1975), 188.

17. Cage, *Silence,* 12.

18. Ibid.

19. Kirby and Schechner, "Interview with John Cage," 50.

20. Walter DeMaria, "Meaningless Work," in *An Anthology of Chance Operations,* ed. LaMonte Young and Jackson MacLow (New York: Heiner Friedrich, 1970), n.p.

21. Reproduced in H. Sohm, *Happening and Fluxus* (Cologne: Koelnischer Kunstverein, 1970), n.p.

22. Where the dates of composition for Fluxus pieces are published, I have included them parenthetically in the main text.

23. Benjamin Patterson, *Variations for Double Bass,* in "Fluxfest Sale," ed. George Maciunas, *Film Culture,* winter 1966, 6.

24. Jill Johnston, "Fluxus Fuxus," *Village Voice,* July 2, 1964, 7.

25. Paik, in Sohm, *Happening and Fluxus,* n.p.

26. Paik's *Suite for Transistor Radio* is similar in this respect to a scenario described by Italian futurist Filippo Tommaso Marinetti in his manifesto "The Variety Theatre" (1913). Marinetti suggests a similar disjunctive juxtaposition of classical and popular musical forms when he proposes to "put life into the works of Beethoven, Wagner, Bach, Bellini, Chopin, [by] introducing them with Neapolitan songs" (in Kirby, *Futurist Performance,* 184).

27. Mellers, *Music in a Newfound Land,* 182.

28. The graphic score for Maciunas's *Solo for Violin* is reproduced in Sohm, *Happening and Fluxus,* n.p.

29. The written score for Maciunas's *Homage to Richard Maxfield* is reproduced in Sohm, *Happening and Fluxus,* n.p.

30. Maciunas's score does allow for what he calls a "chicken variation": "just rewind the previously played tape of R. Maxfield without erasing."

31. Scores for all of the Brecht pieces discussed here appear in *Water Yam* (Surrey, U.K.: Parrott Impressions, c. 1975). The set was originally published by Fluxus in 1963.

32. I argued recently that such theater practitioners as Jerzy Grotowski and Augusto Boal abandoned theatrical performance as such altogether when their interests compelled them to undo the distinction between performers and spectators. See my *Liveness: Performance in a Mediatized Culture* (London: Routledge, 1999), 56.

33. Michael Nyman, "George Brecht," *Studio International,* November–December 1976, 258.

34. Scores for the Knowles pieces mentioned here appear in *By Alison Knowles* (New York: Something Else Press, 1965).

35. Scores for the pieces by Kosugi and Shiomi discussed here are reproduced in Sohm, *Happening and Fluxus,* n.p.

36. Attali, *Noise,* 137.

37. Popular musician Beck (Hansen), grandson of Happenings artist Al Hansen, claims to have been influenced by the spirit of Fluxus through his grandfather. See the

interview "Folk-Punk Poke-Fun(k) Hip-Hop Knee-Drop Kick," *World Art* 19 (1998): 92–96.

38. Peter Frank, "What/Who/When/Where/Why Is/Was/Has Been/Will Be Fluxus?" in *Young Fluxus* (New York: Artists Space, 1982), n.p.

39. *Casta* * was recorded as *Casta Bertram* by double bassist Bertram Turetzky for Nonesuch Records (LP H-71237). The score is reproduced on the album cover.

40. Robert Palmer, *Rock and Roll: An Unruly History* (New York: Harmony, 1993), 228.

41. Paul Friedlander, *Rock and Roll: A Social History* (Boulder, Colo.: Westview Press, 1996), 124.

Michael Vanden Heuvel

"Mais je dis le chaos positif": Leaky Texts, Parasited Performances, and Maxwellian Academons

> The best light is obtained in the mingled region of interferences between two sources, and this region vanishes if the two flows have no common intersection. If each center claims to be the sole source of light . . . then the only compass readings or pathways obtained are those of obedience.
>
> Michel Serres

"In a household where children make peanut butter and jelly sandwiches," asks Murray Gell-Man in *The Quark and the Jaguar,* "isn't there a tendency for the peanut butter in the jar to acquire an admixture of jelly and for the jelly jar to get some dollops of peanut butter in it?"[1] The commonplace observation disguises a set of profound truths (the subtitle of Gell-Man's book is *Adventures in the Simple and the Complex*), but it first of all points to something quite elementary: things are more likely to become mixed and randomized than they are to remain ordered and discrete. What prompts Gell-Man's question is his realization that, in the face of this scientific fact, we continue to seek the simple even as we're stalked by the complex.

While we nostalgize, celebrate, or theorize the "death of the avant-garde" we do well to note another commonplace, that is, that the crucial issues raised by this collective insurgency are resolved only at the cost of the complexity it helped to constitute as a defining feature of modernity. One of the more significant ruptures that remains open after more than a century of avant-garde activity involves the subject of this collection, that is, the vexed relations between textuality and performance and the issues of power and authority they have forcefully brought to bear. This, too, has become an "adventure in the simple and complex," because in order to evoke the transgressive energies of performance, the avant-garde has often posited "the text" as the paradigm of carceral simplicity and order against which it would pitch its pataphysical bomb balls. Yet the results of this tactic have been mixed at best, resulting too often in the simple reversal of terms and concepts. So it is that today, all attempts to avoid an eternal return to some form of simple textuality must look retroactively to the avant-garde for inspiration in the quest for new forms of complexity that move beyond what the earlier practice has already produced.

Still, one wonders if such an advance will remain only a thing devoutly to be wished, given the extent to which even today the debate surrounding relations between paradigms of textuality and performance remain locked in the same binary formation originally put forth by the historical avant-garde. As evidence we can look to a recent forum conducted on the pages of *TDR,* where William Worthen elegantly rehearses the argument that, as new performance studies programs emerge from theater departments at research centers and universities, a "romantic sentimentality" often fixes the terms of the discussion, "opposing 'performance' (transgressive, multiform, revisionary) to the (dominant, repressive, conventional, and canonical) domain of the text."[2] Using Barthes's oft-cited essay "From Work to Text," Worthen reveals that, in fact, "both strategies of authorization—literary and performative—share similar assumptions, what we might call a rhetoric of origin/essence."[3] That rhetoric, to no great surprise, turns out to be merely the mystification of an anterior absence that belies any attempt to reproduce the essence or innate meaning of any work. Since both texts and performances "are materially unstable registers of signification" that nevertheless "remain haunted by a desire for authorization," what distinguishes the textual paradigm from its seemingly transgressive Other is not an ontological fact of performance as such, but rather "power . . . the way we authorize performance, ground its significance."[4]

Worthen's point can't be dismissed, but what I find more interesting is that this debate should be framed as a strategy unique to this historical moment and its institutional crises. The attempt to enforce boundaries between two knowledge domains looks, in fact, like yet another in an interminable series of modernity's efforts to keep discourses separate in order to keep them simple rather than complex (that is, to determine in advance that they will conduct the work of legitimating knowledges by assuring that they are able to produce operational methods and data sufficient to satisfy criteria of predictability and control). That such an effort at maintaining simplicity should be on the decay, and thus in need of the stabilizing force of institutional power, should also come as no surprise: Isn't this, rather, modernity's necessary response to the process of the peanut butter of textuality inevitably finding itself tainted by dollops of performative jelly (and vice-versa)? And isn't the result an equally necessary dismissal of the dynamic interaction between seemingly segregated, autonomous discourses inherently finding their way toward random admixture and disorder, their relation becoming more complicated as a result?

I think that what is being exercised by the strange dance between the need for textual order and its promise of final signifieds on the one hand and a desire to unknot its logic through performance on the other is not the validity of what text or performance means as such, but rather a larger heuristic activity being conducted across the academy and culture at large. In this enterprise, every attempt to distinguish between and to simplify textual and performative paradigms produces, not greater clarity, but further reflection regarding their complementarity and complicity because, in a very real sense, that is the only way we can speak of them. I agree with Bert States, who recently wrote that he is "convinced that a definition of performance, as we have been pursuing one, is a semantic impossibility," and I think the same applies to textuality.[5] But the lack of a fixed definition does not preclude the usefulness of the terms, and the residue created from the clash of these competing (or at least interactive) paradigms is not an altogether insignificant thing. Worthen writes that the "desire to ground the meaning of theatrical production by attributing its authority either to the work or to the institutions of the stage afflicts both the popular and the academic concept of theatrical meaning," and as a general statement this is obviously true.[6] But his formulation dismisses the possibility that such an afflicted understanding of authority is just what provides a site or space of resonance from which new, emergent notions concerning how meaning is both produced and analyzed may arise. The fact is of course that theatrical meaning and the authority to constitute it never remains a simple thing, and never presents itself absolutely along the axis of either conventional textuality or transgressive performativity. Not even the most dour textualists or retrograde directors actually believe, Pierre Menard–like, that they are on a quest "to produce pages" (in Borges's words) "which would coincide—word for word and line for line—with those of Miguel de Cervantes."[7] On the other hand, few with even the strongest investment in performance theory are likely (not anymore, anyway) to insist on the absolute freedom of performance to transgress authors and texts in the project of releasing an unlimited play of significations.

Most productions of meaning, theatrical and otherwise, seem to me "conflicted" rather than "afflicted." That is, textuality and performativity, in theory and in practice, always appear complementary and yet at the same time contestatory: as in Bhabha's formulation of difference, "each objective is constructed on the trace of that perspective that it puts under erasure."[8] Worthen is right to judge that a good deal of institutionally produced theater work and criticism forgoes the challenge of such difference, yet there is no reason to assume from this conclusion that processes of translation and transference cannot instead act to proliferate the ways in which texts and performances can produce meaning. Trite as it may sound, the truth of the relation between stage and page always lies somewhere in between, though not always in the *same* place in between. And, as I hope to show, there's nothing boring or afflicting about such interstitial spaces.

Thus the question might be not so much which paradigm (based in textual or performative signification) enjoys the most power in current institutional discourses, but rather why it is that the two remain so complicitous, why, despite our best efforts to enforce one paradigm or the other, we keep coming back to thinking only about the relations *between* the them. So long as textuality and performance are locked, and are institutionally segregated, in a binary fixed by relations of power, each will appear by itself simple and focused on an illusory quest for presence. Only when they are conceived of as a *complex system,* that is, as necessarily related and interacting with one another, mutually transforming the other even as each element continues to act with relative independence, can textuality and performance allow for emergent, and possibly dissident, effects. Worthen appears to arrive at just this conclusion when he speaks about the "rich, contradictory, incommensurable ways that [the paradigms of text and performance] engage one another." Yet he offers as a strategy for coping with such incommensurableness, not that we allow such unpredictable dynamics to flourish, but rather that we exercise "a little negative capability" when it comes to offering and supporting new critical practices that are actually "captive to the spectral disciplines of the past."[9]

Amen. But the trouble with negative capability is that it always remains potentially oxymoronic. What does negativity make capable? Like so many current theoretical exercises, Worthen's effectively and usefully deconstructs the ground of both text and performance and leaves their figural remnants left to the buffetings of "power" and "authority." But we might ask: what grounds these? What keeps power and authority pure and instrumental when everything else devolves into the more indeterminate terminology of "discourse" and "narrativity"? Worthen himself writes that we live at "a moment of undisciplined, interdisciplinary flux, euphoria, uncertainty, mystery and doubt," yet he cedes to power the capacity to discipline, to "authorize performance" and "ground its significance."[10] Here power, as in most debates surrounding issues of textuality and performance, seems always already both exterior and anterior to both. But could not power itself be understood more productively as something *within* the system that already contains textuality and performance, which thus finds itself conflicted by the same instabilities that underlie them? In such a formulation, power would exert itself, not as a steady, disciplinizing stream, but as a rather more "quantum," that is, spasmodic and unpredictable, force governed by its dynamic relations to the other components of the system of which it is a part.[11] This would allow us to ask what sort of dynamics emerge from the complex, three-body problem of the interactions among text, performance, and power.

"The capacity to think about reality across disciplinary and cultural borders," says Herbert Blau, "requires something less formulaic than the going historicism or the mantras on power arising from an overdose of Foucault."[12]

And it's true that a kind of compulsive symmetry underlies both contemporary formulations of power and the exercise of it in historical and cultural analysis. The "containment/subversion" oscillation of so much new historical work too often produces a sense of effete (L. "no longer bearing offspring") equilibrium in which, as Barbara Riebling says, "for every +1 there will arise a −1, so that all human equations result in 0."[13] Power in this case, despite its boundless regime and ceaseless operation, turns out to be not so much a transient and unpredictable affair as it is the universal constant or invariance that guarantees that such relations will remain dynamic but in equilibrium, fixed in linear and reversible correlations. To return to the subject of Worthen's essay, then, we see (the markers being arbitrary) the +1 of the traditional textual paradigm oscillating with the −1 of performativity, with institutional power directing their correspondence and leaving us holding negative capability as the single remaining strategy to enact. "Power circulates," laments Riebling, "but nothing really changes," while all the time, warns Blau, "invisible power is laughing up its sleeve."[14]

If the evolution of a paradigm of performance through the effort of the avant-garde is to produce tangible results that may direct our current practice and theory—that is, if we are to look at avant-garde theater as a means to get past envisioning performance as just another instance of instability locked in binary relation to stability, waiting on power—then we must also take the next step and recognize the unpredictable nature of power itself. As Bhabha writes:

> contingency as the signifying time of counter-hegemonic practices is not a celebration of "lack" or "excess" or a self-perpetuating series of negative ontologies. Such "indeterminism" is the mark of the conflictual yet productive space in which the arbitrariness of the sign of cultural signification emerges within the regulated boundaries of social discourse.[15]

The quest for a system made up of both arbitrariness and regulated boundaries, in fact, guides much of avant-garde theater's history, which moves through an arc where performance is posited as the sole philosophy by which to hammer conventional forms of textual signification. Always implicit in such work lies the potential for a kind of postmodern, deconstructive form of performative textuality in which, as Worthen recounts, the ontological instabilities of both conventional textuality and performance are evinced. However, such deconstructive "negative ontologies" have in avant-garde theater often produced just the sterility mentioned by Blau and Riebling because the doubt or "−1" they ask us to live in is so overwhelming that it threatens to become just another form of certainty. (To believe in nothing, a current bumper sticker admonishes, is to fall for anything.)

However, our historical position within late capitalism may present an opportunity to move beyond such an impasse because under these conditions power itself is experienced as both so widespread and yet at the same time so unstable and dispersed that it no longer seems to organize and segregate discourses effectively or consistently, even as it constitutes the world. Today we may be better positioned to recognize the simple (and also complex) fact that one never encounters instances of unfettered difference (that is, the complete absence of power) any more than one encounters absolute redundancy and perfect order (or the full presence of carceral power). The "adventure," to return to the title of Gell-Man's book, resides in the unpredictable interactions between the simple and complex rather than at one or the other extreme. Future, "post-avant-garde," performance and critical discourse that hopes to embody the dynamics of a culture that Blau describes as "neither a logic nor a law but rather an environmental totality of forces and tendencies only predictable within the shadowy limits of the indeterminacy principle" will thus have to find the means to compound power and powerlessness, law and indeterminacy, structuralism and poststructuralism, textuality and performance in new and innovative ways.[16] The result will likely lack the boldness of existing theories of conventional textuality or postmodern performativity, as well as the theoretical scope of either structuralism or poststructuralism. But as Ian Stewart has said of theories of symmetry-breaking in mathematics (another hybrid of sorts): "It isn't the long-sought Theory of Everything . . . but we believe it to be a Theory of Something, which may be a better idea."[17]

In order to move toward the better idea of such somethings, I want first to argue that the development of avant-garde theater has always been conflicted by issues of power, or, more exactly, by its engagement with discourses of *powerlessness* that circulated intensely throughout the nineteenth century and that continue to haunt us at the end of the millennium.[18] Avant-garde performance was launched at a moment when widespread anxieties over the specter of the loss of power to organize the energy that constitutes the material world and discourse *at all* infiltrated both elite and mass culture. For in the midst of an archive that showcased the Victorian era as one of imperial might, colonial expansion, and panoptic social organization, emergent counterdiscourses were at work that shadowed the cultural imaginary in profound ways. Indeed, the very specularizations of power staged in the period in the form of industrial exhibitions, ethnographic narratives and displays, new forms of geographical mapping, and strategies of social engineering would seem to indicate, not a simple confidence in energetic expansion and organization, but rather a compensatory reaction to a felt sense that the power underlying such practices was on the wane. Modernism, of course, is fraught with anxiety and a deep sense of dread at the prospect of things falling apart, but the specific form of powerlessness I wish to address is not primarily existential (that is, an effect of subjectivity and the loss of organizing cultural narratives) but material, a powerlessness inherent in things and signs made evident by the sciences of physics, biology, and information. Such a focus seems both natural and necessary for a period quintessentially bound up with both the utopian promises and the grinding constraints of materialism.

From the two great scientific discourses of the last century, thermodynamics and evolutionary biology, there emerged a problematics of matter and life that were quickly translated into a problematics of art and culture. "It is possible," offered Michel Serres in his groundbreaking interdisciplinary study *Hermes III: La traduction,* "that science is the set of messages that are optimally invariant for any translation strategy."[19] Certain kinds of scientific "messages," particularly those dealing with the dissipation of energy in dynamic systems, can be useful for translating the fraught relations between text and performance. For, structurally speaking, the problem of thermodynamics, of entropy, is quite similar to the problem that renders difficult any attempt to constitute relations between textuality and performativity: that is, the instability of power and also of meaning. The notion that entropy (albeit of a different kind) may *be* linked to meaning as well as physical systems becomes evident after the development of information theory from thermodynamics in the twentieth century, and has recently been mentioned by Blau, who—evoking his not-quite-former life as a chemical engineer confronting the second law of thermodynamics as something that "wasn't very good"—asks why, in light of everything science has had to say about the nature of matter, time, and space, "we haven't learned to live in doubt."[20] In light of the monolithic models of power and discourse current in cultural studies, he reminds us that, while the entropy principle does not (yet) necessitate yielding "all of reality to the aleatoric," it does insist that we respect the fact that "there is still a leak in the universe."[21] What leaks out from the (w)hole according to the second law of thermodynamics is order, redundancy, and organized simplicity, that is, both ground and figure of panoptic power. What leaks in is randomness, contingency, and complexity, experienced as a form of powerlessness and doubt that makes the gaze wander and repetition stutter.

Such links between organic and cultural spheres are, I would thus insist, more than metaphorical because the second law exerts its force over both matter and information, essential adjuncts to the signifying systems of theater—particularly avant-garde theater—as well as the cultural production of power. That is, the performing body is not just a thing "that" matters in

Judith Butler's sense, but a thing that "is" matter, as well as a matter of some importance when we speak about how meaning is authorized—and, in avant-garde theater, deauthorized—through embodied performance. More so than any other human activity, performance highlights the effects of entropy. Theater's "difference," it has been argued by everyone from Plato to Augustine through Artaud and Derrida, consists of the temporality and liveness of performance, especially as these are incarnated in the material performing body. And, as Jonathan Kalb has said, this leads naturally to the recognition that it is the *de*composition of that body, "not . . . the living actor but the dying actor" that most powerfully expresses theater's difference from other forms of representation.[22] As well, performance is where fixed meanings and clear messages go to die, where power as a function of information meets its decline (knowledge, too, is said to come in bodies). Thermodynamics has always operated, as Bruce Clarke says, "in the interstices between physical theories and cultural desires,"[23] and avant-garde theater became a particularly intense site of such mediations.

Given that both things and the words that name them are susceptible to forms of entropy, the question becomes: Is the difference engine of the logos therefore doomed to the same heat death as that which awaits matter? This is certainly what Clausius and Kelvin suggested to the Victorian world, leaking randomness and uncertainty into a century primed to ride its machines into a glorious future of limitless power fueled by the general reservoir of British energy (it should be remembered that *energeia* is a term first found in rhetoric, and refers not to physical forces but the force of language). "Within a finite period of time," intoned Kelvin, "the earth must again be unfit for the habitation of man as at present constituted."[24] His implication is clearly that if "man as at present constituted" can only reconstitute himself as a more orderly and knowing entity, he can somehow outflank the deterministic effects of the second law. Chastened by the report ("Bad news from Paris!" exclaims *Arcadia*'s vivacious savant Thomasina. "It concerns your heat engine. Improve it as you will, you can never get out of it what you put in"), various Victorian thinkers and writers inaugurated compensatory narratives to plug the leak, staunch the flow. These responses, as N. Katherine Hayles and others have pointed out, "link these scientific predictions with the complex connections among repressive morality, capital formation, and industrialization in Victorian society."[25]

The most complex of these heuristic narratives is James Clerk Maxwell's infamous "demon," which through an act of superhuman will and memory sorts threatening differences (in molecular temperature) and segregates them so that the entropy of one side of a thermodynamically closed chamber decreases (i.e. it gets hotter) while the other remains constant. This violates the second law and assures that an improbable, but statistically possible, concentration of potential energy could be maintained even in the face of the universe's impending heat death, so long as an appropriately nimble-fingered and mnemonically powerful sorting agent could be found or created.[26] Thus the century that received the legacy of Linnaeus's *Systema Naturae* and its taxonomies could find further evidence for the benefits derived from the rigorous segregation of different orders: *Felis leo, Felis tigris, Felis pardus;* fast/hot molecules, slow/cool molecules; energetic races, insipid races; but never peanut butter *and* jelly.

However, in one of the great ironies of modern thought, Maxwell's attempt to save the universe from the second law by rendering its randomizing, disordering effects probabilistic rather than bound to physical law as such (and thus deterministic) helped initiate a broader statistics-based movement within physics that, as Hayles says, "culminated in quantum mechanics, which when it abandoned the notion of causality drove Einstein to the riposte that God does not play dice with the universe."[27] Maxwell's heuristic demon tries to stem the leakage of organized matter and clarity into randomness and noise by policing the borders between them. More, the demon (like another before him) holds out to humanity the promise of eternity by creating in his thermodynamically sealed box a perpetual motion machine, a generalized heat reservoir beyond entropic expenditure. Yet with the same demonic gesture, Maxwell ushers indeterminacy and probability into the privileged seat from which Heisenberg and Bohr will later announce their humbling theories of uncertainty and complementarity. Seeking to segregate and taxonomize the different orders of heat and language, Maxwell's demon paradoxically clears the ground for a physical and discursive world in which *res cogitans* and *res extensa* collapse into "event fields" and language picks up more and more noise: "the incomplete knowledge of a system must be an essential part of every formulation in quantum theory."[28] Thus the demon, seeking to stabilize the real within a paradigm of conventional textuality and fixed signification ("Being"), instead produces the real-as-performance ("Becoming"): indeterminate, contingent on the intrusion of noise and dirty speech, in a word, processual.

Many forms of avant-garde performance are shot through with narratives of entropy and its subtexts of incompleteness and powerlessness. Emerging at precisely the moment when the (old) new sciences of thermodynamics and evolution first gained a toehold in the popular imaginary, the historical avant-garde was among the first cultural formations to read the subtext of entropy theory and to invest it with a paradoxically utopian thrust. The breakdown of the old order, Zola and Ibsen could claim, will produce the new. However, as the second-phase avant-garde began to question and move away from the social utopianism of the historical avant-garde, the defining gesture becomes primarily a destructive one. Performance, in the form of cabaret, futurist *sintesi,* and dada soirees became the sharp instrument for eviscerating the order of semiosis as it was organized within conventional textuality. Often demonic themselves in their intensity, avant-garde theater artists nevertheless arranged themselves as antidemons to Maxwell's guardian of the reservoir. Performance was the friction that negated any attempt to impose invariance or a universal constant on meaning and affect, creating the clinamen that brought into being the nonlinear interactions that rendered impossible the process of keeping noise and chaos separate from order and message. Interestingly, such difficulties have proved equally bad for Maxwell's demon, for it was eventually remarked that the door through which it ushered its segregated molecules would produce friction, hence would require an expenditure of work to operate and thereby increase the system's entropy. The door meant to segregate becomes instead the frictional parasite drawing energy from the system and randomizing its elements. Similarly, the avant-garde, often characterized as parasitic in relation to the culture in which it operated, projected itself and its art as the bad mathematical difficulties that upset the (too) smooth operations of cultural segregation and taxonomizing, wore down the orders (sexual, psychological, linguistic, and so on) that produced the bourgeois imaginary, and parasited the cultural archive in order to mock it by deriving a living from its very cast-offs and garbage (think especially of Duchamp's readymades).

From the beginning, then, avant-garde performance set itself firmly against what it conceived of as the repressive instrumentality of the "demonic" or highly organized texts of culture, and defined its own agenda by this difference. Yet, for all the liberatory rhetoric these theatrical innovations released, such significatory systems, in the several forms they take across the range of avant-garde theatrical practices, were already built upon a kind of closure because they were predicated on maintaining a segregated difference between textuality and performativity. Locked into what was sometimes portrayed (as in Artaud) as a death struggle between the insurgent valencies of performance and the deadening effects of the textual masterpiece, avant-garde theater created a hierarchized system of text and performance that reversed, but did not eliminate, an earlier one in which texts enjoyed a position of privilege and anteriority over performances.

The notion of "system" that has been shadowing my argument to this point is another translation from science that may illuminate this impasse. Serres writes in "The Origin of Language: Biology, Information Theory, and Thermodynamics" that the conception of system has passed through three stages in history. First, systems were conceived as axioms or equations independent of any time variable: Serres refers to such systems as "logico-mathematical."[29] After Newton, however, systems came to be seen as sets "which remain stable throughout variations on objects which are either in movement or relatively stationary," that is, differential sets of interacting, law-bound elements that behaved the same moving forward in time as they did moving backward. Such time-reversible systems Serres calls "mechanical" because "the ordinary mechanical system depends on time but not its direction." Until the nineteenth century, these mechanical systems were idealized and therefore eternal, but after Fourier's discovery of the nature of heat and Carnot's work on temperature differentials, says Serres, "they become motors. They create movement, they go beyond the simple relation of forces, they create them by energy or power." Such systems Serres terms "thermodynamic," and, as soon as one can build them, "the notion of time changes."[30] Having now to account for the effects of the second law, idealized *mechanicques rationnel* must be replaced by real motors creating heat and friction, material engines dissipating energy and increasing their entropy levels. "From this moment on," remarks Serres, "time is endowed with a direction. It is irreversible and drifts from order to disorder, or from difference to the dissolution or dissemination of a homogenous mixture from which no energy, no force, and motion can arise."[31] Hence Maxwell's need for a demonic sorter to resist such homogenization.

Significantly, all three formulations of system described by Serres are built on very specific forms of closure. A system can remain outside time (logico-mathematical), oscillate reversibly between past and present (mechanical), or degrade across irreversible time (thermodynamic), but in each case the outcome is determined in advance and cannot be altered. Such systems remain closed and predictable because each is predicated on absolute and segregated relations between order and disorder. In the first disorder simply does not exist (or is dealt with algorithmically through perturbation theory), while in the second all relations between order and disorder are governed and balanced by invariant physical laws. In thermodynamic systems, as we have seen, disorder holds sway over order, causing all organization to leak. Until quite recently, these models of systems helped constitute, and limit, scientific as well as cultural discourses, both mobilizing and constraining certain ways of understanding physical laws and processes of signification and making visible a limited understanding of the dynamics of systems.

A variety of avant-garde performance practices developed from the last quarter of the nineteenth century is built on interactions between textuality and performativity that align them with one or another of such systems. Ritual forms of avant-garde performance, for example, such as some forms of early modern dance (Wigman for instance) and the various holy theater predecessors and avatars of Artaud, articulate technologies of representation that are meant to embody formalized and timeless gestures, iconic attitudes and other forms of "animated hieroglyphs." Because such gestural grammars, as for instance those (mis)read by Artaud when he witnessed Balinese dance, "make useless any translation into logical discursive language," they evade the mortal vocabularies of speech and remain immanent, transcendent. Such "masterfully applied conventions," Artaud goes on to say, have "the evocative power of a system," one that verges on "mathematics."[32] The theatrical event becomes a "logico-mathematical" procedure in which the performance of unchanging codes is evoked in order to embody a system at classical (that is, nonthermodynamic) equilibrium. The system in this instance is the human body and perhaps as well the body politic, and the competing forces to be kept in balance (or returned to a balance lost to modern life) include darkness and light, autonomy and possession, healthy humors and pathological ones, and so on. So long as the microcosmic body is purged of difference and thereby returned by cruelty or some other medium to a ritualized equilibrium, it does not know time, and the macroscopic universe similarly remains static and identical to itself (Artaud's "Life" as opposed to the "life of Man"), impervious to entropy because without movement, save for the laminar fall of atoms in a timeless void. Cruelty and holy theater become the vehicles by which one dances back to this tribal morn, penetrating to the heart of such stasis in order, as Grotowski would say, to (re)dis/cover the miracle lying at the center of being.

Of course, not all avant-garde performance is directed toward such static ends. Much of the most memorable work from the first half of the twentieth century in fact seems quite the opposite of anything associated with ritual or stasis. Yet even the cacophonous dada evenings and furious sonic explosions emanating from futurist *intonarumori* gained their substantial power, not simply from what they were, but from what they very self-consciously were *not*. They astounded their few patrons because they acted as a clinamen to the existing system of theatrical and cultural representation by presenting an excess of exactly that which should never have the capacity to *be* exceeded—that is, idealized machines. The "system" of classical (that is, Aristotelian) theater projects the universe not only through technologies of representation, but literally *as* technology, as a perfect machine. Prefiguring the model provided by later Western science, classical theater posited the world as a dynamic, yet mechanical, system in which objects and forces are distributed in and move through absolute space and time governed by irrefutable laws. This is the science, and the theater, of Serres's mechanical systems: of calculable trajectories and integrable systems, of determinism, simple causality, and Laplace's computational demon capable of predicting and retrodicting the location of every bit of matter in the universe without the "hypothesis" of a deity. The Aristotelian plot must contain exposition, recognitions, and reversals: it moves in time and is satisfyingly dynamic. Yet these lunges into past and future time "must grow out of the arrangement of the plot itself by its being so constructed that each succeeding incident happens necessarily or according to probability from what has happened previously," and of course any use of such disorderly and unpredictable devices as the deus ex machina is to be shunned.[33] Strictly linear and causal, classical emplotment pushes its narrative trajectories toward a climax that is rigorously predetermined in accordance with fundamental logical, moral, and religious invariances that produce, not the surprise of the unexpected or impossible, but an "epiphany of law," to use Northrup Frye's felicitous phrase, "of that which is and must be." Since what is "must be," then what "was" also must have been: so if the plot of *Oedipus Rex* were to be written as a differential equation, and negative variables were substituted for positive ones, nothing significant in the shape or outcome of the equation would change when it ran backward, and one could push it forward again using positive variables and it would replay perfectly, like a motor running in forward or reverse. The aesthetic payoff of such systems is similar to that which classical science pursues, that is, the phenomenon of proportionality in which the response of a system is always perfectly congruent to the stimuli that alter it. Serres calls such machines *stateurs* because, based on (again nonthermodynamic) equilibrium, one that recognizes time but not its direction, they remain essentially immovable. They are like idealized motors, the revolutions of which might rise or fall slightly, but which must eventually return to their law-bound mechanical operation.

When avant-garde performance emerged from the intersection of forces that included the new knowledge of entropy, the notion of mechanical systems and heat reservoirs had changed substantially. They could now be seen, as heretofore they could not, as motors emblematic of irreversible time, of decay and the loss of proportionality. Now machines were *nonlinear,* in the sense that their future states could be predicted only within specific limits because the size of the input did not determine the size of the output—small fluctuations (in temperature, friction, and so on) could cause massive irregularities in their function. In a sense, motors could represent what they had been created specifically to exclude, that is, the end of progress and the breakdown of mechanical order, predictability, and stable geometries into the dissipated energies of thermodynamic equilibrium. Responses to such a connotative reversal varied, but among avant-garde theater artists, particularly the futurists, a new fascination emerged with representing the flamboyant expenditure of power and *energeia* run amok and beyond predictable control (here again in both senses, given the notorious rhetorical flights of Marinetti). The exaltation of power, speed, and machinery characteristic of futurist manifestos and performances is always tinged with the anarchic, destructive power of such technologies ("The Variety Theatre destroys all our conceptions of perspective, proportion, time, and space") as well as their ability to force the audience's collaboration and thereby make it active in the expenditure of its own energy ("In its swift, overpowering dance rhythms the Variety Theatre forcibly drags the slowest souls out of their torpor and forces them to run and jump").[34] The first work Marinetti considered futurist, his 1904 poem *Destruction,* contained a canto addressed to "Le Demon de la vitesse" celebrating both pandemonium and the exuberant life force that, it is said, breaks through all barriers and randomizes all form.

Machines of course are featured as characters in avant-garde performances (*The Race between the Sewing Machine and the Typewriter*) and utilized as training devices (Laban's "Space Crystal"), but they also metaphorically structure the implied relationship between conventional, literary theater and non-ritual forms of avant-garde performance art. If the elements of classical drama take the form of ideally integrable components running systematically to produce a linear and time-reversible signifying machine, then futurist performance will rev up that engine until it smokes and wears down. As Serres has observed, by the beginning of the twentieth century inquiry into the nature of matter and biological life had developed a vocabulary and syntax that allowed artists and thinkers like Bergson to bring "that language within the domain of the social sciences, language, and texts."[35] Investigating the texts of classical drama, the avant-garde exploded such *stateurs* with the time-irreversible, performing body of the second law. In this way, the entropized body of performance was already inhabiting the third, thermodynamic system described by Serres and achieving similar disorganizing effects. In a powerful essay on the means by which J. W. M. Turner "translates" thermodynamics into painting *avant le lettre,* Serres describes how first Turner, then nineteenth-century science, frees matter from "the prison of diagram" and drawing and shows art the way to "a new world [that] will soon discover dissolution, atomic and molecular dissemination."[36] Avant-garde performance could indulge in similar dissolution and even more effectively embody it through the entropic breaking down of its own semiotic machinery (spoken language, causal plot, the performer's body, redundant information, a unified audience response, and so on). In avant-garde performance of the dada and futurist variety, the exhaustion of available organization seems to be an end in itself, conveying the sense that, as Günther Berghaus writes, "better a short life of exultation that ends in early death, than a slow and long existence, where all human potential lies dormant."[37] As well, such superconducting expenditures of energy offered the artist (but never his reviled foe the *passatista*) the agency to metaphorically bring on an Armageddon that was anyway already predetermined, just as Freud would argue that thanatos, far from being a simple death wish, was the expression for a certain kind of death and thus the ultimate expression of human agency and self-organization.

Still, despite the fitful *explosions illuminantes* of such a performance practices, the system they created between text and performance, or between order and disorder, remained a closed, thermodynamic one. One walks through Florence or Paris or Zurich surrounded by emblems of bourgeois solidity and permanence and then enters the Cabaret Voltaire or the Théâtre de la Madeleine and witnesses in performance the dissolution of meaning, language, and sense. The movement is from order to disorder and, just as one can't unstir the jelly out of the peanut butter once it's been randomized there, one can't (nor should one feel compelled to) reclaim order from a dada or futurist performance: to do so would be to misconstrue the whole point of the event.[38] The performative grammar in which such work is structured guarantees that redundancy (the foundation of order and the single necessary component in any notion of a text) will be denied as much as possible, as an idealized "Variety" theater seeks to negate the very possibility of repetition. Text and performance are not in any sense in dialogue or open exchange, then, but remain in a binary the polarity of which has simply been reversed.

The futurists, therefore, like other modernists such as Klee, Ernst, and Duchamp in painting and the vorticists in poetry, succeeded in creating new kinds of meaning-making machines; but, as David Porush points out, they were machines still restricted to notions of closed systems that differed little from Maxwell's thermodynamically sealed black box.[39] No surprise, then, that the surrealists imaged the conscious and unconscious as discrete entities polarized along a rigid gender binary, or that the elaborate linguistic formalizations developed by Raymond Roussel have been termed *les machines celibataire* (autonomous [bachelor] machines) because they attempt to be utterly self-contained and free from ambient noise, thus marking an extreme attempt to segregate all aspects of meaning and organization.[40]

Similarly embachelored futurists and other avant-garde theater artists working within a system that privileges performance over textuality, therefore, did not allow performance and textuality to "marry" and thereby interact and produce results that would not be determined in advance. Lacking was a notion of what Serres calls a "chaos positif" built upon an understanding of the dynamics of open (that is, biological and informational-cybernetic) systems, those that exchange a triple flow of matter, energy, and information in order to adapt and evolve. Open systems are nonlinear, and so their future states are impossible to predict, though one can know in advance that periods of both order and disorder will emerge in something like the punctuated equilibrium and blending of Darwinian chance and self-organizing order now used to describe evolution.[41] Still, even though early avant-garde performance may have often lacked this nonlinear dynamic, its reversal of the conventional text/performance binary was not without profound effect. It liberated performance to expend its own matter and information in an uninhibited thermal release that stoked the fires for effects much more complex: for, as Serres says, "the furnace is the engine for going back toward chaos."[42]

"Chaos" has the potential to be as materially an unstable signifier as either text or performance, and recent work in what is properly called "low dimensional, deterministic, nonlinear dynamical systems theory," but which is known popularly as chaos theory, has complicated the term further still. Without rehashing the genealogy of the term, let me isolate what is most important for the argument here, that is, that chaos can no longer be understood only as the weak effect in a fixed linear, or binary, relation to order.[43] Indeed, systems in which such stable dichotomies do exist are now described in many contexts as uninteresting: as Bruce J. West writes, "all interesting natural and psychological phenomena are fundamentally not linear, or said differently, all interesting phenomena are nonlinear."[44] This means that terms like *order* and *disorder* signify only by and through the interesting, unpredictable manner in which they interpenetrate and transform one another nonlinearly. Neither order nor disorder can maintain absolute authority over the other, and one may make visual sense of such complex dynamical systems only by modeling them as chaos science's famous "strange attractors," which evince *both* basins of order and redundancy interacting with complexity and unpredictable difference. Translated into other discourses, this means that power and powerlessness, textuality and performativity, mutually constitute and undo one another to produce emergent properties.

Despite this fact, we are daily presented with different kinds of idealized demons (authors and academics among them) who mark boundaries and, with "invisible power laughing up [their] sleeve," create the illusion of both mechanical or textual stability and their own agency in maintaining it. But demons are also more worldly imps and parasites who, as Michel de Certeau notes, "with a proliferation of tricks and fusions of power that are devoid of legible identity" may undo an old order without assuming management of the new, organic order they haphazardly create.[45] From the model of chaos theory, however, neither demon in its extreme or in isolation creates a very inviting environment, but joined as a complex system, in dialogue, they can be extremely productive. For anything to ensue, however, such demons and imps first must meet in a space where power can speak to powerlessness, where mechanical systems can communicate with process-oriented organisms, and where order (or textuality) can speak with disorder (performance).

That space might well be made possible only by entropy, the simple translation of which is "transformation," itself semantically linked to a deformation or "shaking" of organized matter or information. In "Performance as Metaphor," Bert O. States produces both a rigorous genealogy of performance as well as an intriguing attempt to isolate the "phenomenal sense . . . the without-which-not of performance."[46] Interestingly, after a series of brilliant questionings of the term's use by the usual suspects of performance theory (Goffman, Turner, and "insider theorists"—those who make "metonymical" connections in order to extend "the performance concept into contiguous fields of application"—such as Peggy Phelan and Richard Schechner), States discovers the ontological basis of performance embodied not in anthropological or sociological discourse but instead in the philosophy of science.[47] In *The Play of Nature: Experimentation as Performance,* Richard Crease argues that (in States's paraphrase) "theatre [is not] a metaphor for what goes on in science: theater and science stand in mutual relationship in which the same specified features appear, mutatis mutandis."[48] Moreover, the "without-which-not" of performance erecting the bridge between science and theatre, claims States, is "transformation . . . a fundamental pleasure at the core of mind and memory."[49] Given the semantic link between entropy and transformation, then, we might ask whether or not there exists a "fundamental pleasure" in the very heat death of information and matter taking place in performance. Further, this begs the question of whether or not there exists another notion of system, one that allows emergent properties to arise from the dissipation of an orderly system.

In order for transformations to have the heft to provide pleasure and for entropy to become an enabling force, there must be an exchange and a continuing interaction between what already exists and what comes into being out of its decline. Such interactivity is not possible in orderly, linear systems because of the principle of proportionality, which dictates that the sum of a system is always equal to its parts—that is, that the total output of such systems will always be proportional to the sum of the individual responses of each of its components. As West expresses it, "It is only with nonlinear phenomena that a property not explicit in the underlying elements can emerge through the interaction of the elements"; that is, only with nonlinearity may we model a whole that is greater than, and qualitatively different from, the sum of its parts.[50] If we put this in terms drawn from information theory, the story might go as follows: in any transmission through a channel between a sender and a receiver, the information can only lose specificity, may only degrade entropically. It cannot gain specificity or greater organization.[51] Therefore, if no noise interrupts the communication, the message will be clear but utterly redundant and without variety. Such perfect communicative acts are impossible idealizations against which analyses of Claude Shannon's "entropy of the message" are launched in information and communication theory. Thus noise, as a marker of entropy, transforms and parasites the original message by muddling it, randomizing its information, enforcing an opaque veneer of forgetting and disorder onto the palimpsest of the text. From the perspective of the sender or receiver, informational entropy thus acts to distort clarity, and so produces a kind of heat death of communication. In this classical reading of noise, nonlinearities are considered weakening effects. But if one is positioned as an observer of the channel, the information mixed with noise is now actually more complex, for it contains both the message and also random bits of incoherent information, that is, noise. The result is a qualitative transformation in the system, an increase in overall variety and complexity.

Significantly, however, if noise overwhelms the system and all redundancy (or organized information) is destroyed, then the dadaists get their wish and communication becomes utterly nonfunctional and the system disintegrates. For anything truly surprising or productive (that is, both information-bearing and containing variety, each defining the other by its difference) to emerge, both simplicity and complexity must exist, and must transform one another simultaneously. "Randomness," says the biologist Henri Atlan, "is a kind of order, if it can be made meaningful."[52] Just as importantly, order is a kind of randomness that has already been made meaningful, but that can be transformed by noise to mean something more complex.

Interestingly, it is powerlessness and the consequent weakening of order and memory—but *not* their disappearance—that makes this possible. The crux of Maxwell's demon as it relates to information is found in the fact that the demon's sorting capacity acts as a kind of recall. For some time, Maxwell's original desire to refute or probabilize the second law was replayed by scientists who thought that massive mnemonic technologies like supercomputers could be devised to perform this task of sorting and storing information in such a way that informational entropy and its consequent debilitating complexity and unpredictability could be avoided. But it was soon shown that, since every technology of repetition and memory was finite, energy would always be expended in the act of destroying information to clear the way for new data.[53] Without an infinite storage capacity, information cannot be kept discrete from noise, and without such sorting and differentiation of noise and message there can only an entropy of the message. The demon, we now see, is thus both necessary and a necessary failure. The activity of segregating meaningful organization from utter randomness, of producing negentropy through a coding of difference, is the basis of life (in terms of the genetic code) and culture, the means by which the second law is confronted by the forces of evolution and consciousness. Yet the struggle against complete noise will always, itself, be transformed by the effects of entropy so that order never achieves absolute power over it. Neither order nor disorder, textuality or performance, can assume the status of an essential power, and so the demon is always a double: a kind of differential effect, a knot or loop produced by and lodged within the transformative space between order and disorder.

States would doubtless caution me that entropy is just another example of the metaphorical "drift" and transitivity of the term *transformation,* yet his description of transformative effects in performance resonate compellingly with what entropy theory now tells us, not only about machines but about the nature of biological and informational systems as well. Further, he locates the dynamics of the most productive transformations in what Crease calls "artistic performance," which is where emergent properties materialize through "actions at the limit of the already controlled and understood."[54] Importantly, this formulation revises significantly the practices of earlier avant-garde theater by insisting that the truly new and surprising emerges at the selvage of what currently constitutes meaning, and thus cannot materialize simply by attempting to forgo meaning entirely. Entropy is deterministic, and the second law among the most powerful produced by science, so the theory creates a ground on which we may base certain knowledge over the process of energy transformation; yet, more so than any other law of physics, entropy also sets limits on what human knowledge can control and understand by rendering phenomena nonlinear, stochastic, and time-irreversible. It is also (to go back to Gell-Man's *The Quark and the Jaguar*) the tour guide on the "adventure from the simple to the complex" because entropy breaks down systems that are highly organized (and thus simple in the sense that a minimum of information is needed to describe their structure) and renders them complex (because the distributions of elements are randomized and thus in need of endlessly more information to describe and map them). As described by Atlan, complexity

> expresses the fact that we do not know, or do not understand a system, despite a background of global knowledge which enables us to recognize and name this system. . . . Complexity implies that we have a global perception of [a system], together with the perception that we do not master it in its details. That's why [complexity] is measured by the information that we do not possess, and would need in order to specify the system in its details.[55]

States similarly aligns the fundamental pleasure of performance with a system that combines both global knowledge and a productive mnemonic powerlessness when he quotes Gerald Edelman's observation, "Memory [itself] is transformational rather than . . . replicative." As States goes on to say:

> Hence the endless ability of "the brain to confront novelty, to generalize upon it, and to adapt it in unforeseen fashions." All perception, all memory, is creative, which is to say adapted to the specifications of the organism, and performative art-making (of all kinds) is one of the extensions of this principle into the collective life of the community.[56]

Thus entropy (as the transformation of matter and information *and* as the transformation of memory) introduces a creative powerlessness, a kind of forgetting that randomizes—or as States suggests, drawing on terms familiar from dramatic theory, that "defamiliarizes," "estranges," or "deconceals"—the known and thereby acts as the clinamen of disorder that frees the system from sterile replication. "Knowledge is made by oblivion," wrote Sir Thomas Browne, "and to purchase a clear and warrantable body of Truth, we must forget and part with much that we know." We understand that such "artistic" knowledge emanates from what Joseph Roach describes in *Cities of the Dead* as "the three-sided relationship of memory, performance and substitution."[57] Tracing performances of what he calls "public acts of forgetting," Roach finds these rituals of surrogation at the source of the construction of complex historical identities. Such an introduction of randomness into a system through (in the case of colonized peoples, enforced) acts of forgetting thus drives the entire cultural system toward dissipation, confusion, and surrogation. These processes in turn push the system to a bifurcation point, at which time they transform the system into one evincing a complexity lying at the edge of the already known. Constituted in part by the imposed repetitions and laws of a dominant class, such identities nevertheless perform unpredictably within hegemonic orders, thus creating strange attractors whose orbits, although constrained by history and power, also fluctuate nonlinearly and thereby complexify them both.

It is perhaps, then, through the kinds of performances that enact such self-organization from chaos that we are offered a model of post-avant-garde practice in both theater and theory, one in which islands of order and the known remain as the trace through which, repeated with the addition of noise, disorder and variety find the means to speak productively. "Repetition," Roach reminds us, "is an art of re-creation as well as restoration,"[58] and the simple affirmation that we create as, and because, signifying systems are (as Newton said of matter) "always apt to be on the decay" allows us to envision modes of performance that operate according to principles of powerlessness and dissipation. A rather shocked Bruno Latour once asked Serres if he were "going to make weakness the prime mover of history," and the response is instructive: "Yes, all human evolution passes by way of this weakness, which creates time and history—even Darwin's time. . . . We advance through problems and not through victories, through failures and rectifications rather than by surpassing."[59] One could hardly imagine a better statement of the aesthetic and ideological purpose behind the performances of Roach's circum-Atlantic cultures, or that of the more conventionally deconstructive spectacles of the Wooster Group and the signifyin' history plays of Suzan-Lori Parks.

In an important essay, "Geographies of Learning," Jill Dolan admits that "theatre studies hasn't yet claimed new metaphors through which to visualize its work."[60] Her suggestion of a "newly mapped geography" based in difference and a "determined inclusion of other(ed) geographies, other(ed) desires, and bodies othered by what hegemony has refused to allow seen" gives us, I believe, a generalized cartography in and through which to seek such metaphors.[61] "Masking" (Gloria Anzaldúa), "unassimilated otherness" (Iris Marion Young), and "world-traveling" (Maria Lugones) all capture for Dolan the necessary sense of identities, positions, and paradigms in transformation and enabled by the act of traversing borders.[62] Yet she also recognizes that "feminist critiques need to account for the political effects of emotion that is compelled on the basis of identification."[63] Difference alone, she indicates, cannot a theater (or politics) make, when the desire for identification, redundancy and order are still felt and politically necessary. Yet, as Dolan notes, we can hardly return to conventional notions of identification based in an uninflected presence or simple collations between self and other. Turning to Elin Diamond's notion that identification is, itself, an act of constant psychic transgression, Dolan finds solace in the fact that (in Diamond's words) "We are constantly taking in objects we desire, continually identifying with them or imitating these objects, and *continually being transformed by them*."[64] Such transformations, says Diamond, are an effect of "temporality," or in the terms of this essay, of the irreversible arrow of time imposed by the entropy principle and its insistence that we respect the leak in the universe, recognize that we must find a means to live in doubt, and yet find purpose in erecting the spider webs of order we construct to capture the avalanche of noise in our attempt to organize it temporarily. In a sense, then, we may through notions like entropy, dissipative structures, and entropy claim the metaphors Dolan seeks, and discover that they are just the right kind of motors to drive us toward the theater and criticism we pursue: for, as the poet Norman Dubie writes, "The four terrific agents of movement are air, earth, metaphor, and water."[65] Interesting that his revision of the fundamental elements places *metaphor* in the position usually reserved for fire, the furnace that returns us to chaos. He might just as well have mentioned peanut butter and jelly.

NOTES

1. Murray Gell-Man, *The Quark and the Jaguar: Adventures in the Simple and the Complex* (New York: W. H. Freeman, 1996), 218.
2. William Worthen, "Disciplines of Performance/Sites of Performance," *Drama Review* 39, no. 1 (1995): 14.
3. Ibid., 15.
4. Ibid., 23, 15.
5. Bert O. States, "Performance as Metaphor," *Theatre Journal* 48 (1996): 3.
6. Worthen, "Disciplines of Performance," 14.
7. Jorge Luis Borges, "Pierre Menard, Author of Don Quixote," in *Ficciones*, trans. Anthony Bonner (New York: Grove Press, 1956), 47.
8. Homi Bhabha, *The Location of Culture* (London: Routledge, 1994), 26.
9. Worthen, "Disciplines of Performance," 23.
10. Ibid.
11. The problem is reminiscent of the debates regarding current historical criti-

cism. Alan Liu, for instance, has written that if history is reduced to a mere play of difference, it can provoke only "Foucauldian laughter, wonder, shock, and irony. . . . But irony is not by itself criticism" (*Wordsworth: The Sense of History* [Palo Alto: Standford University Press, 1989], 457). Foucault, of course, had shown movement from a rather more monolithic view of power as conceived in such early work as *The Order of Things* toward something closer to what I am describing here. See the first volume of *The History of Sexuality:* "Power's condition of possibility . . . must not be sought in the primary existence of a central point, in a unique source of sovereignty from which secondary and descendent forms would emanate; it is the moving substrate of force relations which, by virtue of their inequality, constantly engender states of power, but the latter are always local and unstable" (*The History of Sexuality: An Introduction.* vol. I, trans. Robert Hurley [New York: Pantheon, 1978], 93). The image of power I have before me in this essay has been developed from such passages by critics like Alan Sinfield, as for instance in his formulation of "dissident reading" in *Faultlines: Cultural Materialism and the Politics of Dissident Reading* (Oxford: Clarendon Press, 1992). Sinfield opposes dissident reading to subversive reading because the latter implies that "something was subverted" and that, since hegemony is still evident "containment must have occurred." For Sinfield, dissident reading describes a "refusal of an aspect of the dominant, without prejudging the outcome" (49), and in this regard his view of power seems close to the one I offer here through models of chaos theory and dissipative structure.

12. Herbert Blau, "Forum: Forty-One Letters on Interdisciplinarity in Literary Studies," *PMLA* 111, no. 2 (1996): 275.

13. Barbara Riebling, "Remodeling Truth, Power, and Society: Implications of Chaos Theory, Nonequilibrium Dynamics, and Systems Science for the Study of Politics and Literature," in *After Post-Structuralism: Interdisciplinarity and Literary Theory,* ed. Riebling and Nancy Easterling (Evanston, Ill.: Northwestern University Press, 1993), 178.

14. Riebling, "Remodeling Truth Power, and Society," 178; Blau, "Forum," 275.

15. Bhabha, *The Location of Culture,* 171–72.

16. Blau, "Forum," 275.

17. Ian Stewart and Martin Golubitsky, *Fearful Symmetry: Is God a Geometer?* (London: Penguin, 1993), xix.

18. For an insightful overview of the foundations of such doubts, see Crosbie Smith, *The Science of Energy: A Cultural History of Energy Physics in Victorian Britain* (Chicago: University of Chicago Press, 1998).

19. Michel Serres, *Hermes III: La traduction* (Paris: Minuit, 1974), quoted in William R. Paulson, *The Noise of Culture: Literary Texts in a World of Information* (Ithaca, N.Y.: Cornell University Press, 1988), 45.

20. Blau, "Forum," 274.

21. Ibid., 274–75.

22. Jonathan Kalb, *Beckett in Performance* (Cambridge: Cambridge University Press, 1989), 148.

23. Bruce Clarke, "Allegories of Victorian Thermodynamics," *Configurations* 4, no. 1 (1996): 80.

24. William Thomson, Lord Kelvin, *Mathematical and Physical Papers* (1881), vol. 1 (Cambridge: Cambridge University Press, 1911), 514.

25. N. Katherine Hayles, *Chaos Bound: Orderly Disorder in Contemporary Literature and Science* (Ithaca, N.Y.: Cornell University Press, 1990), 43; Clarke, "Allegories of

Victorian Thermodynamics"; Peter Allen Dale, *In Pursuit of a Scientific Culture: Science, Art, and Society in the Victorian Age* (Madison: University of Wisconsin Press, 1989), 130–36, 225–32; Greg Myers, "Nineteenth-Century Popularizations of Thermodynamics and the Rhetoric of Social Prophecy," in *Energy and Entropy: Science and Culture in Victorian Britain,* ed. Patrick Brantlinger (Bloomington: Indiana University Press, 1989): 307–38; Paulson, *The Noise of Culture,* 35–36; Crosbie Smith, "Natural Philosophy and Thermodynamics: William Thomson and 'The Dynamical Theory of Heat,'" *British Journal of the Philosophy of Science* 1 (1976): 293–319.

26. Maxwell originally called the sorting agent simply a "neat-fingered being": the anthropomorphism was supplied by Kelvin, and as late as three years later Maxwell voiced a preference for conceiving of the demon as simply a "valve." See Clarke, "Allegories of Victorian Thermodynamics," 68–72.

27. Hayle, *Chaos Bound,* 42.

28. Werner Heisenberg, *The Physicist's Conception of Nature,* trans. Arnold Pomerans (New York: Harcourt, Brace and World, 1958), 36.

29. Michel Serres, "The Origin of Language: Biology, Information Theory, and Thermodynamics," in *Hermes: Literature, Science, Philosophy,* ed. and trans. Josué Harari and David F. Bell (Baltimore: Johns Hopkins University Press, 1982), 71.

30. Ibid.

31. Ibid., 71–72.

32. Antonin Artaud, *The Theater and Its Double,* trans. Mary Caroline Richards (New York: Grove Press, 1958), 55.

33. Aristotle, *Poetics,* trans. S. H. Butcher, in *Criticism: The Major Texts,* ed. W. J. Bate (New York: Harcourt Brace Jovanovich, 1970), X.

34. Filippo Tommaso Marinetti, "The Variety Theatre," trans. R. W. Flint, in *Futurist Performance,* ed. Michael Kirby and Victoria Nes Kirby (New York: Performing Arts Journal Publications, 1971), 183, 181. For the modernist uses of machines, see Hugh Kenner, *The Counterfeiters* (New York: Doubleday/Anchor, 1973).

35. Serres, "The Origin of Language," 73.

36. Serres, "Turner Translates Carnot," in *Hermes,* 58.

37. Günther Berghaus, *Futurism and Politics: Between Anarchist Rebellion and Fascist Reaction, 1909–1944* (Oxford: Berghahn, 1996), 21.

38. See for instance Bert O. States's comment that "the true performance of performance art occurs between whatever form it takes and the background presuppositions whose gravitational pull it sought to escape. . . . I see nothing essentially original about performance art, by which I mean only that it isn't doing anything different from what art has always done: waged an eternal struggle against the strangulations of its own repetitions" ("Performance as Metaphor," 11 n. 41).

39. David Porish, "Literature as Dissipative Structure," in *Literature and Technology,* ed. Mark L. Greenberg and Lance Schachterle, Research in Technology Studies 5 (London: Associated University Presses, 1992), 298.

40. The brilliant exception to such bachelor logic is Duchamp, whose *The Bride Stripped Bare by Her Bachelors, Even or Large Glass* (begun in 1915 and left unfinished in 1923) has been cleverly analyzed by Linda Darymple Henderson as an allegory of various modernist scientific discourses. See "Ethereal Bride and Mechanical Bachelors: Science and Allegory in Marcel Duchamp's *Large Glass,*" *Configurations* 4, no. 1 (1966): 91–120.

41. See Stuart Kaufmann, *At Home in the Universe: The Search for the Laws of Self-Organization and Complexity* (Oxford: Oxford University Press, 1995).

42. Serres, "Turner Translates Carnot," 61.

43. There are now several score books available that explain chaos theory for the nonscientist. See for instance the following: Mitchell Waldrop, *Complexity: The Emerging Science at the Edge of Order and Chaos* (London: Penguin, 1994); Roger Lewin, *Complexity: Life on the Edge of Chaos* (London: Phoenix, 1993); David Ruelle, *Chance and Chaos* (London: Penguin, 1993); Stephen Kellert, *In the Wake of Chaos: Unpredictable Order in Dynamical Systems* (Chicago: University of Chicago Press, 1993); Nina Hall, ed., *Exploring Chaos: A Guide to the New Science of Disorder* (New York: Norton, 1991); John Briggs and F. David Peat, *The Turbulent Mirror* (New York: Harper and Row, 1989) and James Gleick, *Chaos: The Making of a New Science* (New York: Penguin, 1987).

44. Bruce J. West, "Chaos and Related Things," *Journal of Mind and Behavior* 18, nos. 2–3 (1997): 106.

45. Michel de Certeau, *The Practice of Everyday Life,* trans. Steven Randall (Berkeley and Los Angeles: University of California Press, 1984), 95. Bruce Clarke writes that the demon appears in updated form in literary theory as "a mythopoeic code for uncertain intermediations—the uncanny or disruptive supplement, the noise or excess infecting or reorganizing transmission in matters of reason, cognition, writing, self-identity, desire and so forth" ("Allegories of Victorian Thermodynamics," 69).

46. States, "Performance as Metaphor," 13.

47. Ibid., 8.

48. Richard Crease, *The Play of Nature: Experimentation as Performance* (Bloomington: Indiana University Press, 1993), 22.

49. States, "Performance as Metaphor," 21.

50. West, "Chaos and Related Things," 106.

51. "The general theorem about entropy, 'disorder can only increase in an isolated system,' amounts to saying that noise can only degrade the orderliness of the message; it cannot increase the particularized information; it destroys *intent.*" Moles, *Information Theory and Esthetic Perception,* trans. J. Cohen (Urbana: University of Illinois Press, 1966), 86.

52. Quoted in Paulson, *The Noise of Culture,* 110.

53. Hayles, *Chaos Bound,* 46–47.

54. States, "Performance as Metaphor," 22.

55. Quoted in Paulson, *The Noise of Culture,* 108.

56. States, "Performance as Metaphor," 21–22.

57. Joseph Roach, *Cities of the Dead* (New York: Columbia University Press, 1996), 2.

58. Ibid., 286.

59. Michel Serres and Bruno Latour, *Conversations on Science, Culture, and Time,* trans. Roxanne Lapidus (Ann Arbor: University of Michigan Press, 1995), 188.

60. Jill Dolan, "Geographies of Learning," *Theatre Journal* 45 (1993): 418.

61. Ibid., 421.

62. Ibid., 436–39.

63. Ibid., 439.

64. Elin Diamond, "The Violence of 'We': Politicizing Identification," in *Critical Theory and Performance,* ed. Janelle Reinelt and Joseph Roach (Ann Arbor: University of Michigan Press, 1992), 396.

65. Norman Dubie, *Clouds of Magellan* (Santa Fe: Recursos Press, 1991), 13.

III. Textual Spaces, Theatrical Spaces, and Avant-Garde Performance

Mike Sell

Bad Memory: Text, Commodity, Happenings

(Mis)remembering the Happenings

Allan Kaprow, the artist and pragmatist who coined the term *happening,* once described the Happenings as "the myth of an art that is nearly unknown and, for all practical purposes, unknowable."[1] In order to understand the peculiar, chaotic, philosophically petulant edge of the performance form that arose in the shared margins of avant-garde painting and theater in Manhattan during the late 1950s and 1960s, we must understand how the phenomenological processes of remembering and forgetting were exploited within the Happenings, how "being unknowable" was aided and abetted by a politicization of memory within American capitalist culture that accompanied the development of mass media such as radio, film, and television. By considering the ways in which the Happenings (a term I use to include the performance dimension of the Fluxus collective as well as destruction-oriented events of all kinds)[2] challenged memory and critical judgment, we will be able to place the Happenings within a marginalized tradition of antitextualist, avant-garde performance that includes the likes of Elsa von Freytag-Loringhoven, Arthur Cravan, and Johannes Baader on the margins of dada and surrealism, and Neal Cassady among the Beats and the counterculture, "artists of everyday life and small-time scandal" who courted fame but refused any but the most ambiguous and shifting presence within the precincts of literary history. Like Freytag-Loringhoven and her colleagues, the Happenings made only fitful liaisons with the literary text, considering it merely the pretext for much more significant artistic production. The work of Kaprow, Claes Oldenberg, Emmett Williams, Alison Knowles, Jill Johnston, and others compelled a "fetishization of the text" that attempted to cause a pleasurable, often ironic failure of memory and narrative coherence. Thus, their work marks the limits to a certain kind of literary history: that is, that which depends on the text, shared critical standards, and linear models of history.

Memory was disrupted by the fragmented "structure" of the Happenings. In his memoir of life in New York's East Village during the 1960s, Samuel Delaney describes his experience as a "participant-member" of Allan

Kaprow's *Eighteen Happenings in Six Parts,* the event—part theater, part collage, part dada, part thought-experiment—that introduced the term *happening* into the American cultural stream. "The only truly clear memory I have of the performance proper," Delaney writes, "was that I wasn't very sure when, exactly, it began."[3] Delaney does remember, if less precisely, the tiny loft (recently become the "Reubens gallery") divided into three distinct chambers by mostly opaque pine and polyethylene flats. He remembers the windup toy chattering and clicking around the floor. Most significantly, he remembers his unsatisfiable desire to know what was going on on the other side of the flats. Typical of most Happenings, the performative gestures and stage properties of Kaprow's piece were not linked together in any logical or even systematically illogical way. They moved and transformed, as Michael Kirby was to describe them a few years later, in an "a-logical" way.[4] Even though most of the Happenings were rehearsed and planned with great care, in the moment of performance things tended to "just happen." Many of those things that just happened were noticed by only a few of the spectators—and perhaps not by the critics, academics, and historians who were present.

There is a lot that doesn't make it into Delaney's account of Kaprow's piece that one might find in other accounts—the persons marching rigidly in single file, the malfunctioning slide show, the violins and ukuleles played badly, the fractured dialogue of two women muffled by the flats—but that is to be expected. Delaney might not have known they were there; Kaprow split the audience up so that no spectator could achieve a synoptic vision of the piece; moreover, he cluttered each "part" of the happening with a unique hodgepodge of sound and lighting effects, nonsensical gestures, and incongruous stage properties—all of which were prone to the improvisations and accidents of the performance. Delaney's rather fetishistic focus on the little robot couldn't be helped; one of the necessary effects of Kaprow's particular variety of Happenings is the pressure it put on the viewer's ability to organize, narrate, and, above all, to remember.

Such bad memory was not, however, debilitating. It could prove enormously empowering to individual expression. As a writer of autobiography, Delaney uses his bad memory of Kaprow's piece and his expertise in postmodernist theory to empower his understanding of his place within the complex relationship of capitalism, memory, and the Greenwich Village community in the late 1950s. Delaney informs us that in 1956, three years before Kaprow's seminal event, white-collar workers in the United States exceeded in number blue-collar and agricultural workers combined, signaling a shift in the class structure of American culture and supplying a first clear indicator of the advent of a so-called postindustrial era.[5] Though he does not specify how inflated milk prices and mass-transit tokens were related to his inability to criticize or remember Kaprow's happening properly, he insists on their connection, relying on rhetorical conjunction to support his assertion. Recalling his feelings about the event, he writes:

> I, of course, had expected the "six parts" to be chronologically successive, like acts in a play or parts in a novel—not spatially deployed, separate, and simultaneous, like rooms in a hotel or galleries in a museum. I'd expected a unified theatrical audience before some temporally bounded theatrical whole. But it was precisely in this subversion of expectations about the "proper" aesthetic employment of time, space, presence, absence, wholeness, and fragmentation, as well as the general locatability of "what happens," that made Kaprow's work signify: his happenings—clicking toys, burning candles, pounded drums, or whatever—were organized in that initial work very much like historical events.[6]

Likewise, the audience was organized very much like the massed but isolated individual characteristic of the Cold War. The texture of Kaprow's Happening as a whole is actually an aggregate of the individual responses and partial views of the audience, an audience that includes ourselves, historians and critics four decades after the fact. The Happenings function as a theatrical version of what Roland Barthes called the "writerly" text, the text that foregrounds the desires of a reader invested with genuine "author-ity." Like the writerly text, the Happenings allowed themselves to be altered and reconfigured by the spectator, to be "put forth as a force" in the world.[7] The individual elements and memories of Delaney's particular experience in the audience act as if they, like common commodities such as milk and tokens, had been subjected to inflationary pressure, as if words, gestures, and windup toys were expanding under some deep and unsuspected shift in the cultural weather systems of self, community, and history. To adequately analyze a particular Happening, one would have to understand, among other factors, the particular community of participant-members that were in attendance.

Like milk and subway tokens, the signifiers and acts of signification in Kaprow's Happening were torn from the associations that commonly surrounded them, were torn from their traditional conceptual matrices of subjectivity, sociality, and tradition, from the commonly held information structures of memory and value that are commonly known as plot, character, and moral.[8] Divorced—or "de-matrixed," to use Michael Kirby's important term[9]—from their traditional context by the aesthetic hiatus of performance, a toy robot's connotative meanings (childhood, ingenuity, science-fiction B movies, automation) could be set wandering like displaced laborers, a few of which migrated close to Samuel Delaney and were critically "reinvested" in a book about Greenwich Village, the 1960s, and Samuel Delaney published many years later (and discovered by myself some years after that, etc.).

I do not want to forget the generally positive implications of Delaney's critical performance as member-participant in Kaprow's Happening, nor how his experience dovetails with Barthes's description of the empowered reader, nor how his autobiography functions as a kind of reinvested memory. Nevertheless, I would suggest that the politics—the embodied and critical experience of self, community, and history—of the Happenings were intimately bound to the alienating and repressive dynamics of American capitalism in the late 1950s. Empowered as Delaney and his fellow spectator-participants might have been in some regards, they faced the same kinds of conceptual difficulties most people experience within capitalist culture, dominated as it is by the unprecedented dynamic of ignorance and forgetting sponsored by the culture industry.

I tend to agree with critics who argue that such ignorance and forgetting is part and parcel of the development of commodity culture. However, unlike Theodor Adorno or Guy Debord, I tend to think the commodity's politics are difficult to define once and for all. As a form of communication, the commodity can encompass incredibly diverse contexts in deceptively seamless fashion, challenging our sense of meaning and value—occasionally in profoundly progressive fashion. As I will demonstrate, the communicative experience of commodification parallels the communicative experience of audiences at Happenings. By recognizing the pressures that the Happenings placed—and continue to place—on communication, memory and criticism, we can begin to comprehend how they functioned as an effective tactic to modify and reform capitalism without wholly abandoning the logic of capitalism. The use, abuse, and fetishization of texts—scripts, scores, treatises, memoirs—within Happenings reflect this urge to modify and reform capitalism without wholly abandoning it. When, in *The Smiling Workman* (Judson Church, 1960), Jim Dine drank the paint with which he had written "I LOVE WHAT IM [*sic*]" just a few moments earlier and then crashed through that text into an offstage space, he was announcing a bickersome, if pleasurable marriage of performance, antitextualism, and vanguard consumerism.

As Dine's full-body transgression of the text suggests, the Happenings worked within the dominant cultural logic of their time, a logic that, as advertised by Madison Avenue and promoted by industry, promoted the new, the exciting, the spontaneous—and the systematic forgetting of self, community, and history. The end of the 1950s marked the birth in the United States of a kind of "regime of spontaneity" that favored the improvisational and impermanent as a strategic means of growing the American market. Given this contradictory situation—for nothing is so contradictory as marketed freedom—it is no surprise that the Happenings reflected, appropriated, and diverted the logic of this regime in highly ambiguous and ironic ways. The Happenings exploited a cultural logic that alienated the self (as do aggressive marketing, standardized production, fascinating commodities, and overwhelming media events); deconstructed assumptions concerning self, community, and history (the "severing of traditional bonds" in which capitalism specializes); and promised an irresistible cosmopolitanism (as did the military-industrial complex and the "nuclear continuum"). Much like the innovations of capitalism, the Happenings promised new possibilities of expression, new forms of discourse, new qualities of subjectivity—but at the cost of unified critical and historical perspective.

The innovative commodity, as both a metaphor of American abundance, as material proof of that abundance, and as a suggestive and flexible stage property, supplied an ambivalent weapon to the post–World War II American avant-garde, one not available to other contra-capitalist avant-gardes such as dada, Meyerholdian constructivism, or surrealism. The Happenings demonstrate a kind of "strategic self-commodification" enabled by the sheer quantity of commodified goods and the pervasiveness of the capitalist logic of alienation and obsolescence in the Manhattan community. Such a strategy empowered the Happenings people to create an art form that retrieved objects and energies from the calcifying matrix of American capitalist subjectivity, sociality, and tradition—from its information structure of memory and value—in order to enable a degree of subversive spontaneity for their audiences and a certain degree of invulnerability from critical judgment for the artists and artworks. For the Happenings people, the commodity was more than metaphor—it was, terrifyingly, all there was.

The Avant-Garde of Capitalism

The Happenings were not the first movement in modern times to exploit the ambivalencies of capitalism.[10] In "Modernism and Mass Culture," Thomas Crow argues that the historical advent of the avant-garde is inseparable from the self-divestiture of political power by the French middle classes during the crisis of 1848 to 1852. The takeover by Louis Bonaparte signaled not only the rise to power of a "law and order" regime uncannily similar to those of our own times, but also the cultural effects of the domestic re-entrenchment of surplus capital following the defeat of Napoleon's armies earlier in the century. The fortunate offspring of this class crisis were the impressionists, artists who capitalized, so to speak, on new forms and places of perception, expression, leisure, and freedom. As Crow argues, the parks, prostitutes, and cabarets so dear to the early impressionists embodied forms of liberty that compensated for the compelled sharing of political power with what we would now call the "military-industrial complex." It was the impressionists who pioneered that quirky anticulture we call the "avant-garde," though the military-inspired epithet wouldn't be appended until after the far more radical crises of the great depression of the 1870s and 1880s.[11]

The situation in lower Manhattan a century later was rather different. After all, the American 1950s was an age of conformity and smooth, rapid economic expansion; conformity buttressed by the growth of television networks and the systematic purging of liberals from all levels of the power structure; expansion enabled by the creation of overseas markets and—crucially—the intensive marketing of everyday life within the United States. The Happenings therefore mark an effective, if momentary, response to a brief conjuncture of the long-standing relationship among (1) resistant forms of play and consumption, (2) the commodification of those forms of play and consumption by an innovative capitalism, and (3) highly performative forms of representation. The text—script, score, treatise, and memoir—helped to mediate these distinct forms. The performances of those texts helped to explode the contradictions that flowed among them.[12]

Though it is certainly true that Carolee Schneemann's *Meat Joy* (Judson Church, 1964) was in no way a meditation on Hegelian idealism or the tactical limitations of working-class organizations, it certainly confronted the paradoxical pleasures of the American economy. The simultaneously titillating and repulsive "flesh celebration" of young bodies covered in the bloody scraps Schneemann had recovered from the small butcher's shop around the corner certainly reflects the vertiginous forms of alienation and liberty available in an age of McDonald's hamburgers, *Playboy*, abstract expressionism, and the early echoes of radical feminism. The devalorization of the art object, the courting of scandal, and the deconstruction of critical perspective are traditional tactical moves of the avant-garde artist against the invasive forces of capitalism. But unlike the dadaists, who could count on the shock caused by the presence of garbage, kitsch, and vulgarity in art contexts, the Happenings people had to work in a context in which everything was becoming a commodity (especially the work of the dadaists, newly rediscovered in the 1950s by Manhattan museums and collectors), regardless of its status vis-à-vis high culture, low culture, or refuse. This was by no means an entirely negative situation; it guaranteed certain kinds of freedom as well. As Tom Frank has written, "When business leaders cast their gaze . . . around them [in the late 1950s], they saw both a reflection of their own struggle against the stifling bureaucratic methods of the past and an affirmation of a new dynamic consumerism that must replace the old."[13] Taking into account the vigor of capitalism during the era, with the exception of the breathtaking recession of 1957–58, the American 1960s proves in retrospect to be not only an era of political liberation, struggle, and the rise of new social movements; it was also an era of unprecedented capitalist saturation, market expansion, and popular subversion.

The Happenings are inconceivable outside the context of this expansion and saturation; for they confronted the structures and habits that shielded everyday life from commodification and reification, structures and habits that were precisely the targets of Madison Avenue—most notably, art and the basic banality of everyday life. Like the judo artist who uses the momentum of the enemy against that enemy, the Happenings attempted to divert the invasive momentum of postwar capitalism. While the market attempted to exploit and control by way of an intensive saturation of daily life by the commodity form, the Happenings attempted to expand and liberate daily life. They did this by appropriating the logic of the commodity for other purposes; namely, the expansion of our concept of artistic merit and the rejection of tradition (except as a fund of materials to use and abuse at will). As Richard Schechner once put it, "A very interesting basic freedom is involved" in art that appropriates the degraded materials of Madison Avenue.[14] If fantasy and daily life could be commodified, the Happenings person asked, then why don't we just start doing it ourselves and on our own terms and in such a way that only the participants themselves can possibly understand it?

As painter and performance artist Claes Oldenberg described this odd situation, "one could be anti-bourgeois by being bourgeois. It got very complicated."[15] The scandal of the Happenings is that not only did they blur the line between art and life, but between art and commodity, life and commodity, and—horror of horrors—the avant-garde artist and the entrepreneurial capitalist. Schneemann's *Meat Joy* combined Artaud, Beat poetry, and the sensory assault of the meat market and certainly embodied a profound ambivalence toward consumption and production. As Delaney demonstrates to us in his memoir, the contradictory feelings evoked by the Happenings—in the case of *Meat Joy,* disgust and titillation—do not allow traditional kinds of history or criticism, only highly individualistic, paradoxical forms of "bad memory." The impact of revulsion and titillation is contradictory, unassimilable.

By situating the Happenings within a shockingly intrusive mass-mediated capitalism, we can better understand the politics of their formal innovations and their impact on memory. The first of these innovations was identified by Michael Kirby in his foundational essay "The New Theater." In that essay, Kirby describes the Happenings' utilization of objects, bodies, and language without regard to narrative logic or totalizing critical perspective (what he called "abandoned information structures") as a kind of "de-matrixing" of signifiers from their traditional contexts. Examining Happenings such as Kaprow's, Kirby argues that the epitomous innovation of the form is the dematrixing or "liberation" of objects, bodies, and signifiers from their expected roles and relations. In Kaprow's germinal event, for example, the conversation of women, the playing of music, the splashing of paint, even the audience itself functioned as "things-in-themselves," circulating like displaced workers or newly minted coins. In a typically minimalist Fluxus event such as George Brecht's *Word Event* of 1961 ("Exit"), an action is itself the content of the artistic work, rendered valuable and desirable at the very moment of its disappearance and silence.

The second formal principle of the Happenings is "participation," best described by Richard Schechner in his recently reprinted *Environmental Theater.* In his chapter on participation, Schechner asks, "What happens to a performance when the usual agreements between performer and spectator are broken?"[16] As he demonstrates, quite a bit happens; in fact, when the bodies and desires of the audience are made part of the performance and, as a result, the ability to fully plan or even complete a performance is endangered, narrative structure, aesthetic presumptions, and, most significantly, critical judgment are put to the stake. In the case of Happenings that split the audience up into small groups, or chased them with lawnmowers, or wrapped them in aluminum foil and hung them by their feet in the New Jersey woods (techniques used in some of Kaprow's other Happenings), the "usual agreements" regarding the role of the theater spectator in the recognition of form and meaning were simply abandoned. As a result, diverse forms of critical judgment and aesthetic pleasure were allowed to bloom like the proverbial thousand flowers. The critic became a stage property and the audience member a performer.

By dematrixing objects, actions, and signifiers from their traditional contexts, the Happenings people dialectically inverted the ontological and epistemological pressures of commodification. The commodity, after all, is itself a dematrixed object; as Marx demonstrated, the commodity has no intrinsic relationship to its context of consumption nor any trace of its context of production. As a result, the commodity enables that seductive and ultimately oppressive form of "bad memory" known as "commodity fetishism."[17] By utilizing the risky rhythms of audience participation, the Happenings people dialectically inverted the pressures of social management. Social management, after all, is a form of participation; but as Marx demonstrated, such participation entails no memory, no tradition, no real freedom.

The characterization of the 1960s as an era of simultaneous liberation and control sheds light on the politics of Happenings and Fluxus; in particular, a number of very brief scripts written and performed by Alison Knowles, scripts and performances that engage with the commodity logic and divert its invasive force through ironic performance and aesthetic production. In the early 1960s, Knowles created a number of performance scripts designed to dissolve the boundaries between the public and the private, between a cosmopolitan, transnational realm of value and fame (the realm of idealized and aestheticized capital; i.e. art) and the banal, cyclical spaces of domestic labor (labor rarely acknowledged in capitalist systems). In works such as *Proposition* of 1962 ("Make a Salad") and *Variation #1 on Proposition* of 1964 ("Make a Soup") mutual deconstruction occurs between art and the everyday rhythms of the domestic space. Such works were intended to challenge certain conceptual and economic distinctions such as that between the "serious" and the "not serious" or between "beauty" and "taste." In these pieces, the pretense or hiatus of aesthetic perception enables the abstract quality of the performance script to stand in a dynamic dialectical relationship with (1) the singular, unrepeatable, absolutely contextual qualities of the performance and with (2) the private pleasures and conflicts of domestic space.

This tension is emphasized in Knowles's *Child Art Piece* of 1962: "The performer is a single child, two or three years old. One or both parents may be present to help him with a pail of water, a banana, etc. When the child leaves the stage, the performance is over." The presence of an untrained, potentially volatile performer in the charged and unsettling context of performance (1) threatens intention and expertise, (2) compels recognition that the ontological and epistemological challenges of performance are integral to the world of child-rearing, and (3) reveals how the pressures of artistic innovation have invaded the home, threatening to reorganize family relationships. Perhaps the most suggestive use of Knowles's scripts is in the home by nonartists. By allowing the logic of artistic production to inform domestic labor, Knowles allows a space for consideration and criticism to open—a kind of lacuna or appendix in the American historical memory (and we must recall that the linear, "great man" vision of history still predominated in American schools and universities). Like a new washing machine or fondue set, Knowles's scripts and the ethic they embody enter the home and quietly reorganize it. Not surprisingly, the logic established by Knowles's microscripts supplied a number of effective conceptual and organizational tactics for the burgeoning feminist movement.

The Text as a Fetish/Performance as Subversive History Writing

If the Happenings as *events* demonstrate a kind of "strategic self-commodification" in their use of objects and audience, the texts that have survived the era of Happenings enable other forms of critical subversion. Like the Happenings themselves, the textual remains possess a peculiar power to disrupt and reorganize memory. In the case of the texts left to us by Fluxus—a group always conscious of the inevitability of commodification—this power is simultaneously exploited and preserved. Thus, our readings of Fluxus scripts are "micro-Happenings" that empower and surprise the reader in a fashion Barthes would have appreciated.

The complex interconnections of intentional misremembering, avant-garde performance, and the text are exemplified by a fascinating bit of graffiti that can be discovered on the Internet, downloaded, printed, and taped to the wall next to one's desk (http://www.panix.com/~fluxus/FLUXUS_ONLINE/FLUXON_ART/WRITE/Dont_Let_It_Be_Forgot/_Emmett_William3.JPEG). In its original form, the graffito isn't all that impressive: a small sheet of paper with a machine-printed poem and a handwritten addendum at its bottom. But when we examine the dynamic of reading sponsored by the piece, we discover not only something significant about the Happenings, but also something about ourselves and the place of criticism. The piece comes to us by way of the Fluxus artist Emmett Williams (I assume it's his handwriting on the original), known best for his 1961 event *Duet for Performer and Audience:*

> Performer waits silently on stage for audible reaction from audience which he imitates.

And there is his 1962 event *For La Monte Young:*

> Performer asks if La Monte Young is in the audience.

A duplicate version of Williams's little paean to the golden age of post–World War II American performance still retains a certain capacity to fascinate, to draw one into a potentially endless reverie on history, performance, and memory. It accomplishes this by defacing one of the more pernicious and promising myths of history (the Kennedy "Camelot") with a highly personal, even petulant, mark or trace—the monument is marked with graffiti. Appropriating the myth of Camelot—what one might call the "Kennedy commodity"—Williams defaces it, at once undermining its monumentality and inflating the significance of his own presence in the early 1960s.

"Don't let it be forgot
That there was once a spot
For one brief, shining moment
Called ~~Camelot~~."
FLUXUS

Williams's graffito is an historiographical and critical gesture in perfect accord with the spirit of Happenings, a highly performative meditation on the relationship of memory, commodity, and text. Because it condenses these tensions, it functions as a kind fetish, simultaneously distancing the event and bringing it breathtakingly close. And the original is worth quite a bit of money.

A kind of Happenings script in disguise, Williams's text compels its reader to perform the relationship of memory, valuable/antique commodity, and text. It presses us to abandon the clarity of concept and theory in favor of more personal forms of consideration similar to those that performers in the original Happenings attempted to inspire. Such nontraditional, but highly charged ways of conceiving performance are put to effective use by Knowles in *Proposition;* in that case, in the energetic and quiet dynamic of habitual actions (cutting greens for a salad), situated cravings (no radishes tonight, please, I had them for lunch), social concern (but does *she* want radishes?), brute necessity (if I don't eat soon, I'll die), and purified action (the quiet of the act itself which, if entered completely, may cause us to ignore realities such as the burning lasagna and the hushed conversation in the other room). By placing domestic labor and the banal pleasures of so-called private life at center stage, Knowles challenges our notions of artistic significance and interiority, deconstructing the lines between private and public. Like Williams's performative defacement of myth, Knowles's *Proposition* allows the situation of the performer to serve as a lever against critical assumptions concerning artistic excellence and timelessness. Like Williams's document, the original script of *Proposition* is worth a great deal of money.

Such nontraditional ways of conceiving anticapitalist performance often functioned effectively within and against specific performances of Happenings texts, allowing the relations among the artists to serve as fodder for situational criticism of the artistic community itself. Such criticism occurred in a performance of John Cage's *Music Walk.* Unlike the original 1958 performance, which featured Cage and David Tudor, the 1962 performance at the Manhattan YM-YWHA featured a "dancer," Jill Johnston. Johnston describes the performance as a high point in her career as a performer.[18] Cage characterized the piece as "a composition indeterminate of its performance." *Music Walk,* in this case modified into *Music Walk with Dancer,* was performed according to an arrangement of ten graphs whose intersections determined the characteristics of sound and action that would be performed in some fashion by the performers. Johnston relates that she forgot her script (her stack of cards fell in a puddle on the way to the event, ruining them and forcing her to improvise). Rather than sticking to what she remembered about the script—in which she was to "do a slight dance action on stage, slow and vampy (wearing heels, a floppy hat, and red dress)," she decided to utilize other memories and "went mainly as a Mother."[19]

I will not ask whether Johnston accidentally or purposively forgot her cards. It is certainly true, as she puts it, that she "took the 'life-art' equation seriously then." She writes, "I was a critic moonlighting as a mother of two small children, or vice versa. I chose a number of sound-action implements that I moved around my apartment every day: a frying pan and bacon, a Savarin coffee can, a broom, a baby bottle with brush, a pull-toy, vacuum cleaner, etc."[20] Surprisingly, her improvisations annoyed Cage: "[A]fterwards, Cage reprimanded me for not 'giving up my ego,' meaning acting on my own, by choice, according to my likes and preferences [which, I assume that Cage assumed, involved vamping in high heels]. But of course, the carload of household equipment I brought with me, like his pianos and radios, already indicated plenty about choices we had made in our lives, whether 'preferences' or not."[21]

By insisting on the critical significance of her experience (an increasingly important political gesture as the 1960s progressed) as fundamentally more important than any preexisting communicative or aesthetic structure and exploiting the opportunities for improvisation in the script and performance context, Johnston forced the event to answer to her needs, to her situation, to her own memories. Johnston utilized the peculiar capabilities of the Happening against itself, ironically reminding Cage, the founding father and chief guru of the Happenings, that despite the fact that certain artists and certain audiences are no longer making essential distinctions between art and nonart activities, the relations between art and nonart are no less in need of continued interrogation. In short, the line between art and life must be continually examined and continually subverted. As Kaprow wrote in "The Education of the Un-Artist, Part I," "The art-not-art dialectic is essential."[22]

As Johnston's critical subversion of Cage's graphs suggests, the textual remains of the happening are essentially unstable and continually available for critical interrogation. But unlike most texts, the textual remains of the Happenings compel us to *perform* that instability and interrogation, compel us to spatialize and temporalize our readings. Because they demand a deconstruction of the distinctions between artist and audience, expert and amateur, public and private, the peculiar, hitherto private desires and fantasies of the critic are compelled to enter the field of criticism. Claes Oldenberg demonstrates how such fantastic, fetishistic criticism might function. Ruminating on the textual remains of the various Happenings that were created in the performances he staged at the Ray Gun Mfg Co, Oldenberg called them "Love objects. respect objects. Objectivity high state of feeling" [*sic*].[23] As he diddled about his combination small business/gallery/performance space after his performances, he pondered the "subordinated pieces which may be isolated, souvenirs, residual objects."[24] And he reminded himself that he must "be very careful about what is to be discarded and what still survives by itself. Slow study & respect for small things . . . Picking up after is creative."[25]

Oldenberg's souvenirs, much like Williams's graffito, seem to embody the kind of longing described by Susan Stewart: "[T]he direction of force in the desiring narrative is always a future-past, a deferment of experience in the direction of origin and . . . eschaton."[26] The paradoxical tension of characterless, iconic form and the traces of the producer's hand in these souvenirs of performance would seem to mirror Stewart's understanding of the "pure semiotic": "Hence the notion of a 'pure semiotic' realm of exchange, a realm analogous to the most reductive account of a pure 'poetic language' (Hugo Ball, for example), would find its locus in the gift shop and in the deliberate superfluousness of 'tokens of affection.'"[27] However, Stewart's description of the "affective commodity" does not wholly fit Oldenberg's simultaneously endearing and threatening hamburgers or Williams's incomplete obliteration of Camelot.

In his gallery/store, Oldenberg modeled a form of critical activity; in this case, his personal desires and situations inevitably inform his consideration of performance and text, rendering a peculiarly anecdotal, taste-versus-concept-oriented form of critical consideration. Moreover, both the artist and his artworks self-consciously engage with their status as commodities. The Happenings text becomes a "love object," a "respect object"—and a souvenir for sale. Performance, for Oldenberg, was a productive process, an historical event, and a critical self-analysis. The resulting art object (say, a script or a Day-Glo ice-cream cone) is a commodity, a memory, and a critical/historiographical statement. The resulting art object therefore compels new Happenings. The ice-cream cone as conceived by Oldenberg is a combination text/art object/fetish that allows for a diverse variety of readerly performances:

> There is first the ice-cream cone as it is. This would be one imitation. Then begins a series of parallel representations which are not the ice-cream cone but nevertheless realistic or objective: f. ex. the ice-cream cone in a newspaper ad. The ice-cream cone or any other popular shape as a fetish object. The ice-cream cone in altered scale (giant). The ice-cream cone as a symbol etc. Only the created object—my parallel cone—will include and/or concentrate several of these.[28]

Such an ice-cream cone, as the objective remainder of a specific performance at Oldenberg's studio, is a complex condensation of multiple meanings, emotions, histories, economies, and memories, at once a script, a stage property, and a souvenir. Oldenberg's hope was that such souvenirs would somehow retain the fundamentally "organic and psychological" qualities of the production context.[29] For Oldenberg, the Happening was the liberated zone that the artist opened in the rifts between the standardized, characterless objects of consumer culture and the deeply contextual gesture of the hand.

Such entanglement of text, memory, and desire was one experience aimed at by Ben Vautier in his *Audience Variation No. 1* (date unknown):

> The audience is all tied up together using a long string. Performers in the aisles use balls of string, throwing string over the heads of the audience to opposite rows of performers. Balls are thrown until all the string is used up in creating a dense web over the audience. Enough string must be used to entangle the whole audience, tying them to each other, to their chairs, etc., making it difficult for them to leave. After this has been achieved, the performers leave the hall. The audience is left to untangle itself.

Like the participant-members of Vautier's event, historical study of the Happenings is inevitably tangled up with an unruly, one-time-only hodgepodge of competing interests, tiny turf wars, and absent artists—many of these insistent pressures on the scholar's own work. Whatever perspective can be shed on the experience will be partial—this is critical common sense. But such partiality veers into fetishism in the Happenings. Like the toy burro one might purchase on the rim of the Grand Canyon, criticism of Vautier's event should be precious, partial, perhaps too personal to be widely meaningful, a kind of souvenir of the performative moment. As Vautier's piece demonstrates, the Happenings press their viewers to abandon the kinds of historiography and formal analysis favored by university departments in favor of essentially anecdotal forms of "bad memory" or essentially abstract forms of theoretical consideration.

Williams's document, like virtually all Fluxus and Happenings scripts and scores (and all the memoirs and treatises surrounding them) is, to invoke a complex notion, a fetish. Texts like Williams's, Knowles's, or Vautier's are crises in miniature, souvenirs of production, objective correlatives of bad memory that demand performance and new Happenings. The texts that have survived the Happenings are purposefully tangled with myth, memory, and the scholar's own desires. And if they are not tangled, then the criticism is indecorous, off-target, and rude. Rather, the scholarly work of untangling the various meanings and chance meetings of the event should lead to surprise coincidences, accidents that are perhaps scary, perhaps seductive, chance events that need not be the intent of the artist (who has, after all, long since left the building). In any case, memories of the events and readings of the scripts should be hopelessly tangled in stuff that isn't supposed to make it into criticism and historiography (the bad breath of the stranger tied to one's leg, boredom, the hit-and-run spat with our spouse the event has somehow caused). If the critic ignores such aleatory materials, he will be missing the very spirit of the Happenings.

To return to Williams's graffito, what is "happening" in that defaced text is complicated both in terms of content (the historical references and emotional cues that saturate the piece, many of which are more or less "lost" to contemporary scholarship), form (its banal objecthood, its kitschiness, its apparent lack of artistic "seriousness," its simplicity, its nostalgia), the demands and authority it invests in the reader/performer (the lack of "instructions" as to how the thing is to be made meaningful, made to happen), and its value as an art object. Because it is a kitschy commodity, a trace of graffiti, and a valuable treasure, Williams's text threatens to break down the very narrative machine of history and criticism. Like sugar in a gas tank. Or a symphony through a hole:

> *Symphony No. 1*
> Through a hole.
> George Brecht (1962)

Williams's document and Brecht's score both exploit the effervescent politics of bad memory. (One might note that the original score of Brecht's *Word Event* consists of the word "Exit" positioned next to a large black dot, as if the text itself affords an egress from whatever space it is found in.)

Williams's paean to the "golden age" of American politics and performance is not so much an object as a locale or occasion for a new Happening. As the spike heel functions for a certain breed of "pervert," Williams's text serves as a screen upon which the conflicting memories of trauma, production, and pleasure that constitute the matrix of self, community, and history are formally, if temporarily, resolved. As Naomi Schor demonstrates, "Accurate in every detail, [fetishes] paradoxically conserve apparently indifferent events, while contemporaneous events of great importance . . . go seemingly unremembered, unrecorded."[30] For the fetishist confronted simultaneously with irrecoverable loss and the self-consciousness of productive power, the moment of confrontation with loss and power is often so intense that any attempt to narrate it is bound to failure. As a result, that which is lost is replaced by a souvenir, an object that helps the memory both maintain the source of pleasure and simultaneously consign it to a mythologized past in a kind of pathological or touristic gesture of historicization. As Susan Stewart puts it, "The souvenir seeks distance (the exotic in time and space), but it does so in order to transform and collapse distance into proximity to, or approximation with, the self. The souvenir therefore contracts the world in order to expand the personal."[31]

Looking back again to Williams's graffito and the hundreds of events composed by participants of Fluxus (as if compulsively documenting the vertiginously paradoxical freedoms of postwar America), we notice that the Happenings scripts and memoirs are oddly melancholy textual souvenirs. Like the exquisitely sculpted shoe of the lover, the Happenings script is, as Laura Mulvey has described the fetish, "always haunted by the fragility of the mechanisms that sustain it."[32] Thus, the Happenings script functions as a thing of inflated value, a "memorial, marking the point of lack (for which it both masks and substitutes). . . . It is in this sense that the fetish [i.e. the textual component of the Happenings] fails to lose touch with its original traumatic real and continues to refer back to the moment in time to which it bears witness, to its own historical dimension."[33] The thing about Happenings that makes them so fascinating—and potentially useful for dissident subcultures—is that they are a textual form of "bad memory" that is always available for new performances. As scripts, they continually allow one to reconfigure the past for present purposes. As commodities that can be easily reproduced and transmitted, they circulate freely and freely sponsor new fetishisms, new entanglements, and the production of souvenirs. Like the clown artist in Jim Dine's *The Smiling Workman* who drank from his can of paint before plunging through the text, the critics of Happenings must necessarily interrogate the line between art and life in their own situations, plunge through text into very specific, local performances.

By intentionally challenging our ability to remember performance and mythologize the past, the Happenings compel us to use the signifiers and significatory activities of culture as stage properties in our own critical improvisations, our own scholarly and teacherly Happenings. As John Cage explained to Schechner and Kirby, "I think of past literature as material rather than as art. There are oodles of people who are going to think of the past as a museum and be faithful to it, but that's not my attitude. Now as material it can be put together with other things. They could be things that don't connect . . . as we conventionally understand it."[34] The Happenings are the myth of an art form that compels us away from the past and into our own localities.

There exists an unbridgeable gap in our ability to know the Happenings. Robin Williams's truism abides: If you can remember it, you weren't there. The politics of Happening are the politics of memory itself in a commodity-saturated culture; the materiality of the event, the desires of the moment are left behind like well-thumbed promptbooks or the sweat of a line-worker. The result is a strange kind of liberty for the events and their participant-members, a peculiarly unalienated existence in the history and criticism of radical performance quite different from other anticapitalist movements of the 1960s. As Kristine Stiles has argued, while political groups that shared theoretical ground with the Happenings people—most notably the Situationist International—have seen their work virtually canonized by cultural studies, the Happenings themselves "remain outside critical discussion despite these artists' effort to create an aesthetic strategy that would *insert* their aims into the discourses of art and its history."[35] The entangled, situational qualities of the Happenings remain unalienated by the academic industries of criticism and historiography. "Bad memory" marks the politics of Happening, a politics that works against textuality and academic commodification of performative dissidence.

Significantly, by the late 1960s, the Happenings had more or less disappeared from the scene. Their visible absence should not fool us, however; for their influence on subsequent theater and performance has been profound—as has their influence on subsequent political organizing and demonstration.[36] It is worth recalling—if ironically—the criticism leveled at the Happenings by the now-canonized Situationist International, the ultra-vanguard that instigated the dematrixing of intellectual capital and the mass participation of Parisian students and workers during the singular events of '68. In "The Avant-Garde of Presence," the SI argued that "the happening is an attempt to construct a situation . . . on a foundation of poverty. . . . In contrast, the situation defined by the SI can be constructed only on a foundation of material and spiritual riches."[37] The question of wealth and poverty aside for the moment, it is worth noting that nearly one hundred years after Manet's *Le Déjeuner sur l'herbe,* the imagination of freedom by students and workers in 1968 still remained dependent on the cultivation of scandalous desire, the reappropriation of commodified pleasures, and the stealing of stolen time.

While the Happenings may have been founded on a basis of material and spiritual "poverty," it is nonetheless true that Routledge has recently released a luxurious new edition of *Society of the Spectacle.* Meanwhile, despite the publication of Mariellen Sandford's excellent sourcebook *Happenings and Other Acts* (Routledge: 1996), the original Happenings themselves, the events, remain strangely absent from our scene. Theory and script—like all commodities—can only tease us with memories of community and pleasure. Our absence from the events themselves ensure that the Happenings remain, to recall Kaprow once more, "the myth of an art that is nearly unknown and, for all practical purposes, unknowable."

NOTES

1. Allan Kaprow, "Happenings Are Dead," in *Essays on the Blurring of Art and Life,* ed. Jeff Kelley (Berkeley and Los Angeles: University of California Press, 1993), 61. Kaprow knew the works of John Dewey well. He characterized his work as antiart, but in a distinctly American, distinctly pragmatic tradition of antiart: "[A]nti-art isn't something the dadas invented. There's a whole thread of 'life is better than art' dating at least to the time of Wordsworth, right through Emerson and Whitman, to John Dewey and beyond, emphasizing art as experience, trying to blend art back into life—this tradition [dada] influenced me very much. But anti-art is an old Western theme" (qtd. in Susan Hapgood, *Neo-Dada: Redefining Art, 1958–62* [New York: American Federation of Arts in association with Universe Publishing, 1994], 115).

2. For discussion of the latter, see Kristine Stiles, "Synopsis of the Destruction in

Art Symposium (DIAS) and Its Theoretical Significance," *Act* 1 (spring 1987): 22–31; and "Sticks and Stones: The Destruction in Art Symposium," *Arts,* January 1989, 54–60. The latter contains a meditation on the relations of Happenings to literary and art history that I will cite near the end of the essay.

3. Samuel Delaney, *The Motion of Light in Water: Sex and Science Fiction Writing in the East Village, 1957–1965* (New York: Arbor House/W. Morrow, 1988), 186.

4. Michael Kirby, "The New Theatre," *Tulane Drama Review* 10, no. 2 (1965): 32.

5. Delaney, *Motion of Light,* 183.

6. Ibid., 189.

7. Roland Barthes, *S/Z,* trans. Richard Miller (New York: Farrar, Straus and Giroux, 1974), 3–4.

8. Another one of the Happenings people, Claes Oldenberg (who will be discussed at length ahead), comments on this inflationary pressure vis-à-vis the lumpy, garish commodities on sale at the combination studio/gallery/theater he called Ray Gun Mfg Co: "Volume: Increased flatulence. Model: a balloon. Pressure from center out. From inside. Skin over matter straining out (Claes Oldenberg and Emmett Williams, eds., *Store Days: Documents from the Store, 1961, and Ray Gun Theater, 1962,* [New York: Something Else Press, 1967], 44). Fredric Jameson, examining the "freeing or unbinding of social energies" in the form of ethnic forces, movements, regionalisms, and struggles of all sorts during the 1960s, argues, "The 60s were in that sense an immense and inflationary issuing of superstructural credit; a universal abandonment of the referential gold standard; an extraordinary printing up of ever more devalued signifiers" ("Periodizing the 60s," in *The Ideologies of Theory: Essays 1971–1986,* vol. 2: *The Syntax of History* [Minneapolis: University of Minnesota Press, 1988], 208).

9. Kirby, "The New Theatre," 26.

10. I have explored the relationship between the Happenings and American capitalism in greater detail elsewhere. See "The Avant-Garde of Absorption: Happenings, Fluxus, and the Performance Economies of the American Sixties," in *Rethinking Marxism* 10, no. 2 (1998): 1–26.

11. Thomas Crow, "Modernism and Mass Culture in the Visual Arts," in *Modernism and Modernity,* ed. Benjamin H. D. Buchloch et al. (Nova Scotia: Nova Scotia College of Art and Design, 1983).

12. For a more detailed discussion of the relationship between capitalism and the poised avant-gardism of the Happenings and Fluxus communities, see Sell, "Avant-Garde of Absorption."

13. Quoted in Rick Perlstein, "Who Owns the 60s? The Opening of a Scholarly Generation Gap," *Lingua Franca,* May–June 1996, 36.

14. Michael Kirby and Richard Schechner, "An Interview with John Cage," *Drama Review* 10, no. 2 (1965): 53.

15. Qtd. in Hapgood, *Neo-Dada,* 129.

16. Richard Schechner, *Environmental Theater,* 2d ed. (New York: Applause, 1994), 40.

17. Laura Mulvey asserts that commodity fetishism is the result of "a problem of inscription"; namely, the inability to establish once and for all how "the sign of value come[s] to be marked on a commodity" (*Fetishism and Curiosity* [Bloomington: Indiana University Press, 1996], 2).

18. Jill Johnston, "Dada and Fluxus," in Hapgood, *Neo-Dada,* 93.

19. Ibid.

20. Ibid.

21. Ibid., 94.

22. Allan Kaprow, "The Education of the Un-Artist, Part I," in Kelley, *Blurring of Art*, 98–99.

23. Oldenberg and Williams, *Store Days*, 110.

24. Ibid.

25. Ibid.

26. Susan Stewart, *On Longing: Narratives of the Miniature, the Gigantic, the Souvenir, the Collection* (Baltimore: John Hopkins University Press, 1984), x.

27. Ibid., 6.

28. Ibid., 48.

29. Ibid., 52.

30. Naomi Schor, "Fetishism and Its Ironies," in *Fetishism as Cultural Discourse*, ed. Emily Apter and William Pietz (Ithaca, N.Y.: Cornell University Press, 1993), 95.

31. Stewart, *On Longing*, xii.

32. Mulvey, "Visual Pleasure and Narrative Cinema," *Screen* 16 (autumn 1975): 7.

33. Ibid., 11. My quotation of Mulvey purposefully excludes the central metaphor of her essay: the phallus. While there is no doubt that woman is fetishized in many of the Happenings (not least by Kaprow) and that such fetishization is often explicitly thematized and diverted in others (particularly in the work of Carolee Schneemann and Yoko Ono), I am attempting to discuss fetishization here in a way that takes account of the "experience itself" divorced of any theoretical apparatus or historical context. Fetishism is often a very effective response to crisis (and, as Mulvey demonstrates, a window that allows us to see into the very constitution of the crisis itself). The Happenings are such a response, too.

34. Kirby and Schechner, "Interview with John Cage," 53.

35. Stiles, "Sticks and Stones," 54.

36. Recently, Doric Wilson has asserted that the off-off-Broadway theater scene, in which professional, amateur, and avant-garde theater mixed freely, provided a wealth of practical advice, performance principles, and participants for both the antiwar and women's movements. Comment made on the panel "Excavating the Underground: Towards an Archaeology of Off-Off-Broadway," Association for Theater in Higher Education Conference, New York, August 8, 1996.

37. Situationist International, "The Avant-Garde of Presence," in *Situationist International Anthology*, ed. and trans. Ken Knabb (Berkeley: Bureau of Public Secrets, 1981), 110–11.

James M. Harding

Dissent behind the Barricades: Radical Art, Revolutionary Stages, and Avant-Garde Divisions

Paris est un vrai paradis.
Gustave Courbet (1871)

Avant-Garde Divisions: Disunity in the Reconciliation of Radical Art and Radical Politics

In the fall of 1968, just as the journal *TDR* was sending to press a seminal essay on European experimental theater, its author, Jean-Jacques Lebel, asked that a postscript be added. As if questioning the entirety of the essay, the postscript to "On the Necessity of Violation" began, "Something has changed." The immediate something to which Lebel referred was the boundary that had been crossed in French theater during the events in Paris in May 1968. The crossing was perhaps nowhere more prominently signified than in the student-led occupation of the Odéon Théâtre de France. Having decided against an assault on the senate, the Louvre or the ORTF (the French Radio and Television Offices), the students together with others sympathetic to their cause seized the Odéon just as a performance by the Paul Taylor Ballet Company was concluding.[1] Almost magically, the Odéon was transformed into an arena where, as Julian Beck recalled, virtually anyone who wanted to "could become an actor" and where many of Paris's leading artists appeared and engaged in a dialogue on the theater.[2] During the occupation, the Odéon thus ironically lived up to its long-standing commitment to avant-garde theater. For better or worse, it became the center of a metatheatrical spectacle contesting the previous boundaries of avant-garde performance. Though Lebel was correct in recognizing that overnight the course of French theater had shifted, the events of May, like the occupation of the Odéon itself, only fleetingly embodied the theatrical "pure spontaneity" that Lebel embraces at the end of his postscript.

Amid the play of spontaneity in the Odéon, far more enduring polarizations were resurfacing, polarizations along both theatrical and political lines. Initially the occupation of the Odéon appeared to revitalize a version of the avant-garde languishing since the years directly following the Paris Commune, "when many of the young French artists who had flirted with anarchy and socialism" forged an "alliance of political and artistic radicalism."[3] As Poggioli notes, the alliance was short-lived. Surviving only until about the time that *La Revue indépendante* was founded in 1880, the political and artistic avant-gardes split soon afterward. The reasons for this split were complex, but one thing is clear: the earlier alliance, intertwined as it was with the idealism of the Paris Commune, became a kind of ideé fixe in the collective unconscious of the avant-garde. The desire to reconcile radical art with radical politics—however elusive that desire proved to be—became a powerful source of inspiration and innovation. But it also proved to be as divisive as it was inspiring. The surrealists, for example, attempted to unite an "a spirit of revolt with revolutionary action" by associating their "intellectual, artistic, and moral preoccupations with the aims and methods of communism."[4] Yet in the end their efforts at reconciliation had done more to divide them than it did to reunite radical politics with radical art. In many respects, the dynamics of this late-nineteenth-century split, which had resurfaced and bitterly divided the surrealists just four decades later, set the stage for the dramatic conflict in the avant-garde that commenced with the occupation of the Odéon. In fact, the seeds of division were being sown even as the students stormed the doors of the theater.

With the occupation, the pivotal issue was once again the desire to reconcile radical politics with radical art, and once again a pattern emerged that had also left its decisively divisive mark on the surrealists. In this respect, the frequent description of the events of May as "surrealism in the streets" was far from gratuitous, at least as far as the march on the Odéon was concerned.[5] On at least two counts, the occupation echoed the surrealists' efforts to reconcile the artistic and political avant-gardes. First of all, a rigidly political notion of authentic theater governed the occupation, one that equated artistic authenticity with direct action or *engagement.* Functioning as a kind of litmus test, this politicized notion of authentic theater initiated a course of action that recalled the internal political strife and personal rivalries that characterized the surrealist "revolution" in the 1920s and 1930s. Pursuing this notion of direct action, the shift from Taylor's experimental ballet company to an open forum for what Lebel called "the most extreme expression, contestation, and communication" gestured initially toward an irrevocable erasure of the lines separating "the 'doers' and the 'lookers'" in theater.[6] The gesture was simultaneously framed in irreversible moral imperatives like those expressed in the bulletins on the occupation that were issued by the Comité d'Action Révolutionnaire (CAR). Affirming the revolutionary cultural significance of the occupation, the committee maintained that "the only theatre is guerrilla theatre" and, more importantly, that "the slightest relaxation of [this] revolutionary agitation . . . would be betrayal of the *elan* which was revealed on the barricades."[7] For Jean-Louis Barrault, friend and disciple of Artaud and now director of the Théâtre de France, the proclamation of such moral, political, and theatrical absolutes had to have had a vaguely familiar ring, reminiscent as it was of Breton's purging of the surrealist ranks in the late 1920s.[8] Artaud himself had been a casualty of those purges, and now Barrault found himself at odds with other members of the avant-garde who ironically claimed to have made Artaud's Theater of Cruelty their own.

Breton's purges had had distinctly personal undertones, which also seemed to find their way into the dynamics of the occupation. For Barrault, the shock of the occupation was compounded by the recognition of artists in the crowd whose work he, as director of the Odéon, had supported. Though twice invited to perform at the Théâtre de France, Julian Beck, Judith Malina, and the other members of the Living Theatre, for example, had nonetheless led the insurgent students and *enragés* through the streets once the decision to occupy the theater had been reached, and it was to Beck and Malina "that Barrault first addressed himself when he mounted the stage" to respond to the demands of the occupiers.[9] Barrault's memoirs do little to hide his sense of being personally betrayed by those whose political actions were dressed in admonishments against betrayal. Consequently, it would be easy to characterize the polarizations in the Odéon merely as a conflict between personal and political loyalties.[10] But this would overlook the more profound historical allegory of the avant-garde that the occupation of the Odéon set in motion once again. Unknowingly following the precedent set by the surrealists, Beck and Barrault were but representative players in a fundamental conflict that has characterized the avant-garde since the late nineteenth century.

That conflict has less to do with the goal of uniting radical art with radical politics than it does with the means to that goal, and on this note the occupation of the Odéon was again following a precedent set by the surrealists, specifically a precedent to be found in the dynamics of what has been called the "Aragon affair," that is, when Louis Aragon was officially charged with sedition after writing a rather unsurrealistic *poem de circonstance* that advocated the murder of cops and social democrats. Though Breton mounted a vigorous and largely successful defense of Aragon against those charges, he ended up alienating him because "as the affair progressed, ... [Breton's efforts] became less a matter of defending Aragon from prosecution, than of defending the Surrealist conception of poetry against those who, in Breton's opinion, were prepared to sacrifice the integrity of art to the needs of propaganda."[11] In short, Breton's defense of Aragon simultaneously criticized him for writing propaganda poetry. Angered by Breton's backhanded support, Aragon resigned from the surrealists and denounced them as counterrevolutionary. The relevance of this controversial affair to the occupation of the Odéon is not what one might initially assume—although the relation of art to propaganda was certainly an issue raised by the events of May. Far more important were the differences between Breton and Aragon that the affair revealed with regard to the nature of revolutionary art. As Robert Short observed shortly before the student unrest of the 1960s spilled in the streets of Paris, the differences between Breton and Aragon pivoted on a subtle but important disagreement about communication:

> For Breton, a writer's "meaning" lay in the words he wrote and the intention behind them; their subversive value was latent within them. For Aragon, meaning lay solely in the interpretation made by the reader or by the majority of society at any given time.[12]

This qualitative distinction between intent and reception, while initially applied to poetry, later proved to be equally applicable to direct action and guerilla theater as well. Indeed, the parallel between the "Aragon affair" and the occupation of the Odéon centers precisely on this distinction: with Beck, like Breton before him, vigorously defending the subversive revolutionary intent of the occupation (and ultimately of *Paradise Now*) and Barrault, like Aragon before him, maintaining that the subversiveness of events like the occupation can be measured only by the interpretation and/or reception that they received by "the majority of society at any given time." As the coming arguments will show, in this small but crucial sense Beck and Barrault, like Breton and Aragon before them, found themselves on opposites sides of the same coin of radical aesthetic expression, both laying claim to the same radical tradition of the avant-garde and both also moving in seemingly opposite directions with the radical political thought of their time.[13] For the surrealists that political thought was largely associated with Communism, but by the time that students were filling the streets in 1968, Paris was abuzz with the radical reassessment of Marxism by Guy Debord and the situationist critique of the society of the spectacle.

With regard to the occupation of the Odéon, both Beck and Barrault implicitly laid equal but mutually exclusive claims to this critique. Perhaps rightly so, since the divisions that emerged at the Odéon had their counterparts among the situationists as well. First of all, the situationists had strong ties to the dadaist and surrealist avant-garde traditions, and like their surrealist predecessors the situationists not only "sought to [finally] transcend the distinction between revolutionary politics and cultural criticism" but also (again like their surrealist predecessors) succumbed to "arguments and a major split" as a result.[14] More importantly, as the political philosophies of Debord and the situationists were reshaping the radical political landscape of Paris, the avant-garde was returning to its nineteenth-century anarchist roots, and the situationists were very much a part of this tendency in the years leading up to May 1968: "Like all revolutionaries stranded in a present without revolution, the situationists looked back. It was the Paris Commune that represented *'the only realization of a revolutionary urbanism to date.'*"[15] But it was not so much the uplifted image of the Commune that was significant for the occupation of the Odéon; it was rather situationist interpretation of the Commune as "festival." For the interpretation ultimately situated the opposing gestures of Beck and Barrault within the same avant-garde tradition. While the Commune as festival and saturnalia may have been reincarnated in the radical spirit of May 1968, the origins of festive carnival were evoked in Barrault's biting response to the occupation in *Rabelais,* the piece he finished during the occupation and then produced later that fall.[16]

The Enemy within Us: Spontaneity, Occupation, and the Spectacle of Direct Action

The occupation of the Odéon, which Julian Beck described as "the most beautiful thing . . . [he had] ever seen in a theatre" and which he likened to the "great anarchist dramas," was in many respects a profound realization of a long-neglected potential in avant-garde improvisational theater.[17] Not only did Beck consider the pandemonium in the Odéon to be one of the first moments of honest and authentic improvisation; he specifically linked the improvised spontaneity of the occupation with freedom, political freedom.[18] This conscious linkage of improvisation and politics appeared finally to reconcile "the rebels of art" and "the rebels of politics" who had struggled to find stable common ground since their split in the late nineteenth century.[19] Whether an embrace of improvised spontaneity actually fosters larger political freedom is certainly debatable, but this was the assumption underlying Beck's account of the occupation, even when the occupation failed. However fleeting the liberation of the Odéon might have been—so the logic went—one must first taste freedom in order to understand and pursue it. The action thus served its purpose: to subvert reified consciousness through an immediate experience of liberation. In this respect, Beck's later rationale for citing the Happenings as a precursor for the work of the Living Theatre is understandable.

The Happenings were important to Beck largely because of what Michael Kirby has described as their "nonmatrixed" pattern of performance. This pattern, which Kirby compared tentatively to jazz and which he traced directly back to dada and "the 1916 performances at the Cabaret Voltaire in Zurich," was characterized by a combination of a decentering "compartmented structure" and an unpredictable indeterminacy of form.[20] Positioned in opposition to traditional theater's reliance on repetition, representation, and textuality, the compartmented structure and indeterminacy of the Happenings offered a seemingly ideal antistructure for the decentered authority and anarchical conceptions of political freedom that underlie the guerrilla theater tactics adopted by the Living Theatre and the students during the occupation of the Odéon. These same Happening structures underscored a kind of experiential immediacy that Kirby maintained was always beyond the grasp of traditional theater and, more importantly, that was of obvious relevance to the political objectives pursued during the occupation. Whereas traditional theater might have political intent, Kirby argued that it nonetheless inevitably succumbed to the virtually insurmountable trappings of a "manufactured reality."[21] Limited to "the clichés of exposition," creating and thus confining itself to a "matrix," or "artificial, imaginary, interlocking structure," traditional theater could talk about and even represent freedoms, but in the final analysis (at least according to Kirby), traditional theater was caught in the webs of its fabrications and could at best cultivate a longing for what it had to acknowledge as absent and beyond its grasp.[22] That Beck emphatically concurred on this point is evident in pronouncements like the following: "You cannot be free if you are contained within a fiction," and his concurrence is a crucial aspect of the reconciliation of radical art with radical politics that he sought in adapting the innovations of the Happenings for direct political *engagement*.[23] Following a very similar logic then, the occupation not only realized a political freedom on a local level and thus suggested to Beck and many of the student participants that political liberation could be achieved on an even larger scale. It also positioned the reconciliation of radical art and politics in direct contrast to a text-based institutional structure for theater, in other words in direct contrast to the mainstays of bourgeois theater.

From an historical perspective, the opposition has been a consistent strategy of the avant-garde. Indeed, nowhere has the attempt to reconcile radical art and radical politics been more evident than in the stormy relationship that the avant-garde has had with bourgeois culture—a culture that has proven itself to be at least as resilient (if not more so) as the avant-garde is innovative or radical in its opposition to it.[24] Peter Bürger has argued that among its many different manifestations the avant-garde has consistently positioned itself as a force against "institutional enclosure" and as a mechanism "to shock the recipient," that is, as a mechanism *pour épater les bourgeois*.[25] While this latter function is typical of modernism, Bürger notes that, unlike other works of modernism that sought to shock their recipients into "a contemplation of the work [of art]," the historical avant-garde radicalized modernism's calculated shock aesthetic by attempting "to intensify [it] . . . in order to change immediately the receiver's attitude."[26] With regard to the avant-garde's attitude toward institutional enclosure, the occupation of the Odéon was in many respects an embarrassing wake-up call to long-standing members of the Parisian avant-garde. On this note, Beck was a particularly powerful spokesperson—in part perhaps because of a concern that after the students had left the streets and de Gaulle had been reelected, the occupation of the Odéon was in danger of losing its relevance altogether. However one might rightfully criticize Beck for being selective in his memory, naive in his idealism, or unskilled in his political calculations, one has to admit that he, perhaps more than anyone else, understood the demoralizing implications of not salvaging the occupation from annals of defeat. His response to these implications was very much in tune with Breton's defense of surrealism during "the Aragon affair": for Beck, it was not the conservative backlash but rather the intention of the occupation that mattered.

In what could equally be called either a brilliant moment of insight or major piece of rationalization, it was Beck who recast the occupation as an end in itself and who in retrospect traded the CAR's revolutionary agenda in on a reassertion of the lines distinguishing avant-garde expression from established institutional contexts. Specifically addressing the unhealthy alliance between institutional authority and the theatrical community, Beck continued to argue years after the occupation,

> It was important to occupy the Odéon . . . [b]ecause the students and their comrades were refusing in May of 1968 to grant the government the privilege of flattering both itself and the public into believing that the state maintains reputable avant-garde *contra-sistemo* art. Any art that the establishment supports it exploits, any art that the establishment supports is already infected. So powerful the germs of corruption. We are fighting a plague. The occupation of the Odéon represented the attempt to occupy one of the mechanisms of co-option.[27]

Ironically reversing a crucial Artaudian metaphor, Beck's recollections supplant the initial revolutionary resistance of the students with a metaphorical battle against a plague emanating from the establishment. Abandoned are the CAR's general political goals of sabotaging "all that is 'cultural'" and of concentrating "all energy on political objectives such as . . . the struggle in the Streets against State Power." Forgotten is the CAR's admonishment that "never again must a single ticket be sold at the ex–Theatre of France."[28] These earlier goals held the occupation of the Odéon to be a means to a larger end, a stepping-stone on a path leading toward an as yet unrealized political terrain, whereas Beck finally turns the occupation into a circular end in itself:

"the occupation of the Odéon represented the attempt to occupy . . ." Occupation for occupation's sake, as Graham White has noted of much of the theater during the period of the counterculture, may have served "the invaluable roles of the emotional lightning rod . . . [and] the political rally," but when the intoxicating, emotional highs of the rally subside, the crucial question is whether the political rally has ignited a fervor and *engagement* that is the source of genuinely radical politics and of lasting progressive change.[29]

Elements like the circular nature of Beck's comments or the fumbling, presumably inadvertent, reversal of Artaud's metaphor of the plague suggest a painful retreat from the revolutionary agenda that swept the students through the streets in May 1968. Though Beck was able in retrospect to represent the occupation as a struggle to release the avant-garde from the stranglehold on bourgeois culture, the very attempt to salvage the occupation by changing its objectives after the fact is indicative of how much Beck and the students had underestimated the strength of that hold. Indeed, it was indicative of the extent to which bourgeois culture proved itself capable of containing the student unrest within what Lebel called "the first stage of *any* revolution," that is, within the "theatrical" realms.[30] Such containment was, however, tantamount to a continued split between art and politics and indicative ultimately of a failure to reconcile the radical artistic expression of the occupation with the radical politics of the time. The containment was not merely a conservative backlash reestablishing the order lost to radical activism. Rather, it arguably resulted from the students' inability to push themselves beyond the limits of their own socialized, reified consciousness and beyond what in the final analysis amounted to the intoxicating appearance of radical politics. The transience of gains like the ephemeral liberation of the Odéon led many subsequently to question whether the physical occupation of a building could actually subvert institutional enclosures when the institutions themselves were the product of reified social attitudes that, amid all the tumult in May, had nonetheless remained intact. A good example of this questioning subtly pervades Richard Schechner's recollection of events in October later that same year when the Living Theatre performed *Paradise Now* at New York's Fillmore East. In many respects an adapted reenactment of the occupation of the Odéon, this production of *Paradise Now* culminated when, as Schechner recalls,

> Julian Beck began chanting "FREE THEATRE, FREE THEATRE, FREE THEATRE, FREE THEATRE, FREE THEATRE, FREE THEATRE." (Later he told me that he knew people were ready to "take the Fillmore—to go into Paradise on one leap.") Hundreds rushed the stage, someone took a microphone and announced that "The Fillmore East is liberated!" A dozen or more arguments erupted simultaneously. Who would run the theatre? What

would be done in it? Would the night's program go on? Who represented "the community"?[31]

Unlike the events in Paris, this performance ended in a negotiated settlement, and the "liberators" of the Fillmore gained the opportunity to move beyond the theatrical stage of revolution when the director of the Fillmore, Bill Graham, reluctantly "agreed to turn the theatre over on Wednesday nights." The problem was, as Schechner curtly notes, that "the community" had no idea what to do next: "they couldn't agree on how to use . . . [the concession they had won], did nothing, and finally Wednesdays reverted to Graham."[32] If the underlying assumption of the performance at the Fillmore was, as with the occupation of the Odéon, that one must have a direct, unmediated experience of freedom in order to understand and pursue it, then the floundering in the weeks that followed the event would suggest that no such experience had occurred. At best the performance of *Paradise Now* had achieved a kind of "spectacularized" dissent that, since it forced "no breakthrough beyond the aesthetic context," was thus itself "implicated," "recuperated," and contained from the very start.[33]

Spectacular Liberation and the Context of *Rabelais*

For many, such flounderings were all too typical and were the inevitable consequence of the mistaken notion that one could take up residence in the house that the oppressor built—whether that house was a theater or a factory. Certainly this was the stinging assessment of the situationist Raoul Vaneigem, whose *Revolution of Everyday Life* (1967) had profoundly influenced the students who had taken to the streets in 1968. In a 1972 postscript to his book, Vaneigem pointed specifically to the occupations as examples of where the student activists were unable to move into authentic revolutionary consciousness because they could not bring themselves "to destroy what can *only* be destroyed (through sabotage and subversion—not occupations)."[34] Compounding this inability to adopt a genuinely radical political course of action was the general realization of the extent to which "entrenched power . . . [had been far more] intelligent and artful in its control" than the students themselves had been in their opposition to it, and on this note there was a very clear echo of Aragon's concern with the interpretation of political activism by the majority of society at a given historical moment.[35] Indeed, in the aftermath of the events of May groups across the spectrum of radical activism encountered a post-May assessment of the student unrest by the situationists that sounded very much like Aragon's criticism of the surrealists thirty years earlier and, more importantly, that challenged the understanding of direct action and the conclusions about the occupation offered by figures like Beck: "it is not so much the clarity of communication achieved in direct action which decides its effectiveness as the dramatic intensity of its resultant representation. It is this which decides whether the activist achieves a progressive intervention, or the spectacle's inscription remains secure."[36] Having been unable to achieve a course of protracted direct action, the occupiers of the Odéon had also to contend even with a loss of control over the representation of the occupation. Some, in fact, had maintained all along that the occupation and its representation were being co-opted even before the CRS (the riot police) came and cleared the theater.

The rationale for these arguments had much to do with the shock value of the occupation itself. However much one might agree with Bürger's characterization of the avant-garde's opposition to bourgeois institutions and consciousness, the occupation of the Odéon underscored the extent to which the two characteristics are not always manifest in tandem: opposition to "institutional enclosure" does not necessarily work in concert with a shock-induced transformation of bourgeois consciousness, because aesthetically induced shock is highly unpredictable. As Bürger has noted in *Theory of the Avant-Garde,* shock may very well "strengthen existing attitudes because it provides them with an occasion to manifest themselves."[37] The overwhelming support for de Gaulle's government after the events of May offers strong support for such claims. But the occupation of the Odéon tends also to suggest that aesthetically induced shock is not only unpredictable in its effect on the public; it also has the potential to become blindingly intoxicating for its practitioners. However dramatic the shock value of the act of occupying might have been, it too easily served as a diversion unto itself and kept those directly involved too distracted to critically examine whether in the occupation of the Odéon authentic revolutionary direct action or merely its semblance was taking place. Such at least was the opinion of the person most directly affected by the occupation, its director Jean-Louis Barrault.

Though dismissed as a bourgeois relic, Barrault too was concerned with co-option and exploitation by the establishment. But while Beck spoke of severing the avant-garde from the tutelage of state-sanctioned institutions, Barrault was gradually becoming conscious that he and everyone in the Odéon were playing into the hands of a far more resilient, indeed more pernicious, form of containment. Thinking along lines that, ironically, were consistent with Guy Debord and the situationists, Barrault understood the occupation of the Odéon to be little more than a spectacle of revolution, that is, a revolution dramatized rather than a revolution enacted. Barrault's understanding coincided with situationalist arguments like Debord's suggestion that the "false models of revolution" that modern society offers "to local revolutionaries" are comparable to the pseudogratifications provided by the commodities and spectacles of the marketplace.[38] Indeed, when René Viénet, a member of Debord's circle, claimed that the occupation of the Odéon was "a farcical enactment of the decomposition of the state power," his criticism found an echo of affirmation in Barrault's speculation about why de Gaulle's government had initially offered no opposition to the students.[39] Barrault recalls:

> I was beginning to understand what the role of the Odéon in those historic events would prove to have been. The government, unable on 15 May to use the police because of that unfortunate night of the rue Gay-Lussac, had allowed the Odéon to be taken as one gives a bone to a dog. The Odéon had become a fixation abscess. Because of this the Académie, the Senate, the Louvre and the ORTF were spared. The police could then reappear prudently—and, very soon, as saviors.[40]

Despite such insights into political maneuvering, Barrault, like many intellectuals across Europe, was unprepared for the events of May. Caught between the students and de Gaulle's government, Barrault lost his position as director of the Odéon. But as a consequence, he gained an important critical position from which he challenged the false dichotomies that were central to the representation of the events leading to his dismissal. However spectacular or illusory the liberation of the Odéon might have been, the occupation of the theater thus ultimately proved to be liberating for Barrault. Though sympathetic with the students, he did not subsequently seek to regain favor with the dissenting voices of May but rather took the opportunity afforded him by the loss of his position to reassert a voice within the avant-garde that the events of May had eclipsed.

The voice was by no means new. As the clamor on the streets subsided and Barrault's company regrouped, their activities initially might have suggested that the month's volatile events and specifically the efforts to reconcile radical art and radical politics—if they had achieved nothing else—had succeeded once again in bitterly dividing the avant-garde into different factions. While this is true, it tends to overlook the extent to which these same avant-garde factions, though polarized, were still in pursuit of similar if not identical ultimate goals. Viewed in light of more dominant trends in the history of the avant-garde, the seemingly rival factions represented by Beck and Barrault were but the most recent manifestation of the contradictory dynamic that has long characterized the avant-garde's relation to radical politics. The form that this dynamic assumed in 1968 had been identified earlier in the decade by Poggioli, who in *Theory of the Avant-Garde* (1962) had maintained that, as was later the case in Paris, historically the avant-garde has flourished in the dialectical tensions between its activist and agonistic (i.e., sacrificial) impulses.[41] Poggioli's comments occur within a rather dismissive but certainly debatable assertion that the avant-garde would have neither "reason [n]or chance to exist within a communist society" because of its fundamentally anarchistic propensities, but the comments nonetheless provide a theoretical framework that helps to situate Barrault's own aesthetic response to the occupation within the larger context of the dynamics of the historical avant-garde: "the activist impulse leads the artist . . . of the avant-garde to militate in a party of action and agitation, while the agonistic and futurist impulses induce him to accept the idea of sacrificing his own person, his own movement, and his own mission to the social palingenesis of the future."[42] There is little doubt about where and how the activist impulse manifested itself during the student unrest during May 1968. One need look no further than the guerilla theater tactics of Julian Beck and the Living Theatre for an example. The agonist impulse, on the other hand, was more subtle, but it clearly was at play as Barrault pieced his theater company back together and moved toward a production of *Rabelais*.

A few days before his dismissal, in that uncertain period directly after the CRS had "reliberated" the Odéon from its student liberators, Barrault reconvened his company in the theater only to be overcome with a sense that the Odéon itself was a casualty. Examining the now empty, repossessed theater, Barrault pronounced it dead. He compared the Odéon to "a man tortured to death" and argued, "Someone had been killed: a place that had had life."[43] Though the pronouncement commiserated the loss of twenty years of his company's work, Barrault's metaphor evinced a nascent awareness of the larger significance that the occupation of the Odéon would have not only in the historic events of May but also in the history of avant-garde theater. Consciously or unconsciously, the metaphor of a tortured death equated the destruction of the Odéon with the agonistic impulses of the avant-garde and thereby placed the political divisions of May within dynamic tensions of the historical avant-garde.

Coupled with a sense that the destructive side of the occupation had defiled the sanctity of the Odéon, Barrault's personification of the theater in the image of a man who died cast the events of May in a religious metaphor and allowed Barrault to conceptualize the assault on the Odéon as a holy sacrifice, in other words as a kind of avant-garde passion play with the theater cast in the role of Christ. Framed in these sacrificial terms, the spectacle of the occupation assumed an eschatological significance. The loss of the Odéon was not a permanent end, that is, a death without hope of rebirth or resurrection. For Barrault, this agonistic hope of resurrection was intimately intertwined with *Rabelais,* the piece that he completed while the students still occupied the

Odéon and that he subsequently produced at the Élysée-Montmartre in December of that same year. Certainly, the production at the Élysée-Montmartre was a personal victory for Barrault after having been fired by André Malraux, de Gaulle's minister of cultural affairs. For the public who knew Barrault, it would have been hard to miss the expression of that victory in the prologue to *Rabelais* when, Barrault, in the role of the "Orator of the Company" implicitly identified himself with his sixteenth-century predecessor:

> Between those two calamities called Order and Disorder, Rabelais . . . . belongs to the party of Tolerance. That has always been the minority party. Excommunicated by one side, rejected by the other, what is man to do? Lose heart? Despair? Never![44]

That Barrault was once again standing center stage was evidence that he had neither lost heart nor succumbed to despair. Yet the December production of *Rabelais* became more than Barrault's triumphant return to the stage. Speaking later on behalf of his theater company, Barrault recalled that in the enthusiastic reception of the first public preview of *Rabelais,* the Compagnie Renaud-Barrault "witnessed the rebirth of . . . [their] theatre."[45] It was a rebirth facilitated by the kind of Nietzschean quirks of history that Theodor Adorno refers to in *Aesthetic Theory.*[46] Warning against being too strict in historicizing art, Adorno argues that, having once become "false in the course of historical time," an artwork can nonetheless "reveal its truth a second time when the conditions which undermined its truth in the first place are changed."[47] Rebirth for Barrault's company was conceived in the recognition of precisely the type of socioconditional change that Adorno alludes to in his admonishment. In the events of May Barrault had recognized the emergence of cultural and political conditions that potentially could revitalize for a "second time" the dialectical critical edge of François Rabelais's *Gargantua and Pantagruel.*

Word Made Flesh: Textuality, Overlapping Histories, and the Doctrine of Real Presence

Stating both in the preface and the prologue of *Rabelais* that "Rabelais's times are our times," Barrault portrayed the sociopolitical turmoil of France in 1968 as an atavistic echo of the socioreligious turmoil of Rabelais's sixteenth-century world. Barrault's adaptation posited, in short, an argument by analogy. His drama underscored the parallels between the political, theatrical rivalries polarizing the avant-garde in May 1968 and the spiritual, theological rivalries polarizing France in the early Reformation. Of particular interest to Barrault in this regard were Rabelais's controversial handling of sixteenth-century attitudes toward the written word, his critical attitude toward contemporary debates over the doctrine of real presence (transubstantiation), and his skeptical stance toward religious communal structures. Attracted by the carnivalesque character of Rabelais's theological concerns, Barrault concluded that "in his soul . . . [Rabelais] is 'theatre.'"[48] The conclusion implicitly suggested that the theater is a nexus of ritual, ceremony, and popular carnival: a contradictory and subversive meeting of the holy and profane. The implication was nothing new for Barrault. Artaud had admired his earlier work precisely because Barrault "brought back the religious spirit by using profane means."[49] Since Rabelais was embroiled in, even persecuted for, a similar agenda, Barrault not only saw in Rabelais a writer of kindred spirit. He also saw in Rabelais's work a profoundly irreverent medium that when adapted and performed could embody many of the goals of the occupation while simultaneously questioning the assumptions those goals had about the relation of theater and politics. As Rabelais had positioned *Gargantua and Pantagruel* in a debasing parodic relation to the theological debates that had surfaced in sixteenth-century France, Barrault positioned the drama *Rabelais* in a debasing parodic relation to the divisions in the avant-garde that had surfaced during the occupation of the Odéon. Responding to the categorical dismissals of text-based theater and to the radical liberties of direct action, Barrault offered a profane textuality and the liberties of festive carnival. In both of these offerings, Barrault was still very much concerned with the reconciliation of radical art and politics that had been primary motivation of those who had stormed the doors of the Odéon in May.

Typical of the rebellious attitude that the historical avant-garde had for categories like authorship, Barrault's decision to adapt Rabelais's work for the stage rather than to compose an original piece for the theater himself was significant because it permitted Barrault to work from within avant-garde traditions while questioning the assumptions made by those who had occupied the Odéon. The piece was antiauthoritarian in its opposition to authorship, in its challenge to the logocentric authority of the written word and in its strong support of plebeian folk traditions. Relying on Rabelais's controversial relation to the written word, Barrault was thus able to challenge the notion that "manufactured" dramatic realities necessarily succumb to what Kirby called "the clichés of expositions" and the notion that fiction and freedom are diametrically opposed, as Beck had claimed. The suitability of Rabelais's work for this task had as much to do with his notions of textuality as it did with the festive carnival traditions that were central to his writings and to the anarchistic sentiments of the avant-garde. These notions were probably nowhere so manifest as in Rabelais's uncritical embrace of the vernacular. At a time when many across Europe had begun to translate the Scripture into local vernaculars, Rabelais engaged in a course of writing that transgressed the presumed holiness of the written word. Rather than redeeming the vernacular by bringing the Scripture to it, Rabelais elevated the vernacular by codifying its concomitant oral traditions into written form. That which presumably was reserved for the sacred and holy he profaned with plebeian vulgarity. In a similar manner, Barrault, by drawing upon the carnival traditions of Rabelais, offered a pointed critique of the avant-garde's skeptical attitude toward textuality, and in the aftermath of the student revolts the critique was implicitly aimed at guerilla theater and at the notion that direct action circumvented the restrictiveness of texts. For Barrault, the issue was not whether dramatic texts were transgressive or restrictive but rather whether dramatic texts could help to orchestrate a context for disrupting the habitual patterns of reified consciousness that, much to the chagrin of occupiers of the Odéon, had unfortunately surfaced even during the unrest of May.

More than a mere return to a text-based theater, Barrault's use of Rabelais's writings laid the foundation for a profound critique of the basic assumptions of Beck's notion of freedom. Underlying Barrault's production of *Rabelais* was a fundamental question as to whether Beck (and Kaprow) had his equation skewed in the rigid opposition between fiction and freedom that he maintained. From Barrault's perspective, the association of scripted performance with restriction had to have been too simple. Indeed, it may very well have elided the Living Theatre's most important point of self-reflection regarding their participation in the events of May 1968, overlooking as it did the subtler implications of one of their earlier performances at the Odéon. That event was their production of Kenneth Brown's *The Brig,* which, at the invitation of Barrault, the Living Theatre performed at the Odéon in 1966 and which Beck specifically identified as the pivotal piece in the Living Theatre's evolution toward "free theater."

Though Beck could place the piece in the continuum of the Living Theatre's evolution, the problem is that it arguably had implications that were in fact counter to that evolution. Indeed, the very characteristics of *The Brig* that Beck most admired offer an important but subtle contrast to the assumptions governing the occupation of the Odéon two years later. As Beck recalled: "Kenneth Brown had written a play in which the action was bound by rules, but within those rules only improvisation was possible. He provided a situation in which improvisation was essential. It was real."[50] For many members of the avant-garde—and Barrault's continued work with text-based theater locates him within this group—the authenticity that Beck recognized in the Living Theatre's production of *The Brig* was achievable only because of the situation constructed by the play. Not only did *The Brig* demand improvisation from its performers, the play arguably facilitated the emergence of improvisation and freedom as viable possibilities, possibilities that otherwise could not exist or emerge on their own. According to this line of thought, the situation created by *The Brig* promoted "real" improvisation because the play first thwarted bourgeois consciousness and thereby established a context of resistance where authentic improvisation and freedom could thrive (however fleetingly). The implication here—and it was one that applied to the improvised spontaneity of the occupation as well—was that while improvisation may very well be related to freedom, not all improvisation is synonymous with freedom. The implication of *The Brig* and also of Barrault's highly visible text-based dramatic response to the occupation was that without some deliberately orchestrated aesthetic context of resistance, improvisation will never depart from the clichés of bourgeois consciousness. While Beck maintained that the spontaneous, improvised occupation of the Odéon forcefully resisted bourgeois theater and gave the students a taste of freedom that in turn would cultivate a desire for more freedom, the fundamental question about the occupation—which echoes from the example of *The Brig*—is whether during those crucial days of the occupation the Living Theatre, the students, and the *enragés* actually achieved a period of immediate actual freedom or whether they were deluded by the mere "spectacle" of freedom.

The divisions that emerged among the avant-garde during the events of May were obviously not limited to mutually exclusive claims about the role of textuality in thwarting bourgeois consciousness and cultivating radical freedoms. But the polarizations over these issues were historically typical of the avant-garde's attempts to unite radical art and radical politics: they resulted in division not over ends but means to those ends. The same tendency was evident in the seemingly different notions of historical precedent that Barrault and Beck used to justify their actions. Though drawn from radically different sources, the precedents claimed by each led back to the avant-garde's close ties with anarchistic sentiment. The authority granted by precedent was certainly not lost on Barrault. Having found himself cast outside the seemingly progressive currents of history, Barrault acknowledged, "One is never really aware of the image one has in the eyes of other people."[51] Rather than resigning himself to this image, however, his response was to contest the terms by which he (and those who had occupied the Odéon) would be judged. His turn to Rabelais, as the piece itself shows, evinced a sharp awareness that theater, even guerrilla theater, is grounded in repetition and draws its authority from tradition and historical precedent. The question was which precedent? Though brilliantly argued through his adaptation, Barrault's assertion that Rabelais's times are our times was not the historical analogy his audience most likely would have drawn with regard to the political unrest in Paris '68. Nor would they have likely looked to Rabelais as a source of legitimacy for avant-garde expression. Indeed, with regard to historical precedence—both political and theatrical—*Rabelais* articulated a counternarrative to the striking parallels between the student activism of 1968 and the Paris Commune of 1871.

On a political level, Paris itself was the site of radical history, and the student barricades were unmistakably reminiscent of the barricades erected during the Commune. Other events underscored this visible parallel, events like the attempts of the students to reach out to the unions and workers in the factories. These attempts (unsuccessful as they were in the bitter final analysis) echoed the "decree [issued during the Commune that] encouraged workers' co-operatives to take over abandoned factories and workshops."[52] While during the Commune few workers actually followed the encouragement, during May 1968 the workers' initial support was short-lived. After massive strikes in support of the students, "the so-called 'Communist' party and its unions came to de Gaulle's rescue and accepted a ridiculous compromise. The workers were persuaded to go back to work by their bureaucratic 'leaders.'"[53] Even the occupation of the Odéon echoed the turbulent period of the Commune. For during the siege of Paris, the Odéon was transformed from a conventional theater into a hospital.

The cultural politics of the occupation also recalled the Commune. Just as the Council of the Commune passed general responsibility for the theaters "into the hands of the Commission of Education" so that it could concentrate on other matters and so that the commission could establish an agenda for Parisian theater, so too in 1968 did the CAR decide "to move on to other things in other places" while remaining fundamentally at the disposal of the Committee of the Occupation of the ex–Theatre of France.[54] Indeed, while the CAR, in expressing its "solidarity and sympathy with the Committee of the Occupation of the ex–Theater of France," echoed the Council of the Commune's decision that all theater "companies and troupes should henceforth be run as self-managing co-operatives," this expression of solidarity included an acknowledgment only of guerrilla theater.[55] On this point the CAR was also in sync with its late-nineteenth-century predecessor. Not only did the precepts of guerilla theater, that is, to readapt theater in order to "teach" and "direct toward change," echo the sentiments articulated in the manifesto of the Federation of Artists of Paris that the communards read at the "School of Medicine at the Sorbonne," but both the CAR and the Council of the Commune pushed for artistic expression "free of commercial considerations."[56]

With so many similarities between the student upheavals in 1968 and the Paris Commune of 1871, one may question whether across the centuries, debates in theology and in theater have enough in common for the type of parallel that Barrault sought in *Rabelais*. It certainly did not hurt that Alfred Jarry had also adapted Rabelais for the stage. Nor did it hurt that Guy Debord had in part laid the foundation of Barrault's adaptation of the festive carnival traditions of Rabelais when he called the Paris Commune the biggest festival of the nineteenth century. While these were important supports to the work that Barrault was doing, his adaptation of Rabelais had far more depth than what Baz Kershaw calls the "orthodoxy among performance analysts to associate performative excessiveness with notions of carnival and festival—bacchanalic riotousness."[57] Barrault found in Rabelais a profound historical relevance to the events of May that blossomed into a full-scaled critique of those memorable days of unrest.

The historical context of *Gargantua* was greatly determined by the *Affaire des Placards* in 1534 when Paris awoke one October morning and discovered that the city streets had been covered with posters vulgarly denouncing the pope, the priesthood, the Mass, and "the doctrine of Real Presence." Those responsible for the publication of the placard were much divided about the prudence of its uncompromising severity, and some argued that the placards "would alienate the sympathy of many, and thus retard, instead of advancing, the cause it advocated."[58] The forebodings proved correct. The repressive backlash to the placards, felt for years to come, was more brutal and violent than any measures taken in 1968 by the hated CRS. Despite the disparity in repressive measures, Barrault recalled that the situation toward the end of the occupation reminded him of that very "business of the Placards."[59] It is little wonder why. The slogan "The only theater is guerilla theater" not only appeared in the bulletins of the occupation. The slogan along with dozens of placards and countless graffiti was plastered all along the streets of Paris. When the streets had been cleared and official order reestablished, backlash propelled de Gaulle to a landslide reelection.

Barrault matched the parallels in historical context with parallels in content. The founding link between Rabelais's writing and Barrault's drama pivots on Barrault's adaptation of Rabelais's use in *Gargantua and Pantagruel* of liturgical imagery as a metaphor through which to criticize the irreconcilable heterodoxies emerging in the sixteenth-century church. After seemingly endless anecdotes about the insatiability of Gargantua, Rabelais's narrative abruptly shifts attention to an invasion of Gargantua's homeland while he is a student in Paris. Summoned home by his father, Grandgousier, Gargantua returns to defend his homeland against the armies of the neighboring King Picrochole. The pretext for Picrochole's ambitious attack is an argument between shepherds keeping watch over vineyards and bakers taking bread to the market. The argument escalates into a full-scaled invasion, a campaign conducted by bakers of bread against vineyard watchmen, in other words bread against wine. This subtle allusion to the sacraments of bread and wine is nothing less than the beginning disintegration of the central sacraments of the Christian faith, a polarization of the body and blood of Christ. Bakhtin, one of the few critics who has given the allusion consideration, cites

Rabelais's use of the liturgical complex of grapes and cakes as an instance of debasing parody (since, according to the narrator of *Gargantua,* the combination of grapes and cakes has the purging effect of a laxative). Bakhtin cites this parody of the sacraments as another example of Rabelais's festive carnival. But it is carnival embedded in a harsh critique of the irreconcilable divisions that were splitting the sixteenth-century church.

Equally harsh and critical was Barrault's staging of the invasion by Picrochole's armies. Rabelais had positioned himself outside the factional divisions of the church by personifying his criticism in Gargantua, whose origins were in oral festive traditions. Barrault, in turn, positioned himself outside of the factional divisions of the avant-garde by equating the oral festive traditions in *Gargantua* with the "style of Alfred Jarry's *Ubu Roi,*" and he staged the invasion with a corresponding "circus atmosphere."[60] Just as Jarry's *Ubu* had "promoted a bitingly satiric denigration of bourgeois values via parodies of existing nineteenth-century theatrical styles," Barrault used *Rabelais* in a bitingly satiric denigration of the naïveté of the guerilla theater troupes who forced their way into the Odéon.[61] The invading armies in the Picrocholine War were cast as "a noisy political demonstration, waving all sorts of banners, placards and portraits, and bellowing imaginary national anthems."[62] The allusion here was difficult to mistake because it was so fresh in everyone's memory. Six months earlier the streets had been alive with identical images of students turned would-be revolutionaries. Indeed, when Julian Beck and Judith Malina had led the group that occupied the Odéon, they had done so "waving black anarchist flags" and "singing the 'Internationale.'"[63] In this single image of placards, banners, and song, Barrault took the occupation of the Odéon and insinuated that its divisiveness within the avant-garde was equivalent to the destruction of sacraments with redemptive power.

Given Barrault's appeal to the theater of Alfred Jarry, not to mention his reliance on the irreverence of Rabelais's own work, the critical alternative he offered to proactive guerilla theater was far from a mere reactionary reassertion of bourgeois pieties. Skillfully blurring the scatological with the eschatological and touting the tradition of what Yeats in a fit of disgust with Jarry's *Ubu Roi* had called the emergence of the "Savage God," Barrault laid claim to the earliest, offensive manifestations of avant-garde performance when appealing to Jarry's theater—Jarry the infamous offender of bourgeois culture who arguably fathered the avant-garde when his Ubu delivered the opening line "Merde!"[64] As Christopher Innes has noted, the uproar at *Ubu Roi*'s premier "was so violent" that the play continued only with the accompaniment of "catcalls and vociferous arguments between rioting factions in the audience."[65] While such pandemoniac displays certainly recalled the forums conducted during the occupation of the Odéon, Barrault's staging returned in kind the scatological performances that the occupiers of the Odéon themselves had advocated and indeed pursued. To Beck's "Shit on everything rather than the sterile power clean machine," to Lebel's "It's time for mass shit-ins," but above all to those who had transformed his theater company's wardrobes into a "soup . . . filled with excrement," Barrault offered a Rabelaisian salute, a crude flaunting of the grotesque body and its fluids.[66] Turning his back to the audience and the activists, Barrault staged Rabelais's "The Arse-Wiper":

> To reply to all the Putherbes, to all the *enragés:* sacroshams, creeping Jesuses, gullygutses, church vermin, mealymouths, devourers of men's substance who, with Genet as a pretext, had as good as called in the police to have us banned and arrested. Just as, four centuries earlier, they did to the priest of Meudon. All the *voyeurs,* the chicken-arses, the hypocritical sanctimonious sorbonnizing right-thinkers, had made me determined to stage the arse-wiping scene.[67]

Despite Barrault's obvious desire to settle the score with those who had ransacked his theater and his work, the decision to stage the scatological arse-wiping scene transcended the instance of getting even. The scene wrestled for the mantle of tradition and precedent, vying for the authority conferred by the legacy of Alfred Jarry. The combination of Jarry and Rabelais—a volatile mixture by any measure—underscored the paradoxical nature of the grotesque body in Rabelais's oeuvre: at once holy, at once profane and thus emblematic of a liberating redemption from the prevailing pieties of Rabelais's day and of Barrault's. But this same grotesque body was also emblematic of a radical tension within the avant-garde.

In his criticism of earlier, comparable divisiveness in the church, Rabelais seized upon a central ambiguity in Christian discourse. The body of Christ, as the Church is so often called, split over questions like whether the sacraments were or were not the actual body of Christ. Rabelais inverted the structure of this ambiguity, transforming the dispute over "the doctrine of real presence" into a more general question regarding the authenticity of the Church itself. Giving narrative form to an allegorical polarization of the sacraments, Rabelais implicitly questioned in *Gargantua* whether a church could still provide spiritual guidance when it was so bitterly and irreconcilably divided over the issue of transubstantiation. Whether the symbols of faith actually became the objects of faith, or, more simply put, whether signifier and signified were one and the same in the holy sacraments was certainly an important question even for Rabelais as a humanist, but he did not view the question as litmus test for determining the true Church.

It is not very difficult to see why in 1968 Barrault was attracted to Rabelais's concerns with the church doctrine. In addition to its direct relation to the agonistic traditions of the avant-garde, the question of whether the sacraments were a symbolic representation or an immediate manifestation of the body of Christ could easily be manipulated into a question of whether the collective activity of the students was merely a symbolic representation or an immediate manifestation of revolutionary theater. By playing upon the ambiguity in Christian discourse that allowed the "body of Christ" to signify both the sacraments and the Church, Rabelais afforded Barrault the opportunity to appropriate the debate over the doctrine of real presence and turn it into an allegorical reflection on what constitutes real theater. The occupation of the Odéon centered on that question as well. But the occupiers had turned it into an either/or proposition. Like different factions of the early French reformers accusing one another of heresy, those who had occupied the Odéon asserted the dramatic legitimacy of their spontaneous action by denouncing the legitimacy of any other theater. (In this respect, they not only followed the precedent set by the French reformers but that set by the surrealists as well.) Like Rabelais, who in *Gargantua and Pantagruel* had distanced himself from such binary propositions, Barrault attempted to push his drama beyond the ideologically calculated dilemmas offered during the month that the Odéon was occupied. In doing so Barrault ultimately challenged the underlying assumptions of guerilla theater, questioning its notions of immediacy and direct action by placing them in a context of theatrical representation.

While on the one hand one might argue that this act was fundamentally at odds with the very essence of direct action, it also emphasized the "spectacular" nature of all direct action and underscored the extent to which, even on the streets, guerilla theater never could legitimately claim immediacy or fully escape the trappings of representation. Even as figures like Julian Beck maintained that the citizens in May had demanded nothing less than "the miracle: paradise now," Barrault was concluding his post-May vision of the theater with the image of Rabelais on his deathbed asking, on the one hand, for the very sacraments whose status could not be determined and then calling in the next breath for the curtain to fall. In this final image, Barrault sidestepped the doctrine of real presence by suggesting that even in dying we, like the sacraments, are also caught in that contradictory space between immediacy and representation.

Mock Utopia: Of Communal Societies and Paradise Then and Now

If the historical and theological analogies of Barrault's piece were too rarified on their own, Barrault compensated with staging practices that, like his staging of the invading armies of Picrochole, conjured familiar images and parodied the naively utopian underpinnings of direct action. Nowhere was this compensation more evident than in Barrault's staging of Rabelais's Abbey of Thélème. With a refined sense of mimicry and caricature—Barrault was after all a master mime—Barrault directed that "the Abbey of Thélème should reveal complete freedom of expression, with each person improvising in harmony with the ideas of the others." Accentuating this "staged improvisation" was a relaxed atmosphere of sexual liberation. Women with scantily covered breasts danced with "youths with provocative codpieces," while other "'Hippy' couples . . . [lay on the floor] making 'love not war.'"[68] Variations of such images could be found across the spectrum of the youth movement in festivals and concerts, but for those involved in student activism and/or political theater, the quasi-utopian image of the Abbey of Thélème bore a rather satirical resemblance to the Living Theatre's *Paradise Now*—all the way down to the G-strings. Indeed, it is no small coincidence that the one-clause antirule "DO WHAT YOU WILL" that governs Rabelais's Abbey of Thélème later resurfaces, albeit in modified form, in Beck's philosophical clarifications of *Paradise Now*.[69] The dictum, "There is no grace: there is no guilt: / This is the Law: DO WHAT THOU WILT" (which Beck appropriated from Malcolm Crowley) is central not only to *Paradise Now* but also to the conception of political freedom that guided the Living Theatre's entire political *engagement* in the theater.[70] Given Beck's own sense of the irreconcilability of fiction and freedom, the subtle allusion that Barrault's staging of the Abbey made to *Paradise Now,* inasmuch as the allusion associated with repetition and representation, had rather damning implications, suggesting among other things that *Paradise Now* was caught in its own web of fictions.

As was the case regarding the occupation of the Odéon, here too with *Paradise Now* the accusation was that the Living Theatre was naively advocating fictional freedoms—if not also participating in its own brand of special pleading. Again, Barrault was not a sole voice in this implicit criticism. At one level, Beck and Malina were acutely aware of the fictional trappings of the paradise that they performed and experienced, and, they worked hard to distance themselves from those trappings or at the very least the appearance of them. Though describing their productions as "ritualistic," Beck and Malina maintained nonetheless that *Paradise Now* was not an enactment but rather "the act itself," that it was not a reproduction but rather "always . . . a new experience" and "different from what we called acting."[71] Such descriptions were only partially satisfactory and circumvented a more fundamental question, one raised not only by Barrault but also by the same *enragés* whom Malina described as those "Parisian revolutionary kids who . . . can play *Paradise Now* like no other audience."[72] Those same revolutionary kids, the ones who had earlier liberated the Odéon despite its antibourgeois reputation, questioned the revolutionary character of *Paradise Now* despite the Living

Theatre's claim that "*Paradise Now* was . . . [their] contribution to the revolution." Under pressure from the *enragés*'s criticism, Beck finally conceded that the piece and the Living Theatre "were caught in the same trap that the rest of the would is caught in."[73] Though the concession referred specifically to the *enragés*'s efforts to get the Living Theatre to withdraw from the Avignon Festival—something the Living Theatre only did when they were censured by the Avignon city authorities—the criticism was arguably a much more general statement about the degree to which the Living Theatre, for all its antibourgeois, revolutionary sentiment, was still caught within the spectral realms of the society of the spectacle.

Though bitter and critical of the Living Theatre, Barrault was not primarily concerned with Beck's preoccupation with the contrast between reproduction and "the act itself," nor was Barrault all that concerned by the ostensibly restrictive relation of text to performance (i.e., of "word made flesh"). His concern was more about the ease with which revolutionary theater could deceive itself into believing that it had escaped the trappings of representation and had entered the immediacy of revolutionary politics. He was concerned, in short, with the false or fictional unification of radical art with radical politics. This concern—a not so distant echo of Aragon's criticism of Breton—while separating Beck and Barrault in the immediacy of their historical moment, ironically united them within a long tradition of the avant-garde: that gesture which strives toward the unification of radical art and radical politics but always divides its own ranks.

NOTES

1. Taylor was by no means a stranger to avant-garde circles, having worked, as Sally Banes notes, with "John Cage and Merce Cunningham in their experiment at Black Mountain College in 1953" and collaborated with the likes of Robert Rauschenberg, Jasper Johns, Ellsworth, and Alex Katz ("Meaning in Motion," *Connoisseur,* March 1985, 94).

2. John Tytell, *The Living Theatre* (New York: Grove Press, 1995), 232.

3. Renato Poggioli, *Theory of the Avant-Garde,* trans. Gerald Fitzgerald (Cambridge: Belknap Press of Harvard University Press, 1968), 11.

4. Robert. S. Short, "The Politics of Surrealism, 1920–36," in *Left Wing Intellectuals between the Wars,* ed. Walter Laquer and George Mosse (New York: Harper, 1966), 3.

5. Sadie Plant, *The Most Radical Gesture* (New York: Routledge, 1992), 101.

6. Jean-Jacques Lebel, "On the Necessity of Violation," in *Happenings and Other Acts,* ed. Mariellen R. Sanford (New York: Routledge, 1995), 283.

7. Ibid., 275.

8. In an effort to give surrealism revolutionary credibility, Breton had at that time denounced and expelled those surrealists who would not sign on to his notion of a collective political program. As bitterly divisive as the purges were, they hardly brought the surviving surrealists much more than the appearance of radical politics; the

purges certainly did little to bring them much closer to the revolutionary forces of the Communist Party.

9. Pierre Biner, *The Living Theatre* (New York: Horizon Press, 1972), 203.

10. This portrayal would at the very least accentuate the underlying assumptions of Guerrilla Theatre in which, as R. G. Davis notes, "there is to be no distinction between public behavior and private behavior. Do in public [Davis admonishes] what you do in private, or stop doing it in private." See "Guerrilla Theatre," *Drama Review* 10, no. 4 (1966): 131.

11. Short, "The Politics of Surrealism," 16.

12. Ibid., 17.

13. In this respect, the tension between Beck and Barrault offers an important additional dimension to Jon Erikson's more general definition of the avant-garde's notion of its relation to art. In *Fate of the Object* (Ann Arbor: University of Michigan Press, 1995), Erikson argues, "An antiart movement arises when it becomes obvious that art has become indentured to systems of meaning congruent with, if not dependent upon, systems of cultural repression. Thus antiart is a desire for the preservation of the force of art as autonomous from corrupt and determining powers, which use art by incorporating formerly effective autonomous art into their own meaning systems" (34). While there is little to disagree with in this succinct clarification of the underlying desires of "antiart," the examples of the occupation of the Odéon and the politics of the surrealists would suggest that the indentured status of artistic expressions is always subject to multiple and contradictory interpretations.

14. Plant, *The Most Radical Gesture,* 56.

15. Greil Marcus, *Lipstick Traces: A Secret History of the Twentieth Century* (Cambridge: Harvard University Press, 1989), 140.

16. Though not citing the situationists' impact on the events of May, Christopher Innes arrives at very similar conclusions about the nature of the Commune. In *Avant-Garde Theatre: 1892–1992* (New York: Routledge, 1993), he posits a conceptual parallel between the anarchistic Bakunin and the literary theorist Bakhtin (particularly Bakhtin's interest in Rabelais) in order to argue that the anarchistic irreverence and abusive parodies characteristic of the avant-garde follow a tradition beginning in the folk traditions of Rabelais. Innes sees in this confluence not only a foreshadowing of the "sexual liberation and social revolution [that] formed the core of the Living Theatre" but also a foreshadowing of figures like Alfred Jarry and Jean-Louis Barrault (8).

17. Julian Beck, *The Life of the Theatre* (San Francisco: City Lights, 1972), 91.

18. For Beck, this gesture had a number of important precursors, not the least of which were the "the improvisatory flights of jazz" that he was careful to relate historically "to the experiments of Dada and Surrealism" (ibid., 45). Beck openly acknowledged his troupe's attempt to emulate the example of jazz improvisation and its conscious rejection of a preestablished score. Disavowing the Living Theatre's own productions of works like Pirandello's *Tonight We Improvise,* Beck rejected script just as jazz had rejected score. In seeking a model for this rejection, Beck looked to more recent trends in avant-garde performance and attempted to politicize the theatrical spontaneity found in the work of Allan Kaprow and the Happenings. Since jazz improvisation was associated with an artistic expression of resistance, the logic here was ultimately to equate the antitextual attitudes of the Happenings with freedom itself.

19. Poggioli, *Theory of the Avant-Garde,* 11.

20. Michael Kirby, "Happenings: An Introduction," in Sanford, *Happenings and Other Acts,* 17, 5.

21. Ibid., 5.

22. Ibid., 4–5.

23. Beck, *Life of the Theatre,* 45.

24. An acute sense of the resilience of the bourgeois, that is, of its recuperative powers, was not overlooked by those widely reputed to be the intellectual force behind the student unrest in 1968, the situationists. Not only were the situationists the only group to have accurately predicted the events of May, but they arguably saw the course that those events would ultimately take. As Sadie Plant notes in her history of the situationists, "The situationists argued that it is as a consequence of these recuperative powers that 'the ruling society has proved capable of defending itself, on all levels of reality, much better than revolutionaries expected.' It should never be forgotten, they warned, that *'the bourgeoisie is the only revolutionary class that ever won',* and all revolutionary criticism must recognize the failures of the past and learn from the implications and effects of this failure" (*The Most Radical Gesture,* 77). Despite the admonishments, the students played right into to de Gaulle's hands.

25. Peter Bürger, "Adorno's Anti-Avant-Gardism," *Telos* 86 (1990–91): 52–53.

26. Ibid., 53.

27. Beck, *Life of the Theatre,* 91.

28. Lebel, "Necessity of Violation," 275.

29. Graham White, "Direct Action, Dramatic Action: Theatre and Situationist Theory," *New Theatre Quarterly* 36 (1993): 331.

30. Jean-Jacques Lebel, "Notes on Political Street Theatre, Paris 1968, 1969," *Drama Review* 13, no. 4 (1969): 112.

31. Richard Schechner, "Radicalism, Sexuality, and Performance," *Drama Review* 13, no. 4 (1969): 93.

32. Ibid.

33. White, "Direct Action, Dramatic Action," 332.

34. Raoul Vaneigem, *The Revolution of Everyday Life,* trans. Donald Nicholson-Smith (1967; London: Rebel Press, 1993), 276.

35. Davis, "Guerrilla Theatre," 132.

36. White, "Direct Action, Dramatic Action," 329.

37. Peter Bürger, *Theory of the Avant-Garde,* trans. Michael Shaw (Minneapolis: University of Minnesota Press, 1984), 80.

38. Guy Debord, *The Society of the Spectacle,* trans. Donald Nicholson-Smith (New York: Zone, 1995), 37.

39. René Viénet, *Enragés and Situationists in the Occupation Movement, France, May '68,* (London: Rebel Press, 1992), 53.

40. Jean-Louis Barrault, *Memories for Tomorrow,* trans. Jonathan Griffin (London: Thames and Hudson, 1974), 319.

41. Poggioli, *Theory of the Avant-Garde,* 66.

42. Ibid., 99–100.

43. Barrault, *Memories for Tomorrow,* 320.

44. Jean-Louis Barrault, *Rabelais,* trans. Robert Baldick (London: Faber and Faber, 1971), 22–23.

45. Barrault, *Memories for Tomorrow,* 329.

46. Aside from their both having some affiliation with the avant-garde, Jean-Louis Barrault and Theodor W. Adorno would seem to have very little in common. The notable exception is that, when European students took to the streets in the late sixties, both Barrault and Adorno unexpectedly found themselves to be the recipients

of strikingly similar expressions of contempt and scorn. Adorno, humiliated while trying to give a lecture in Frankfurt, packed up his notes and left the lecture hall while students chanted "Adorno as an institution is dead!" Barrault, director of the Odéon Theatre de France, encountered similar pronouncements from students who occupied the theater during the events of May 1968. In fact, newspaper accounts of the occupation were prefaced by the headline "Barrault Is Dead." Ironically the papers attributed this student slogan to Barrault himself because he repeated it when responding to the students' sarcastic invitations for him to address them from the stage. The pronouncement foreshadowed the end of his relationship with the Odéon Theatre.

47. Theodor Adorno, *Aesthetic Theory,* trans. C. Lenhardt (New York: Routledge, 1970), 60.

48. Barrault, *Memories for Tomorrow,* 328.

49. Jean-Louis Barrault, *Reflections on the Theatre,* trans. Barbara Wall (London: Rockliff, 1951), 41.

50. Beck, *Life of the Theatre,* 45.

51. Barrault, *Memories for Tomorrow,* 311.

52. Rupert Christiansen, *Paris Babylon* (New York: Viking, 1995), 319.

53. Lebel, "Political Street Theatre," 112.

54. Christiansen, *Paris Babylon,* 347; Lebel, "Necessity of Violation," 275.

55. Lebel, "Necessity of Violation," 275; Christiansen, *Paris Babylon,* 347.

56. Davis, "Guerrilla Theatre," 131; Christensen, *Paris Babylon,* 317.

57. Baz Kershaw, "Fighting in the Streets: Dramaturgies of Popular Protest, 1968–1989," *New Theatre Quarterly* 51 (1997): 265.

58. Henry Baird, *Rise of the Huguenots* (New York: Scribners, 1879), 165.

59. Barrault, *Memories for Tomorrow,* 319.

60. Barrault, *Rabelais,* 43.

61. Michael Huxley and Noel Witts, *Twentieth Century Performance Reader* (New York: Routledge, 1996), 214.

62. Barrault, *Rabelais,* 44.

63. Tytell, *The Living Theatre,* 232.

64. Since its articulation at the close of the nineteenth century, this line has echoed repeatedly through the antiestablishment avant-garde. Peter Brook gave as good an explanation as any when in 1968 he argued in *The Empty Space* (New York: Atheneum, 1968): "If we find that dung is a good fertilizer, it is no use being squeamish; if the theatre seems to need a certain crude element, this must be accepted as part of its natural soil" (66).

65. Innes, *Avant-Garde Theatre,* 22.

66. Beck, *Life of the Theatre,* 13; Lebel, "Necessity of Violation," 283–84; Barrault, *Memories for Tomorrow,* 318.

67. Barrault, *Memories for Tomorrow,* 327.

68. Barrault, *Rabelais,* 75.

69. Ibid., 159.

70. Beck, *Life of the Theatre,* 48.

71. Julian Beck and Judith Malina, "Containment Is the Enemy," *Drama Review* 13, no. 1 (1969): 26, 24–25.

72. Ibid., 32.

73. Ibid., 32–33.

Conducted by James M. Harding

An Interview with Richard Schechner

February 1997

Some theater historians have complained about the undue influence that English departments have historically had in shaping our conceptions of drama and performance. In short, they complain about a disproportional emphasis on the literary rather than the performative dimensions of theater. This concern would seem to be of particular relevance when considering the history of the avant-garde. Do you think that the presumptions of a literature-based classroom blind us to crucial dimensions of avant-garde performance?

I don't know if an emphasis on dramatic literature blinds one to performance as such, but the two are different subjects. Your question is like asking, "Does chemistry blind you to architecture?" Literature and performance: they're different subjects. Is the object of study behavior or writing? Literature is behavior mostly at the moment it is being written and to a lesser degree—if you believe certain kinds of reception theory—at the moment it is being read. Of course, in this sense *everything* must be "read," i.e., "received" in order to be understood. What makes performance different is that it is very contingent, supple, changing, flexible as it is being "written" or "composed" and as it is being received; and that often the moment of composition and the moment of reception are identical. This is even true of a so-called fixed text, a scored drama or dance; that is because even in fixed texts there is a great deal that is loose, that varies from instance to instance. Much more so than in a written text or film, where the item to be received is fixed and what changes are the circumstances of reception and the audience.

In this regard note that I categorize movies as a form of literature, not as performance. The *source* of the material from which films are made is performed behavior; but the finished film itself—what an audience sees—is as fixed as any novel or poem. The behavior on the screen does not vary, cannot vary, from showing to showing. When a certain radical reception occurs, as in *The Rocky Horror Picture Show* where teenagers came knowing the script by heart and enacting it—or counter-acting it—in the theater at the moment of screening, a definite performance activity of the spectators supplemented the literary activity of the movie. Movies are behavior when they are being filmed, but once in the can they are like print.

Behavior is marked by qualities of presence and contingency, both contested terms. *Presence* means that the author or producer of the behavior is there actually behaving, actually doing at the same moment and in the same space with the receivers. *Contingence* means that no score is perfectly reenacted time and again. Every instance is either an original or there is no original anytime. You can't have a "manuscript" or a "master print" of a performance, a single source from which everything else is a copy. Media means there is at least an implied original, or first thing, which is then "treated" in such a way, mediatized, and then copied and broadcast, or broadcast as a potentially endlessly replicating item. But what is comparable to an "original" in theater, for example? A "first night"? But what is first night? It is the end point of a series of rehearsals, nothing more. The first night does not fix the performances that come after, once and for all. That is why theater reviewing is so different than book reviewing. The theater reviewer is examining one instance; a book reviewer is examining the thing itself. What is largely ephemeral in terms of books is fundamental to theater. I mean the mode of presentation. The binding, paper quality, and typeface are of course important adjuncts to literature, but not nearly as decisive as the words, the sentence structure, the shape of the whole work as literature. But in theater, the mode of presentation is part of the core of the thing—and that includes who is playing the roles, who has directed: a whole bunch of contingencies and variables. Yes, everyone who admires criticism and scholarship wishes performance were easier to pin down, more fixed. And writers about performance act as if performance was as settled a category as literature. But it isn't. If one honestly indexes one's *experience* in doing or receiving a performance, you have to acknowledge that performance is open and subversive of fixity. Even the tightest score is flexible. I who have spent so many years of my life in rehearsal rooms know how impossible it is even when you're working with the strictest discipline to fix something, nor do I want to. What I want is a tension between that which can be fixed, that which can be predicted to a certain degree within a certain range (where you move, how you speak, etc.) and that which cannot (the quality called "presence," what Walter Benjamin called "aura"). But even in the most strictly scored ballet, the leg goes up and it may not go up exactly the way that it did before, with the same muscular tensions, the same kind of ease, and those differences do affect how both the performer and the spectators experience the lift; and as the experience varies, so do all meanings and associations. That subversion of fixity is what fascinates people like Judith Butler—who extend the notion of subversion and flexibility to gender: according to Butler, one is the gender one performs. Looking at this another way, biology is destiny means gender is like literature, written in the genes; but if one thinks of gender as performance, than whatever the genes may *suggest,* one can play them out differently. Also there is the whole different notion of error that obtains in the physical production of a book and the physical production of a performance. If you pick up a book and see blurred type or a typo, you the reader read right through the error, make the correction, see the way it ought to be, the way it was written in the first place. If the author is lucky, and there is a second printing, the errors are corrected. But errors are much harder to identify in performance. You watch a show—a stage play or a performance in everyday life, a gender display, whatever—and something uncomfortable or "passing strange" or funny happens; and you wonder: Was this meant to be, or is this a mistake? And every actor can tell stories about mistakes that improved the show, that were kept the next time round.

To get back to the classroom, once scholars were asked to be teachers first and researchers second, to be educators ahead of being thinkers, i.e., once college became the place where youth was educated—which is not what the universities always did—then teachers needed fixed and reliable texts. These texts were often written by people other than the teachers. This is not the Socratic method at all. Socrates interrogated his students with ideas that were his own. He may have referred to other philosophers, but what he taught, first and foremost, was Socrates. Not so our ordinary teacher these days. The ordinary teacher, the good teacher even, interprets, reads, cites, and to a great degree passes on knowledge and opinions that are not his or her own. Today's teacher is a pipeline, not a source.

The notion of textual interpretation can be tied to the history of exegesis. The humanities *did* come out of religion, a child of the marriage between trusting empirical observation (the development of modern sciences) and the art of interpretation. The Bible was *logos,* the Word, it was what it was, unchangeable but interpretable. In the Renaissance and during the epoch of positivism, observable phenomena became Nature's Word, unchangeable (or at least regular, predictable, lawful), but interpretable. The humanities emerged with a high regard for the Word, for the book, for who authors the book or can convincingly interpret it, the author and her/his interpreter, the authority. What was done with Bible studies was transferred to the study of literature: keep the words intact, but change their meanings through interpretation.

But behavior-based outlook, a performative outlook, introduces the ability to change the primary text, or whatever you want to call it. More, the performative approach insists that there is no primary text, what appears to be primary is actually fluid, unfixed. This subversion of fixity applies not only to interpretation but to what's being interpreted. There develops a dancing relationship, a continuously shifting relationship, between two variables: the performance text and the interpretation.

And this is true also of ritual?

Well, yes. Rituals are much more dynamic than are usually thought. That is why they persist. They obviously have certain things that remain the same, certain core gestures. But, as Emile Durkheim observed more than eighty years ago, rituals are actions, they are performances, so they follow the laws of performance, they are unfixed and subversive. Ritualists—priests, shamans, and so on—may try to give rituals the quality of fixity, to make them like the Word, but this attempt can never be wholly successful because rituals are transmitted corporally, through the bodies of its practitioners. Rituals thereby carry within them a severe tension between their encoded text (the sequence of actions to be performed) and who performs them. And the performers of rituals not only vary what they do, how they do it, the style in which it is done, they also more often than is ordinarily supposed change the encoded text itself. Ritual may change less rapidly than other kinds of performance, but ritual definitely is in motion, changes over time.

Furthermore, one of the most interesting things about ritual performances is that sometimes the most powerful, the most charismatic are not the best performances. In other words, there are many people who may be better public performers than the pope, but only the pope is the pope, and therefore only the pope projects the pope's aura. The pope's gestures as he faces the crowds gathered in St. Peter's Square may be faint and frail, "ineffective," at the end of his life, but despite this failure to be a good actor, the pope is going to get much more attention than an actor playing pope. So here is a paradox. What is "real" in these cases is the power invested in a particular person, and this power infuses whatever that person does. An actor, like Plato's shadow in the cave, is at a remove from such reality. Ritual confers on its performers the reality of a particular line of belief, a sometimes very long history of performance. This reality is fused with the body of the ritual performer. Knowing that this is the "real pope" and not an imitation makes all the difference to the believers who have assembled to see the pope, however frail and ineffective, and not some fake. What is happening is that the ritual supports the performer, the pope, even as the pope performs the ritual. Or to put it another way, the pope becomes his own body text. This is also true of all other persons who are who they are by virtue of the "authority" conferred into their bodies—judges, generals—those people Jean Genet in *The Balcony* identified as the Great Figures. This authority then gives their words and gestures particular power. With stage acting, aesthetic acting, you want the person who can perform the role best. But in ritual, you want the person in whose body the authority has been vested. One could generalize and say that aesthetic performances "make believe" while rituals performances "make belief."

But to get back to your question about teaching. It's harder to teach the *performances* of *Hamlet* than the text of *Hamlet*. Simply put, the text is there; but performance is not. Or maybe one or two performances are—you take a class to the theater, you look at a videotape. But these are only instances. What you can teach is not mostly an interpretation of the play, but a method of approaching performances. And those are very different things.

Literature scholars would say that you have hold of a text.

Right. You have hold of a text. In performance studies, the text would be a performance everyone has seen together or a videotape of a particular performance. From there you can say something about the meaning of the production, you can interpret it. But what is most interesting to me is to point out the variables possible, the basis for subversion, the multiple relationships opening up among author, actors, director, spectators. At present I am teaching a large undergraduate introductory course in performance studies, "Worlds of Performance." Each student has to go to at least four events; each is invited to make a performance—as well as the ordinary requirements of reading and writing. The students select four of seven events, ranging from Chinese New Year, to Gospel church, to an orthodox drama or dance, to a baseball game, to a Native American powwow (in Manhattan). There is no way that we can discuss performance just by reading or just by watching videos. Once the class has seen something, the discussion gets very concrete, about this particular performance on this night in this place. The questions raised are not only abstract ones about meanings but concrete ones about the techniques of staging. The students learn that the differences between art and life is not the "mirror held up to nature," but a more porous continuum or spectrum of activities, that art and life blend into each other; that a lot of ordinary life is staged and played out "artistically" even as a great deal of art—performance art especially (and I use the term both as a particular genre of performance and as the generality)—draws very directly on life, incorporates the actualities and contingencies of daily life into the act.

How are the demands of avant-garde performance, then, different from the more traditional performance?

Well, I would say that today's avant-garde is traditional. The avant-garde, as you're probably using the term, doesn't exist in 1997. In 1980, I thought that there were two avant-gardes. Now I think there are five. I categorize them briefly in the introduction to *The Future of Ritual*. There is the historical avant-garde, the current avant-garde, the forward-looking avant-garde, the backward-reaching avant-garde, and the intercultural avant-garde. Certain performances can be in more than in one of these categories. The current avant-garde is whatever journalists and scholars say is avant-garde. That is why it doesn't exist now. It exists only as a marketing strategy. It exists because people have named it, but if it means that which is "in advance of," there is nothing that is being done now that is being done "in advance of." What we call the avant-garde—say, what Richard Foreman does or the Wooster Group or Robert LePage, or me—is simply another style.

There was a real "current avant-garde" from the end of the nineteenth century with the burst of naturalism through various other movements (symbolism, futurism, dada, surrealism, etc.) until around 1980, maybe not that recent. During this period, what happened among those who were experimenting in the arts was picked up and disseminated. The avant-garde really was just that: in advance of. The classic example is naturalism. When Ibsen first did his plays or Strindberg his, they were shocking. Later they became part of the mainstream. But this kind of movement from fringe or shock to mainstream doesn't happen anymore. Nothing is really very shocking; there are many mainstreams. The work of people like those I've mentioned is not in advance of anything. Environmental theater, which I was one of the pioneer of, is Disney World. I can't imagine what an avant-garde would be. Of course, that doesn't mean that another one won't burst forth at some future time, maybe even tomorrow, for some reason. But I doubt it. I think we've entered what will be a very long period of stasis, a kind of neomedievalism.

The historical avant-garde, though, was particularly excited with advances in technologies, the futurists for example. There was a real fascination. Do you not think that current technologies offer fertile ground for the "in advance of" of a new avant-garde?

Don't fall for the hype! Name me an advance in technology that wasn't here fifty years ago. I mean if you're talking about three-dimensional or virtual reality or the Internet—the idea of communicating personally instantly over long distances and the transmission of images and words over long distances—has been with us since the development of the telephone and television, since the twenties and thirties. What we are seeing now is its extension, its globalization. That globalization is important and different, and it gives rise to what I call the intercultural avant-garde. The big issue today is how to maintain cultural diversity even as people everywhere want to acquire a general technical sameness: advanced communication, transportation, and so on, what is called development. The extension of technology and its integration into daily life on a worldwide scale is having profound consequences socially, not to mention environmentally and ecologically. Technologically we're elaborating on basic discoveries of the nineteenth and early twentieth centuries. The next step, if there is a next step, would be real science fiction. You know, "ziipp!" and you're dissolved and you reappear someplace else. *That* would be transportation! We can imagine it, but it doesn't fit our conception of the world, a universe limited by the speed of light.

Returning to the issue of staging, let me ask you about the issue of space. Is there an "avant-garde space" that literary histories overlook?

Some of the most radical experiments in space, environmental theater space, for example, were made by people interested in what I call the backward-looking and the intercultural avant-garde (Grotowski or myself for example). We found our models for staging—as well as other aspects of our theaters—in nontechnological cultures as well as in earlier versions of Western culture, in archaic and ritual practices. I think most theater histories—I don't know about literary histories—slight these experiments in organic spaces, audience participation, and the like: the cusp between ritual and aesthetic performance. Most theater histories adhere to an old-fashioned idea about the so-called origins of theater, that theater began as ritual and that there is an evolutionary development. This actually is Aristotle's idea, elaborated on by the Cambridge anthropologists at the turn of the century, and supported by a kind of social Darwinism, again of the nineteenth and early twentieth centuries, that "primitive" peoples were earlier or vestigial than so-called civilized (read, European) cultures. It's all bullshit. Ritual in the religious sense can't have been evolutionarily first. Did the early protohumans, the ones closest to the apes, *begin* with religion? Of course not. Nor did they begin with theater as we know it. They most probably began performing something that was neither and both. I don't want to go further into that here—I've written about it extensively elsewhere. But to get back to your question, theater history books are organized around the performance of plays, not the development of spaces, audience interactions, and so on. Such histories ignore the wide range of performance activities: popular entertainments, rituals, public ceremonial and so on.

What some in the avant-garde of the 1960s to 1970s did was to bring into the aesthetic theater practices and ideas from non-Western theater (both classical as from India, Japan, China and animist as from Australia, Papua–New Guinea). These practices involved actions common in religion and ritual: the body as a site of performance, sharing of food, audience participation, performances that extend in space and time. These traditional practices were combined with more technical practices deriving from film especially, montage, overlay, close-up. The theory of montage of texts (Grotowski) was developed from Sergei Eisenstein's montage of images. Eisenstein studied with theater director Vsevolod Meyerhold. Meyerhold developed the notion of biomechanics, or how to make human performers more like machines. Meyerhold, at one point in his life, was very fascinated with the beauty and efficiency of the assembly line. And the assembly line is in its own way a kind of montage. The item being manufactured comes into being through the addition of disparate parts. A textual montage is also the assembly of a whole from disparate parts. Montage plus ritual plus the full use of space plus audience participation equals a strong tradition in the avant-garde, one which has not yet had proper scholarly attention.

Now when Disneys get hold of the avant-garde, they give it a little pizzazz even as they make it safe. The performance takes place all around you, your chair spins, you feel mice crawling onto your feet—but you know it's all make-believe, totally controlled, without risk. Somewhat like Disney are the many restored villages and living museums, some more elaborate than others, more historically accurate. Plimoth Plantation and Colonial Williamsburg are among the best known. Original buildings are restored as in Williamsburg, or a complete simulation is constructed as at Plimoth, where the original site three miles away is all built up. The sponsors say that everything is real, but of course it's not. It's a kind of movie set, and the interpreters are actors. The script is an enactment of researched actual events mixed with probabilities. This kind of thing draws not only on the avant-garde but on a long tradition of colonial expositions, worlds' fairs, and amusement parks. Remember, in the U.S.A. at least, the midway, sideshow, museum, theme park, and trade fair are close relations.

But to get back to the avant-garde—what I want to know is how can we study avant-garde directors or auteurs in such a manner that does not immediately inscribe them into a literary paradigm?

The avant-garde director is an author, but of the performance text not the dramatic text. Let's look at theater, music, and dance. In theater, the dramatic text is a freestanding narrative that can be used to evoke a behavior, the play as performed. But you can interpret the dramatic text by itself, and to do so, at least at a certain level, you don't need any more special skills than it takes to read a novel. People in fact used to buy the plays of modern writers like Shaw, Pirandello, Miller, Williams simply to read them for pleasure, whether or not one went to the theater. But when you move to music and dance, things change radically. Although there is Laban or other notation for dance and music notation, without special training an ordinary person can't read them. Most people can't pick up a score and say, "I'll read a little Beethoven tonight before I go to bed." And even fewer can say, "I'll read some Balanchine." Most people experience music and dance *only* as performance (whether live or mediatized), while drama lives two lives—as literature and as performance.

Insofar as a director takes the dramatic text not as the cause or the prior authority but simply as material, as the spoken part of the performance text, used either as written or as part of a montage (deconstructed and put together with other texts, spoken, sung, moved), then the director is the author of the performance text. In most of my theater work, I do not make a textual montage, but radically interpret a prior text which I accept more or less as written. So my *Three Sisters* is staged in four different time periods in different acting styles; or my *Oresteia* is done by Beijing Opera Chinese performers in *jingju* style. Others, like Grotowski, put together the uttered text as they do the movement or scenic texts, from a variety of sources—including their own and their actors' original compositions.

I believe I retain the texts because I want to engage these texts in a kind of dialectic, I want to interrogate the texts, and make them signify in ways they haven't previously done. When I did *The Bacchae* (*Dionysus in 69*) I made a lot of changes; and when I did *Makbeth* and *Commune* I constructed textual montages. But for the most part, I've honored the texts of the plays I've directed. But I have not honored the scenic or acting intentions of the authors. Now how would one study these productions? They can't be approached in a literary manner. One would have to put together a good deal of documentation in terms of videos, slides, program notes, and other data in order to get at the performance texts. It's not easy to do, and that's why it's rarely done.

Currently I am teaching a course called "Redirecting the (Realist) Classics." The students have to take plays by people such as Williams, Miller, Chekhov, Ibsen, etc. and stage scenes any way that they want, but not realistically. In this way the students see that realism is simply a style among styles, that realist texts can be restaged in totally different ways. When they are staged differently, their meanings radically change also! That is, the meanings of these plays does not reside only or even mostly in the words, the play texts, but in the interaction among words, staging, scenography, and audience reception. That may seem obvious, it is a theoretical truism, but to see it actualized in a class is very exciting indeed.

That means, of course, that any dramatic text is always fraught with a multiplicity of possibilities.

Exactly. Very flexible. Again, that subversivity and flexibility of performance. Because it's not that the texts are inherently supple, but that performance makes them so.

I think that your resistance to even my use of the term "avant-garde" is rather interesting in the way that it forces discussion back to that multiplicity of possibilities, that is, to the multiple particular possibilities of performance. And that is where the real stakes are for you.

Absolutely. I am as much an anthropologist as I am a director. What fascinates me are the minute particulars of concrete social encounters at specific times. In theater, everything important is specific. You have to start with this performer on this stage or in this space doing that thing for those people. From there you can derive certain things, but you can't assume, as people do with literary criticism, that there is a Hamlet separate from *that* Hamlet enacted by *that* actor or by *this* actress. For me there is no Hamlet—no more than there is "the King." There is Henry IV, Queen Elizabeth I or II, King George I to VI, and so on. If you begin to study enough of them specifically, you may begin to get some general idea—some Platonic ideal about kingship or about how kingship worked in this or that society over this or that span of time. If I ask you to "Take me to the king," you've got to escort me to some specific person. But if I ask you to tell me about Hamlet, you may pull out Shakespeare's text. But what would you be doing? Talking abstractly? Offering your own performance of Hamlet? I would prefer you to discuss Olivier's Hamlet or Joseph Papp's. For me, there is no ideal or general *Hamlet* the play or Hamlet the person. There isn't even "Shakespeare's *Hamlet*." The Shakespeare play is the pretext (in both senses of the word) of an actualized event—or, rather, very long and still unfinished set of events.

That seems to coincide with your feelings about the avant-garde, or about implicitly being asked, "Show me the avant-garde." But let me revert back Daryl Chin's article "The Avant-Garde Industry," which we were discussing before the interview technically began. He argues that the avant-garde conceptually can't exist without a tradition.

He's right. The avant-garde is a tradition. The avant-garde is itself a tradition.

Well, that is his complaint: that it has become a tradition.

It always was a tradition.

That is where you seem to disagree, because Chin suggests that the historical avant-garde established itself in a challenge or opposition to tradition and authority. One could argue that this is negative tradition, but basically Chin maintains that without being developed in a clear opposition to authority the avant-garde can no longer exist. My question is, what authority? Is this an authority of previous performances?

Let's take the notion of tradition. *Tradition* is etymologically related to the idea of trade. It means handing something down, taking something from an elder. Tradition suggests that whatever you are doing someone else did it before roughly in the same way. Certainly this can't be the avant-garde. The avant-garde prides itself on the "tradition of the new." The avant-garde is in opposition, is rebellious. But I am saying there are two ways in which the avant-garde is traditional: the tradition of rebellion, which in the West goes back artistically and politically to the French or American revolutions or even the Protestant Reformation—a long time. So there is a tradition of antinomious behavior. In England, the rebellious tradition goes back to the beheading of Charles I and the establishment of the Commonwealth. In other words, the Renaissance spawned the idea of revolution or rebellion. This idea was different than the struggle among royalty and in the higher echelons of the church for power. The Renaissance idea was that ordinary people, forces from below, the vox populi, could overthrow established authority. Authority soon enough included not only state and church, but manners, styles, and all kinds of accepted behavior. The avant-garde became part of that spirit of overthrow, of rebellion against taste, values: whatever was established. Artists practiced this kind of overthrow, which can be connected to individuality, a market economy, and entrepreneurship. Ironically, even when on the left, as artists often were, they are identified stylistically with individualized local capitalism. When the Left actually came to power, as in the U.S.S.R., the avant-garde artists were reined in, destroyed. The first thing Stalin did was kill his immediate enemies. The second thing he did was kill the artists, the experimenters from Mayakovsky to Meyerhold. What the avant-garde artists are uncomfortable with is state power, not the Right or Left as such.

But the avant-garde is traditional also in the sense of particular lineages, trading down through time techniques and concerns. If you work backwards, you can get from Grotowski to Osterwa to Meyerhold to Stanislavsky. Art is handicraft. It is people who work with people—passing on techniques and values.

How is it then that the avant-garde gains the reputation of being antitraditional?

Well, I think that's because the avant-garde largely set itself against normative, mainstream, orthodox behaviors and values. This marks it as bohemian. Its politics of opposition puts it mostly on the left in France, England, and the United States—because governments there have been predominantly right. A truly radical left government in Western Europe and North America is very rare to nonexistent. The avant-garde is sexually open in places where sexual repression and/or Puritan hypocrisies operate. Once straight sex without marriage became OK, the focus shifted to gay sex. Once language taboos came down, body taboos were explored. And so on. There are always boundaries, borders not to be crossed in the mainstream. And it is at those borders that the avant-garde operates. This is predictable. This is the tradition of the avant-garde. Thus, if pushed, I would define the avant-garde not as in advance of, but as against the grain.

Is there still a grain to go against?

There is a grain to go against, but many people are less likely to go against it. Once the National Endowment for the Arts was legislated in 1965, people had to write grants. The avant-garde went to school for development. People applied for money to be offensive. We expected the money, our right, our entitlement. But it also made us like house pets. A little soil on the national carpet. And even so, it became harder and harder to shock. Shock became a questionable value. Pretty well everything imaginable short of mayhem, torture, and murder has been done as a performance. The value of shock is questionable. The idea of doing something offensive is no longer interesting. I know it's been said, but TV offers up a vast medley of images and actions; and if you add to broadcast channels and cable what's available on videotape, just about everything is there to be seen. We are both overstimulated and deadened simultaneously. Not a nice place to be in.

I'm interested in the fact that there was a time when people could be shocked, but I am not sure what that means or what it means that we no longer capable of being shocked. At one level, I think that perhaps that is good, but at another . . .

I don't know if it's good or not. I am not that much of moralist. I don't think that it is so hot. I turn on the television and I actually see people starving to death in Zaire. How can I react to that? Is it right to take such photographs and broadcast them? I know that starvation has long been with us. How many starved to death in Ireland in the past? What does it mean that the graphics are right there in my face? It's like walking past the homeless. Information circulates so widely and quickly. It's hard to get a handle on whether the world is worse off or just that we get wind of stuff more often. What is sure is that we appear to absorb all the horror rather easily. But again I know how awful London was a couple of hundred years ago, with crime rampant, lots of public hangings, disease, and all that. Weren't many people, those who were better off, inured to those who were suffering? Are we going to hell any quicker than previous people?

In the arts, shock is no longer—at least for me or for the artists that I know—a positive value. There are other ways to go against the grain. As I said before, we are at the verge of a neomedievalism that includes a profound acceptance of what is, a localization of violence. Twenty-five years ago, people were frantic with fear of World War III. Today, a world war is not thinkable. Yes, a terrorist or even a nation may launch some nuclear weapons. But even that would not immediately ignite the apocalypse. On the international level, as on television, we tolerate a local violence, a Bosnia or Rwanda (or wherever the next horror erupts), without fearing that the war will spread until everyone is in it. That kind of anxiety and panic is reserved for disease (Ebola, AIDS). The Cold War has been psychically replaced by fear of disease and ecological destruction.

But the problem of the apocalypse is that it can come unexpectedly, right?

The only reliable prediction is that, in the long run, most of what's predicted won't happen.

There is a really wonderful, short essay by Raymond Williams entitled "What Was Modernism," in which he talks about "avant-garde" as a critical term that has unfortunately attained a kind of ahistorical status. Your comments earlier in the interview really coincide with his own concerns, but the end result is that it makes it difficult to talk or ask questions about the avant-garde. The problem here—especially while the interviewer's tape recorder is running—is how best to recover and how best to find a language that doesn't succumb to the same ahistorical trappings.

Well, the historical avant-garde was, and maybe something like it will come again. But it hasn't been here for a long time, for at least twenty years. Most of those who want to go against the grain are now a part of the grain. And the very poor—the real underdogs, the real against-the-grain people—are not making art or using it as a weapon. Also, American society is so multiple, so intricately local, compared to what it was, that a person can now almost always find a fairly substantial community to be with, to identify with. To be historical is to recognize that sometimes terms run out of steam. Maybe *avant-garde* is one of those.

IV. Reflections on the Institutions of the Avant-Garde

Sally Banes

Institutionalizing Avant-Garde Performance: A Hidden History of University Patronage in the United States

The performance avant-garde has historically positioned itself as an oppositional, anti-institutional movement. The usual narrative of the birth of avant-garde performance locates its nineteenth-century roots both in the little-theater movement in France and England (which protested against the commercial practices of mainstream theaters) and in various *salons des refusés* (which protested against the entrenched conventions of visual arts museums and galleries) and avant-garde visual art movements. Eschewing (or having been rejected from) mainstream theater and art world institutions, avant-gardists founded a terrain of their own in unofficial spaces like garrets, basements, cabarets, lofts, and private apartments.[1]

Yet, like most myths, the romantic legend of the anti-institutional nature of the avant-garde is both true and false. Avant-garde performance *has* often operated in an alternative arena. But in stressing the ingenuity, nonconformism, and agonism of advanced experiments in performance, this narrative fails to acknowledge two key points. One is that the avant-garde has regularly formed its own alternative institutions, which in turn have been co-opted by the mainstream to become establishment schools and venues. The second is that, particularly in post-World War II America, intellectual and religious organizations—in particular, colleges, universities, and churches—have played a central role in the development of avant-garde performance, serving as research and development centers, venues, catalysts, and patrons.[2]

There are other sources for American postwar avant-garde performance (broadly defined), including not only government funding and private funding by individuals, corporations, and foundations, but also trust funds from wealthy parents, more modest support by middle-class parents, and even real-estate speculation.[3] To analyze the entire complex financial underwriting that supported the blossoming of American avant-garde performance in the second half of the twentieth century would be a significant chapter in the history of American performance, but it is far beyond the scope of this essay. The present essay focuses on support for avant-garde performance by American colleges and universities.

I should note that in discussions of postmodernism in recent years, the question has been raised as to whether, in the 1990s, one can still speak of a living avant-garde tradition of innovation and insurgency. Certainly in an era when college students are as likely to study Karen Finley's and Annie Sprinkle's performances as Duchamp's *L.H.O.O.Q.*—not to mention the *Mona Lisa*—the issue of whether anything can now shock or surprise the bourgeois sensibility (Jesse Helms and Donald Wildmon notwithstanding) may be moot. And indeed, some may argue that if my claim in this essay—that support for the avant-garde is by now an established part of our American academic economy—is true, to call these arts activities avant-garde is simply an oxymoron. But I want to propose an alternative reading of university patronage of avant-garde performance, a reading that sees arts funding as a result of the dynamic interplay of forces. Avant-garde expressions of opposition and resistance (especially at present) are always the product of negotiations and compromises. And the avant-garde's peculiar historical relation to the university exemplifies this process. I want to argue that there remains a variegated arena of art activity we can still identify as avant-garde, despite its changing political and cultural functions and contexts, as well as its present recirculation of traditional forms. It is avant-garde partly because it identifies itself as breaking with hegemonic artistic, cultural, and/or political discourses, and partly because it remains (whether by choice or not) largely marginal to the established mainstream presenting institutions (other than universities)—for example, Broadway theaters and established arts museums.

As American academia becomes distanced from mainstream society, some (though certainly not all) of its cultural events develop in what anthropologist Victor Turner calls a "liminoid" space, where "anti-structural" activity and "ludic" invention can take place outside of normative social constraints. Turner argues that "universities, institutes, colleges, etc., are 'liminoid' settings for all kinds of freewheeling, experimental cognitive behavior as well as forms of symbolic action," from theoretical science to fraternity initiations.[4] Still, as I will show, avant-garde performance has not entirely stepped outside of the culture or the economy, for the backing the academy provides is still (relatively) mainstream compared to the bohemias of Paris and Greenwich Village.

I should also note that one can (and should) raise crucial questions about the ways in which until very recently definitions and histories of the avant-garde have been based on biases of class, race, and ethnicity, but that is a very complex story beyond the scope of this essay.

Patronage and the Performing Arts in the United States

In looking at the issue of patronage for avant-garde performance in the United States, it might be useful first to sort out briefly the differences between various kinds of financial support for the arts in general. Judith Huggins Balfe points out that patronage—which she defines as "the deliberate sponsorship of the creation, production, preservation, and dissemination of the so-called 'fine arts'"—is just one category of (and therefore not identical to) the broader class of support for the arts. Support also includes earned income, or the direct financial contributions of arts consumers (i.e., audience members, museum-goers, and so on). As Balfe points out, patrons are traditionally active on the "supply side" (that is, they work with artist, commissioning and often influencing the making of the artwork), while audience members occupy the "demand side" of art (they are the artwork's consumers after it is finished—as is, of course, the patron, too). In recent debates about public arts funding, Balfe observes, problems have arisen partly because many seem to assume that the consumer should exercise the patron's traditional right to control the artistic product.[5]

But, one might ask, why would patrons choose to sponsor avant-garde art in the first place, since either as an activity or product, avant-garde art often—in principle—resists control by both patron and consumer? Avant-garde arts, especially avant-garde performance, seem to call for a special kind of patronage, one that endorses experimentation and artistic risk for its own sake (or for some other purpose or interest, such as the educational value of art making), one that tolerates or even encourages social and political resistance, and one that is willing to forgo artistic control over the final product. For numerous reasons the university fits this description.

It is often said that the performing arts in general (implicitly, those associated with "high" or elite culture) require intensive financial support by patrons exactly because they are so expensive to produce; if theater, dance, and music groups had to rely on box-office sales for support, they would have to sacrifice much of their vision and quality. This was the argument often advanced to advocate federal funding for the arts in the early 1960s, prior to the establishment of the National Endowment for the Arts. The government, advocates of federal funding asserted, should become an active patron of the arts because they are vital to a democratic culture.

The statistics published by the Ford Foundation in 1986 indicate that the need for subsidy has not diminished since the 1960s. Experimental theaters, the foundation discovered, earn only 35 to 45 percent of their operating income through ticket sales (as opposed to the 65 to 70 percent earned by large nonprofit theaters)—in keeping with various assessments of the labor- and capital-intensive nature of the performing arts.[6]

Just in order to proceed without the need for wealthy patrons, state support, or large audiences—in order to be beholden to no one—avant-garde performers have often adopted a low-technology, antispecialist modus operandi. A case in point is the well-known story that the early realist director André Antoine borrowed his mother's furniture for the set of Zola's

Jacques Damour, given by his Théâtre Libre in Paris in 1887. (In 1887, of course, theatrical realism itself was avant-garde.) Another is the birth of the Living Theater, whose first performances the codirectors, Julian Beck and Judith Malina, presented in their New York City apartment in 1951.

My first example above comes from France and the second from the United States, but it is important to keep in mind the drastically different systems of patronage for the arts in the United States and Europe and, therefore, the different role and status of both mainstream and avant-garde arts in the two cultures. In Europe, the model may vary from one country to another according to whether state support for the arts is centralized or decentralized. But in general, from the Renaissance to the present, both church and state (whether royal, democratic, or totalitarian) have sponsored the arts financially. In the United States, by contrast, we have had direct federal support for the arts for approximately thirty-five years (with the notable exception of the arts projects of the Works Progress Administration from 1935–39, which were, in effect, relief programs to put people back to work, rather than arts subsidies). The National Foundation for the Arts, established by President Kennedy in 1963, eventually grew into the now-embattled National Endowment for the Arts in 1965. In 1964, arts councils were established in thirteen U.S. states. Prior to 1963, arts patronage flowed primarily from private individuals, foundations, and corporations (although prior to 1963, the U.S. government did promote American art abroad, but not domestically, as a form of Cold War propaganda,[7] and local governments helped to support some arts projects, such as the municipally assisted City Center of Music and Drama in New York City).

In establishing the National Endowment for the Arts, the U.S. federal government did take on the role of patron, but only to a limited extent, especially compared to the extensive government arts patronage in Europe, Canada, and Latin America. The limited state funding situation in the United States places other types of patronage (that is, nonstate patronage) under different kinds of stresses and demands.

The Value of Art as Pedagogy

In arguing not only for federal funding for the arts, but for a national appreciation of the arts that would match Europe's, early advocates of the National Endowment for the Arts had to join battle with an old quarrel against state patronage: centuries of American rhetoric against federal patronage as an emblem of royalist regimes and a symptom of the elitist luxury and decadence of both church and state in Europe.

As cultural historian Neil Harris has remarked, the entrenched American attitude of anxiety not only toward patronage but toward art making itself has roots in the very beginnings of American culture—not, as one might expect, as the result of Puritan moralizing, but rather, as the product of a utilitarian political agenda. Art in the early days of the American republic was seen as a frivolous luxury—much as it is seen now, in an era of downsizing and budget cutting. And, since art, like other forms of luxury, required money, it was seen as a superfluous extravagance, as well as an unhealthy link to the aristocratic cultures of the Old World. Moreover, art was seen as capable of stirring up the emotions and supporting tyrannical regimes, both secular and religious, of all kinds.[8]

Eventually, Americans began to value art for its utilitarian purposes and to create hierarchies of types of art according to their relative usefulness. Alexis de Tocqueville noticed, on his trip to America in 1831–32, that in the United States,

> the general moderate standard of wealth, the absence of superfluity, and the universal desire for comfort, with the constant efforts made by all to procure it, encouraged a taste for the useful more than the love of beauty. Naturally, therefore, democratic peoples with all these characteristics cultivate those arts that help to make life comfortable rather than those that adorn it. They habitually put use before beauty, and they want beauty itself to be useful.[9]

Besides comfort and advertising, utilitarianism in regard to the appreciation of art came to include art's functioning to provide moral uplift, and in particular, art's relation to education as a form of moral elevation. Crucially for the history of arts patronage in the United States (and for the story I want to tell here), as early as the late eighteenth century the rhetoric of pedagogy became the most effective means for advancing the establishment of arts institutions for exhibition and training.[10] American arts patronage, that is, has historically harnessed itself to what is seen as the higher political and moral good of education.

But avant-garde work seems to forsake, indeed to criticize radically (and often actually to fulminate against), traditional American views of art as well as traditional views of society. As I implied earlier, it is certainly not in the utilitarian interest of the state (or of the wealthy) to support art that criticizes it and threatens the status quo. Nor does avant-garde work generally command mass commercial audiences. Thus one needs to ask what institutions or individuals are likely to support or commission antiestablishment, avant-garde work, and for what reasons. In a capitalist marketplace, where the special financing of the avant-garde may in fact be a political contradiction, for whom is it a necessity (or at least a strong attraction)?

It may not be directly in the university's interest to teach and sponsor avant-garde art—and much of its sponsorship may be ad hoc and even unwitting—but it is nevertheless in the interest of many people involved with the university, for a variety of reasons, ranging from the noble to the pragmatic to the parsimonious. Some students want to learn how to enter their chosen arts professions as cutting-edge innovators of the upcoming generation; besides, they are of an age when they like to rebel in general, which is part of forging their own identities, even as professionals. Their parents, who are willing to sponsor arts training as long as it comes earmarked with a college degree, support them in this demand; teachers whose research and teaching areas include the avant-garde want to show their colleagues and students how developments even in the mainstream arts came from avant-garde inquiries in and among the disciplines; administrators uphold the teachers' and students' avant-garde proclivities because it shows they tolerate free expression. The innovative avant-garde telos fits with the research university's mission to create new knowledge, and the avant-garde's critique of the status quo suits the liberal arts college's mandate to foster critical thinking. And, in a crude economic sense, to hire marginalized avant-gardists as faculty or guest artists (whether because that's what they really are by choice or because they haven't yet succeeded in joining the mainstream) is much cheaper for the university administration than to hire established artists.

Perhaps there is even a certain cachet attached to avant-garde performance from which university administrators derive various benefits. Just as avant-garde artists sometimes serve as a catalyst for the gentrification of neighborhoods, so they can also function as honeypots to sweeten the university administration's fund-raising efforts or even its glamour quotient.

Certainly not all universities or colleges are hotbeds of avant-garde activity. But if there is an interest in this activity by faculty, staff, or students, participation of various kinds can take place surprisingly easily. And this is not, as Michael Mooney paranoiacally suggested in 1980, because there is a secret alliance among Congress, the White House, business, and the academic "knowledge industry" to foist a radical left-wing, avant-garde cultural policy on an unsuspecting nation.[11] At the beginning of the twenty-first century, when Congress and the White House are at loggerheads and both corporate and federal arts patronage are shrinking, the university still supports the avant-garde; indeed, it has taken on an increasing burden of avant-garde support as other sources dwindle. Rather than a conspiracy by a unified "ministry of culture," university patronage survives because it is one of the few places in an increasingly conservative American culture where the avant-garde can still flourish and find protection from the demands of the commercial marketplace—where insurgency and both social and artistic criticism may be protected by the principle of academic freedom.[12]

In terms of performance art, Laurie Anderson may earn income on hit records, and Spalding Gray, Eric Bogosian, Willem Dafoe, John Leguizamo, and Steve Buscemi may find work in Hollywood films and on television. But for every Laurie Anderson or Spalding Gray there are scores of performance artists who either shun the capitalist marketplace and showbiz, or find their work shunned by popular and mass-media venues. Teaching jobs and guest residencies in the university system can sustain those noncommercial avant-gardists with both money and research time.

However, rarely is the avant-garde patronage function of the university, even the part that flows from economic self-interest, acknowledged in the literature about arts patronage, either journalistic or scholarly. (Two important exceptions to this lack of recognition are *The Arts at Black Mountain College,* by Mary Emma Harris, and *Off Limits: Rutgers University and the Avant-Garde, 1957–1963,* edited by Joan Marter.)[13] For instance, Gideon Chagy's 1972 book *The New Patrons of the Arts* emphasizes the increased patronage of the arts by corporations in the late 1960s. His historical survey of traditional patronage in Europe and the United States encompasses not only merchants and corporations, but also the church, the state, wealthy individuals, and foundations. But, except for one mention of courses offered in arts administration, Chagy refers to universities only as examples of recipients of corporate giving for arts buildings and other capital projects.[14]

More recently, a 1986 Ford Foundation working paper lists the sources of support for the arts as individuals, corporations, government, the marketplace, and foundations. It traces the history of arts funding in the United States and of the Ford Foundation's generous patronage of the performing and visual arts since the mid-1950s, with its major grants to key institutions in the early sixties and its support, since the late eighties, of both experimental work and ethnic diversity in the arts. Yet it never mentions the important role universities have played in furthering the foundation's priorities. In fact, the word *university* shows up only three times in this publication—two of them in a citation of a study on foundation support for the arts, for the work cited, *Non-Profit Enterprise in the Arts,* was written by Paul DiMaggio of the Program on Non-Profit Organizations at Yale University's Institution for Social and Policy Studies and was published by Oxford University Press.[15]

However, it is worth noting that even this small citation, so easily overlooked, illuminates two different ways in which universities more and more play key roles in advancing the arts: by studying (and making recommendations for) arts-funding policies, and by publishing books (through university presses) about the arts.

Even major foundation grants for innovative work are now frequently funneled through universities, and thus become coproductions with universities, which supply the overhead. For instance, as I noted above, the Ford Foundation has long supported avant-garde performance. But in 1981, for the first time it linked its Arts and Culture program to its Education program.[16] Beginning in 1994, the Ford Foundation's mission in funding the arts shifted to support a new area: "cultural institutions in the United States that are trying to 'internationalize' their multidisciplinary performing arts programs . . . involving collaborations between artists from the United States and artists in the developing world." As the 1995 Ford Foundation annual report states, "this program builds on the Foundation's continuing interest in new interdisciplinary performing arts activities but broadens that work to involve regional cultural institutions and universities that have strong program interests in the arts and cultures of Asia, Latin America, and Africa."[17]

In 1996, the Lila Wallace–Reader's Digest Arts Partners Program gave implementation grants to proposed projects involving Arizona State University, University of Colorado–Boulder, Stanford University, and Lafayette College for avant-garde projects. It gave planning grants to projects involving California State University, Los Angeles; St. Mary's University; Miami Dade Community College; University of California Extension; University of Arizona; University of Kentucky; and University of Wisconsin. And, it gave a $750,000 grant to National Performance Network, a thirteen-year-old touring organization for avant-garde performance; approximately one-fourth of NPN's tours include residencies for artists of at least one week's duration through university partners.[18]

Finally, the National Endowment for the Arts itself increasingly funnels its funds for artists through universities and colleges. The fiscal year 1998 NEA application guidelines state specifically that "independent components that meet [criteria for eligible applicants] often will be part of a university/university system or part of a cultural/community complex." The guidelines give as examples of these independent components (i.e., eligible to apply separately, even though the NEA accepts only one application per organization) "a presenter, literary magazine or press, museum, radio station, theater, etc., within a university campus or larger university system." Although "academic departments of colleges and universities will not qualify as independent components," conceivably (given the guidelines quoted above) five or more units within a university could receive NEA funding in a single year.[19]

The ways in which foundation and government funds are currently funneled through universities (which provide the necessary institutional home and overhead for large, complex projects, as well as for smaller-scale residencies) and the ways in which university personnel currently work with foundations and the government both testify to the increasing role universities play in supporting the arts, and the avant-garde arts in particular.

Perhaps the universities remain invisible in public and scholarly discourse about arts patronage because their support often comes in forms that are indirect, rather than direct grants and contributions to individual artists. But there are still myriad ways in which universities and colleges support the arts. And, given the changing support system for the arts since the 1960s, as well as the changing nature of the university since the 1960s, avant-garde performance has been one of the beneficiaries of this hidden underground stream of arts patronage.

Two Early Models of American Avant-Garde Patronage

Two early, unique models of artistic nurture in American academe in this century exemplify the stress on pedagogy that links fostering artistic freedom with upholding academic freedom. Neither the New School for Social Research, founded in New York City in 1918, nor Black Mountain College, established near Asheville, North Carolina, in 1933, originally envisioned the fostering of avant-garde art and performance as part of its mission, but for complex reasons, both created congenial grounds for artistic experimentation.

The foundings of both were prompted by faculty outrage at encroachments on academic freedom at other universities. Both the New School's and Black Mountain's pedagogical principles were also inspired by John Dewey and, generally, the progressive movement in education. This movement led to the founding of such schools as Bennington College and Sarah Lawrence College, as well as to changes in curriculum at established colleges like Bryn Mawr, Swarthmore, Reed, Antioch, and Columbia. For Dewey, the arts served as a practical, exploratory, experiential model for creativity in general, and therefore they were intimately linked to the democratization of education, because they could form students with inquisitive, critical minds.

In furthering these goals that yoked the practice of art with liberal democratic humanism, both schools hired modern artists; sponsored innovative projects in the arts by faculty, students, and visiting artists; and attracted creative students who eventually came to populate the avant-garde movements of the 1950s and 1960s. A most important influence on postwar avant-garde performance activities at both schools, leading to a broader avant-garde influence in American performance in the 1960s, was the presence of the composer John Cage.

The New School for Social Research, established by historians and political scientists, grew out of ideas regarding academic freedom and democratic education that reached a crisis in 1917, when two Columbia University faculty members were fired and several others subsequently resigned because they disagreed with the university administration's support of President Wilson's war policies. The funding for the school originally came from philanthropist Dorothy Straight, heir to the Whitney fortune. Influenced not only by Dewey's ideas about progressive, democratic education, but also by Thorstein Veblen's writings on the institutional reform of universities, the founding group opened an antihierarchical school for adult education—as its name suggests, focusing on research carried out by teachers and students—that initially stressed graduate and professional education. But over the course of the school's existence, its emphasis has oscillated several times between the social-science orientation of its graduate faculty and the cultural-enrichment aspect of its adult education division.[20]

Although in the early years of the school very few courses in the arts were offered, beginning in 1923 (when Alvin Johnson assumed administrative leadership of the school and it moved to Greenwich Village), the New School became a center for both innovative artistic and intellectual life in downtown New York. Johnson saw the appreciation of and participation in the arts, and in particular, the new modernist movements in the arts, as instrumental to social change. Not only were young artists and critics hired to teach courses and to give occasional lectures, but also Johnson commissioned a new building in the modernist International style to house the school, which included an auditorium shaped like an ancient Greek amphitheater, symbolizing the school's commitment to liberal democratic values as well as providing a venue for its arts events.

By hiring artists as teachers, Johnson in effect was also buying them time for "research," or artistic creativity. In the 1920s, and especially during the depression years in the 1930s, Johnson attracted a diverse group of modern composers, including Aaron Copland, Henry Cowell, and Hans Eisler. He also hired choreographer Doris Humphrey, the leading modern dance critic John Martin, visual artists Stuart Davis, Seymour Lipton, and Berenice Abbott, and the art critic Meyer Schapiro to teach at the school.

Also, importantly, Johnson hired the German avant-garde political theater director Erwin Piscator, who had earlier influenced Bertolt Brecht's notions of the epic theater. Piscator established the Dramatic Workshop at the New School in 1939; it not only offered an academic curriculum, but also sponsored three semiprofessional off-Broadway theaters, a repertory theater, a children's theater, and other performance activities. Piscator's Dramatic Workshop lasted at the New School until 1949, when it became an independent entity in New York for two years, continuing until the director returned to Germany in 1951. Among other students of the Dramatic Workshop (many of whose acting and directing remained in a more mainstream mode), Judith Malina studied with Piscator from 1945–47 and was partly inspired by him to start the Living Theatre.[21]

In the late 1950s, the liberal arts components of the adult education division of the New School flourished, although music and dance thrived less than literature and the visual arts.[22] Still, John Cage (who had himself studied briefly with Henry Cowell at the New School in the 1930s and occasionally substituted for Cowell in the 1940s) began in 1956 to teach a course in "Composition of Experimental Music" at the New School that had an enormous impact on the development of Happenings, Fluxus, and performance art, as well as music and poetry, in the 1960s and after.[23] According to Cage, when he decided to teach in a formal way in the 1950s, "It never entered my mind to teach in any other place in New York City than the New School. Nor is it likely that any other school would have accepted me, since my work and ideas are controversial."[24] Cage's students included composer Toshi Ichiyanagi, poet Jackson Mac Low, Happenings makers Allan Kaprow and Al Hansen, and Fluxus members Dick Higgins and George Brecht.[25] Also among his students was Robert Dunn, a composer whose own dance composition course at Merce Cunningham's studio, modeled after Cage's music composition course, was the seedbed for postmodern dance.[26] Thus the lively avant-garde performance scene of the 1960s may be traced back in large part to the New School, although in the late 1950s, there was another university outpost of avant-garde activity in the New York City area at Rutgers University, involving other Happenings- and Events-makers, who included faculty member Allan Kaprow, students Lucas Samaras and Robert Whitman, and neighbor George Segal.[27]

Black Mountain College was founded by faculty members from Rollins College who had either resigned or been dismissed over issues of academic freedom. Its initial funding came primarily from Mr. and Mrs. J. Malcolm Forbes and was raised by one of the founding faculty, Theodore Dreier, whose wealthy family in New York was active in promoting social reform, women's rights, poverty programs, and the arts; Dreier's aunt Katherine had been (with Marcel Duchamp and Man Ray) a founding member of the Société Anonyme, a private collection of modern art. From the start, Black Mountain was an alternative educational establishment with a radically democratic structure. And also from the beginning, the school included visual art and theater as an integral part of its liberal studies instructional curriculum.[28]

For a variety of reasons, including the interdisciplinary, democratic, and participatory theory of education it espoused, Black Mountain always stressed (even more than did the New School) practical studies in art as a core aspect of the curriculum. In this it also differed from most other undergraduate colleges, where, as historian Mary Emma Harris notes, the arts were often relegated to noncredit or extracurricular status. At Black Mountain, the arts were seen as foundational, not in order to train students as professional artists, but because, following Dewey's ideas in *Art and Education* and *Democracy and Education,* the college's founders saw in the arts a means of stimulating creativity and independent thought in all realms of life.[29]

Black Mountain was also deeply influenced by the Bauhaus in Germany, which was closed down by the Nazi government in 1933, the same year that Black Mountain was founded. The Bauhaus influence was both indirect, in the college's adherence to a utopian communal ethos based on practical work in the arts, and direct, in that Josef Albers (one of the Bauhaus master teachers) and his wife Anni Albers (a weaver who also taught at the Bauhaus), were immediately invited to join the Black Mountain faculty, and other Bauhaus teachers later followed. Josef Albers became one of the Black Mountain faculty's most influential members.

During the depression and war years, Black Mountain became known as a center for experimental, modernist art, especially the abstraction espoused by Albers. And, although it was an institution of higher learning, the college staked out an antiacademic position regarding both the study of the artistic canon and the practice of art.[30] On the Bauhaus model, the students learned art, design, and craft in a practical, functional way—including weaving, photography, graphic design, typography, bookbinding, music, drama, dance, and creative writing. Xanti Schawinsky, who had been a student at the Bauhaus and had collaborated with Oskar Schlemmer on several productions in the 1920s, joined the Black Mountain faculty in 1936 and for two years worked with the students to create a nonnarrative, nonmatrixed theater of "total experience," based on music, light, movement, and masks.[31] In the early 1940s, Eric Bentley taught history, literature, and drama, and he directed the student theater group, most notably in readings from Bertolt Brecht's *The Private Life of the Master Race,* which Bentley was then translating.

In addition to its core curriculum, Black Mountain College sponsored many artistic residencies and collaborations from the time of its founding. Special summer institutes in the arts, initially meant to educate teachers, began at the college in 1944. Guest teachers included Walter Gropius, Robert Motherwell, Lyonel Feininger, and Charles Olson. Olson eventually joined the regular faculty and became rector of the college. After World War II, more and more arts students were attracted to study at the college. According to Harris, "by 1945 the college had become 'a natural gravitational force' for those interested in the arts," eventually drawing students like Ray Johnson, Ruth Asawa, Robert Rauschenberg, Sue Weil, Kenneth Noland, Arthur Penn, and Joel Oppenheimer.[32] And by 1948, when John Cage, Merce Cunningham, Willem de Kooning, Buckminster Fuller, and Richard Lippold were on the summer faculty, Black Mountain fostered the emergence of a specifically American avant-garde art, no longer beholden to European models, especially the functional modernism of the Bauhaus. Importantly, these American teachers were not yet established artists. According to Harris, "In 1948 these people, most of whom had been living a hand-to-mouth existence in city apartments, were all thankful for room and board for the summer, a modest salary, and an opportunity to work in a sympathetic community of artists and friends."[33]

Two crucial events happened during the 1952 summer session. One was the beginning of a long collaboration and a meeting of like minds in the encounter of Cage and Rauschenberg. The second was a groundbreaking postwar performance event: John Cage's untitled chance-composed event, which, on the one hand, was inspired by futurist and dada events and, on the other, was a precursor of Happenings.[34] Also at around this time, Black Mountain faculty member M. C. Richards was translating into English several essays by Antonin Artaud, which were eventually published as *The Theater and Its Double*.[35] John Cage showed those essays before they were published to Malina and Beck. The influence of those essays on the avant-garde and experimental theater of the 1950s, 1960s, and after, is incalculable.

The New School and Black Mountain were founded as alternative institutions. Thus, like other schools including Bennington, Antioch, and Mills Colleges, they created a framework in which avant-garde arts activities were supported and encouraged as part and parcel of the institutional raison d'être. But for a variety of reasons, by the 1960s even mainstream universities offered a home for the avant-garde.

The University as Patron since the 1960s

In the late 1940s and 1950s, returning servicemen, under the GI Bill, had entered college in large numbers and forced certain changes in arts education. The mission of the university in regard to the arts altered in the postwar years as well. A 1965 Rockefeller Panel report shows that the function of the university in relation to the art world shifted after World War II from training students in appreciation of the arts to a complex, multifunctional support, training, and patronage system.[36] The report explains that by the early sixties institutions of higher learning were increasingly taking on the role of training performing artists. This was because the costs of conservatory and independent arts schools had risen and ideas about higher education had changed, while an expanding broad economic base of public and private support at universities allowed for more experimentation. Of course, in order to do this, universities hired professional artists to train students, thereby setting up another layer of patronage: they provided salaries and other benefits (including space, materials, and time for research/creative work) to their full-time and part-time faculty.

A change took place during the 1960s in regard to the expansion of performing arts programs in universities. As universities, with the help of foundations, were building up their theater programs, the lack of innovative work in the academy—in contrast to the lively performance scene, for instance, off-off-Broadway—was much commented upon in the midsixties. However, shortly after these reports were issued, university campuses underwent drastic transformations, not only politically but also artistically.

In the late 1960s, a generation of baby boomers entered college in large numbers and swelled the ranks of students enrolling in arts and humanities programs. More theater departments were formed, sometimes by splitting off from speech or communications departments. The political upheavals taking place at many universities in 1968 (and after) swept both radical political theater and artistically experimental theater onto American college campuses. Not only were there national tours by the Living Theatre, the San Francisco Mime Troupe, the Open Theatre, and other groups, but also, those troupes left in their wake students who were galvanized to form local guerrilla theater groups that used theater for political agit-prop and local artistic collectives that used performance for artistic exploration. Although both the tours and the local activities, sponsored either by student organizations or political groups, often simply bypassed the official theater departments, many theater departments also were deeply influenced by political and experimental work in the 1960s and 1970s.

In the 1980s and 1990s, however, the focus of many theater departments is on faculty-student productions, and many are forced, either by the necessity of relying on earned income or by the training requirements for students, to cater to middle-brow taste. Thus, small-scale or imported performances may more easily happen in formats more familiar to dance and art departments. College and university dance departments have since the 1930s sponsored tours and hired artists in residence. Art departments invite visiting artists, including performance artists, to teach and critique student work.

In 1957, what is now known as the Association of Performing Arts Presenters was founded, primarily to present classical music and dance concerts. Those presenters eventually added avant-garde events, such as performance art and postmodern dance, to their classical music series. Of the fifteen hundred presenters belonging to that association in 1997, 38 percent were affiliated with universities.[37]

In summary, although avant-garde arts were supported in academia in various ways before the 1960s, since the late 1960s universities and colleges have dramatically increased their patronage of the performing arts, including avant-garde performance. These include hiring artists, critics, and scholars to serve on departmental faculties—as either full-time or part-time employees—where they may receive both salaries and grants to do their creative work, as well as having access to in-kind contributions of space, materials, and staff support. University patronage also includes hiring nonacademic artists, critics, historians, and theorists to do lectures, performances, workshops, and master classes, as well as to do guest residencies of various lengths, from a week to a semester or a year. And universities sponsor museum exhibitions and installations, university press publications by artists and scholars, conferences, appointments to research institutes, and the preservation of artists' archives. As well as financial and in-kind support, universities provide symbolic capital to avant-garde artists in the form of prestigious honorary degrees.

Since the 1970s, arts administration programs have been established at major universities; these programs train those individuals who will eventually serve as fundraisers and company managers for performing artists. Finally, since the 1980s, the outreach components of many university performing arts programs have mushroomed. While many of these practices and programs may originally have centered on educating audiences for mainstream high art—in outreach, bringing classical music to schoolchildren, for instance—to a large degree, the same infrastructures are now being used to support innovative and avant-garde work in the arts, including performance.

The Academic Mainstreaming of Avant-Garde Performance

As universities expanded with the influx of baby boomers and simultaneously underwent radical political and institutional changes in the late 1960s, many of their arts programs gravitated toward supporting innovative work by faculty, students, and guest artists. By the early 1970s, students and faculty from these academic milieux were moved to found alternative galleries and artists' spaces, where avant-garde performance took place outside of the academic or museum setting. But what may have looked at the time like a gesture *against* academia, in favor of small-scale alternative institutions, in time took on the shape of a lively interchange, as the two situations fed one another and activists in alternative galleries and performance spaces eventually rejoined the academy.

By the mid-1970s, the loose confederation A Bunch of Experimental Theaters facilitated tours of avant-garde groups to campuses. For instance, at the University of Pittsburgh, a program called the Pittsburgh 99 Cent Floating Theatre sponsored performances in the 1970s by many visiting companies from A Bunch, including Charles Ludlam's Ridiculous Theatrical Company, Meredith Monk and the House, Mabou Mines, the Iowa Theatre Lab, the Medicine Show, and others.[38]

But also, in the 1970s and 1980s many avant-garde artists of the 1960s and slightly younger baby boomers joined the cohort of faculty populating the visual and performing arts departments. There, themselves formed by the experiments of the 1960s, they began to institutionalize avant-garde history and practice through teaching, research, and publication, producing new generations of avant-garde practitioners as well as a new level of scholarly and public discourse about the avant-garde. For instance, the Experimental Theater Wing in the New York University Department of Undergraduate Drama was formed by Ron Argelander in 1976 to create a situation in which students could work directly with avant-garde artists; Anne Bogart, Richard Foreman, and Robert Wilson have directed student productions, and ETW graduates include Kate Valk and Jeff Webster of the Wooster Group and performance artist Gayle Tufts.

As the economy shrank in the late 1980s and early 1990s, many avant-garde artists who had not previously been affiliated with academia began to seek the economic security—including not only salaries, but health insurance and retirement plans—of university teaching positions, while still carrying on their experimental and avant-garde theater activities. Antioch College's theater department, for instance, which is part of the American Theater Festival Campus Diversity/Cultural Research Initiative, is chaired by Louise Smith, a solo performer who has appeared with Otrabanda and Ping Chong, and it regularly sponsors guest artists and experimental productions by students and faculty.[39] The Barnard College Theater Department faculty includes Amy Trompeter, formerly of Bread and Puppet Theater, and Deni Partridge, formerly of the San Francisco Mime Troupe. John Bell, another Bread and Puppet Theater alumnus, teaches at New York University.

Yet the myth of the natural antagonism between the avant-garde and academe persisted into the 1990s, despite overwhelming evidence that, at least since the 1950s, much of the radical activity in American avant-garde performance has been sponsored and supported by universities and colleges, whether those (like Black Mountain or more recently the Naropa Institute) that were or are committed to experiment or those (like Rutgers University or Kutztown University) that simply have allowed pockets of radical artistic activity to occur among interested faculty and students.

Avant-garde chronicler Richard Kostelanetz, for instance, upholds the myth by staking out a pure antiacademic stance. In his 1993 *Dictionary of the Avant-Gardes,* under the entry "Academic Critics," he writes:

> When professors discuss avant-garde art, particularly literature, they tend to focus upon the more conservative, more accessible dimensions of an artist's work, in part to make their criticism more digestible to the ignorant (e.g., students and colleagues), rather than pursuing radical implications to their critical extremes. . . . Academics tend as well to reveal incomplete familiarity with new developments (especially if they would be unknown to their fellow professors). . . . When a professor writes three words about an avant-garde subject, one of them is likely to be superficial and a second to reveal ignorance.

And, he concludes, "Genuinely innovative art measures itself as avant-garde by a healthy distance from the academy."[40] Kostelanetz may disparage academic criticism. But he himself, willy-nilly, acknowledges the myriad important ways in which the university supports the avant-garde when he records, for example, Cage's important work carried out during various university residencies.[41] *HPSCHD* (1969), one of Cage's "most abundant pieces" according to Kostelanetz—a collaboration with Lejaren Hiller that took place at Assembly Hall, a sports arena, at the University of Illinois, Urbana—probably could not have taken place anywhere in the United States but a university setting, because of the resources available there both for the performance itself and for the preparation of the sound tapes. *HPSCHD* involved enormous projection screens, film projections, fifty-two slide projectors, fifty-two tape recorders playing computer-generated tapes, and seven live harpsichordists. A later performance at the Brooklyn Academy of Music (under nonuniversity auspices) had to be drastically reduced.[42]

The university can provide the kind of time needed for the long incubation of artistic creation. In her article on the New World Performance Laboratory, a joint project of the University of Akron and the Cleveland Public Theatre founded by two actors who have worked with the late Jerzy Grotowski, Lisa Wolford explains that "within university theatre departments Grotowski sees a possible site of resistance against the superficiality and slapdash craft dictated by the culture industry." Since university theater departments "enjoy a basic level of funding, access to work space, and a relatively stable population of unpaid student actors," they "provide a structure which allows for long-term, systematic work; and, [Grotowski] argues, are relatively free to negotiate the constraints which plague commercial theatres." Under these auspices, "would it not be possible to spend months or even a year preparing a single performance?"[43]

The Wexner Center, a major presenter of avant-garde performance, is a part of the Ohio State University; the Walker Art Center, long an avant-garde venue but most recently infamous for its controversial hosting of Ron Athey's performances in 1994, is independent but closely connected to the University of Minnesota at Minneapolis. The Haggerty Museum, part of Marquette University, has presented performances by Adrian Piper, Rachel Rosenthal, Ping Chong, and others. National Performance Network brings groups like the Five Lesbian Brothers, Spiderwoman Theater, Eiko and Koma, and the Hittite Empire to many campuses.

By the mid-1980s, it was clear that much work in performance art and its documentation and criticism was underwritten by both long-range and short-term academic support. It was also evident that much training for performance artists was taking place in academia or art schools that offer college degrees.[44]

But of course it's not only short- or long-term residencies by artists, or faculty and student support, that constitute patronage for the avant-garde. Sustenance also includes university-sponsored publications, including preeminent journals covering avant-garde performance like the long-lived *Drama Review,* edited by Richard Schechner and published by MIT Press, but housed and staffed at New York University's Department of Performance Studies, and the newer *TheatreForum,* edited by Theodore Shank and housed and staffed at the University of California, San Diego. Patronage in the form of publication includes, as well, books on avant-garde performance increasingly published by university presses, as changes in commercial publishing over the past decade or so have made small print runs of books nearly impossible without subventions from large institutions like universities. Wesleyan University Press has long produced books on avant-garde performance, from John Cage's *Silence* to C. Carr's *On Edge: Performance at the End of the Twentieth Century.* Other publishers of books on the avant-garde include the University of Michigan Press (in fact, the publishers of the present volume), Duke University Press, MIT Press, and Indiana University Press.

Academic conferences about avant-garde performance, too, are a form of patronage. Since 1995, the Performance Studies conferences hosted by New York University, Northwestern University, the Georgia Institute of Technology, City University of New York, and the University of Wales have featured not only scholarly presentations but also performances by both academic and non–academically based performance artists. The Performance Art, Culture, Pedagogy Symposium held at Pennsylvania State University in November 1996 showed just how entrenched avant-garde performance in academe has become. Indeed, the theme of the conference was performance art pedagogy "as an emerging form of arts education," and the majority of the presenters were academics.[45]

Conclusion

The question arises as to whether the funding of avant-garde performance by academic institutions is good or bad, and further, whether, if this activity is being funded by a mainstream institution, it may still be considered avant-garde. According to antiacademic critics like Kostelanetz, the university is inimical to avant-garde activity by definition. Surely one result of the institutionalization of avant-garde performance by the mainstream university is that much postmodern performance of the 1980 and 1990s has been driven by criticism and theory—that of poststructuralism and identity politics—rather than, as was predominantly the case previously, serving to spark criticism and new theories. Insofar as one way of defining the avant-garde since its emergence in the nineteenth century might be that it contests academic critical discourse, this new turn suggests that sustenance by the mainstream university has co-opted, if not killed off, much avant-garde performance. However, here it should be noted that some of the most exciting avant-garde performance of the last fifty years has emerged partly as a result of artists' exploring the histories and theories of their practice. So to embrace Kostelanetz's position seems to be to endorse a naive romanticism that flies in the face of historical reality.

There is another way of looking at the university patronage system, one that I, as a historian, curator, reconstructor, and sometime participant in avant-garde performances, as well as a university professor and author of university press books, must take seriously. We *do* live in a capitalist marketplace, where—especially since recent NEA cuts and the discontinuation of NEA grants to individual artists—the bulk of what scanty arts funding there is in the federal budget goes to support mainstream institutions like symphonies, art museums, regional theaters, and major dance companies (which may occasionally present an avant-garde work but are not dedicated to the avant-garde project). In the pre-NEA early 1960s, a lively avant-garde performance scene flourished without any federal support and only sporadic university support. Although presently our economy is booming, the costs of both living and making art have risen astronomically in the 1980s and 1990s. That the university now provides a protected haven—however random or small-scale—for experiments in performance; that it animates in the next generation of young artists ideas—however embattled—about innovation and originality; that it literally feeds those who make iconoclastic, deviant, or alternative art; and that it supplies dissident voices within the university system itself; all these aspects are crucial politically as well as culturally—not to mention pedagogically.[46]

NOTES

1. See Noël Carroll, "Performance," *Formations* 3, no. 1 (1986): 63–79, for an account of performance art and art performance since the 1970s as two interrelated and intertwined strands of activity with separate roots in avant-garde theater and visual art.

2. I should note that I am consciously using the word *America* here interchangeably with *United States.* I recognize that the arts practices and funding situations in Canada and Mexico, not to mention Central and South America, differ from that of the United States. But in the interests of an efficient prose style, references to American art, American institutions, and American society should be understood to mean those of the United States.

3. I am grateful to Philip Auslander for suggesting that a "real-estate theory" would partly explain the economic base for postwar avant-garde performance activities in New York (personal communication). In this context George Maciunas, in particular, was instrumental in buying and establishing several low-cost artists' cooperative loft buildings in the Soho district, which included living, working, and performance spaces.

Maciunas was a key figure in setting precedents for the legal exemptions and rent controls that allowed for an explosion of artists' living and working lofts in Soho in the 1960s and 1970s. See my *Greenwich Village, 1963: Avant-Garde Performance and the Effervescent Body* (Durham, N.C.: Duke University Press, 1993), 64–65, for a discussion of Maciunas's real estate activities, which he modeled on ideas inspired by early Soviet arts cooperatives as well as Soviet collective farms. Also see the various Fluxnewsletters and other documents reprinted in Jon Hendricks, *Fluxus Etc.: The Gilbert and Lila Silverman Collection, Addenda I* (New York: Ink &, 1983), 170–228.

4. Victor Turner, "Liminal to Liminoid in Play, Flow, Ritual: An Essay in Comparative Symbology," in *From Ritual to Theatre: The Human Seriousness of Play* (New York: Performing Arts Journal Publications, 1982), 33.

5. Judith Huggins Balfe, ed., *Paying the Piper: Causes and Consequences of Art Patronage* (Urbana: University of Illinois Press, 1993), 1.

6. *Ford Foundation Support for the Arts in the United States: A Discussion of New Emphases in the Foundation's Arts Program* (New York: Ford Foundation, 1986), 10.

7. See, for instance, Naima Prevots, *Dance for Export: Cultural Diplomacy and the Cold War,* Studies in Dance History (Hanover, N.H.: Wesleyan University Press/University Press of New England, 1998); and Robert Haddow, *Pavilions of Plenty: Establishing American Culture Abroad in the 1950s* (Washington, D.C.: Smithsonian Institution Press, 1997).

8. Harris, *The Artist in American Society: The Formative Years, 1790–1860* (1966; New York: Simon and Schuster, 1970), 28, 34–36.

9. Alexis de Tocqueville, *Democracy in America,* trans. George Lawrence, ed. J. P. Mayer (New York: Harper Collins, 1988), 465.

10. Harris, *The Artist in American Society*, 90–91, 94.

11. Michael Macdonald Mooney, *The Ministry of Culture: Connections among Art, Money, and Politics* (New York: Wyndham, 1980).

12. In response to NEA cuts, in 1999 the Creative Capital Foundation was formed by over twenty foundations and individual philanthropists "to support artists who challenge convention." (Judith H. Dobrzynski, "Private Donors Unite to Support Art Spurned by the Government," *New York Times,* May 3, 1999, sec. E, 1).

13. Mary Emma Harris, *The Arts at Black Mountain College* (Cambridge: MIT Press, 1987); Joan Marter, ed., *Off Limits: Rutgers University and the Avant-Garde, 1957–1963* (New Brunswick, N.J.: Rutgers University Press, 1999).

14. Gideon Chagy, *The New Patrons of the Arts* (New York: Harry N. Abrams, 1972). Chagy mentions arts administration courses on p. 67.

15. *Ford Foundation Support,* 6–7.

16. The rationale for this change is given in ibid., 18.

17. Ford Foundation, *Annual Report, 1993,* <http://www.fordfound.org /AR.93 /AR9311.html>; Ford Foundation, *Annual Report, 1994,* <http://www.fordfound.org /AR.94/AR9413.html>; Ford Foundation, *Annual Report, 1995,* <http://www.ford found.org/AR.95/AR9513.html>.

18. Lila Wallace–Reader's Digest Fund, "1996 Grants," <http://www.lilawal lace.org/ 96grant.htm#writer>; telephone interview, Cathy Edwards, managing director, National Performance Network, February 21, 1997.

19. National Endowment for the Arts, FY 98 Application Guidelines, 7.

20. Peter M. Rutkoff and William B. Scott, *New School: A History of the New School for Social Research* (New York: Free Press, 1986).

21. *The Diaries of Judith Malina, 1947–1957* (New York: Grove Press, 1984), 463.

22. Rutkoff and Scott, *New School,* 229.

23. See John Cage, "[The New School]," in *John Cage,* ed. Richard Kostelanetz (New York: Praeger, 1970), 118–20; Ellsworth Snyder, "Chronological Table of John Cage's Life," in Kostelanetz, 39. On the influence of John Cage's class on Fluxus, see Philip Auslander's essay in this volume.

24. Cage, "[The New School]," 119.

25. See ibid.; and also Al Hansen and Dick Higgins, "[On Cage's Classes]," in Kostelanetz, *John Cage,* 120–24.

26. On Dunn's class, see my *Democracy's Body: Judson Dance Theater, 1962–1964* (Ann Arbor, Mich.: UMI Research Press, 1983; rpt. Durham, N.C.: Duke University Press, 1993), 1–33.

27. See Phyllis Tuchman, *George Segal,* Modern Masters (New York: Abbeville Press, 1983), 13–15; Michael Kirby, *Happenings* (New York: E. P. Dutton, 1965), 53; Barbara Haskell, *Blam! The Explosion of Pop, Minimalism, and Performance, 1958–1964* (New York: Whitney Museum of Art and W. W. Norton, 1984), 41.

28. My information about Black Mountain College relies on two important sources: Martin Duberman, *Black Mountain College: An Exploration in Community* (New York: E. P. Dutton, 1972); and Harris, *Arts at Black Mountain College.*

29. Harris, *Arts at Black Mountain College,* xix, xx, 7.

30. For instance, John Rice, one of the founders of Black Mountain, trained as a classicist, wrote a spirited response to Robert Maynard Hutchins's experiments in general education at the University of Chicago, in which Hutchins posited "a common stock of fundamental ideas" that would make "education everywhere the same," teaching "correctness in thinking as a means to . . . intelligent action," but "leav[ing] experience to life." Rice argued against "a common stock of fundamental ideas" and claimed that other modes than the written word (such as the arts) could contribute to education. Further, he expostulated that the classics should be seen as products of their times, not as eternal truths, and that "Gertrude Stein's *Lectures in America* is headier than Aristotle's *Poetics* or Horace's *Ars Poetica*" (Harris, *Arts at Black Mountain College,* 15).

31. Ibid., 40; see Xanti Schawinsky, "From the Bauhaus to Black Mountain," *Drama Review* 15, no. 3a (1971): 30–44. On nonmatrixed performance, see Michael Kirby, "The New Theatre," in *The Art of Time: Essays on the Avant-Garde* (New York: E. P. Dutton, 1969), 78–80.

32. Harris, *Arts at Black Mountain College,* 122.

33. Ibid., 151.

34. For several, often conflicting, descriptions of this event, see Duberman, *Black Mountain College,* 370–78.

35. Antonin Artaud, *The Theater and Its Double,* trans. Mary Caroline Richards (New York: Grove Press, 1958).

36. *The Performing Arts: Problems and Prospects,* Rockefeller Report on the future of theater, dance, music in America (New York: McGraw-Hill, 1965).

37. I am grateful to Michael Goldberg for these statistics.

38. Attilio Favorini, personal communication.

39. John Fleming, personal communication.

40. Richard Kostelanetz, *The Dictionary of the Avant-Gardes* (Pennington, N.J.: A Cappella, 1993), s.v. "Academic Critics." Despite my disagreement with Kostelanetz on the antipathy of academia toward the avant-garde, I do appreciate the fact that he singles me out, along with some other full-time academics—Gerald Janecek, Roger Shattuck, Michael Kirby, Mark Ensign Cory, Jack Burnham, Hugh Kenner, Laszlo

Moholy-Nagy, Jo-Anna Isaak, and the classicist Donald Sutherland—as having written intelligent books on avant-garde art.

41. Ibid., s.v. "Cage"; Snyder, "Chronological Table," 36–41.

42. Kostelanetz, *Dictionary of Avant-Gardes,* s.v. "*HPSCHD.*"

43. Lisa Wolford, "Re/membering Home and Heritage: The New World Performance Laboratory," *Drama Review* 38, no. 3 (1994): 128–29. I thank Claudia Nascimento for referring me to this article.

44. In *The Amazing Decade,* Moira Roth documents the work of fifty-three women performance artists active from 1970 to 1980, including Laurie Anderson, Eleanor Antin, Judy Chicago, Leslie Labowitz, Linda Montano, Pauline Oliveros, Adrian Piper, Yvonne Rainer, Faith Wilding, and Martha Wilson. Of those fifty-three, twenty noted in the biographies published with their documentation that they either had teaching positions in or graduate degrees from universities and colleges. One can assume the number was in fact higher, since several artists mentioned neither their graduate education nor whether they earned money through college teaching.

45. Guest speakers at the Performance Art, Culture, Pedagogy Symposium included not only active performance artists working for the most part outside of the university, like Tim Miller and Guillermo Gómez-Peña (although they, of course, often teach and perform at universities), and curators of museums and performance spaces, but several historians and theorists of performance, including Kristine Stiles (Duke University), Peggy Phelan (New York University), Henry Sayre (Oregon State University), and Moira Roth (Mills College). Perhaps most significantly, the symposium roster also included a number of performance artists who are tenured professors at a wide variety of institutions, including the conference organizer, Charles Garoian (Pennsylvania State University), as well as Suzanne Lacy (California College of Arts and Crafts), Joanna Frueh (University of Nevada, Reno), William Pope (Bates College), Jacki Apple (Art Center College of Design and University of California, San Diego), Lin Hixon (School of the Art Institute of Chicago), John White (University of California, Irvine), Roger Shimomura (University of Kansas), and Daniel Collins (Arizona State University). Allen Kaprow (professor emeritus, University of California at San Diego), the eminent creator of Happenings and performance art since the late 1950s, was the conference's opening speaker. At the time I wrote this article, the webpage for the symposium could be viewed at <http://is04.ce.psu.edu/c&i/PACP.html/>.

46. In addition to those individuals who either corresponded with or spoke to me, already acknowledged in notes above, I would like to thank all those who responded to my email survey regarding university support for avant-garde performance. I am also indebted to Agatino Balio, David Bordwell, Laurie Beth Clark, Kevin Kuhlke, Meredith Monk, Michael Peterson, Stan Pressner, Mark Russell, Arthur Sabatini, and Dan Wikler, who spoke with me in illuminating ways about, and provided factual data for, many of these issues during the writing of this essay. Finally, I would like to thank my editor, James Harding, for suggesting this topic; Phil Auslander and Lynn Garafola for their careful readings of an earlier draft; and, especially, Noël Carroll, without whose insights, questions, and criticisms this essay could not have been written.

Kristine Stiles

Never Enough Is *Something Else:* Feminist Performance Art, Avant-Gardes, and Probity

Censorship and *Something Else*

"To write," Gilles Deleuze claims, "is certainly not to impose a form (of expression) on the matter of lived experience. Literature rather moves in the direction of the ill-formed or the incomplete."[1] He also notices that "a writer is not a patient but rather a physician, the physician of himself [*sic*] and of the world."[2] Deleuze supports this metaphor by quoting French writer Jean-Marie Gustave Le Clézio: "One day, we will perhaps know that there wasn't any art, but only *medicine.*"[3] And then Deleuze adds: "Literature appears as an enterprise of health." But it is a strange kind of health, a health wracked with "delirium," a delirium played out between what he identifies as the poles of "disease" and "resist[ance]."[4] Deleuze leaves his assertions intentionally ill-formed, namely unresolved, a strategy that he secures by locating them in the incomplete condition of always becoming. "Writing is inseparable from becoming," Deleuze insists.[5]

However sympathetic one may be to Deleuze's application of an organic, philosophical model of becoming to writing and being, or to his alliance with what resembles Victor Turner's anthropological interest in the relation between the liminal function of art and social healing, one still needs to ask: How would the "inseparable" relation he proposes between writing and becoming be different if one did impose "a form (of expression) on the matter of lived experience"? And how could one not, if writing (and art, following Le Clézio) is a kind of physician, an enterprise of health? More importantly, what criteria would be constructed to administer this medicine? How may those who write (or produce art) be held responsible for their practices if writing (as physician) is to have a social function in an actual political space? Does this mean that something akin to the code of medical ethics embodied in the Hippocratic oath would be solemnly sworn to by writers (and artists)? How and who would administer that code of ethics? Of what might it consist?

These questions are particularly compelling to me because of the unpredictable ways in which the present state of this essay came into being. Indeed, "essaying" is a more accurate term for this text, which was written over a period of four years, on divergent subjects, for distinct reasons, in response to multiple requests from various people for diverse contexts, in different countries, and on different continents.[6] Under such conditions, writing itself never ceases becoming, as I shall explain.

The article with which the present essay began was called "Never Enough." (It appears below as the second section.) "Never Enough" was commissioned by Danish performance artist Kirsten Justesen for *Body as Membrane,* an exhibition of women's performance art photographs that Justesen organized with Austrian performance artist Valie Export.[7] To my surprise, Justesen cut my essay from the catalog in December 1995. She refused to publish it because I had raised questions about the ways in which the photographs in the show demonstrated attitudes that I described as self-denigrating and self-destructive, a criticism that implicitly challenged Justesen's exhibition itself. Justesen justified her censorship by stating that my views represented "American Puritanism with a thin candy coating."[8]

Ten months later, when I attempted to include an excerpt from the still unpublished "Never Enough" in a different catalog essay (this time on Carolee Schneemann), to my utter astonishment this very section was censored by Marcia Tucker, then director of the New Museum.[9] The section of "Never Enough" that I had attempted to include (entitled "Apples and Stems" for the Schneemann essay) addressed the ways in which Schneemann's theory and practice have been usurped for years by artists and critics who often neither credited nor supported her work. When I learned of Tucker's cut, I requested that an asterisk be added to the heading of my catalog essay to alert readers to the fact that an important part of the text was missing, and that it had been deemed "not appropriate" for publication.[10] In response to my request, Tucker responded that I had been "edited"—not censored.[11] She further asserted that everyone who had read my text, including Schneemann, was "troubled" by the "angry and defensive tone" of the "Apples and Stems" section.[12] I responded to Tucker this way:

> Have I—without the slightest intention to do so—breached a museum code of decorum much in the manner [that] Schneemann herself [does in her art]? . . . Why was a section of the "Apple and Stems" part of my essay deemed "inappropriate" as I was told? Why have the quotation marks I had placed around the word appropriate been struck from my [requested] note? Is it because I wrote what needed to be said and named names where The New Museum would prefer to be more polite? Is it because I accurately honed in on, and breached, institutional standards of decorum? If so—and obviously I did—then I, like Schneemann, must be on the right track.

> Moreover, . . . why does taking a position against self-destruction, self-derogation, and the appropriation of Schneemann's theoretical language—that is, taking a position against art that is opposed to everything for which her life's work stands—have to be interpreted as "angry and defensive"? . . . What is inappropriate about anger? What is wrong with defending an artist's work after so many years of misunderstanding, neglect, and abuse? Why, even as we embrace the visionary work of a revolutionary artist, must we politely whisper about (and thus protect) the forces which systematically have conspired against her? Indeed, I find it distressingly paradoxical, if not hypocritical, that in our profession all forms of the most extreme sexuality, violence, masochism, sadism, "abjection," and so on, may be shown, written about, and even celebrated as "transgressive," but a critique of these very behaviors is described as "angry and defensive." It is more than ironic that my text should be censored when, for so many years, I wrote about destruction and violence in art when no one else would. What a strange world we make![13]

Tucker never responded. When I saw her at Schneemann's opening, Tucker remained her congenial and warm self.

I let the whole matter of both censorship experiences pass until January 1997, when I was again contacted by Justesen, who invited me to "respond" to an article by English art historian Katy Deepwell on the exhibition *Body as Membrane* in the now defunct Finnish art journal *Siski.*[14] The insult of being solicited to retort to a debate sparked by my own work, by the very person who had censored it, was unmistakable. In the intervening months, Justesen had realized that my essay potentially motivated an extended discussion of her show. So she distributed my text to numerous individuals, among them Tania Ørum (a critic for *Kritik*), Deepwell, and others. In order to further the discussion of the whole affair, Justesen herself (not Deepwell) had shifted the focus from the problems I had raised (about the ways feminist performance artists represent themselves) to a spurious competition about the differences between "American and European feminists." (Divide and conquer has always been the best smokescreen to avoid grappling constructively with real conflict.) I agreed to respond to this contrived debate only when John Peter Nilsson, editor-in-chief of *Siski,* resolved to publish the full text of my censored catalog essay—"Never Enough."[15]

In the summer of 1997 an article by Tania Ørum, an assistant professor in the Department of Comparative Literature at Copenhagen University, was published by *Siski* as part of the chain of responses to the "debate" my essay prompted. In her article, Ørum—a friend of Justesen—charged that it was I who was the one to be held accountable for lamenting the self-representations of the artists exhibited in *Body as Membrane.* "If anybody is guilty of perpetuating the image of woman as victim and part of a chain of interchangeable bodies which may be replaced by each other at any moment irrespective of individual characteristics," she wrote, "it must be feminists like Kristine Stiles."[16] Ørum also repeatedly described me as an "old" feminist and associated me with Jill Johnston, a lesbian activist and 1970s essentialist feminist. However inaccurate a personal description of me this was, I did not find it insulting to be called either old and essentialist or lesbian, as she intended. On the contrary, Ørum's polarizing strategy simply recalls Justesen's attempt to pit American against European feminists in an effort to shift the questions I raised in "Never Enough" from substantive cultural issues to personal attacks. Justesen's and Ørum's behavior, as well as the censorship of my essay, are object lessons in feminist discourses and politics. Feminists do, can, and must disagree. This is the only objective I hold "essential" to the health of feminism. That my work was censored in a feminist context, by feminists, and that I continue to be misrepresented and maligned by feminists in avant-garde contexts, only proves how important such disagreements are to us all.

Now, Justesen and Tucker are both intelligent, responsible, and creative women, highly informed about contemporary art. Tucker is an articulate, longtime champion of contemporary aesthetics and cultural theory. Justesen is a feminist artist herself, practicing performance art, one of the most controversial forms of art making. Who could predict that of all people they would censor? Certainly not I, who never set out to write anything worthy of censorship, even though I realized that my essays did not conform to the celebratory tone of conventional catalog entries. But I felt that "my textual contribution [was] in keeping with the fierce quality of the works themselves."[17] Moreover, neither Tucker nor Justesen could conceive that they could censor. Rather, Tucker held that she had "edited," and Justesen stated that she "refused to publish" a text that was "inappropriate" for her exhibition catalog.

The professional positions alone of these two women must compel further consideration of the issues I raised in "Never Enough," if only because it would appear that Justesen and Tucker possess a certain kind of power, authority, experience, and knowledge. That these attributes are real or recoverable in any larger context is, of course, at question. For there is a critical difference between the appearance of power and the actual ability to exert power in culture at large. If Tucker and Justesen had any real authority, it is doubtful that they would have found the need to censor within the confines of art history and criticism. And is it not a lack of essential confidence and authority that drives the censor in the first place?[18]

According to William Gass, censors perform their tasks for a higher value, one known best to them, and which they alone determine for the others:

> The censor cuts; the censor veils; the censor confines; the censor denies. All this is done for the sake of something higher: the stability, the good, of society. . . . There is always a position of power and privilege at risk when the censor snips, for what stone tree would fear the woodcutter's tiny saw?[19]

Regardless of their defenses, Tucker and Justesen did censor. The difference between "editing" and "censoring" depends on *who* has the power (at any given juncture) of representation.[20] My authority as an author was usurped without my agreement and without consultation with me. I had the feeling of one whose mouth was "stopped," as Gass so powerfully pointed out about the effects of censorship when he remarked: "You wish to stop her mouth from voicing her thoughts, thoughts that you would see silenced, frightened into formlessness."[21]

Why do censors uphold what they themselves believe to be unthinkable? Because *something else* has been spoken that they sense must be suppressed in order to protect someone or something else from exposure. This repressed virtual content then requires endless exposure, in the manner Gass described "To expose, to lay bare . . . how many layers of concealment had to be removed? Seven veils? And each one symbolic, through and through of political, sexual, [institutional], and educational enstiflement."[22] Whether faced with censorship or not, the writer's responsibility—especially if s/he is to let writing perform the physician's ministrations—is to reveal and accuse. My essay was censored *not* because of its actual content, but because of that *something else,* that virtual content at work within it. The voice that both Justesen and Tucker deemed necessary to stifle (in order to secure the illusion of uncontested exhibitions) was the voice within the text that changed my discourse into what Deleuze described as "a kind of foreign language within language." In other words, although I said one thing, I was also saying *something else,* that virtual content Deleuze associated with what Virginia Woolf might have considered to be the very rightful concern of the writer: "The writer does not speak about it, but is concerned with *something else.*"[23]

So I have been required to interrogate myself, asking: What is this *something else,* this foreign language, lodged within my discussions of art that caused censorship by those who could not imagine themselves to censor? My answer is this: I brought value judgments culled from my personal expectations about the ethical behavior of avant-gardes (and of those associated with them) to my experience of writing about them. My *something else,* in the first instance, was my temerity to describe as negative the performances and self-representations of women performance artists in *Body as Membrane,* and, in the second instance, my critique of the unethical behavior of those associated with representing avant-garde art. Moreover, in addition to exercising value-judgments that clashed with doctrine, rules, and rites regarding the behavior of, and institutional practices associated with avant-gardes, my text searched for a something I shall describe below as *probity* within avant-garde practices. The evocation of that *something else* raised the censors' dread and panic, and it was *that* fearsome *something else* that the censors tried to hide, transgressing even their own creeds in order to silence words from being voiced.

These events of censorship further caused me to confront the fact that this *something else* hovering in my texts is akin to what Deleuze described as a kind of "delirium," the "disease" of the process of writing that underpins the "physician" who, through writing, acts on herself:

> Literature is delirium, and as such its destiny is played out between the two poles of delirium. Delirium is a disease, the disease par excellence, whenever it erects a race it claims is pure and dominant. But it is the measure of health when it invokes this oppressed bastard race that ceaselessly stirs beneath dominations, resisting everything that crushes and imprisons, a race that is outlined in relief in literature as process.[24]

Indeed, in this essaying—this never enough—writing *became* the physician through which I encountered how thought may invoke what it also wishes to resist, the delirious process that releases the cure—namely that *something else* which resists oppressive domination. When the physician that is my writing required me to examine why my work had been censored, I realized that the *something else* haunting my text was my insistence on the enactment of personal codes of *probity*. By this term, I mean to draw attention to personal accountability and responsibility: the integrity, rectitude, candor, fair play, justice, scruples, and accountability with which those engaged with avant-gardes must operate. My concern with probity must have been the subtext, the *something else,* that summoned the censor's scissors. Is, then, the censure of my work simultaneously the register of its delirious conjuring, a resistance to the "bastard?" Does the *something else* of that delirium also have to do with writing and art themselves, with their dual possibility to minister health, with their instrumental ability to interrogate with probity, and with their recuperative role as a means to operate in the dissociative breach between delirium and resistance?[25] Finally, is it not probity that requires us to search, to delve beneath the surface, to dig into the substance not only of events but of the measure of those events in the institutions erected around them?

"PROBITY!" a surprised Laura Cottingham, wrote to me: "What an unheard of suggestion for the 20th century, [insofar as] this is a shared or at least understandable assumption . . . of accountability, integrity, probity."[26] On further reflection, the feminist writer and lesbian activist added:

> I BELIEVE in probity. I believe in it politically, intellectually, emotionally and spiritually. My concern with your essayistic assertion is still that the weight of your assertion does not, for me, weigh in against the strength of understanding currently operating against it. That's all—in other words, I see you doing a David and Goliath here. And yes I know who won that battle, but that was a myth![27]

When I call for avant-garde art to operate with probity, as I shall at the end of this essay, it is *not* a call for ethical or moral fundamentalism, nor for a simplistic grand principle, but for a pluralistic accountability that may be virtuous *or* monstrous. Cordelia's answer to King Lear's question to his three daughters is exemplary of virtuous probity. Lear asks: "Which of you shall we say doth love us most?" Cordelia testifies, in contrast to her obsequious sisters: "I love your majesty according to my bond; no more nor less." If Cordelia's scruples impress some as too righteous, Pier Paolo Pasolini's film *Salo* is an excellent model of the heinous. In *Salo,* Pasolini takes up the marquis de Sade's theme of perversion with a fierce probity and horrible aesthetic in order to investigate with uncompromising and brutal integrity the violent clash between the limits of individual desire and the boundaries of human freedom demanded by the social contract.[28]

Several sections follow. "Never Enough," as I have said, is the original essay censored from *Body as Membrane* and published in *Siski,* to which I have made minor emendations. The next section, "Feminist Performance Art," widens the discussion of the feminist avant-garde begun in "Never Enough" with special attention to the problem of drawing parallels between the work of Schneemann and such artists as French performance artist Orlan. In the section "Probity, Avant-Gardes, and Radical Originality," I first consider feminist performance in the context of widely discussed theories of the historical avant-garde. Next I reflect on the relationship between radical*ism* and radical, and the difference between a specious "ism" and an authentic originality, before ending with a discussion of the value of probity in the identity and behavior of avant-gardes. Finally, "Women Taking Action" concludes—for the time being—with a call for more intensified practices of probity, the *something else* driving this essaying essay, these many remarks.[29] Taking probity as an ethical premise, these sections weave together interdependent critiques of feminist performance and avant-garde practices, providing not only a reevaluation of each, but a theorization of their relationship to each other.

Never Enough

"Is this where it all ends?" *Time* asked of Ivana Trump, Czech-born wife of U.S. billionaire Donald Trump, in its December 24, 1990, coverage of the "scrumptious scandal." Ivana had been granted $25 million and a divorce after thirteen years of marriage and three children. The judge handed down the decision in only ten minutes "based on Mr. Trump's cruel and inhuman treatment." Ivana, forty-one at the time, had been discarded for a twenty-six-year-old actress, Marla Maples, who not only remarkably resembled the first Mrs. Trump but also produced a child for Mr. Trump four years later. Exchanged for a newer, fresher, and better-functioning machine, Ivana "disappeared from high society for a few weeks . . . only to turn up on the May cover of *Vogue* Magazine as a blonde bombshell with a very fresh face [lift] . . . newly single, secure and oh-so-stylish," *Health* reported in July 1991. As if money and body-altering technology could reverse the cultural consciousness and values to which she, regardless of being tall, slender, blond, glamorous, rich, smart, or accomplished (in short the paradigms of desire in Western culture), had been forced to surrender.

Grief and futility overwhelmed me while reflecting upon Ivana's circumstance, not because of her divorce or plastic surgery. No one but Ivana was responsible for turning herself into the caricature of her own youth. I was desolate because no matter who a woman is, what she does, or what she has, she is never enough. I am never enough. And the temporary shift in Ivana's self-representation would not ultimately prevent her from her fate. For, despite momentary triumphs, none of us is exempt from defeat—even women like Marla, who capitalize on the fall of another.[30] Trump's exchange of women represents a phenomenon against which even the youngest, most beautiful, accomplished, and fertile—or, on the contrary, the most enraged, hostile, and man-hating—woman is powerless. In this particular case, Trump's ability to attract and acquire younger women feeds the illusion of the deferment of mortality and the insufficiency that absolute power always knows. And so, one representation is constantly traded for another.

Religious, social, and cultural formations that arbitrarily limit women's potential and use-value to age, beauty, and fertility provide the psychological conditioning that convinces women that we are never enough. Even more depressing, the incessant exchange of women in patriarchy remains fundamentally unaltered despite feminism, consciousness training, gay and lesbian separatism, radical changes in gender and sexual roles and practices, and the theoretical critiques of poststructuralism. What is more, it is exacerbated by the economy and circulation of representations of women as objects of desire. Women have learned that representations that abuse and degrade us—images that also promised to capture male attention—now hold the gaze of many males and females. But this attention is fleeting at best, as the desire for female sexual subservience is transformed into disgust at our pathetic self-abnegation, at the same time as it is fueled for more. We women continue to produce ourselves as victims, feeding this voracious appetite.

My ruminations about never being enough, and about Ivana Trump's dilemma, were prompted by the photocopies sent to me of works that were to be included in the exhibition *Body as Membrane* (for which I had been commissioned to write this essay). While examining them, I found myself asking: "Is this where it all ends?" The cheap photocopies of photographs—still images of live performance events—were pictures that broke my heart and incapacitated my will. They confirmed the desperation of the struggle and the extent to which we women continue to degrade ourselves in a misguided attempt to wrest power over the cultural implications of our representations. For despite pictorial rhetoric, these images were not empowering, but hopeless and sad. I longed for them to be simply fictions. But even as fictions, they would have bespoken self-hatred. And they are not fictions, but residual documents of real actions taken by actual women. Indeed the photographs of French performance artist Orlan, one of the most extreme examples of suffering in the exhibition, demonstrates just how much the contest over representation is one of life and death, as she repeatedly undergoes dangerous spinal blocks in order to retain consciousness during her body-altering performances.

Curiously, however, it was not the black-and-white photocopy of the horrific suicidal mania of Orlan's serial body-reconstructions that reminded me of the dislocated wretchedness of Ivana Trump, posing as a forty-one-year-old ingenue on the cover of *Vogue*. (I had, until this moment, become anesthetized to their gore.) It was the color photocopy, thrice removed from the actual performance, of *Dog Bites* (1992)—an action by the Finnish artist Eija-Liisa Ahtila—that prompted my ruminations.[31] The visual remove of the photocopy enabled me to distance myself from the usual aesthetic function of the slide transparency and photograph. Their spotless, glamorous surfaces (made ready for consumption) technologically enhance viewing. But to see *Dog Bites* at the distance of the poorly reproduced black and white photocopy was to grasp not only the commercial function of the slide and glossy photograph, but also to visualize the dejection of Ahtila's act. There she is: cropped, dyed red hair. Harsh black lines traced carefully on her eyebrows and around her eyes. Lips thick with color. The artist glowers expectant, penetrating, distrustful, but analytical. Her partially revealed breasts are squeezed together and contorted. Her hand is raised in the gesture of a dog, paw up. Her title insists that she is ready to attack. But what I see is not a biting dog. I see an untouched woman who might rather roll over, more likely to be petted and licked (by man or woman) than to bite. She is pure emotional pathos. The body here is a membrane of pain.

Some terrible gnawing psychophysical self-doubt, self-hate, self-revulsion, and annulment pervades these images. In *Hyperventilation,* Heli Rekuli wears a gas mask with the phallic oxygen hose inserted into her vagina. While Rekuli makes a connection between the life-sustaining function of the oxygen hose and the life-giving capacity of the birth canal, her red-greased body, animalistic pose, stained fingers, and menacing eyes suggest rather a sadomasochistic fantasy of some variety of vicious bondage. Rather than controlling her own body and restricting the elements that sustain it to a female origin, Rekuli's image insists upon the constriction of the female body within the repressive and humiliating sexual technology of a male domination fantasy.

Similarly Joan Jonas's disembodied bodily image *Mirror Piece* (1970) resembles Hans Bellmer's disemboweled dolls, anticipating the recent violently dismembered mannequins in Cindy Sherman's photographs of the early 1990s. In *Satisfaction* (1994), Elke Krystofek masturbates before a public with objects inserted into every genital orifice—anus and vagina stuffed with what (in the photocopies I was sent to study) resemble a dildo and a knife. Krystofek's action seems to be an aggressive, if not ironic, reply to the Rolling Stones' whine, "Can't get no satisfaction." But her satisfaction is one of lonely exhibitionism in an environment that she suggests (because of the objects with which she surrounds and impales herself) offers only brief respite from duties of ironing, vacuuming, and other domestic tasks conventionally associated with women's subordination. Is Krystofek free merely because she can abandon her chores and masturbate in public to a primarily male crowd? Isn't this scenario simply a staged version of any number of stock male fantasies—to see a woman as beautiful as Krystofek masturbate for them? Such an action is not the same as entering a porn theater, as Valie Export did in 1968, in order to stop the show by inviting the audience to touch and experience a real female body. Is Krystofek in possession of her self-representation, or is she a woman completely out of touch with the dignity of her own body? As an Austrian, has Krystofek been conditioned by Wiener Aktionismus, a consummately male genre of performance art, to abase herself in public?

Krystofek is the antithesis of Mary Kelly, whose body has disappeared, hidden in a black monolithic costume and replaced by texts, narrative histories, and heraldic shields. Kelly's cosmetic makeup equally camouflages her and suggests that her self-confident pose, her apparent invulnerability, derives from a conditioned disembodiment, rationalized by the patriarchal logic of language handed down from Plato and protected by the polished wooden floors of exhibition spaces. Rather than debase her body, Kelly abandons it, like the

> bourgeois subject [who] substitutes for its corporal body the rarefied body of the text. . . . The carnality of the body has been dissolved and dissipated until it can be reconstituted in writing at a distance from itself. As the flesh is derealized, representation, which becomes at last representational, is separated from it and puts in train a mode of signification for which, to borrow a word from Derrida, the body has become supplementary.[32]

The body is anything but supplementary for Annie Sprinkle, who claims to be "sexually excited" by the production of her own image. But what is presented superficially as a parody in *Prostitute/Porn Star Turned Sex Guru/Performance Artist* and in *Anatomy of a Pinup Photo* (1991) is, I think, a thin pretense for asserting and protecting the "real," and that which may not be substituted.[33] *Anatomy of a Pinup Photo* is simultaneously natural and artificial, an image of fecund desire and barren repulsion. In this work of art, Sprinkle verbally emphasizes the "realness" of her pendulous breasts by describing them as "sagging," while also attempting to overcome their inevitable insufficiency (insufficient because they will always be replaced—as Marla replaced Ivana) by encrusting them with pearls. Sprinkle's emphasis on her "real" breasts divulges a craving to be associated with anything she might consider real.[34] For the one element of her image that the self-appointed "sex guru/performance artist" insists is real—except the pain she endures from wearing shoes that are too small and a corset in which she can not "brethe" [*sic*]—is her enormous breasts. It is her one irreplaceable special aspect that few other women share. No wonder Sprinkle seeks to assert the "reality" of her breasts by apologetically noting their vulnerability to gravity ("sagging") or describes her corset as hiding the actual girth of her "very big belly."

Similarly, the Hottentot Venus that Renée Cot summons in *Hott-En-Tot* (1994) has strap-on prosthetic breasts and buttocks that reinforce the stereotype of African "primitive" sexual appetite. But these prosthestic appendages equally visualize the extended temperament of the colonialist mind Sander L. Gilman has carefully theorized.[35] Much like the commodity that the black Hottentot became for nineteenth-century society, a commodity whose genitalia remain on display at the Musée de l'Homme in Paris, Kirsten Justesen presents herself as a commodity. In *Lunch* (1975), Justesen is stuffed naked into a grocery cart situated on a country road in a pretty landscape. She appears to glory in the bucolic environment (of both her own body and the lovely terrain), becoming a fetish of the supermarket of images asking to be consumed and devoured. In another image, she appears as a mermaid, but her fishy tail has replaced her head (creating the male fantasy of the woman who won't talk back) and leaving her ravishingly voluptuous body mindlessly intact for consumption.

One after another, these photocopies overwhelm me with their thinly veiled anxiety, anguish, and futility. Even Alison Knowles, ordinarily the picture of serenity and self-acceptance, appears catatonic in her self-portrait, *The Identical Lunch.* Regardless of the fact that this is one of the most benign images in the exhibition, Knowles looks sphinxlike. This naked woman on a New York rooftop seated by her lunch might just be resting, meditating, or enjoying the sun. But her pose is stiff and strained in the chair where she sits objectlike, rectilinear, an automaton shackled to the rotations of the wristwatch she wears, a technological reminder of the incessant march of time that regulates the social usefulness of her female body and its decline so poignantly present (but denied) in Sprinkle's work.

"By what 'system of power' are certain representations authorized while others are blocked, prohibited, invalidated, or ignored?" Margaret R. Miles has asked.[36] Her question is rhetorical since it already identifies a system of power as the means by which certain kinds of acts are validated. This observation offers a key to how we might understand that the images exhibited in *Body as Membrane* belong to the very system of oppression against which they ostensibly contend. The images in *Body as Membrane* surface in a culture of female abuse precisely because the culture is conditioned to representing women in this manner. Despite much theorizing to the contrary, and regardless of who has the power over representation, the semiotics of female degradation has been so deeply and systematically established and entrenched that it will be read as misogynic whether produced by a feminist or a misogynist. Consciously departing from Judith Butler's highly influential theory of the 1990s that one may reformulate prohibition as power, I want to clearly state that *women do not empower themselves by perpetrating signifiers of domination and degradation under the signs of feminism or self-representation.*[37] A feminist retheorization of bondage, for example, is not sufficient to change the signification of S-M images in a society acculturated to viewing female bondage through male desire.

The photographs that comprise *Body as Membrane* overwhelmingly testify to the failure of feminist art and theory—my own included—to resist the continued and even accelerating degradation of women. These images reinscribe it and suggest that the cultural conditioning of women is so complete, and the situation so extreme, that we will—in the name of self-empowerment—rerepresent ourselves within the same vulgar exploitative system of signification. Valie Export's *Genitalpanik* (1969) and *Eros/ion* (1971) succinctly summarized this state over twenty-five years ago. Perhaps that is why her photographs are among the most compelling in this exhibition. Her work addressed the fact that women's bodies are tortured and carefully taught to reiterate the wounds in self-inflicted acts of pain and subjugation *(Eros/ion);* and that we remain in a profound condition of genital panic *(Aktionshose: Genitalpanik)* attempting, it would appear in vain, to defend that space while simultaneously aiding and abetting our exposure.

I recognize how conservative this position may appear, and that such a perception would break with the history of my own scholarship. But when faced with the photocopies of representations in *Body as Membrane,* I honestly could not recognize the values I had previously stood for, even when I had defended some of these images in the past. Why? The context of looking at these pictures—as a whole representation of women's performance art—has the overwhelming impact of showing me something I have never been able to see before: *how, under the empty slogan of self-representation, women have become the handmaids of the system of our own abuse against which we must struggle and never capitulate.*

For example, in an article on Orlan published in 1993, U.S. critic Barbara Rose defended Orlan's "theater of operations" as a reworking of the ancient Greek artist Zeuxis's art. "Zeuxis," Rose wrote, "made a practice of choosing the best parts from different models and combining them to produce the ideal woman."[38] What Rose forgot is that Zeuxis's male construction of an impossible female ideal is the originating source of Orlan's wounds. Such deep damage cannot be recuperated through irony, or healed by mere imitation of the same process. Rather, by drawing on Zeuxis, as Rose claims, Orlan reiterates the system she seeks to expose. In this act, Orlan is assisted by the increasingly brutal efficiency of contemporary patriarchal technology, the very technology that fostered Ivana's disappearance and "fresh" new look, and the reproductive technology that threatens to make women's bodies obsolete altogether.

Decades have passed since Carolee Schneemann offered the justification for a female artistic practice that Rose uses to account for Orlan's motivation and accomplishment. Schneemann wrote, "Not only am I an image maker, but I explore the image values of flesh as material I choose to work with."[39] Schneemann also claimed in her essay "Istory of a Girl Pornographer" that: "I WAS PERMITTED TO BE AN IMAGE/BUT NOT AN IMAGE-MAKER CREATING HER OWN SELF-IMAGE."[40] Reworking Schneemann, Rose wrote: "Orlan remains in control of her own destiny [as] the artist and the woman [who] will never play the victim. . . . [She] is both subject and object, actress and director, passive patient and active organizer." Does Rose's defense of Orlan mean that after thirty years of ignoring Schneemann, the critic has finally learned something from her? Does this mean that Rose's consciousness has been raised after decades of contributing to mainstream culture and supporting male artists associated with Greenbergian formalism, the very art world patriarchy that has suppressed Schneemann's work for so long? I think not. It means that Schneemann's discourse has been co-opted.

Rose is able to defend Orlan because, like Donald Trump, she represents and reifies systems of power validated by patriarchy. The very culture that replaces Schneemann with Orlan (Marla for Ivana) is the culture that never empowered Schneemann in the first place. Another vivid example of this brand of sexism is a letter I received from the chief curator of a well-known museum in the United States. In refusing my proposal for a retrospective on Schneemann's work, he wrote: "In the case of Carolee [Schneemann], we were compelled by the case that you made but, while she may indeed be the stem, we felt that our audience would be better served by the apple."[41] In other words, this curator would prefer to exhibit an artist *in the style of* Schneemann rather than the artist herself.

What is at stake in the dynamics of desire and representation? Why serve the public the apple and not the stem? The apple (Marla/Orlan) is sweet, juicy, fecund, and new before it drops off the gnarled life-supporting stem (Ivana/Schneemann). The obvious irony of the fresh/stale, new/old paradigm is its profound instability. Orlan is not new and fresh. Aging, indeed, is what motivates her current work (and Barbara Rose's interest in it). Like Carolee, Marla, and Ivana, Orlan is already being substituted for by someone else. Is it you, Elke Krystofek? Or you, Heli Rekuli? Someone still in gymnasium? Who will she be?

My point is that the appropriation of once-subversive actions into the cultural mainstream merely provides another spectacle of victimization. One should not be surprised to learn in this regard that as Rose uncritically and proudly points out, "Pierre Restany, Achille Bonito Oliva and Hans Haacke get prominent billing [in Orlan's work] because they have supported [her] work in the past." Indeed! Support by such powerful male critics and artists merely validates Rose's discourse.

Orlan's work and many other works in *Body as Membrane* make me ache with misery for us all: men and women alike. For it appears that much of what we see has been disciplined and managed back into the system of marketable and profitable "apples." And after one shiny red apple loses its luster or is consumed, a bushel more women each awaits her turn. The biting tone of this essay is not directed at the artists, curators, or even critic Barbara Rose. Nor do I mean to pit Schneemann against Orlan. All of us, like Marla and Ivana, take our positions at victims of the patriarchal system that abuses and uses us as replacements for each other at some point or another. My anger is directed at our culpability, at all of us who sacrifice our bodies as membranes to capital and patriarchy in the name of fame, sex, love, and theory. *Body as Membrane* marks a critical turning point for me in my recognition of the insurmountable gap between feminist intentions and theories, and their actual effect in visual and discursive practices vis-à-vis avant-gardes (to which I shall return in a later section).[42] Despite many significant theories, many women artists remain confused and misdirected with regard to how to bridge this abyss in the visual domain. The enormous value of an exhibition like *Body as Membrane* is to instruct us visually in how far discourse is from rectifying the abusive conditions of women's representation and carnal knowing.

If we learn anything from *Body as Membrane,* it is that we fail to exempt ourselves from patriarchal economies and end up supporting them unwittingly if prevailing discourses or visual practices approve of women's images of self-denigration. Let me close this section with a parable that might be instructive for the ways in which power, despite one's best efforts at self-empowerment and self-representation, quite frequently gains its own ends:

> There were two starving artists living in the kingdom. The king offered them both a stipend to become his court artist. The one said to the other, "I can not accept this offer as it would jeopardize the integrity of my work." The other said, "Then you should not. But I will accept so that I can live and work." The one artist died of hunger. The other became a successful court poet. The king fulfilled his will both ways.[43]

Feminist Performance Art

My last pronouncement would seem to have ended the discussion. But not so fast. Returning to the questions I raised earlier, let me move closer to that *something else* that motivated the initial essay "Never Enough." That *something else* had to do, in large measure, with the vehicle that hauls the cart of apples and stems, namely the avant-garde, in which the delirium Deleuze identified as the poles of "disease" and "resist[ance]" is played out in the domain of visual art. For what the avant-garde might be, and how it might operate, is the *something else* that was the intuitive underpinning of my initial response in "Never Enough."

Justesen and Export positioned their exhibition *Body as Membrane* within the history of the feminist avant-garde. As a result, the exhibition itself must answer to that context. They wrote, for example, that *Body as Membrane* belonged to the tradition of "the feminist exhibitions [that] have emerged in Europe and the USA," and within the events they believed "rapidly changed" the ways in which "women, environment and art" were represented and treated in the international economy of art practices, institutions, and markets.[44] They located the origins of their show in the famous feminist exhibition Export organized in 1975, *Magna Feminista: Kunst und Kreativität.*[45]

In short, they positioned *Body as Membrane* as a contemporary incarnation of feminist avant-garde practice/performance in order to establish an illustrious lineage for younger artists and Justesen herself. They achieved this goal by juxtaposing the work of relatively unknown artists with images of such now-canonical performances as Export's *Tapp und Tast Kino* (1968), Joan Jonas's *Twilight* (1975), Mary Kelly's *Post-Partum Document* (1973–78), Gina Pane's "Azione Sentimentale" (1974), Carolee Schneemann's *Interior Scroll* (1975), and Hannah Wilke's *Intra-Venus* (1992–93). The very presence in *Body as Membrane* of feminist pioneers lent unquestionable avant-garde authority and cachet to the rest of the exhibition, and any question about the exhibition was perceived as a challenge to the history of feminist avant-garde art.

Avant-garde practices are conventionally marked by revolutionary fervor, radical*ism* that attempts to effect change and innovation in aesthetics as well as in the culture and politics of everyday life. The photographs exhibited in *Body as Membrane* conformed to these common and inherited expectations and representations associated with avant-garde art. Many of them, for example, belonged to the visual conventions of surrealism whose established symbolic discourse historically has canonized art as both radical and avant-garde. Jayne Parke's *Film Still: The Pool* (1991) is a good example. Parke presented a photograph of a naked woman holding a gigantic eel just under her breasts. Her head was cropped out of the image just below the shoulders and her legs are edited (amputated?) from the frame, just below her pubis. This image draws on not only the visual vocabulary of surrealist painting and film, but on ancient representations of fertility goddesses in biblical and mythic lore. But most of the works in *Body as Membrane* utilized extra-artistic contexts also conventionally associated with avant-garde strategies to infiltrate everyday life. Indeed, the photographs exhibited in *Body as Membrane,* if encountered in another context, might very well have been perceived as belonging to life, not art. Where else, for example, might Alison Knowles's very beautiful and poignant *Double Production* (1964)—an x-ray image of her belly pregnant with twins—be found, except perhaps in a medical archive? That she presented her pregnancy as performative conforms precisely to the genre and conventions mandated by avant-gardism.

Annie Sprinkle's photograph *Anya, a Goddess* (1990) recalls nineteenth-century pornographic daguerreotypes—too obviously composed to be erotic, too corny to be provocative—pornographic only because her Rubenesque body is solicitously displayed for the gaze as a visual stimulation for other pleasures. Heli Rekuli's *Untitled* (1995) is a color photograph of a naked woman sitting propped up on the floor, slouched against a wall like a limp doll, head covered entirely in a black rubber hood with Mickey Mouse ears, and into whose mouth a large, black phallic object (perhaps a dildo) is shoved. This image could be found only in the context of sadomasochistic literature, since in everyday life few venues (except an avant-garde exhibition space) would support, much less permit, the representation of such a helpless, debased, and humiliated woman.

Orlan's work also fits neatly into the avant-garde practice of bridging public and private life. In her photographic poster *I Have Given My Body to Art* (1993), the artist represents herself with black-and-blue, heavily bruised eyes, distorted nose, swollen lips, and ragged, greasy, multicolored hair. It is a picture of pure abjection, pain, and suffering that would make an excellent warning poster for the prevention of family violence. Such an image reinforces the fact that the only artists who have systematically achieved canonical status in art history are those who have belonged to, or been associated with an avant-garde in one way or another. It is fitting, then, to place Orlan's self-inflicted violence in the context of a kind of domestic violence, the abusive family histories of a pseudo-avant-garde, whose achievement is neither a visionary nor revisionary changing nothing at the root (as anything associated with the original meaning of the word "radical" must do).

As the apologist for Orlan, the critic August Ruhs defined Orlan's aesthetic aim in these ways:

> irreversibly alter her physical and social identity—in order to blaspheme as well as to rebel. . . . since to Orlan it is not enough merely to read the body—and in particular her own body—she literally sacrifices it to art to perform a Demiurgic and parthenogenetic act through plastic surgery, so that she transcends the limits of traditional body art in an unprecedented way—hardly any other artist achieves this aim as radically as she does.[46]

Such a statement makes it clear that the production of (art) history as a game of high stakes (since the nineteenth century) has now reached life-threatening proportions. Writing with utter sincerity and surprising naïveté, Ruhs continues to applaud Orlan's "efforts" as "ethical, especially since their intention is to do good."[47] Oh, that intent had the power to cause reality to become so!

Furthermore, Ruhs understands Orlan's work to be "basically a community project [because] art's essence is an integral part of the political opposition against categorization, which turns similar to [it] in the end." Ruhs also claims that Orlan's "fight" is on "two fronts: Where trespassing is done against the actual state of nature—and against the naturalness of culture."[48] To suggest that plastic surgery that endangers a woman's body represents a "community project" flies in the face of sociological facts. Starting in 1983, Pulitzer Prize–winning journalist Susan Faludi pointed out, "the American Society of Plastic and Reconstructive Surgeons launched a 'practice enhancement' campaign, issuing a flood of press releases, 'pre- and post-op photos,' and patient 'education' brochures and videotapes . . . bill[ing] 'body sculpturing' as safe, effective, affordable—and even essential to women's mental health."[49] Faludi explains that by the mid-1980s they were filling magazines and newspapers with "low monthly payment plans" for such surgery, and that the campaign worked. "By 1988, the cosmetic surgeons' caseloads had more than doubled, to 750,000 annually . . . counting only the doctors certified in plastic surgery; the total annual figure was estimated in excess of 1.5 million."[50] Despite this booming business, plastic surgery "was as dangerous as ever [and] in fact, the operations [especially silicon implants] would become even riskier as the big profits lured droves of untrained practitioners from other specialties."[51] These operations, furthermore, led to

> widespread charlatanry, ill-equipped facilities, major injuries, and even deaths from botched operations. Other studies found that at least 15 percent of cosmetic surgery caused hemorrhages, facial nerve damage, bad scars, or complications from anesthesia. Follow-up operations to correct mistakes filled a two-volume, 1,134-page reference manual *The Unfortunate Result in Plastic Surgery*. Plastic surgeons were devoting as much as a quarter of their practices to correcting their colleagues' errors.[52]

Faludi closed her chilling account of cosmetic surgery—a section of her book entitled "The Breast Man of San Francisco"—by quoting Kurt Wagner, a plastic surgeon who operated on his wife's body nine times: "To me surgery is like being in the arena where decisions are made and no one can tell me what to do."[53]

Orlan's self-punishment—exhibited in the negative ways in which she represents herself, reconstructs her identity in multiples, sexualizes her environment, and engages in self-mutilation (through instigating her own disfigurement at the hands of reconstructive surgery)—resembles the transference of psychopathological dissociative behaviors from the personal to the avant-garde. In this regard, the artist's work suggests exposure at some early point to identity-shattering psychological experiences, the dissociative effects of which now appear in her art in a manner that indicates posttraumatic stress disorder (PTSD). In such instances, a "traumatic event" resides somewhere in the history of the individual, an event defined as "outside the range of usual human experience that would be markedly distressing to almost anyone," in which "the victim becomes 'stuck' . . . when response to trauma cannot be worked through, for whatever reason."[54] PTSD is the dissociative, unconscious, maladaptive, repetitive attempt to work through the traumatic event lost (dissociated) from memory but stuck in the unconscious.[55] Orlan's symptoms might include repeated constructions of alternative identities (the name *Orlan* itself is a fictive identity that, apparently, the artist assumed as a teenager); fixation on breaking social taboos; obsession with sexual display, media attention, and spectacle; self-aggrandizement in the form of associations with God and saints ("Saint Orlan" is one of her identities); and self-abuse in the form of repeated life-threatening operations. Furthermore, Carey Lovelace reported that Orlan planned to adopt a new name, one chosen for her by "a public-relations agency."[56] Lovelace also has pointed out that, among other efforts, Orlan "has displayed her magnified vagina painted red, blue, and yellow; applied pubic hair on Louvre paintings of [pubic] hair-free females; walked down the street in a dress on which was printed an image of her own naked body."[57] In a "mesurage" in 1965, Orlan used her body as a standard unit of measure to compare "the length of streets named after famous men against streets named after other famous men," asking, "why would a 'Chateaubriand' measure 550 *orlans,* for example, and a 'Victor Hugo' only 25?"[58] In this action Orlan fabricated a link (through the device of measurement) between the names of famous French men, the number of times their names appeared on French street signs, and the representation of the size of their phalluses. This metonymy also functions as a metaphor displaced into a representation of herself—"measure[d]" in "550 orlans."

The artist's apparent chronic dysfunction implies some form of long-term, particularly sexual, abuse in which the pain of experience has been sublimated and transformed into guilt, a self-loathing typical of traumatic subjectivity that equates the self with being despoiled and dirty.[59] "She would wash her white clothes in public and capture her gray sweat in a small bottle," Lovelace reports.[60] One of the more definitive symbolic actions indicative of sexual trauma is that Orlan displayed the sheets "with semen stains documenting her sexual encounters" that her mother had saved for her bridal trousseau.[61] This symbolic "display" provides, perhaps, the most direct evidence of the "traumatic event," the primal act of sexuality for which Orlan seems to require and repetitively demand witnesses. Her dialogue of showing and telling, of producing representations, and displaying sexual acts suggests that Orlan desperately needs viewers to confirm and testify to her otherwise dissociated illicit sexual experience(s).

Most telling in this regard is a point that Lovelace notes: "To watch the procedure of Orlan's skin being opened up and flesh removed *feels like witnessing an obscene act*" (emphasis added).[62] Orlan's pathology, I think, involves not only the symbolic reenactment of original obscene acts, but the requirement that their display be witnessed by viewers. This witnessing approximates the testimony necessary for the acknowledgment of her painful experiences, and for her recovery from them. Psychologist Susan Roth and psychiatrist Ronald Batson, health professionals who specialize in adult survivors of incest, point out an aspect of trauma that I think is especially helpful in thinking about Orlan's work. Trauma is always visible, they write, "showing itself to be alive and well, as if one were still living in the past, in a state of terror or terror transformation. The memory is before us, frozen in time, defying attempts at exposure and forcing us to look in unconventional ways for what is right in front of our eyes."[63] In this regard, Orlan's actions also function as both the screen and the image theorized by Jacques Lacan in "Of the Gaze as Object Petit a," the screen upon which her own trauma is simultaneously projected and becomes its own image.[64]

Such acts transfer and displace onto art the artist's own dissociative relation to the source of her pain. But transference is not uncommon in art, especially in performance art, where corporeal experience is the primary material of the artist.[65] Art then serves as both perpetrator and savior. For what could be more of a nightmare than "giving" one's body to art—except representing that gift *as if* it were involved in an abusive and victimized relation, not only *with* art, but *in the name of* art. Not just *any* art, avant-garde art. For the only art worth such a price—the price of one's own body—is an art through which, and in which one *can,* and more importantly *may,* establish one's fame for radical*ism* in the history of art. From there one may transcend the body as nature and find cultural immortality. In a sense, however, for a woman artist this achievement gives only the fleeting and false impression of breaking the cycle of replacement (metaphorically represented by Ivana and Marla), since the voracious appetite of the public constantly demands "the new" from its avant-gardes. The lengths to which Orlan has gone to give her body to the context of avant-gard*ism,* then, proves only that she is willing, finally, "to die to be reborn as a tradition."[66] Moreover, repetitively performing the traumatic dissociative conditions of a cultural context that itself requires replacement through repetition, insures that the artist will always have an environment and audience for her traumatic reenactments. More than living life, Orlan lives for (art) history in a wretched, self-destructive cycle of operations and disruptions to her personal life: "Orlan has been marginalized, fired from jobs, arrested, ridiculed, *and showered with media attention*" (emphasis added).[67] Such are the pitiable histrionics of a scarred body, the visual corollary to a disfigured self-esteem. Her repeated acts of self-abuse and mutilation deserve empathy and a sense of tragedy, not celebration.[68]

At this critical juncture, it is important to distinguish between my method and Hal Foster's psychoanalytic notions of the relation between trauma and the avant-garde. For a discussion of the presence of *real* pathology in avant-garde art is precisely what is missing in theories of the avant-garde. Foster's *Return of the Real* depends heavily upon the psychoanalytic notion of "deferred action," an event that "is registered as traumatic only through a later event that recodes it retroactively, in deferred action."[69] Quoting Jean Laplanche on Freud, Foster takes as a truism the following: "It always takes two traumas to make a trauma."[70] But to propose, as Foster does, that the avant-garde (as a grammatical subject) conforms internationally, transgenerationally, and transhistorically to a set of dissociative symptoms identified with traumatic subjectivity—such as *deferred action*—requires a tremendous leap of theory and imagination. Moreover, the claim that artists associated with Foster's "neo avant-garde" (a concept to which I shall return) have some universalized relationship to trauma is equally untenable even, and especially if, Foster is merely using the discourse of trauma as a descriptive device.[71]

Regardless of the overdetermination of his thesis, there is an even more serious shortcoming in Foster's theory of theories of trauma. Freudian and Lacanian theories seldom function in the *real* (Foster's leitmotif) world of psychotherapy, where *real* psychologists and psychiatrists actually work to heal *real* traumatic subjectivity, since they do not seem to be therapeutically effective theories.[72] Foster's theorizing equally ignores the differences between cultural constructions (theories) and actual trauma victims—*real* people who may not have the ability to recuperate "the real." Those who really live as survivors, dissociated from their own actual experiences, quite frequently are unable to lead constructive lives, lives that would permit them to devote themselves to such things as the *real* production of art. And when they do, their trauma shows; as it does so blatantly in the art of Orlan.[73]

Moreover, to link superrealist painting (like that of Richard Estes) with trauma, as Foster does, is absurd and threatens the urgent needs of *real* traumatized subjects. Foster writes:

> Superrealism is also involved with this real that lies below, but as a *super*-realism it is concerned to stay on top of it, to keep it down. Unlike surrealism, then, it wants to conceal more than to reveal this real: thus it lays down its layers of signs and surfaces drawn from the commodity world not only against representational depth but also against the traumatic real. Yet this anxious move to smooth over this real points to it nonetheless; superrealism remains an art of "the eye as made desperate by the gaze," and the desperation shows. As a result its illusion fails not only as a tricking of the eye but as a taming of the gaze, a protecting against the traumatic real. That is, it fails *not* to remind us of the real, and in this way it is traumatic too: a *traumatic illusionism*.

Such thinking is—as political scientist James M. Glass has argued about the celebration of schizophrenia as a metaphor for poststructuralist theory—not only "naive but dangerous" for the ways in which it trivializes the *real* pain of *real* trauma.[74] Real suffering creates *real* alterity, not pseudoliminality, the affected show of being an "other."

Under a spurious radical*ism* proscribed for the avant-garde and then theorized (by Foster) as trauma, Orlan employs extra-artistic means to present her torment. But to the extent that she performs her distressing misery before the collective gaze, should not extra-aesthetic means be employed to enable her to help herself? If she walked into a psychotherapist's office, would that mental health professional celebrate the purposeful self-mutilation of her body, or draw her attention to her delirium and her need to resist it? Why should the art world revel in its own delirium with pseudo-avant-garde celebrity in the name of an artist's suffering? Can we not assist the suffering in our midst? Can we not demonstrate support among our own ranks on behalf of ourselves? If not, how may we presume to be effective in the social spaces of everyday life?

Liljana Sedlar, a cultural critic from Belgrade, asks similar questions. Writing on the reception and impact of Annie Sprinkle's work (as a self-appointed sex guru of "spiritual orgasms" who displays her cervix), Sedlar observed:

> Although her method of demystification makes visible that which has hitherto been hidden from view on the stage, it fails to transcend itself and culminate in a vision of woman's body, or woman's more complex nature, which differs from the purely instrumental and pornographic. This has to be stressed because spiritual understanding of woman and sex, and expert guidance in these matters, is what Annie Sprinkle sells. . . . Without Annie . . . intending it, the show gave the viewer a chance to have a good, long look at appalling, desperately fought off but ultimately unbreached human loneliness, packaged in the unconvincing high spirits of a seeming sexually and spiritually liberated and fulfilled woman.[75]

Sedlar pointed out that feminism is not exempt from spurious claims to avant-garde status, or from the demands of the market. She also has noticed the desperate lengths to which a woman might feel forced go to garner attention in a society that devalues everything we do.

> In a sense, in her specific field [Sprinkle] strove for the kind of performance that, connecting nothing with nothing, superficially gets things done and keeps things going. She shows the detached, pragmatic concept of knowledge promoted by the establishment: internalized and applied—not to politics or the media, but to our most internal affairs, our understanding and enactment of our primary creativity.[76]

Sedlar closed her remarks on Sprinkle by stating that in her display of the private and interior spaces of a woman's body, Sprinkle "did not really know what to do" with her body and merely used it to convey some sort of conception, "but the conceptions themselves were the problem."[77] Here it is important to reiterate: It is *not* Orlan or Sprinkle or any of the other artists in *Body as Membrane* that I wished to excoriate, but *the conceptualization and representation of women within the codes of patriarchy and the corrupt conditions inherited for avant-garde practice.*

Theater historian Rebecca Schneider summarized another dilemma related to these questions when she discussed the transient fashion of "transgression" in avant-garde contexts:

> One of the complexities that riddles contemporary performance art is the status of transgression in art practice today. Inasmuch as postmodernity necessitates a distinction from modernity, cultural critics and postmodern theorists have made the claim that the avant-garde, and its "bad boy" hope in the political promise of transgression, died sometime in the 1960s. As the argument goes, late capitalism appropriates, incorporates, and consumes transgression into fashionable chic at such a rapid pace that the subversive impact of transgression has become impossible. . . . I find it telling (as have many before me) that the avant-garde and the option of "shock" that it championed should die just as women, artists of color, and gay and lesbian artists began to make critically incisive political art under their own gender-, race-, and preference-marked banners. . . . Abandoning transgression might not be the issue so much as critically confronting the historical licensing of transgression in art practice.[78]

Schneider perceptively distinguished between what is permitted white male artists and withheld from "women, artists of color, and gay and lesbian artists"—though it is still much easier for gay men and men of color to achieve avant-garde status than it is for women. Furthermore, she questioned whether or not the situation in which women make art (that may be called "avant-garde") has changed at all:

> When women as active agents picked up the avant-garde tradition of transgressive shock, as they began to do with a certain *en masse* fervor in the 1960s, the term of transgression necessarily shifted. Female transgression presented a structural impossibility—almost a double shock. After all, men transgress, women resist. Does the structural taboo of "transgressive femininity" relate in any way to the proclamation that transgression is necessarily failed, impossible, defunct—to the point of shutting down the avant-garde among generally male postmodern theorists who strive to re-mark their own present tactics as "resistant?"[79]

The terms of avant-gard*ism did* shift in the 1960s. But the fact that women were suddenly more visible in the arts cannot solely explain the rhetoric of a declining interest in "transgression" as a socially held value. For the multiplicity and synchronicity of invention in all areas of artistic production in the 1960s required a reenvisioning of what might constitute avant-garde activity, a rethinking of the avant-garde itself. Reconsideration of the qualities and values that attain to the avant-garde led, in part, to the widely held view that it was dead, but also to new theorizations of the avant-garde. For while some called for "resistance" to replace "transgression"—Schneider cites Hal Foster as an example—the literature on art and the avant-garde over the past two decades reveals that it became de rigeur (particularly in critical theory) to call for avant-garde models of both resistance and transgression. Indeed, artists might achieve avant-garde status merely by having such terms assigned to their work. In no small measure, this accounts for why some artists, especially women associated with performance art (witnessed in *Body as Membrane*), have gone to extremes to present their work in a context of transgression. This includes the culture's current fascination with abjection, and especially with "bad girls."

In this regard, Laura Cottingham offered a powerful and uncompromising critique of the "bad girls" shows—four exhibitions organized between 1993 and 1994 by museums in London, Glasgow, New York, and Los Angeles. Cottingham charged the curators (Marcia Tucker being primary among them) with refusing "to acknowledge '70s Feminist Art [and] activism and theory of the Women's Liberation Movement."[80] Though in her midthirties herself, Cottingham accused "most women under age forty [of acquiring] their knowledge of feminism from *Newsweek* magazine or some other corrupt site—such as women's studies professors who mistakenly offer fag-hagging, the theories of Jacques Lacan, and inane interpretations of the First Amendment as contributions to feminist theory and activism."[81] Cottingham described the "historicized usage of the term 'Bad Girl' [as] distinctly derogatory [and functioning] to regulate the behavior of women toward self-sacrifice, sexual repression, and assimilation into the heterosexual contract of marriage and family, toward the very 'Good Girl' model" against which the shows were a reaction. She also added that "an appropriation of the good/bad model, from any woman's perspective, even if consciously attempted as subversive, is still nothing more than a parroting of a male supremacist construct.[82] Such rhetoric, she concluded, "relies on a false, pseudo-Hegelian premise that thesis ('good girl') and anti-thesis ('bad girl') will provide synthesis (emancipation)—ignoring how obviously this dialectic willingly writes the terms of women's emancipation according to patriarchy itself."[83] She also pointed out the shallowness of Marcia Tucker's definition of the "bad girl," as "honest, outrageous, contentious, wanton, self-indulgent, and even vulgar." It should be clear from my discussion above (regarding Tucker's "cutting" of my text) that bad-girl contentions are permitted only in the circumstances she herself sanctions. As Cottingham put it:

> That Tucker puts the "Bad Girl" in the same pejorative terms commonly used against women who do what we want—"wanton, self-indulgent and vulgar"—is another instance where her voice and her judgment don't subvert, but directly mimic, the patriarchal voice of woman hating. Much of the rhetoric associated with these exhibitions reeks of such unexamined self-hatred and self-contempt.[84]

Finally, the *Bad Girls* title, Cottingham insisted, was one "the museums chose . . . because of its potential as a marketing device, because it commodifies art, and women, as insubstantial and sexualized objects, [and because] these are sex(y) exhibitions and girl/woman is a synonym for sex."[85]

All of the above is relevant to the parallels many critics and art historians made between Orlan and Carolee Schneemann. Schneemann's performances, too, have been cast as the stereotypical "bad girl," pseudotransgressive works, especially since she (along with such artists as Valie Export and Linda Montano) were interviewed in the famous special issue of *RE/Search* magazine on "Angry Women."[86] In this regard, Schneemann is, herself, partially responsible for encouraging such associations, connections that subsume her otherwise authentically challenging and original performances into a digestible cultural context. But Schneemann understandably points out that the situation is paradoxical: if she refuses to participate in such contexts, her work would never be seen; if she acquiesces, her work is subject to distortions. However, in confronting this dilemma, *if feminist theory and practice are to perform their social imperative, then to become "transgressive" or "resistant" now, in works that mime and mine patriarchal models, is to defeat the very aims of feminism altogether.* So when Schneemann turns up, or places herself in, the "bad girl" context of the 1990s, it "threatens to undermine the very values she has so courageously fought to achieve."[87] As a result, many critics (in their enthusiasm to claim Schneemann as a transgressive model for a feminist avant-garde) have missed the centrality of her aesthetic strategy.[88] For Schneemann's brilliant contribution to the shift from painting to performance was her understanding of the importance of combining the body, in her words, "with the work as an integral material."[89] Schneemann has never been celebrated for this key contribution to the histories of art, for realizing that the fractured planes of Cezanne's protocubist painting suggested corporeal extension into the live body in action. Deprived of this recognition, Schneemann was also dismissed as a "dancer" (rather than the filmmaker, painter, performance artist, etc. that she is) by Annette Michelson. It was this comment that so frustrated and enraged the artist that she performed the infamous *Interior Scroll* (1975), in which she pulled from her vagina a scroll that she read during her performance, the text of which ended with the statement that "we think of you as a dancer."[90] Until very recently, she has been marginalized and scorned as someone who merely wanted to "take her clothes off." While Hannah Wilke found an influential male dealer in Ronald Feldman, and Orlan's work has been supported in part by powerful male figures in the art world, Schneemann still has little institutional support despite the fact that she is the precedent for such practices as those of Wilke and Orlan. Apples and stems, apples and stems . . . Schneemann herself admits that the ways in which she has retrospectively presented her work does "accommodate such interpretations" as those that link her work with that of Annie Sprinkle and Orlan (both of whom she considers friends).[91] Moreover, although she agrees that her work is different in intent and representation than theirs, she observes:

> The social force field in which male artists come together and bond, even with dissension and competition, constitutes a power base even though they may fight with each other. But there is no instance where women associate together with a shared area of concern, and its implicit contention to build a shared base of aesthetic power. The image of this historic situation is Saint Orlan blowing herself up in order to displace an iconic power. As a Saint, she is slightly ridiculous because she has her breast bared and eroticised, and she is wearing the robes of the old patriarchy. But if your attempt to subvert the hagiography fails and your image turns back on yourself so that you are still dressed up as a whore in a saint's costume, then that might be the moment when you take up the ritual knife to mutilate yourself to become an offering in a culture where there can be no sainthood.[92]

Schneemann's deep understanding of Orlan's predicament must increase our empathy for the grave situation in which Orlan tries (and indeed all women try) to make art and try to be enough: tries to stave off her own inevitable transformation from being a shiny apple to becoming a disposable stem.

If Schneemann's options for public attention have been reduced to a feminist context alone, a context that, while significant, also threatens a fuller reception and understanding of her work, is she to blame even though she pays the price? Given this situation, the scope of her extraordinary aesthetic production is circumscribed by cultural criticism, art history, and gender issues. Despite this fact, her work includes drawing, painting, assemblage, environments, happenings, Fluxus, body art and performance, film, photography, and video, as well as a prodigious body of writing that includes diaries, letters, poems, essays, and aesthetic theory. While she may have permitted a reductive view of the breadth and depth of her oeuvre—in her urgency to have her work enter into the discourses of art and its histories—it was feminism that gave her the important historical place she has achieved. Nevertheless, the art historian's task, as I understand it, is to draw out the richness of such an artist's work and to defend it. For there is much at stake in making it possible for the work of a woman artist to be understood outside of the restricted context of feminism, so it may gain recognition for the kind of sweeping cultural contributions to art, literature, and aesthetics that Schneemann has made.

Schneemann created acts of primary observation. She reconstructed the ways in which we see and interpret the world. *Observation that reconstructs interpretation is radical and original.* And it is the radical quality of her vision, her originality, that is worth defending. Schneemann's art has been full of the joy and celebration of female (and male) bodies in and for themselves. Her work is not *essentially* about women only and our bodies, even though she and her apologists have taken advantage of the extraordinary power of her female imagery to further the cause of feminism, feminist art, feminist performance, and theories of gender. Her art is also about the role of art, of vision, of seeing and its relation to the body, of how spaces for the body are conceptualized. For example, anyone who has viewed *Fuses* (1965–68)—the exquisite and erotic film she made of intercourse with her then-husband, composer James Tenney—will realize that much of Schneemann's work is about heterosexual love, relationships, and the joy of bodies in general. Most of all, she has validated all bodies, proclaiming: YOU ARE ENOUGH.

Probity, Avant-Gardes, and Radical Originality

Probity—the real *something else* with which I have been concerned throughout this essay—*is crucial to the foundation of successive avant-gardes if their acts of observation are expected to remake the world.* But before leaping to the conclusion that avant-gardes may contribute to remaking experience, I must ask: What is avant-garde activity and how is this cultural formation conventionally defined?

Art history has long fantasized that one avant-garde leads to another in a long, but broken, line of transformations, discontinuities, ruptures, and displacements from *the* idealized, authentic, *historical,* avant-garde down to successive authentic or spurious *neo*-avant-gardes.[93] Yet even a casual study of the histories of *the* avant-garde suggests a different historical formation than the diachronic, developmental model to which we have become accustomed. I want to describe avant-gardes as plural, existing simultaneously, working in different media synchronistically in local, national, and international settings (each dependent on the context of their practices and politics), and functioning in different social configurations, at different times and for different purposes. Finally, I want to state categorically that the institution of avant-gardes has not, and can never die, as long as revisioning the world in myriad ways continues. Avant-gardes develop through adaptation and alteration among diverse artistic and cultural practices simultaneously. As every artist knows, art comes from art, so that concepts left undeveloped in one avant-garde, medium, and cultural context reappear expanded in an adjacent or subsequent one. I have theorized that this process can transpire in subtle and profound ways. For example, the failure of academic figurative painters to sustain ethical humanist content at the end of the nineteenth century, coupled later with the co-option of figuration by National Socialism in Germany and social realism in both Russia and the United States, made it nearly impossible for artists like Oskar Schlemmer to address what he called the "timeless themes" of figuration. Only the dramatic reemergence of the figure in a presentational form (namely in the artist's actual body, not only in Schlemmer's and Duchamp's work, but in happenings, Fluxus, actions, events, and performance art) vigorously renewed the ethical content of figurative work in cultural discourse.[94] What is more, avant-gardes may be celebrated or not, have commercial success or not, and be institutionalized or not. None of these categories is sufficient to identify what is, or is not, avant-garde.

When the impact of avant-garde practices, including writing, is considered, the stakes become higher than may be reached by theories of radical*ism,* the dismissal of originality, and accounts of how one avant-garde may displace another. While these arguments have served important ends in the past, extreme situations require reconsideration of the very purpose of the social institution identified with *the* avant-garde, and the expectations that accrue to it. For *avant-gardes provide space for communicating determined acts of primary observation.* What I mean by a determined act of primary observation (more commonly thought of as originality) is "to observe" in the fullest psychophysical sense of that possibility: not only to look with one's inner vision and outer gaze, but to bring one's full attention to something, to consider, inspect, become mindful of, and absorbed in, something. As such, the visions and thoughts of multiple avant-gardes (in every discipline and walk of life) provide a framework for rediscovery that challenges ordinary notions of form, meaning, function, and context. Such observation—one that reconstructs received interpretations and predetermined results—is always already radical and original and connects private subjectivity to transmutation in social reality. The function and purpose of avant-gardes, then, may be described as follows: *Avant-gardes perform acts of envisioning and observing able to reconstruct the ways in which events, objects, and the relationships between them may be interpreted and lived. Such singular acts provide a framework for discovery or rediscoveries of the world that challenges epistemological, ontological, and teleological concepts.* As a result, while mandated from within society for its necessary growth and change, avant-gardes are simultaneously, and paradoxically, always in conflict with the given order.

Some twenty years ago, Fred Orton and Griselda Pollock rightly pointed out that the term *avant-garde* had become a "catch-all label to celebrate most twentieth-century art and artists, [and] the pervasive, dominant ideology of artistic production and scholarship."[95] Accordingly, avant-gardes are expected to conform to the rules established for their codes of representation and conduct. Susan Suleiman succinctly summarized this framework of expectations: "The hallmark of an avant-garde practice or project—or dream—[is] the attempt to effect radical change and innovation both in the symbolic field (including what has been called the aesthetic realm) and in the social and political field of everyday life."[96] This widely accepted view of *the* avant-garde keeps faith with normative descriptions of it and automatically consigns avant-gardes' practices to a "dream" in which they are figured as a special vehicle for successive utopian visions. Such a view deprives multiple and simultaneous avant-gardes of their real contributions to (and in) real cultural, social, and political contexts, and fails to acknowledge their effective alterations of conventional ways of seeing and reenvisioning life. Moreover, such a concept of avant-gardes and their practices supposes that radical*ism* is the same thing as being radical (namely changing things at the root), a difference to which I shall soon return. Idealist and materialist views of *the* avant-garde, moreover, deprive avant-gardes of the capacity for "spiritual renovation and artistic innovation." This oversight accounts for some of the reasons that it has been so easy, so often, to proclaim the death of both *an* avant-garde and *the* avant-garde.[97] Both views equally consign multiple avant-gardes to failure, either by constructing a fantasy of transformation within a utopic discourse of reform, or—as in the case of Orton and Pollock's argument—by limiting radical observation and practice to narrowly defined "new discursive frameworks."[98]

When Suleiman states that the avant-garde is recognized for its "attempt to effect radical change and innovation both in the symbolic field (including what has been called the aesthetic realm), and in the social and political field of everyday life," she refers to Peter Bürger's and Renato Poggioli's classic theories of the avant-garde.[99] Bürger's arguments have preoccupied theorists of *the* avant-garde for the ways in which he identified a "historic avant-garde," based on "genuine intentions," and to which he juxtaposed a "neo-avant-garde" that "institutionalizes the *avant-garde as art* and thus negates genuinely avant-gardist intentions."[100] An invention of cultural criticism, according to Bürger, the neo-avant-garde represents the demands of the market (and those critics who do the marketing) for new aesthetic products.

In *The Return of the Real,* Hal Foster attempts to retheorize Bürger's concept of a commercial neo-avant-garde. Chiding Bürger for dismissing the postwar avant-garde as merely a commercial neo version of *the* historical avant-garde, Foster constructs an argument for the continued vitality of successive first, second, and presumably subsequent neo-avant-gardes.[101] In an attempt to rescue his renewed concept of successive neo-avant-gardes from being dismissed as merely commercial, Foster required the function of his neo-avant-garde to recuperate and review moments, themes, questions, and so on, of *the* historical avant-garde. But by reinvesting his version of a neo-avant-garde with the putative value of *the* historical avant-garde, there seems little reason to distinguish between avant-gardes unless there is a residual value (which Foster leaves untheorized) in the valence of originality (Bürger's "historical avant-garde"). Which, of course, there is. Foster further argues that the authenticity of neo-avant-gardes might be achieved by what he describes as "protension" and "retension." By these terms, he indicated the means by which his neo-avant-garde is able to recuperate, repeat, reconstruct, and displace the institution of the historical avant-garde: first, protensively by recovering the historical avant-garde and, second, retensively by offering "a critique of the process of acculturation and/or accommodation," of "becoming-institutional."[102] (In most theories of *the* avant-garde, an original avant-garde is privileged, and neo-avant-gardes are described as merely commercial and competitive with the original avant-garde, displacing and revising, as in Foster, or responding to "new discursive frameworks.") Finally, Foster's theorization of the operations of his neo-avant-garde relies on two concepts: "parallax," which he defines as "the apparent displacement of an object caused by the actual movement of its observer," and "deferred action," which he interprets according to Freud.[103] "In Freud," Foster explains, "an event is registered as traumatic only through a later event that recodes it retroactively, in deferred action."[104]

Foster introduces the concept of parallax to create a model in which the observer "caused . . . . the apparent displacement of an object." The more common context and use of the term *parallax* is in astronomy. There the term signifies the central role that the observer plays in the identification and constitution of the object, and is a term associated with relativity theory, second-order cybernetics, Heisenbergian uncertainty, and reception theory. (Foster contradicts himself in his use of a quasi-scientific metaphor—since he also claims, much later and, significantly, in a footnote that "artistic innovation and scientific revolution are hardly analogous.")[105] Namely, to account for the central role the spectator and critic play in the identification of the avant-garde. The term *parallax* permits Foster to build a theoretical model capable of accommodating his own critical pronouncements about what constitutes neo-avant-garde.[106] In short, Foster's labored theory accounts for the continued institutional function and appearance of successive avant-gardes enabling him to simultaneously construct and confess to his own reflexive role as a self-proclaimed champion of a postmodernist "second" neo-avant-garde. (One of the neo-avant-gardes he champions is feminist, but he only accords avant-garde status only to those artists [he names Mary Kelly, Silvia Kolbowski, Barbara Kruger, Sherrie Levine, Louise Lawler, and Martha Rosler] interested in producing and theorizing "the sexual-linguistic constitution of the subject . . . from the middle 1970s through the middle 1980s."[107])

Moreover, while Foster admits to having portrayed only a "partial" history of the neo-avant-garde and acknowledges that he remains "silent about many events," the subjects about which he remains silent and partial—and his reasons for doing so—are suspicious. For example, feminism itself, to say nothing of the contributions of feminist theory in general to questioning theories of *the* avant-garde, is generally absent from the book, even while feminism is ostensibly one of his theoretical models. Foster borrows the phrase *feminist art* in his text, but when women artists are mentioned, they are drawn exclusively from a postmodernist, poststructuralist, Lacanian-influenced panoply sanctioned by *October.* Indeed, the only women mentioned in Foster's book are Kiki Smith, Maureen Connor, Rona Pondick, Mona Hayt, Kate Ericson, Cindy Sherman, Barbara Ess, Andrea Fraser, Katarina Fritsch, Nan Goldin, Eva Hesse, Barbara Kruger, Silvia Kolbowski, Louise Lawler, Sherrie Levine, Adrian Piper, Anne (and Patrick) Poirier, Yvonne Rainer, Martha Rosler, and Sue Williams. Moreover, Audrey Flack is singled out with James Rosenquist and Don Eddy "among others" merely for "dereliz[ing] the real with simulacral effects."[108] Equally egregious in a book purportedly on the neo-avant-garde, and so thoroughly engaged in the poststructuralist, postmodern problems posed by conceptual art, is the fact that Foster never mentions Joseph Kosuth, certainly one of the founders of conceptual art, if not arguably its most precocious theorist. Is this not a strategy for attempting to write Kosuth out of the postmodernist avant-garde or art history in general: murder by omission? Such an absence certainly reflects the well-known and documented struggle between Kosuth and the editors of *October,* with whom Foster is closely associated.[109]

Despite Foster's apparent openness about aesthetic and ideological preferences, the role of the critic and art historian in the formulation of the concept of the avant-garde is one of the more invisible aspects of the theories of avant-gardes. By contrast, Orton and Pollock carefully explored how critics themselves can "manifest all the symptoms of 'avant-gardism' in [their] inability to account for the avant-garde."[110] Few have been more circumspect (and sardonic) about the role of the critic in the construction of the avant-garde than Thomas Crow, who states that the avant-garde functions, after all, as merely "a kind of research and development arm of the culture industry."[111] Antoine Campagnon is equally as explicit: "At the start, avant-gardism belongs to both the critic and his subject, for it is the critical viewpoint integrated into artistic practice that gives the term avant-garde its meaning."[112]

No real theory of avant-gardes, then, may be written until the tastes and ambitions of critics themselves have been explored. For, as Paul Mann stated in *The Theory-Death of the Avant-Garde:* "The death of the avant-garde is its theory and the theory of the avant-garde is its death."[113] Moreover, in capitalist economic systems, avant-gardes routinely must be pronounced dead in order to resurrect them for a new market. In this respect, Mann has also noted,

> Death is necessary so that everything can be repeated and the obituary is a way to deny that death ever occurred. Under the cover of the obituary artists and critics continue exactly as before, endlessly recuperating differential forms, endlessly manufacturing shabbier and shabbier critical goods. Long after theory proclaims their demise, we still see the same drives to originality, to novelty, to autonomy, to the anti, all exposed, framed, and evacuated in a continuous cycle of discursive commitments. . . . The death of the avant-garde is an event-horizon, a limit of visibility, and thus a discursive phenomenon in the strictest sense: it's death from discourse. The theory-death of discourse itself. In every obituary of the avant-garde criticism writes its own epitaph.[114]

William Gass has further observed,

> Sophists support the status quo until it changes. Then they support the new status quo. They are the friend of every place of power and are beloved by every regime, large and small, because they can offer no reasons for change. Except they aren't fast friends. They wiggle with the wind. And every tribal law is right—but only inside the tribe.[115]

The purported "death" of *the* avant-garde is relevant here, especially to the ways in which women are permitted access to becoming identified as avant-garde.[116] For either there *are* avant-gardes or there are not. The jargon of *neo* does little other than confuse the anthropology of what it *means* to be avant-garde and in what cultural, national, and historical context one becomes so. Feminism—as a real, political, social movement—demonstrated that formal style had nothing whatsoever to do with the cultural conditions of the avant-garde, as Rozsika Parker and Griselda Pollock pointed out two decades ago: "The heterogeneous activities of women in the twentieth century convincingly dismiss any notion of a homogeneous woman's art."[117] Thus, style must not be the determining feature of avant-gardes. The cultural function of avant-gardes (one that becomes political by virtue of being social) *is to provide information about determined acts of observation, and to communicate that knowledge as a means to reconstruct the ways in which events, objects, and the relationships between them may be interpreted and lived.* All the rest is pseudo-avant-gardism, propped up by the cultural institutions of art and criticism from which the value of probity has disappeared.

Now let me turn more directly to the question of probity, through a consideration of the concept of originality. Continuity occurs between and among avant-gardes, in large measure, because they represent social ideals worked out through time. Indeed, the coexistence and pluralism among avant-gardes occurred from the moment when it became evident that there was a contention over the production of cultural value associated with the historical avant-garde. In the 1970s, when feminist theory made it impossible to avoid the facticity of avant-garde pluralism, those who understood *the* avant-garde to represent a diachronic phenomenon began to identify it as dead.[118] In other words, *the* historic avant-garde died when a pluralistic feminist avant-garde was born. It is predictable then that someone like Foster—interested in defending only a particular *kind* of feminist practice—should miss the essential point of avant-garde plurality and attempt to popularize only one kind of feminist practice. Inherent plurality, too, is key to understanding the fierce competition over avant-garde production of values. An awareness of that plurality also accounts for the highly competitive language in the numerous avant-garde manifestos produced during the first two decades of the twentieth century. We have only to think, for example, of the relative simultaneity of futurism and cubism (with its many branches such as Orphism, purism, etc.), the various Russian avant-gardes that drew on cubism and futurism, and the theoretical debates within de Stijl, and so on, to confirm this point. It was, and remains, the accomplishment of radical change in the reorganization of meaning in the symbolic, social, and political fields—namely to be original—over which avant-gardes (and their champions) have always clashed in the construction of value.

Originality is the primary element in any reconstruction of meaning. In this regard, it is important to recall the auspicious success of Rosalind Krauss's 1981 article "The Originality of the Avant-Garde," in which the critic posited just the opposite premise. There she attempted to dismantle what she dubbed "the myth," or "the cult," of originality. This well-known essay does not require rehearsal here. I need only to point out that Krauss opposes originality with "repetition and recurrence" as central to the function of art-making itself, locating her argument in the problem of copyright over the multiple castings of Rodin's sculptures. I wish only to focus on a pair of telling sentences that have been, heretofore, disregarded. In them, Krauss most directly and simply undermines her own argument:

> Now why would one begin a discussion of avant-garde art with this story about Rodin and casts and copyrights? Particularly since Rodin

> strikes one as the very last artist to introduce to the subject, so popular was he during his lifetime, so celebrated, and so quickly induced to participate in the transformation of his own work into kitsch.[119]

One must immediately ask the following questions. If Rodin's work was not original—not avant-garde (by dint of being "so popular . . . during his lifetime")—then how could that art have been transformed into kitsch in the first place? How must the work be described, then, *before* the mechanism of capital changed it (and "induced [him] to participate in the transformation of his own work") into something that could be described as kitsch? *In other words, how could there be kitsch without a counterreferent?* What is the status of that counterreferent? The answer is, of course, there could not be kitsch without originality. Rodin could not have been "so quickly induced to participate in the transformation of his own work into kitsch" if it was not avant-garde and/or original *before* becoming kitsch.

But once this crucial failure in her logic is pointed out—like pointing to the queen who is wearing no clothes—Krauss's theory of the avant-garde is revealed as simply her bold bid for power and authority over the erection or destruction of an avant-garde. Moreover, the particular principles of formalist aesthetics she wished to construct as value (in her celebrated article) were those associated with the avant-garde of minimalism with which she herself was associated: repetition and recurrence. Repetition and recurrence were the values of originality that she would have *appear* to belie originality itself, but are championed nevertheless by Krauss as avant-garde. What Krauss confused is that to place the value of originality *in the value of* repetition and recurrence is different from claiming that repetition and recurrence, in themselves, are phenomena of originality. In this way, the facticity of originality plays around the notion of transformation and is the unacknowledged subtext for Krauss's theories.[120] *Her* theory becomes original, even as she debunks the value of originality in art. Her theory—like that of Foster's "parallax"—transforms the conventionalized secondary position of the critic vis-à-vis the primary work of art, into the primary position once held by the artist. Words take precedence over aesthetic objects. Theory, itself, becomes an aesthetic object. Krauss, as creator, theorizes the world rather than merely commenting on it.

Krauss's concept of the "myth of originality" reflects the continued hegemony of formalism—bound up as it was, ironically, with Greenbergian aesthetics of originality. At the same time, it also followed feminist deconstructions of the concept of genius that Linda Nochlin first discussed a decade earlier in her brilliant essay "Why Have There Been No Great Women Artists?" (1971).[121] Such examinations of the social practices related to the concept of originality and patriarchy were necessary. But is it possible that, in unhinging patriarchy, the critique of originality has been seriously misplaced? Indeed, faith in, and a need for, originality is an ideal shared by all cultures and located in the value societies place on any form of concentrated attentiveness to the conditions of being and making that affirm diverse models of invention. In this regard, originality is a value worth defending. For an ideal is not a myth any more than the social value accorded originality (in any field) is mythic or insignificant. On the contrary. Ideals are important ways in which societies embody needs, desires, and possibilities; and the social concept of originality that expresses such human constructs must be taken seriously if a culture is to maintain a constructive vision of itself and its future. Theory needs to be more than an exegesis on taste, or—as in the case of Krauss—a predilection to admire recurrence in the visual form of modular repetition.

Every discipline has its own concept of originality, its avant-gardes, and its relationship to originality. Imagine how innocent it would appear in the context of physics, for example, for someone to pronounce its scientific avant-gardes dead, or to describe its inventions as myths of originality. Is the effect of the original atom bomb a myth? Similarly, while any particular manifestation of avant-gardism may appear exhausted, certain cultural formations, ideological beliefs, and social practices that produced its particular responses—and that earned the appellation *avant-garde* in the first place—may be displayed in new formations elsewhere. My question is: Why is artistic originality and vision treated with such fear in a cultural context? What is there to be gained, and for whom? The answer seems self-evident to me: discursive power over originality. The last two decades of the twentieth century, in which textual theories declared power over originality, will be understood to have been a kind of fin de siècle and fin de millennium sophistry representative of a period in massive technological and social transition and generally without substantive leadership or shared social values. In this way the historicity of the theory of the death of the avant-garde is tied to concepts of the myth of originality. Both theoretical positions fall short of an account of the recurring and concurrently shifting historical, political, social, and cultural phenomena that give rise to the responses I have identified as avant-gardes. The putative notion of the death of the avant-garde is based on the critique of originality, itself an attack on the concept of authenticity—a value attached to what is esteemed, in part, in the concept of "radical." But this chain of meanings that moves from the uniqueness of something radical (something that changes things at the root), to something authentic and, therefore, original, is seldom considered. *An attack on originality, therefore, is an assault on the very foundations of the notion of the authentic and the radical.*

Moreover, the term *radical* itself has been misused, and its meaning has been depleted and overdetermined in contemporary jargon.[122] Therefore, it must be asked: What constitutes "radical" as opposed to "radical*ism,*" and what is the relationship of radical and radical*ism* to the avant-gardes? Radical*ism* can be understood to embody an attitude about conventions, suspicions, and perhaps even fears of conformity. Radical*ism* always speaks *as if* from a position of alterity, of being outside. And it is as often a self-appointed position of marginality as it is a socially ascribed one. Radical*ism* seldom assumes actual political positions, nor is it usually aligned with any ideology either of the right, left, or center. For radicali*sm* is relational, relative with regard to centers, and may represent any theoretical or ideological position. In this way radical*ism* is as shifting and ambiguous as any unanchored sign, like the sophist identified by William Gass above who supports the status quo until it changes. These are the very reasons why radical*ism* is—and should be—considered dangerous. Radical*ism* is wholly unpredictable. Ted Kaczynski, the man convicted of being the Unabomber, is a prime representation of radical*ism.* He is someone whose native intelligence, race, class, education, and sexuality (for all that is currently known about him) could offer few clues to his disaffection, his radical*ism,* or, more importantly, his violent expression of it. Moreover, radical*ism* almost always—and I can think of few exceptions—means an attraction to violence, and the ability to entertain violence as a method to achieve its end. The more dangerous the radical*ism,* the more interesting, exotic, and sometimes erotic the person who exhibits its traits becomes in the public imagination.[123] But the Unabomber reforms nothing. His radical*ism* is always reduced to a mere curiosity, a social anomaly, but not a social force.

The behavioral manifestations of radical*ism* (unpredictability, involvement in violent change, attraction to violence, and enticement of those magnetized by violence) are very close to the symptomology identified with traumatic response. This suggests to me that radical*ism* itself may be a traumatic response. I don't want to overstate this point, but I do want to link this possible dimension of radical*ism* with another one of its features: radical*ism* is always a struggle with power. Radical*ism* is not—and never can be, by definition—*of* authority even when it may be *in* authority—as was the case with despots like Hitler, Stalin, and Mao, with the Khmer Rouge, and so forth. Radical*ism* is always, somehow, disenfranchised. Of course this disenfranchisement presents the greatest problem: how is a culture to discern actual or imagined disenfranchisement in those who wield enormous power? In this sense, theories of *the* avant-garde have suffered especially from the academic project of Western Marxism, which, having associated itself with the avant-garde, appropriated radical*ism* to itself especially after the failures of the 1968 revolutions and the increasing institutionalization of the leftist throughout the 1970s and 1980s. Ironically, the result has been that most theories of *the* avant-garde prove to be fundamentally conservative and deeply attached to academic dogma.

Radicals are different. *To be radical means to envision and produce in a way that alters observation, changing perception at the root.* Indeed, is this not the very task of the radical? Whether on the left or right, radical deeds are, paradoxically, often accomplished unintentionally. One may become radical by simply going about one's business as usual—if that business is investigating the world, *closely* and with a difference. As a result, one of the most interesting conditions of the cultural position of the radical is that s/he often—although not always—remains nearly invisible. That is, someone fundamentally radical is often imperceptible in, and to, her/his own time, especially during the period of his/her innovations. But how could it be other? For how could knowledge and experience be reshaped if new epistemologies were already known, ontologies lived, and teleologies recorded? This must be one of the most cherished conditions of avant-gardes: the paradox of the general inability to identify what is original in our own time. Does it not stand to reason, thus, that to be authentically radical or avant-garde one must—more or less—be invisible? Radical signifies a phenomenon that militates against encounters with that which *is surprising in itself.* For once something is known, it sheds its original condition and surprise becomes the familiar.

To be radical requires responsibility, a quality that may be impossible to transmit from generation to generation, as Jacques Derrida has observed: "Such is the secret truth of faith as absolute responsibility and as absolute passion that, sworn to secrecy, cannot be transmitted from generation to generation. In this sense it has no history."[124] While Derrida is correct that faith has no history, he exaggerates when he speaks of "sworn secrecy." Faith as absolute responsibility has no need for secrecy. For faith as absolute responsibility *cannot* be inherited, imitated, recuperated, repeated, reconstructed, or displaced. Faith cannot be transmitted from generation to generation. Faith is never neo; it cannot be learned. Faith—as absolute responsibility—becomes, knows itself becoming, understands its absolute responsibility and passion, and is quiet in that knowledge, a quietude and becoming that remains a mystery to all that behold it. For faith represents personal will, unlike trust, which designates interpersonal responsibility. The secret truth *of* avant-gardes is a culture's passion-filled faith *in* insight and vision as absolute responsibility.

In order to credibly uphold such a truth, avant-gardes are culturally constructed and charged with the responsibility to represent *how* such behavior—behavior that is also understood as an aesthetic—is to be accomplished. In conventional discussions of the avant-garde, this passion has been circumscribed to a reductive notion of utopianism, rather than an expanded discussion of probity: namely the degree to which avant-gardes demonstrate integrity, candor, fair play and justice, scruples; and, most of all, the degree to which they are accountable to the social and cultural implications of what they create, represent, and originate. Without probity, how can value have meaning? How might there be a "dream" without probity?

Probity contributes *invisibly* to the health of the social order in constructive, nonideal, material ways because it contributes to an ethical order. As Emmanuel Levinas observed: "It is there, in the ethical, that there is an appeal to the uniqueness of the subject, and sense is given to life in defiance of death."[125] Commenting further, Derrida writes:

> Duty or responsibility binds me to the other, to the other as other, and ties me in my absolute singularity to the other as other. God is the name of the absolute other as other and as unique (the God of Abraham defined as the one and unique). As soon as I enter into a relation with the absolute other, my absolute singularity enters into relation with his on the level of obligation and duty. I am responsible to the other as other, I answer to him and I answer for what I do before him.[126]

Derrida's discussion is exemplary (even when the philosopher conforms to his faith in the Judaic tradition that God is male). For Derrida's discussion locates the structure of social duty and obligation as metaphorically represented in a notion of God as a construct. If one takes a similar position vis-à-vis avant-gardes, they are cultural constructs established to embody the promise and ideal of an ethical order where the potential for change (namely originality) is played out in observing and making based on radical acts of probity. The radical act represented in the cultural construct of the avant-garde is *the concentrated attentiveness to the conditions of being and making wherein personal subjectivity and social reality themselves converge toward acts of probity.*

Women Taking Action

Let me close by returning to the beginning of my delirium, to the beginning of this essaying essay, to the beginning of this my medical act of self-ministration. In *Body as Membrane,* Justesen and Export focused on the theme of the membrane, which they defined as "a border coating between the cell and its surroundings," a "sensitive and soft, porous material (skin) that functions as a transformer [that] transports and transmits any conceivable information," and as "one of the body's vital components, [which] functions as a filter as well as a canvas screen for reception, projection and reproduction."[127] Comparing the photo-emulsion of the photographic medium (the medium through which the performances of the artists selected for the show were exhibited) to the surface of the body, the curators explained that "the physical body is an instrument to test theory practically on a spatial surface."

But the body's somatic spatial surface is also connected to a complex system of social values and practices and psychophysical responses that forever distinguish it from other surfaces immune to such emotive fates. The body is, indeed, an interface between external and internal experience, an object among other objects with values of use, exchange, and many others, like ability. That the body has been deployed as a discursive surface in the visual arts testifies to the extremity of the ontological insecurity of the body, identity, and existence itself in the late twentieth century. That women's bodies are displayed for consumption in all walks of life is a truism that reinforces the traumatized states of dissociation in which so many women live. As a result, when the body, any body, but particularly a woman's body, is presented, there is much at stake. That art might contribute to the remedy of our vulnerability is without a doubt true, but only if we are willing to be vigilant with respect to our own probity, especially if we are feminists. It is the duty of avant-garde art and the institutions and practices attached to it—if they are worth the social values invested in them—to be so. Unless, of course, all of us fail in our effort to maintain society's trust. So, let me repeat myself:

> Why does taking a position against self-destruction and self-derogation . . . that is, taking a position against art that is opposed to everything for which . . . [life] stands—have to be interpreted as "angry and defensive"; and what is wrong, or inappropriate about anger? . . . [It is] distressingly paradoxical, if not hypocritical, that in our profession all forms of the most extreme sexuality, violence, masochism, sadism, "abjection," and so on, may be shown, written about, and even celebrated as "transgressive," but a critique of these very behaviors is described as "angry and defensive" [or American Puritanism with a thin candy coating] . . . What a strange world we make![128]

The many themes and subjects that I have addressed in the process of essaying this essay constitute the unnamed *something else* present in the work that earned double censorship. My work was expurgated for breaching the standards of decorum for institutions and their publications; feminists are expected to celebrate each other's productions, especially in the context of the feminist avant-garde. I was invited into the presentational context of the avant-garde, provisionally accepted because of those privileged invitations, and expected to behave according to the unwritten rule that whatever is exhibited under that sacred umbrella is exempt from the critique of those within its ranks. I was expected to construct a discursive picture of a feminist avant-garde beyond reproach, to close ranks, to perform my ekphrastic duty of explanation and apology. But I bungled my job. I now understand that I earned the censors' mark because of the following infractions: I failed to conform; I had the temerity to disagree; I violated a taboo of *the* avant-garde exhibition catalog by describing in unflattering terms, and questioning, the work of the artists I was hired to praise and celebrate; I explicitly rebuked Justesen both as the curator for the content of her exhibition and as an artist exhibiting in her show.[129] Furthermore, I named names and criticized both an artist (Orlan) and a critic (Barbara Rose).[130] In her position as director, I made Tucker vulnerable to the implication that she was an accomplice to my views if she permitted my words to be published under the aegis of the New Museum.

Finally, just before sending this manuscript off to the editor of this volume, I learned that an essay by Rosalind Krauss had suffered the same censorial fate as mine. A section of Krauss's work critical of artist Jeff Wall was "edited out" of her essay on artist James Coleman by Yves Gavaert, Belgian publisher of Coleman's exhibition catalog for the Vienna Secession Museum.[131] Krauss was led to believe that she had been "unethical" in launching an "attack [on] one artist in a catalogue about the work of another artist." Stunned by the censorship of her work, the first in "thirty years of critical writing," Krauss acquiesced, just as I had. Why? She did not want to hold up the catalog for the artist who was depending upon her essay:

> Given the shortness of time between now and the opening of Coleman's exhibition, however, withdrawing the text will mean that Coleman will not have a catalogue: this is not, then, just my problem alone. So I decided on a second course, I will cut the text for the catalogue but publish the unexpurgated, uncensored version in *October.*[132]

Krauss was clever. She made certain that she could publish her own views by building a powerful and highly visible international context for them in *October.* Most work that is censored, especially when it is by or about women (or both), finds no publisher. Or, as William Gass has pointed out: "It is not that we suppress serious [material] entirely; but in capitalist countries, only on the margins can excellence be located."[133] I am not suggesting that all work at the margins necessarily belongs to the category of excellence. In fact, had "Never Enough" been published, it most likely would have found its place in the dustbin with so many other feminist writings: ignored, and then forgotten.

What the censors proved is that whoever they censor is not intrinsically within their ranks, nor trying to be. Maybe that lack of desire to belong is my most unforgivable breach (and most powerful weapon). As Fredric Jameson once observed: "The reversal of our habits of idealism . . . is a dialectical shock."[134] Fear is what prompted the censors who, in their acts, took it upon themselves to guard the art, guard the public, guard themselves (and their friends), guard the pseudo-avant-garde context. Guard against what? My delirium about probity? Even though taken on their own merits in different contexts, I might sanction the works in *Body as Membrane,* their collective presence—the experience of these works en masse—was not consonant with the probity to which feminist avant-gardes must hold.

"What's really bad for the system," Laura Cottingham has written, "is women refusing to believe in all the myths of history, and taking action to change our present and our future."[135] Taking action as avant-garde feminists, endowed with the absolute passion for responsibility and accountability, means making the act of primary observation and representation itself an act that reconstructs the ways in which women are seen, and refusing to participate in contexts that do violence to those reconstructions. Observation that reconstructs, deconstructs, alters, and reforms the ways in which women are interpreted, empowered, and represented *could be* radical, original, and might connect private subjectivity to social reality to challenge patriarchal epistemologies and change human ontologies.

Much like the *Bad Girls* series of exhibitions, *Body as Membrane* has made it clear that this show was about marketing artists through the vehicle of sex. Images presented in an avant-garde context—*by* women, representing the degradation *of* women—belong to the traffic *in* women and constitute little more than pseudo-avant-garde acts. For unless the lesson is learned that *never enough* is *never again,* the traffic in women that depicts her/us as degraded and subjugated will remain radical*ism,* not radical. As Manfredo Tafuri and Francesco Dal Co have written in another context, we will become pure alienation: "Like the last notes sounded by the Doctor Faustus of Thomas Mann, alienation, having become absolute, testifies uniquely to its own presence, separating itself from the world to declare the world's incurable malady."[136]

I contend that *avant-garde art operates constructively in the cultural, social, and political spheres and must do so with probity that contributes something substantial to the social order within which it is involved.* The provisional term here is probity—defined by the ethics of virtue and justice associated with accountability and responsibility to oneself and to one's society. These are all putative values underpinning any concept of authenticity that is not spurious (though to complicate matters, one can also be spurious, and be so genuinely!).

Avant-garde art—the cultural institution of originality at the radical margins of vision—is, was, and always will be powerful, alive, and a cultural threat operating in the social domain of the political. "Deleuze quoting Le Clézio is interesting," Edward Shanken pointed out after several exhausting edits of this essay. "But Le Clézio got it backwards. The point is not that, as he put it—'One day, we will perhaps know that there wasn't any art, but only *medicine*'—but rather: One day we will perhaps know that there wasn't any medicine, but only *art!*" Knowing this, one cannot help but become infected with the enduring will to insist upon, and search for, a value that must undergird any social institution that is called upon to improve life. If not probity, what would, or could, the charge of avant-gardes be?

NOTES

I would like to thank Edward Shanken for his many careful readings and editing of this essay.

1. Gilles Deleuze, "Literature and Life" (1993), *Critical Inquiry* 23 (winter 1997): 225. This article was first published in Deleuze's final book *Critique et clinique* (Paris: Editions de Minuit, 1993), which later appeared in English as *Essays Critical and Clinical,* trans. Daniel W. Smith and Michael A. Greco (Minneapolis: University of Minnesota Press, 1997).

2. Deleuze, "Literature and Life," 228.

3. Ibid, 228n. 8. See J-M. G. Le Clézio, *Haï* (Paris: Flammarion, 1971), 7.

4. Deleuze, "Literature and Life," 228–29.

5. Ibid., 225.

6. My interest in the process of "essaying" and its relation to the actual unfolding of a person's life began with the discovery in 1976 of *Essaying Essays: Alternative Forms of Exposition* (New York: Out of London Press, 1975), an inspiring anthology of creative writing edited by Richard Kostelanetz. *Essaying Essays* was the model for my own artist's book, *Questions: 1977–1982,* with essays by Kathy O'Dell, Lynn Hershman, and Richard Irwin (San Francisco: KronOscope Press, 1982).

7. Artists in the show, at the Kunsthallen Brandts Klaedefabrik, included Elke Krystofek and Valie Export, Austria; Jayne Parker, England; Heili Rekula, and Eija-Liisa Ahtila, Finland; Kirsten Justesen, Denmark; Orlan, France; Reneé Cox, Joan Jonas, Mary Kelly, Alison Knowles, Carolee Schneemann, and Annie Sprinkle from the United States. In addition, the show included deceased artists Gina Pane (France) and Ana Mendieta and Hannah Wilke (United States).

8. Justesen's justifications were transparently defensive. She knew quite well that for over twenty years my scholarship has been devoted to some of the most controversial performance art in the post-1945 period. My work on destruction, violence, and trauma in art and society is the reason she invited me to write for the catalog. Moreover, she also knew that as an artist I collaborated in performances with African American artist Sherman Fleming on the subject of sex and race, actions that included interracial nudity.

9. In addition, when I presented a history of the censorship of aspects of this paper in the fall of 1996 at a symposium, "Contemporary Exhibiting," organized by Liviana Dan in Sibiu, Romania, I was criticized there for describing Justesen's and Tucker's acts as censorship. Some participants felt that the act of deleting my essay from the *Body as Membrane* catalog and cutting sections of my Schneemann essay were perfectly in keeping with the powers and rights of a museum and curator.

10. While traveling in September, I was initially contacted by Dan Cameron, curator for Schneemann's exhibition, who faxed me an urgent notice in my Amsterdam hotel that Tucker "strongly felt" that the "Apples and Stems" part of my essay was "not appropriate" for the publication and "should be cut" from my essay.

11. Marcia Tucker, letter to the author, October 10, 1996.

12. Early in the editing process sometime in August, I had been advised that the

"Apples and Stems" section appeared to "pit Orlan against Schneemann." I had immediately revised the text since my intention was never to pit the artists against each another, but rather to delineate the structure of competition endemic to the cultural situation itself. After the revision, Schneemann herself told me in a telephone conversation that she was "thrilled" with my essay and later wrote to me that she was "humbled . . . and grateful" for my "insight . . . and loving comprehension" (Carolee Schneemann, letter to the author, August 24, 1996).

13. Kristine Stiles, letter to Marcia Tucker, October 16, 1996.

14. See Katy Deepwell, "Debate: Sassy or Not?" *Siski* (Helsinki) 11, no. 4 (1996): 88–90.

15. When my essay "Never Enough" finally came out, Nilsson changed the title to "Debate: The Empty Slogan of Self-Representation," *Siski* 12, no. 1 (1997): 87–90.

16. Export and Justesen, introduction to *Body as Membrane,* 142.

17. This comment is excerpted from my letter of December 31, 1995, to artist-curator Kirsten Justesen and Lene Burkard, assistant director of the Kunsthallen Brandts Klaedefabrik. I wrote that my text was "ruthlessly honest, passionate, and empathic to the women in the exhibition as well as to my own feminist position" and pointed out that I "I was *not* commissioned to write something sympathetic to the exhibition, nor was I required to be uncritical." I tried to impress upon them that what I wrote needed to be written, and that I had done so "in the spirit of open dialogue." Furthermore, I explained that I believed my essay was "in keeping with the fierce quality of the works themselves." And I lamented the fact that they did not seem to grasp "the inter-relatedness between theory and action, between text and image." Finally, I observed, "In the end, I feel that you betray not only your aims but all of our purposes as feminists by not fairly admitting into the arena of visual and textual discourse an open discussion of the issues." Nevertheless, I stated, "I remain committed to the show and to the artists in it."

18. A year after I wrote this essay, Marcia Tucker was dismissed from her position as the director of the New Museum, more evidence for her lack of substantive power even in the institution she was instrumental in founding.

19. William Gass, "Shears of the Censor: Notes on Excision, Imprisonment, and Silence," *Harper's,* April 1997, 61.

20. For a superb discussion of censorship see Sue Curry Jansen's *Censorship: The Knot That Binds Power and Knowledge* (Oxford: Oxford University Press, 1991).

21. Gass, 60.

22. Ibid.

23. Deleuze, "Literature and Life," 230.

24. Ibid., 229.

25. This is the function of the social contract and what I once naively called "Art-Literature" in my *Questions.*

26. Laura Cottingham, email to the author, July 28, 1997.

27. Laura Cottingham, email to the author, July 30, 1997.

28. I have been preoccupied with the responsibilities of interpersonal exchange—the social contract—since 1980 when, as an artist, I used this term in two works of art. The first, entitled *International Social Contract,* was a collaboration between myself and the San Francisco artist Richard Irwin (now deceased) for an exhibition entitled *Tourism.* It took place in the summer of 1980 at the Heller Gallery on the University of California, Berkeley, campus. Our intention was "to extend the meaning through examining the function of *social contract.*" In a second work I realized in 1980,

entitled *Lettres/Livres,* I wrote letters in little books (which I collaged with images) to twenty-five people in Nice, France. I had found their names in the Nice telephone book. I left a place in the books for the recipient to respond, hoping, thereby, to create a space for responsive exchange and mutual trust. In other words, I tried to engage them in a friendly exchange and a social contract. I hoped that as strangers we would get to know each other by exchanging the books through the international mail. In this way, together we would produce a work of art. No one responded. See my *Questions,* 68–73, 78–85.

29. As if this essaying is never enough, I have been invited to extend these remarks and publish this text as a book. For now that project will have to wait. But it would appear that "Never Enough" named a phenomenon of female struggle, but a personal event of writing that has imposed a form of expression on the lived matter of my personal experience, proving just the opposite of what Deleuze wrote but arriving, nonetheless, at the same conclusion, where "literature rather moves in the direction of the ill-formed or the incomplete."

30. Since the writing of this essay, Trump and Marla have divorced amicably. I paraphrase his reason, as given in a CNN Nightly News program: "Marla prefers things like home and walking on the beach. I would rather be in the office making phone calls for eight hours a day. Ivana was more like me in that way." In a double irony, Marla, too, was not enough—*and* not enough like Ivana.

31. The catalog from *Body as Membrane* was published after my essay was rejected. It contains a statement by Ahtila about *Dog Bites* that states that she is not the figure in the picture. As I was given only the photocopy of Ahtila's action, not her text, and told that these images represented the artist's performances, I could not have known when I wrote my essay (unless I had asked, which I did not), that Ahtila was not the woman in the pictures. The photograph's ability to fool the observer into believing that the image is of the artist depicted (especially when the work is one of performance art) is characteristic of the assumptions that are brought to performance art, where the medium of the artist is the body. I have criticized other writers—among them Henry Sayre and Robert Hughes—for not being attentive to the problematic relationship between the photograph and performance art, and of being duped (especially by Rudolf Schwarzkogler's images of castration, photographs that promoted the myth that he died by castrating himself in a performance). See my "Readings: Performance and Its Objects," *Arts,* November 1990, 35–47. Having fallen victim to the very same error, I acknowledge my own culpability.

32. Francis Barker, *The Tremulous Private Body: Essays on Subjection* (New York: Methuen, 1984): 62–63.

33. I need to remind the reader at this point, that this section of my text was written in the fall of 1995, long before Sprinkle ceased doing these kinds of performances, and before the terrible fire at her boathouse in Sausalito, California, a fire that destroyed the artist's entire belongings. Even before her tragedy, Sprinkle had begun to change her direction.

34. A similar preoccupation with authenticity haunts Madonna despite much postmodern theorization to the contrary. In the last scene of *Truth or Dare,* Madonna appears snuggled in her bed with her dance troupe. In the midst of a playful scene in which they are teasing her, she recoils when someone suggests that a string of pearls she is wearing is fake. Without thinking, Madonna instinctively retorts: "No! They are the real thing!" Hearing her own longing to be associated with something fine and "real," something unable to be exchanged, the woman who has made a career of being cele-

brated as the paradigm of an empowered woman able to invent herself, Madonna resumes her charade. But Madonna's denial of simulation exposed her craving to be *anything but* that decentered, fragmented postmodern construction she has been made out to be.

35. Sander L. Gilman, *Difference and Pathology: Stereotypes of Sexuality, Race, and Madness* (Ithaca, N.Y.: Cornell University Press, 1985), 85.

36. Margaret R. Miles, *Carnal Knowing: Female Nakedness and Religious Meaning in the Christian West* (New York: Vintage, 1989), 5.

37. While a systematic engagement with Butler's highly influential tenet is in order, this is not the place for that encounter. See Butler's *Gender Trouble: Feminism and the Subversion of Identity* (New York: Routledge, 1990). For a more detailed discussion of my thesis that the reformulation of negative signs does not function as a means for self-empowerment, see my "Shaved Heads and Marked Bodies: Representations from Cultures of Trauma" (1993), reprinted with a new afterword in *Talking Gender: Public Images, Personal Journeys, and Political Critiques,* ed. Jean O'Barr, Nancy Hewitt, and Nancy Rosebaugh (Chapel Hill: University of North Carolina Press, 1995), 36–64.

38. Barbara Rose, "Is It Art? Orlan and the Transgressive Art," *Art in America,* February 1993, 82–87, 125. All quotes by Rose are from this article.

39. Carolee Schneemann on "Eye Body" (1963), in *More Than Meat Joy: Complete Performance Works and Selected Writings,* ed. Bruce McPherson (New Paltz, N.Y.: Documentext, 1979), 52.

40. Schneemann, "Istory of a Girl Pornographer" (1974), in *More Than Meat Joy,* 194.

41. Some may wonder why, in this essay that names names, I have left this curator anonymous. The answer is that ours was a private exchange regarding the possibility of exhibiting Schneemann's work. All the names that are named in this essay are already part of a public record.

42. The defeat an artist experiences from co-optation is vividly documented both in Guy Debord's suicide of 1995, and in his biting self-irony in *Comments on the Society of the Spectacle,* trans. Malcolm Imrie (New York: Verso, 1990).

43. Quoted from the back jacket-cover of my *Questions.*

44. See Valie Export and Kirsten Justesen, introduction to *Body as Membrane* (Odense, Denmark: Kunsthallen Brandts Klaedefabrik, 1996), 142.

45. See Export's exhibition catalog, *Magna Feminista: Kunst und Kreativität—ein Überlisk über die weibliche Sensibilität, Imagination, Projektion und Problematik, suggeriert durch ein Tableau von Bildern, Objekten, Fotos, Vorträgen, Diskussionen, Lesungen, Filmen, Videobändern und Aktionen* (Vienna: Galerie Nächst St. Stephen, 1975).

46. August Ruhs, "Orlan's Metaphorphoses," in *Body as Membrane,* 154.

47. Ibid.

48. Ibid.

49. Susan Faludi, *Backlash: The Undeclared War against American Women* (New York: Crown, 1981), 217.

50. Ibid., 218. Faludi points out further that "More than two million women, or one in sixty, were sporting the $2,000 to $4,000 breast implants—making breast enlargement the most common cosmetic operation. More than a hundred thousand had undergone the $4,000-plus liposuction surgery, a procedure that was unknown a decade ago."

51. Ibid., 218–19.

52. Ibid., 219.

53. Ibid., 222.

54. Bennett G. Braun, Center on Psychiatric Trauma and Dissociation, Rush Institute of Mental Well-Being in Chicago, in "Multiple Personality Disorder and Posttraumatic Stress Disorder: Similarities and Differences," in *International Handbook of Traumatic Stress Syndromes,* ed. John P. Wilson and Beverley Raphael (New York: Plenum Press, 1993), 35–36.

55. See also Mardi J. Horowitz, *Stress Response Syndromes* (Northvale, N.J.: Jason Aronson, 1976); and "Post-traumatic Stress Disorders," *Behavioral Sciences and the Law* 1, no. 3 (1983): 9–23.

56. Carey Lovelace, "Orlan: Offensive Acts," *Performing Arts Journal* 49 (January 1995): 15.

57. Ibid., 18.

58. Ibid.

59. See section 5 of Wilson and Raphael, *International Handbook of Traumatic Stress Syndromes,* "The Impact of Trauma on Children and Adolescents," with articles on childhood incest particularly by Arthur Green, Judith Lewis Herman, and others (527–658). These articles also contain an extensive bibliography on the subject.

60. Lovelace, "Orlan," 18.

61. Ibid., 19.

62. Ibid., 18.

63. Susan Roth and Ronald Batson, *Naming the Shadows: A New Approach to Individual and Group Psychotherapy for Adult Survivors of Childhood Incest* (New York: Free Press, 1997), 25. For an excellent general introduction to the symptoms of sexual trauma see Judith Lewis Herman, *Trauma and Recovery: The Aftermath of Violence—from Domestic Abuse to Political Terror* (New York: Basic, 1992). See also P. M. Cole and F. W. Putnam, "Effect of Incest on Self and Social Functioning: A Developmental Psychopathology Perspective," *Journal of Consulting and Clinical Psychology* 60 (1992): 174–84; M. A. Polusny and V. M. Follette, "Long-Term Correlates of Child Sexual Abuse: Theory and Review of the Empirical Literature," *Applied and Preventive Psychology* 4 (1995): 143–66.

64. See Jacques Lacan, "Of the Gaze as Object Petit a," in *The Fundamental Concepts of Psycho-analysis,* ed. Jacques-Alain Miller, trans. Alan Sheridan (New York: Norton, 1977), 67–122.

65. On the relationship between trauma and performance art, see my "Shaved Heads and Marked Bodies," as well as Kathy O'Dell's "The Performance Artist as Masochistic Woman," *Arts,* October 1988, 96–98. See also O'Dell's *Contract with the Skin: Masochism, Performance Art, and the 1970s* (Minneapolis: University of Minnesota Press, 1998).

66. I borrowed this phrase from W. J. T. Mitchell, who used it in quite another context. Nevertheless, I think it is still valuable here. Writing on the subject of abstract painting and language, Mitchell queried: "If we ask when abstraction stopped being an avant-garde movement, dying to be reborn as a tradition that must treat these forbidden subjects as heresies to be repressed, an obvious answer is: at least as early as [Alfred] Barr, who noted in 1935 that 'ten years ago one heard on all sides that abstract art was dead' and who sees his own work as 'in no sense a pioneering effort'" See Mitchell's "*Ut Pictura Theoria:* Abstract Painting and Language," in his *Picture Theory: Essays on Verbal and Visual Representation* (Chicago: University of Chicago Press, 1994), 236, reprinted from *Critical Inquiry* 15, no. 2 (1989).

67. Lovelace, "Orlan," 14.

68. Indeed, after this essay was completed, I met Orlan for the first time at the opening of *Out of Actions: Between Performance and the Object, 1949–1979,* the celebrated exhibition curated by Paul Schimmel on thirty years of international performance art, which opened at the Los Angeles Museum of Contemporary Art in February 1998. I approached the artist and introduced myself. Orlan responded to my self-introduction by commenting that she had heard that I was such a "warm" person, that she did not understand why I wrote so harshly about her work. In the course of a brief conversation under an umbrella outside LAMOCA in the rain, I explained that I was concerned for her life and that I did not want her to kill herself for art. She responded that "life is much harder than art." I replied that I realized she was personally in psychological pain, but that acting it out as physical pain was not the solution, and I urged her to stop punishing herself. I would not stop writing about her work in this manner, I added, until she stopped hurting herself. Her response was to throw her arms around me and burst into tears. There is no way to tell this poignant story—witnessed by my family and two of my graduate students—without sounding melodramatic and self-aggrandizing. Nevertheless, it happened and that matters. Orlan is an artist for whom I have deep respect and boundless empathy.

69. Hal Foster, *Return of the Real: The Avant-Garde at the End of the Century* (Cambridge: MIT Press, 1996), xii.

70. Ibid., 29. See also Jean Laplanche, *New Foundations of Psychoanalysis,* trans. David Macey (London: Basil Blackwell, 1989), 88.

71. I have pointed out that the increase in trauma globally, for example, has produced what I theorized as "cultures of trauma" in some specific nations such as Romania, Rwanda, Bosnia, Yugoslavia, Vietnam, Cambodia, and so on. But in suggesting such a term, my research was grounded in specific examples of actually (not theoretically) traumatized peoples and environments such as I have encountered in work in Romania.

72. Neither the term *deferred action,* nor Jacques Lacan's name, for example, appear among the literally thousands of terms indexed in the *International Handbook of Traumatic Stress Syndromes.*

73. On the relation between cultures of trauma and feminist performance see my *Amalia Perjovschi: Shadows in a Vertical Life* (Bucharest: Soros Foundation, 1996).

74. James M. Glass, *Shattered Selves: Multiple Personality in a Postmodern World* (Ithaca, N.Y.: Cornell University Press, 1993), 158.

75. Liljana Sedlar, "A Letter from Belgrade," *Performance Research* 2, no. 1 (1997): 101, 100.

76. Ibid., 101.

77. Ibid., 102.

78. Rebecca Schneider, *The Explicit Body in Performance* (London: Routledge, 1997), 3–4.

79. Ibid. See Leslie Jones, "Transgressive Femininity," in *Abject Art: Repulsion and Desire in American Art,* ed. Jack Ben-Levi, Craig Houser, Leslie C. Jones, and Simon Taylor (New York: Whitney Museum, 1992–93).

80. Laura Cottingham, introduction to *How Many "Bad" Feminists Does It Take to Change a Light Bulb?* (New York: Afterwords, 1994), 3. Cottingham was hired to write about the show *Bad Girls* in London at the Institute for Contemporary Arts. But when she discussed the implications of the title of the show, the curators "immediately attempted to edit/censor" her work. "Their reasons for justifying the title, or rather their assumed right to eliminate my criticism," Cottingham wrote, "were based in such

specious rationalizations as how many women and artists of color the sponsoring institution . . . exhibits; and how my critique personally insulted their work" (2).

81. Ibid.

82. Ibid., 8.

83. Ibid., 9.

84. Ibid. Marcia Tucker is quoted from Mary Haus's "Funny, Really Funny," *Art News,* April 1994, 27.

85. Ibid., 13.

86. See *RE/Search* 13 (1991).

87. See my "Uncorrupted Joy: International Art Actions," in *Out of Actions: Between Performance and the Object, 1949–1979,* ed. Paul Schimmel (Los Angeles: Los Angeles Museum of Contemporary Art and Thames and Hudson, 1998), 296.

88. Ibid., 297. See also my "Schlaget Auf: The Problem with Carolee Schneemann's Paintings," in *Carolee Schneemann: Up to and Including Her Limits* (New York: New Museum, 1996), 15–25.

89. Schneemann, *More Than Meat Joy,* 52.

90. A discussion of the history of *Interior Scroll* is complicated and beyond the scope of this essay. However, it is important to mention here that the text Schneemann pulled from her vagina and read during *Interior Scroll* was adapted from tape 2 of *Kitch's Last Meal,* a super-8 film she made between 1973 and 1977. In tape 2 she discussed a conversation she had with "a happy man, a structuralist filmmaker," who criticized her films for "the personal clutter, the persistence of feelings, the hand-touch sensibility, the diaristic indulgence, the painterly mess, the dense gestalt, and the primitive techniques" (*More Than Meat Joy,* 238). In an unpublished letter to Carol Wikarska of March 4, 1975, Schneemann identified this filmmaker to be none other than Annette Michelson: "Did I note that 'I met a happy man' from "Kitch's Last Meal" tape 2 is a derelict 'communication' between myself and Annette [Michelson]?" Fictionalized as a male protagonist for *Kitch's Last Meal,* Schneemann transformed the internalized memory of this insult into the external discourse of *Interior Scroll.* She performed this action twice, first for the exhibition *Women Her and Now,* August 29, 1975, in East Hampton, and second at the Telluride Film Festival. She made the decision to enact *Interior Scroll* again when she found—to her "dismay"—that her work has been relegated to the category of "The Erotic Woman," in the program of the Telluride Film Festival. Yet another classification—like "dancer"—that (in the context of the film festival) withheld recognition for her work as a filmmaker must have reminded the artist of being described as a "dancer" in the earlier discussion of her films with Michelson. *Interior Scroll* and *Kitch's Last Meal* tell much about both the artist's working methods, her fierce fight for recognition, and failure of many powerful cultural theorists to acknowledge Schneemann's many significant achievements and contributions. See my forthcoming *Correspondence Course: Selected Letters and Performances of Carolee Schneemann* (Johns Hopkins University Press).

91. Schneemann in a telephone conversation with the author, July 27, 1997.

92. Schneemann in conversation with the author, August 3, 1997, New Paltz, New York.

93. It is not my intention here to write a historiography of the theory of the avant-garde, or to theorize this cultural institution in any systematic way. I want only to comment on aspects of its conceptual formation that are critical to the problem of realizing a probity in culture.

94. See my "Survival Ethos and Destruction Art," *Discourse* 14, no. 2 (1992): 74–102.

95. Fred Orton and Griselda Pollock, "Avant-Gardes and Partisans Reviewed," *Art History,* September 1981, 305, reprinted in *Pollock and After: The Critical Debate,* ed. Francis Frascina (New York: Harper and Row, 1985), 167.

96. Susan Rubin Suleiman, *Subversive Intent: Gender, Politics, and the Avant-Garde* (Cambridge: Harvard University Press, 1990), xv.

97. In "Avant-Gardes and Partisans Reviewed," Orton and Pollock argue that the avant-garde "is not a process inherent in the evolution of art in modern time; it is not the motor of spiritual renovation and artistic innovation; and it is more than an ideological concept, one part of a complex pattern of imagery and belief" (167).

98. Ibid., 168. Here Orton and Pollock argue that an historical avant-garde emerged in the "second half of the nineteenth century [that entailed] a range of social postures and strategies for artists by which they could differentiate themselves from current social and cultural structures while also intervening in them." Moreover, "In this century there has been only one other, successful avant-garde moment when the avant-garde and the definition of appropriate avant-garde practices had to be, and was, revivified and re-articulated." That moment was "in New York in the late 1930s and early 1940s when a new discursive framework was established that enabled some of the artists and intellectuals who gathered there to construct an identity for themselves which was simultaneously an opposition to, and an extension of available American and European traditions."

99. See Renato Poggioli, *The Theory of the Avant-Garde* (Cambridge: Belknap Press of Harvard University Press, 1968); and Peter Bürger, *Theory of the Avant-Garde,* trans. Michael Shaw (Minneapolis: University of Minnesota Press, 1984).

100. Bürger, *Theory of Avant-Garde,* 58.

101. Foster, *Return of the Real,* 8.

102. Ibid., 21–24.

103. Ibid., xii.

104. Ibid.

105. Ibid., 228 n. 6.

106. Ibid. "[A]vant-gardist transgression [shifts] toward a model of deconstructive (dis)placement [based on] the reflexivity of the viewer to refashion the cliché not only of the neo-avant-garde as merely redundant of the historical avant-garde, but also of the postmodern as only belated in relation to the modern" (xii–xiii).

107. Ibid., 59.

108. Ibid., 142.

109. This is not the place to rehearse the battle between Kosuth and the editors of *October,* but for those who wish to follow it, see Joseph Kosuth, "Intention(s)," *Art Bulletin,* September 1996, 407–12.

110. In this respect Orton and Pollock point out the "intentionalist and formalist" history of style Irving Sandler constructed in his account of the evolution of abstract expressionism in New York, while at the same time "conceal[ing] the fact that a section of the New York intelligentsia was intensely preoccupied with the avant-garde in the late 1930s and 1940s." They also note that Sandler made "no mention of the intervention which one member of that group, Clement Greenberg, made at that time in avant-garde theory and American intellectual . . . artistic strategies" ("Avant-Gardes and Partisans Reviewed," 169).

111. Thomas Crow, "Modernism and Mass Culture in the Visual Arts," in *Modernism and Modernity,* ed. Benjamin H. D. Buchloh, Serge Guilbaut, and David Solkin (Nova Scotia: Press of the Nova Scotia College of Art and Design, 1983), 257. For an excellent study of some of the institutional origins of the avant-garde see Robert Jensen, *Marketing Modernism in Fin-de-Siècle Europe* (Princeton: Princeton University Press, 1994).

112. Antoine Compagnon, *The Five Paradoxes of Modernity* (New York: Columbia University Press, 1994), 35. An good example of how critics construct avant-gardes and how those constructions are canonized is exemplified in the way in which Benjamin Buchloh's views have been repeated by Alice Jardine in the particularly influential context of the exhibition catalog *Utopia Post Utopia,* a show that established the identity and pedigree of many critics, art historians, and artists associated with what became accepted as the postmodernist avant-garde. She cited "Benjamin Buchloh's list of radical deconstructionist artists of the late seventies: Dara Birnbaum, Sherrie Levine, Louise Lawler, Martha Rosler, Jenny Holzer." Her repetition of Buchloh's list, in a context saturated with power, is typical of how avant-gardes are constructed, cultivated, promoted, deemed "radical" (or "deconstructionist," which, for a time, was the same), preserved, and how a specific critic's taste and ideology may be institutionalized. See Alice Jardine, "Alice in Wonderland Looking/For the Body," in *Utopia Post Utopia: Configurations of Nature and Culture in Recent Sculpture and Photography* (Boston: Institute of Contemporary Art in Boston, 1988), 116. See also Benjamin H. D. Buchloh, "Allegorical Procedures: Appropriation and Montage in Contemporary Art," *Artforum,* September 1982, 43–56.

113. Paul Mann, *The Theory-Death of the Avant-Garde* (Bloomington: Indiana University Press, 1991), 3. Such "deaths," Mann maintains, are a "more or less explicit . . . kind of cultural feedback or backlash, the revenge of the mainstream after a hundred years of reading its own obituaries in manifesto after manifesto" (36).

114. Ibid., 141, 145.

115. Gass, "Shears of the Censor," 64.

116. Even the linguistic representation of this process is tortuous; for permission is required for access in order to be positioned for becoming identified as avant-garde—all this before recognition as such!

117. Rozsika Parker and Griselda Pollock, *Old Mistresses: Women, Art, and Ideology* (New York: Pantheon, 1981), 137.

118. While the conventional date for the beginning of the historical avant-garde is somewhere around 1850 in the work of Gustav Courbet, as the date of modernism itself continues to be pushed back to the Renaissance and earlier—to periods in which the production of culture is self-consciously analyzed in its own period—the notion of avant-gardes' originality (of vision that revisions the world outside of prescribed institutionalized values) will be discussed in earlier periods.

119. See Krauss, "The Originality of the Avant-Garde," in *The Originality of the Avant-Garde and Other Modernist Myths* (Cambridge: MIT Press, 1985), 157; reprinted from *October* 18 (fall 1981).

120. W. J. T. Mitchell, in his superb essay "*Ut Pictura Theoria:* Abstract Painting and Language," compared Krauss's aesthetics to those of Clement Greenberg, and I fully agree. "Whatever criticism we might make of Krauss's rhetoric," Mitchell writes, "we certainly could not charge her with presenting an eccentric or unprecedented account of the history of abstract art." He continues: "One might even call this an entirely orthodox version of the story, one that has been retold in many ways over the

last ninety years, usually under the rubric of abstractions like 'opticality' and 'purity.'" He concludes: "The abstract artist, as Clement Greenberg put it, is a 'purist' who insists upon excluding 'literature' and subject matter from plastic art" (215–16).

121. Linda Nochlin, "Why Have There Been No Great Women Artists?" (1971), in *Art and Sexual Politics,* ed. Thomas Hess and Elizabeth Baker (New York: Collier, 1973), reprinted in Nochlin, *Women, Art, and Power* (New York : Harper and Row, 1988), 145–78.

122. I gave parts of this section of the text in a talk at *Assault: Radicalism in Aesthetics and Politics,* November 10, 1996, a symposium organized by Joanne Richardson, Svetlana Mintcheva, and Aisha Karim, graduate students in the Literature Program at Duke University.

123. For example, see David Aberbach, *Charisma in Politics, Religion, and the Media: Private Trauma, Public Ideals* (New York: New York University Press, 1996).

124. Derrida, *The Gift of Death,* trans. David Wills (Chicago: University of Chicago Press, 1995), 80. I am grateful to Susan Jarosi for introducing me to Derrida's remarkable book, and for sharing her intellectual passion for, and joy in, Derrida's meditation on responsibility.

125. Levinas, *Noms propres* (Montpellier: Fata Morgana, 1976), 113, as quoted in Jacques Derrida, *The Gift of Death,* 78.

126. Derrida, *The Gift of Death,* 68.

127. Stiles, letter to Tucker.

128. See Tania Ørum's "Fishy Bodies and Closed Minds," *Siski* 12, no. 2 (1997): 88.

129. It may occur to some readers that Valie Export, the cocurator of the exhibition *Body as Membrane,* is curiously absent from my critique. The reason for this is that never at any time did Export have anything to do with the censorship of my essay, as far as I know. Indeed, it was she who was instrumental in recommending I write for the catalog. Moreover, as it should be evident from my comments on the photograph *Genitalpanik* (1969), the entire import of the exhibition itself could have been and was—already in 1969—conveyed in her one work. I deeply admire her act, the image of it, one that is unsurpassed in its elegance, brutality, and depth of content.

130. Barbara Rose, it turns out (as I was informed), "lives in the same building as Marcia Tucker"—whatever that means.

131. Rosalind Krauss, ". . . And Then Turn Away: An Essay on James Coleman," *October* 81 (summer 1997): 32.

132. Ibid.

133. Gass, "Shears of the Censor," 63.

134. Fredric Jameson, "Architecture and the Critique of Ideology," in *Architecture, Criticism, Ideology,* ed. Joan Ockman (Princeton: Princeton Architectural Press, 1985), 60.

135. Ibid., 17.

136. Manfredo Tafuri and Francesco Dal Co in ibid.

Index